# ALL IN ONE LIFETIME

Books by James F. Byrnes

SPEAKING FRANKLY

ALL IN ONE LIFETIME

# All In One Lifetime

## BY JAMES F. BYRNES

HARPER & BROTHERS, PUBLISHERS, NEW YORK

**ALL IN ONE LIFETIME**
Copyright © 1958 by James F. Byrnes
Printed in the United States of America

K-H

Library of Congress catalog card number: 58-11390

# ACKNOWLEDGMENTS

First, I wish to acknowledge the contribution of my capable assistant, Miss Cassie Connor, without whose intelligent and untiring efforts this story could not have been written.

Then I wish to acknowledge the assistance of Dr. George Curry, of the History Department, University of South Carolina, whose search of records, organization of material, and editing of some portions of the manuscript have been very valuable.

To my former associate Walter Brown I am indebted for the use of his diary of the war period. His detailed daily record of what he saw and heard was very useful in verifying my own notes.

To Ben Cohen, Leo Crowley and Porter McKeever, who were associated with me in public life, and to Worthington Miner I am grateful for their kindness in reading and commenting upon certain chapters.

Last, but not least, I wish to record the assistance of my wife, who read these pages, making helpful suggestions and in many ways aiding me in this, as she has in every worth-while task I have undertaken during the last fifty-two years.

# CONTENTS

## PART I.  THE BEGINNING OF A PUBLIC CAREER

## PART II.  THE SENATE

## PART III.  THE SUPREME COURT

## PART IV.  THE WHITE HOUSE

# ILLUSTRATIONS

---

*The following are grouped in a separate section after page 84.*

# Part I

## THE BEGINNING OF A PUBLIC CAREER

# 1 SPEAKING GENERALLY

I have been fortunate in my life in that it has fallen to my lot to serve the country in one capacity or another for half a century. In this book I want to record something of what I learned, what I saw, what I experienced during those fifty years, partly for my own pleasure, I admit, but also in the hope that some who read may be persuaded by my experience of the high satisfaction to be found in a life of public service.

This is a subject on which I feel entitled to write, for I think I may claim without immodesty to know something of the inner workings of government. I have seen it at first hand from the floors of both the House and the Senate, from the vantage point of the Supreme Court bench, from inside the White House, from the office of the Secretary of State, and finally from behind the Governor's desk in South Carolina.

Let me say at once, however, that if I ever had an idea that these offices were important, I was duly deflated one day in June, 1945, by a young sailor. It was in the short period between April 1, when I resigned as Director of Mobilization, and July 2, when I became Secretary of State, and I had just been to see Cordell Hull in the Naval Hospital at Bethesda, Maryland, to talk about foreign affairs. As I drove away I was hailed by a young sailor, who asked for a ride for himself and his red-headed buddy, who was leaning against a telephone pole. When I agreed to take them into town, the sailor at the pole started navigating toward the automobile and I knew the telephone post had performed a useful service. The smaller of the two sat next to me. The inebriated red-head also got into the front seat and put his head back in comfortable relaxation. The little, but talkative, one seemed afraid I might object to the condition of his friend and tried to keep me diverted. He asked what kind of work I did. I said, "Right now I'm out of a job." He seemed sympathetic and asked what my job was when I worked. I said, "I was Director of War Mobilization." His expression clearly showed he had never heard of it. After being quiet for a second or two, he made another effort, "Well, what did you do before that?"

"I was Economic Stabilizer," I said. He had never heard of that one either.

"I mean before the war," he replied.

"I was a Justice of the Supreme Court," I told him, thinking that at least would impress him. He asked, "You mean the highest court?"

"Yes," I said.

With his elbow he nudged the other boy, asking, "How would you like to be a member of the highest court?"

Shaking his head the sailor replied, "I wouldn't like it. No chance for promotion."

This naval deflation of the importance of two of my posts and of the desirability of a third rightly humbled me. It is in this spirit of humility, then, that I have written of my experiences in these and other public offices, recording from personal knowledge some of the virtues and weaknesses of those with whom I was associated and some of the hazards and the pitfalls but most particularly the rewards of a government career.

My call to public service should not go unheeded because of my personal experiences. The chapters that follow have their share of disappointments and defeats, of encounters with selfishness and desire for power, and of frustrating failures in seeking to make the art of the politically possible serve desirable ends. But all these should be just the points of contrast in the picture. The overwhelming impression that should emerge is of the variety and richness of friendships and experiences, the excitement and stimulation of being involved in the nation's responses to its needs, the satisfaction of being a part of, and perhaps a contributor to its moral and political strength.

Frequently I am asked which service I "enjoyed" most. I can answer that question only with the stipulation that it does not involve an appraisal of the relative importance of the various offices or the power exercised in those offices.

In retrospect, I think I enjoyed most my service in the United States Senate. There I was engaged in the consideration of every phase of our national life—our foreign affairs as well as our domestic problems. Present always was the incentive that comes from accomplishment. There was independence of action, and there was the pleasure of competing with men who displayed good sportsmanship and whose friendships enriched my life. However, in arriving at that answer, I take into account that my service in the Senate covered years that offered rare opportunities. When I began that service the country was at the depth of the depression, and after our economic recovery we soon started preparation for the war that came to us in 1941. Not to be overlooked, also, was the fact that I was between fifty and sixty years of age—which could have made a difference in enjoyment.

I am glad, however, that I had first those full rich years as a representative. Service in the House was a liberal education in government and in human relations. Even earlier, as a young man, working as a court stenographer, I had begun to learn that in all relationships in life success and happiness can be achieved only by a willingness to make concessions. I saw how essential this was in the administration of justice. The verdict of a jury was arrived at only by unanimity. Often after hearing conflicting testimony in a case, I wondered how twelve men could come to an agreement. At times I would discuss the case with the jurors after the verdict had been announced. Of course, the methods were as varied as the cases because the people involved differed, and so did the facts.

Similarly in the House and in the Senate the art of legislating is the art of intelligent compromise. No one congressman can have his way; the spirit of compromise is necessary to secure the essential majority. Frequently, an obstinate man, whose political creed is "my will be done," will attempt to justify his course by asserting there can be no compromise when a principle is involved, and he is likely to see a "principle" in every issue, even in determining the amount of money to be appropriated for some unimportant activity. In my experience, there were really few bills in which a great principle was involved; the issues were usually matters of policy, not principle.

When the House and Senate differ about legislation, the committees that are set up to compose the differences usually consist of three or five members from each house, the appointees being the ranking members of both parties on the committee having charge of the bill. The members appointed by the House, for instance, are expected to do everything possible to sustain the action of the House, and if it becomes necessary to make concessions, they must try to effect a compromise that will be approved by the House. Serving as a conferee is valuable training for a legislator.

Now and then in a presidential year when one party unexpectedly wins by a landslide, some mediocre men will be elected to Congress. The explanation is that, at the time the candidate was nominated, his party was not regarded as having a chance of winning and good men did not seek the office. These "accidents" are seldom re-elected. The men who serve many terms usually are men of ability.

I recall hearing a preacher pray that the Almighty grant "wisdom" to the members of Congress. A little wisdom would help us all, but if there was a deficiency in congressmen that would cause me to resort to prayer, my prayer would be for courage. Really, I would need to ask for this gift only during the six months prior to an election. At other times I think their courage would equal that of any other group of men.

Senator Swanson, of Virginia, who was an outstanding senator before becoming Secretary of the Navy, contended that if a senator wanted to be a statesman for five and a half years, he had to be a politician the six months preceding an election and do whatever he thought the majority of his constituents wanted even if he thought them wrong, because he would not have time to convince them in the short period before the election. Whenever he heard a colleague cast a vote he regarded as demagogic, Swanson would say that he had voted like a senator with a six-months "pulse."

The same qualities that make for effective service in the House qualify one for similar service in the Senate. The only difference is that agreement is easier in the Senate because of the smaller membership. There is no magic about success in either body. The qualities that make for leadership and influence are the same as in other fields. A horse that can trot, single-foot and run is always valuable. So is the member of Congress who possesses a good mind, good judgment, character and energy, and who shows consideration for his colleagues. Such a man, if he has the good judgment to attend his committee meetings in the morning and stay on the floor after the house convenes, is certain to attain a position of leadership.

In every branch of government there is room and reward for men of talent. To be sure, government service in a civilian capacity in time of peace lacks the glamour of military service in either peace or war.

Moreover one's character, capacity and habits are frequently exposed to slashing verbal attacks from political enemies. But why should this deter a man who would not hesitate to expose his body to the bullets of the country's enemy?

It is also true that the man who is willing to serve his government in public office should abandon any ambition to accumulate money as does the man who labors only to serve himself. In no public office should one expect the financial rewards to be found in private business. However, a man who has accumulated great wealth in the business world not infrequently finds, after a taste of government service, that business has lost some of its old-time flavor.

Our word "idiot" comes from the name the ancient Greeks gave to the man who would take no part in public affairs. In some periods of our history this was a harsh connotation to apply. But in today's world it is hardly an overstatement.

A free, democratic society functions well only when it commands the active interest of all its citizens and the dedicated involvement in its affairs of a sizable percentage of them. And today the effective functioning of our democracy is not simply a question of progress, it is a question of survival. Recently, Soviet Premier Nikita Khrushchev has said to the United States: "We declare war upon you. . . . We will bury you."[1] He made clear he was not speaking of armed conflict but of the competitive struggle between the Soviet Communist system of political, social and economic organization and our own. The Soviet challenge, he said, will be "relentless" and "will prove the superiority" of the Soviet system.[2]

Thus we have been warned that the entire mechanism of the Soviet Union is being directed toward our downfall. And in the Soviet system this mechanism includes not only the nation's political institutions but its economic organization, its educational system, its science and technology and its organs of communication and propaganda as well.

The ability of a dictatorship to direct the attention of such a wide range of institutions toward a single objective can give it at least an initial advantage. Where those who look upon men as mere cogs in the machine of the state often miscalculate is in their ignorance or disregard of that extra ounce of genius, of energy and of devotion that

[1] *New York Times*, November 18, 1957.
[2] Interview with William Randolph Hearst, Jr., November 22, 1957.

free men can summon when their institutions are challenged. It is
this extra capacity that provides the promise of freedom's survival.
Its presence is reflected directly in the extent and quality of citizen
participation in public affairs.

In my public life I have seen the democratic process win inspiring
victories and sustain stunning defeats. Above all, I have seen the
wonders that a sense of national purpose, stimulated by national peril,
can achieve. I have seen proof of the resourcefulness, the vigor and
the valor of the American people when aroused to meet a challenge.

Khrushchev's warning indicates that an equally deadly challenge
now confronts us. We need to respond at every level of our national
life—in our jobs, our unions and trade associations, our school boards
and institutions of higher learning; in our town, city and state governments, as well as in all the branches of our federal government.

There have been times when men were regarded almost as idiots for
dedicating themselves to public affairs. It was "smart" to describe
politics as "dirty" and politicians as corrupt. There should be an end
to such generalizations. For every public official convicted of corrupt
acts there are many dishonest business and professional men.

In all three branches of the government, public service will be found
rewarding, and particularly satisfying is the opportunity to associate
with men who give their lives to their country in the field of either
national politics or world affairs. Even when one has ceased active
participation he will have the comfort optimistically promised by Tom
Moore in his lines,

> When time who steals our years away,
> Shall steal our pleasures too,
> The mem'ry of the past will stay,
> And half our joys renew.

My joy is more than half renewed when, for example, I recall an experience with Winston Churchill, who during World War II addressed
his messages "To the President from a former Naval Person." In 1945
his Conservative government was defeated. He did not sulk, but he
worried about the future of his country and the future of the world.

A few days after I announced at Stuttgart the policy of the United
States for the government of Germany, I was encouraged by the congratulations of Mr. Churchill, who expressed a desire to see me. He said
he would come to Paris from Brussels, where he was a guest of the

Belgian government, and I sent word I would be happy to see him. I was told by the British Ambassador that the meeting was to be kept confidential and preliminaries were conducted through the American Embassy in Paris. Mr. Churchill evidently did not want to involve the British Ambassador, Duff Cooper, who was holding over in the Attlee government. Of course, I had to have in mind my relations with Attlee and Bevin, who then represented the British government.

In the telephone conversations between the two Embassies which went on a day or two before his arrival, the visitor was either referred to as "Mr. C" or the "gentleman who was to see Mr. Byrnes," and the British staff did not communicate even in this guarded manner with anyone except my secretary or me. Mr. Churchill said that he hoped I would be free on "Saturday evening, September 28th," which sounded like a dinner engagement.

I agreed to go to the British Embassy at five in the afternoon and was asked by the Ambassador if I would mind going in by the "side door." When I arrived there I found Mr. Churchill's secretary all apologies, stating that it was good of me to enter in this manner because the public must not be allowed to know of the meeting. After proceeding through the Embassy kitchen, I ascended by a small service elevator to the library, where Mr. Churchill was installed.

We then began an exchange of views. Mr. Churchill repeated his secretary's apologies, and said he had told Mr. Bevin he wanted to come to Paris to see me, but learned that the British government preferred that he should not do so. However the old Spartan had stood on his rights as a British subject to travel where he pleased and would have put up at a hotel had not the Ambassador insisted that he stay there. He wanted to say that he was so much in accord with what I had been doing that he had to tell me so personally and that he hoped I understood my own importance as the spokesman of the Western world; that I must not be downhearted but must persevere; and that he heartily approved the Stuttgart speech.

Our talk then ranged over other matters. He said he was not kept informed by the British government of what was going on in foreign affairs and was kept abreast of events only by friends in other governments. He had apparently been briefed on the developments at the Peace Conference by Swiss sources when he had recently visited Zurich. I was glad to give him full information not only about the progress of negotiations but also on the various problems throughout the world which were delaying the making of the peace.

Mr. Churchill was philosophical about his defeat. He told me that it was not personal; that during the war the people had been forced to sacrifice too many comforts in civilian life as well as in the army. He said they had been subjected to oppressive taxation, to rationing and many sacrifices they regarded as unnecessary, and they were just "agin" the government.

After a while he suggested that we might go out to dine at a hotel. I knew this was impossible in view of the Ambassador's desire for secrecy and declined. We, therefore, continued to talk until Field Marshal Smuts was announced. I remained with these two great Commonwealth leaders for quite a while. When I arose to leave Mr. Churchill was all for seeing me out, but the Ambassador intervened, and I found myself politely escorted out by the same young secretary, through the same side door.

In a short time I entered the side door of our hotel and was back in my own apartment, having successfully evaded the watchful eye of the Secret Service and an equally alert press. I felt as if I had been playing a role in an exciting mystery story. Recalling the prediction often quoted by Churchill that "there will always be an England," I wished there could always be a Churchill!

The Churchills, the Roosevelts, the Stimsons and Forrestals and Clays are exceptional of course. But my hope is that more and more good men, well-equipped men, will help America meet the Soviet's challenge by seeking public office and assuming the responsibilities that come with power; that they will not be content with merely offering unsolicited advice or harsh criticism from the safety of an editor's desk, a civic group or Chamber of Commerce. Of course, constant and unfair criticism of men who are willing to serve their government is nothing new. More than two thousand years ago Lucius Aemilius Paulus, a Roman consul, who had been selected to conduct the war with the Macedonians, went out from the senate house into the assembly of the people and said:

In every circle, and, truly, at every table, there are people who lead armies into Macedonia; who know where the camp ought to be placed; what posts ought to be occupied by troops; when and through what pass that territory should be entered; where magazines should be formed; how provisions should be conveyed by land and sea; and when it is proper to engage the enemy, when to lie quiet. And they not only determine what is best to be done, but if anything is done in any other manner than what they have pointed out, they arraign the consul, as if he were on trial before them. These are great impediments to those who have the management of affairs; for every one cannot encounter injurious reports with the same constancy and firmness of mind as Fabius did, who chose to let his own ability be questioned through the folly of the people, rather than to mismanage the public business with a high reputation. I am not one of those who think that commanders ought at no time to receive advice; on the contrary, I should deem that man more proud than wise, who regulated every proceeding by the standard of his own single judgment.

What then is my opinion? That commanders should be counselled, chiefly, by persons of known talent; by those who have made the art of war their particular study, and whose knowledge is derived from experiences; from those who are present at the scene of action, who see the country, who see the enemy; who see the advantages that occasions offer, and who, like people embarked in the same ship, are sharers of the danger. If, therefore, any one thinks himself qualified to give advice respecting the war which I am to conduct, which may prove advantageous to the public, let him not refuse his assistance to the state, but let him come with me into Macedonia. He shall be furnished with a ship, a horse, a tent; even his travelling charges shall be defrayed. But if he thinks this too much trouble, and prefers the repose of a city life to the toils of war, let him not, on land, assume the office of a pilot.[8]

This opinion of military critics, expressed so many years ago, can be applied with equal force to the critics of the men who serve their government today in a civilian capacity.

I invite you to come with me into the Macedonia of American politics and learn of the heartaches and the rewards. In every important public office there are close decisions to be made daily on political, social and economic issues. Deciding them on state or national levels may lose you friends—but you may favorably influence history.

[8] Livy, *History of Rome.* Vol. 7, Book XLIV, Chapter 22. Translation by George Baker, A.M.

## 2  TOWARD CONGRESS

*Vote for*

JAMES F. BYRNES—FOR CONGRESS

HE IS A LIVE-WIRE—A HUSTLER. HE IS A SELF MADE MAN.

*As Solicitor he has proven his ability. Success has not changed him.
He is today the same genial Byrnes we knew as Court Stenographer ten
years ago. A vote for him assures able, energetic representation for the
District and gives encouragement to every young man who aspires to
better himself in life.*

In these flattering terms the August 26, 1910, issue of the Aiken *Journal
and Review*, a semiweekly county newspaper, advocated my election to
Congress. Many things had happened since the summer of 1900 when,
as a result of a competitive examination, I was appointed court stenographer by Judge James Aldrich of the Second Judicial Circuit, and
moved from Charleston, where I was born and reared, to the city of
Aiken, where the Judge had his office and home.

I clearly remember the varied impressions of the first week I served
as court stenographer, which happened to be in Beaufort, a beautiful
old town in the tidewater section. Fifty years ago the journey there
was made by railroad, and when I boarded the train on a warm May
morning, the first thing I did was scurry to get a seat next to a window
and to open it as far as possible. This provided a welcome rush of air,
but along with it quantities of cinders and soot which soon lodged in
my eyes, ears and hair. At the depot in Beaufort, at least twenty-five

12

small vehicles were waiting for the fifteen or twenty travelers who disembarked, each driver loudly vying with the others for patronage. The hack fare downtown, I learned, was nominally fifty cents, but if one betrayed little interest or haste the price would rapidly drop by half. The carriages were drawn by tough little ponies, raised on the Sea Islands and known as "marsh tackies." They must by now be extinct—certainly it has been many years since I have even heard one mentioned.

My quarters were in the hotel located on a high bluff overlooking the bay. With a fresh breeze coming into the room, I forgot about the hot train and the cinder bath and simply looked out at the view. Though I have traveled far in the half century since, the picture of blue water and the clear sky as I saw it that promising spring day remains with me yet.

The journey to Beaufort marked my first week away from home and to me it was an eventful one. People whom I regarded as important had come to court, from the nearby islands as well as the mainland, and I was anxious to make a good impression. I had meals with Judge Ernest Gary and other notables. Among these was the massive Colonel Tom Martin, a famous local sportsman who had proved himself an expert gunman in national competitions. The Colonel weighed about three hundred pounds and his voice was as big as his body. I forgot my own appetite while watching him consume an enormous dinner and then give a duplicate order which vanished as speedily as the first.

My change of residence from Charleston to Aiken was destined to influence my future life in many ways, but at the time I was interested only in what an advance in employment would enable me to do for my mother. My father died shortly before I was born, leaving her with two young children and about $200. As soon as she could, she left the children with her mother, went to New York where her sister lived, and studied dress designing for several months. Upon returning to Charleston she started in business as a dressmaker, and by her talent and industry was able to support us all. Through the years she slaved and saved and in time bought the house we lived in. All my childhood recollections of her were in the sewing room, and later, when I had a job, I would find her still at work no matter what time of night I returned home.

When I was about fourteen, impelled by the ambition to help my mother and spare her from toiling day and night, I got work at the law offices of Mordecai, Gadsden, Rutledge and Hagood during the summer holidays. In the fall, when I was due to return to school, I decided instead to continue working and contributing to the family income. Fortunately one of the law partners, Benjamin H. Rutledge, took an active interest in my further education and arranged for my membership in the Charleston Library. He then mapped out a course of reading for me and saw to it that I followed it through. This experience provided a solid background when I later came to study law in the office of Judge Aldrich.

With us at our home in Charleston was my cousin Frank J. Hogan, who was some years my senior; he had been sent south from his native New York State because he was thought to have tuberculosis. My mother insisted that he and my sister Leonore and I study shorthand, and each evening she held informal classes, dictating to us. This training proved in the future to be most valuable to each of us. When my sister was widowed after an early marriage, her shorthand enabled her to support three children and eventually to study law. She was admitted to the bar in the District of Columbia and became assistant to the Solicitor of the Department of Agriculture, some years later rendering valuable service to the Extension Service of that department. Frank Hogan's proficiency in shorthand led him to a position as private secretary to General Bellinger, Quartermaster General of the Army. At the same time he studied law at Georgetown University and later became an outstanding trial lawyer at the District of Columbia bar, representing at one time Andrew Mellon, the former Secretary of the Treasury, Edward Doheney and many other prominent citizens. He was for one term president of the American Bar Association.

In my case, shorthand led, as a first result, to my job as court stenographer. To please me, my mother gave up dressmaking during the first month after my appointment and, with my grandmother, joined me in Aiken.

In those days Aiken was a quiet country town, but for some years it had enjoyed a reputation as a health resort. Its polo grounds and golf courses, favored by many northern visitors, lent it a cosmopolitan air. Life was pleasant and sociable there; I remember playing a great deal of tennis and some golf, enjoying—as far as my means allowed—a carefree bachelor's existence. My court duties occupied about one half of the year and I had time for legal and general reading. Judge Aldrich had to preside in the various counties of the state, but between courts his time was spent in Aiken, where he encouraged me to use his office and assisted me in my study of law.

I passed the bar examination in 1904 and opened an office of my own in Aiken. My shingle attracted many agreeable callers but few paying clients, and therefore it was necessary for me to continue in my job as court reporter, at least for a while, in order to support my mother and grandmother. To supplement my income further, I shortly afterward went into partnership with A. K. Lorenz to purchase the *Journal and Review*. Lorenz, who had just graduated from the University of South Carolina, had no more money than I had, but together we were able to pay the former owners $5,000—after borrowing $4,500 from a bank!

I knew nothing about publishing a newspaper. The business was really managed by Lorenz, who had been interested in it since his college days, when he had worked on the paper during his holidays. But my career in the field of journalism was brief; for after a year or two, when I became a candidate for Solicitor, I thought my candidacy might hurt the paper and that, if I were elected, it would not be appropriate for my newspaper to publish details of cases which as solicitor I would be called upon to prosecute. I therefore sold my interest to my energetic and very capable partner.

While recounting briefly the course of my life before I entered public office, I should give the all-important fact that on May 2, 1906, I was married to Miss Maude Busch of Aiken, whom I had first met while she was a student at Converse College. Both of us belonged to the Outing Club in Aiken and I frequently escorted her to boating and swimming parties and other social affairs. When Maude came home after graduating from college, she sang in the choir of St. Thaddeus Episcopal Church and I frequently accompanied her to rehearsals. Possessing what was then popularly called a "barber shop tenor," it was not long before I was invited to stay and sing with her. For some time I had been attending St. Thaddeus instead of the Roman Catholic church in which I had been baptized when a child.

My marked attentions to Miss Busch soon became a subject of comment in the small community, which doubtless accounted for a tactful comment made to me by the parish priest while on a visit to my newspaper office. He courteously said it was rumored that I was to be married and he thought he should present the position of the Church on "mixed marriages." After some discussion I told him, with equal courtesy, that while I had no immediate plans to wed, I disagreed with the Church's attitude on that subject. Thereafter, though I considered the question seriously, I saw no reason to change this view, and in time Maude and I were married by the Reverend T. W. Clift, rector of St. Thaddeus, and I began attending that church regularly, later formally becoming a communicant.

My decision in regard to church affiliation was difficult because of my devotion to my mother and my desire not to displease her. She was by now spending most of her time in Charleston with my married sister, Leonore. When I told her that I was to be married by an Episcopal rector, she relieved me greatly by saying that, although for several years she had been very much disappointed by my failure to attend the Catholic Church, she would much rather have me go to the Episcopal Church than to none. Nor did she complain when my sister became a member of the choir of St. Michael's in Charleston and after moving to Washington, while retaining her membership in the Catholic Church, sang regularly in the volunteer choir of All Soul's Episcopal Church.

My wife likewise, though a loyal worker for her own faith, has always been tolerant of the religious views of others. Her only brother now living married a Catholic and, though he has remained an Episcopalian, his children have been reared as Catholics. Probably my own independent thinking on these matters accounts for my tolerance of the religious beliefs of others. I cannot believe that in Heaven there are compartments separating the members of various denominations of our Christian faith. I think that my mother, who to the day of her death was a devout Catholic, and to me an angel on earth, has her place there just as will Maude, an equally devout Episcopalian.

For myself, I think a man's religion is a matter between God and himself and I dislike the hypocrite who parades his religious views no less than the bigot who arouses prejudice against other faiths. Time was to show me that these opinions were not shared by some of my political opponents.

To return to more mundane matters, about half the year, as I have said, saw me covering the court circuit of six counties. This of course was before automobiles came into general use, and one had to depend upon the intermittent train service. To reach Hampton County by railroad, for example, a passenger from Aiken had to go seventeen miles in the opposite direction, to Augusta, Georgia, and there board the Charleston and Western Carolina train. Fortunately the dockets of the

courts in Hampton and Bamberg were light, most of the activity of the
circuit centering in Aiken and its adjoining county, Barnwell. But even
to go from Aiken to Barnwell meant taking a Southern Railway train
to Blackville and waiting for hours for another train to cover the remaining ten miles. Today by automobile the entire distance can be
covered in about half an hour.

The magistrates of this period were often picturesque in appearance
and fearlessly independent in judgment; justice from their hands was
likely to be personal and informal. I recall particularly Magistrate Tom
S. Dunbar, quite an impressive figure, who presided in a rural area and
who contended that his court was one of justice, not law. He took the
general view that lawyers were unnecessary, but on one occasion he
permitted a lawyer to plead lengthily for a client. At the noon hour,
after he had been seen to commit some words to paper, he politely
interrupted the advocate to tell him to continue his address but that the
Judge was leaving the courtroom to have his lunch. The verdict, he
added, would be found in the desk drawer!

While I was riding the circuit, many of my evenings were spent at
the small hotels where were gathered the lawyers who had business
in the court. These men were often entertaining talkers, much given
to discussing affairs of state as well as questions of law. In their company I learned not only the strategy of trial lawyers but something of
the art of politics, an art more readily acquired by association than by
study.

In 1908 I decided to seek the office of Solicitor, with duties equivalent, in South Carolina, to those of a prosecuting attorney or district
attorney elsewhere. In addition, at that time the Solicitor attended
sessions of the General Assembly, serving somewhat in the capacity in
which the Legislative Counsel now acts, drafting bills for legislators.
In determining to offer myself for this position I was influenced by the
knowledge that the experience to be gained trying cases in court
would be wider than that ordinarily attained by a young lawyer, especially one who had not inherited an established practice and who
had no influential friends. As a court stenographer witnessing the trial
of all criminal cases, I had become impressed by the importance of the
Solicitor's role and I was vain enough to think that I might do well
in it. I was greatly flattered when I was elected in the first primary,
receiving a majority of the votes cast and carrying every county in the
circuit.

The term of office for a Solicitor was four years and the salary $1,700 per annum. During the two years I served I had to prosecute a number of important murder cases, including some widely publicized ones in which I got money from the Governor to employ a Pinkerton detective. But my work was not all in murder trials.

Shortly after taking office, I was reminded of the reverence our people had for the old Confederate uniform. Among the indictments found by the grand jury and turned over to me for trial was a case of assault and battery with intent to kill against a Negro who had shot another celebrant at what was known in the rural sections as a "hot supper." These festivities were usually held on Saturday night, the menu consisting of fried fish, corn bread and corn whisky. Captain Bill Williams, a notable local character whom I counted as a friend, came to see me in the Court House and asked if I really proposed to prosecute this Negro. When I said that I did, he said, "Why you can't prosecute this man! He is Doctor Peeples' Negro." I told my friend, "If you don't think I can prosecute him, come in here this afternoon and I'll show you how it's done."

The Negro had no lawyer, and when the sentence for an offense was not capital punishment the court was not required to appoint a lawyer for a defendant. It usually meant that the Solicitor made it his business to see that the evidence was fairly presented, that he made no argument, and that the defendant received every consideration. If the Solicitor did not see to this, the presiding judge did.

From the facts of the case as disclosed in the preliminary examination, I had no doubt that the jury would convict this defendant. I called the prosecuting witness, who pictured the start of the fight. When one guest shot out the oil lamp, everyone else dropped to the floor and crawled toward the door. The witness admitted that more than one pistol was fired, but swore he knew where the defendant was and that the defendant had shot him, wounding him slightly. Another colored witness corroborated his story. In his turn the defendant denied having fired a pistol at all and said when the light was shot out it was so dark he did not even see the prosecuting witness.

I then asked Captain Williams, whom I had noticed in the courtroom, if he wished to testify to the defendant's reputation for peace and order. He replied, "No, but I want you to put on the stand a witness who will do so." He asked me to call "Old Matt Ramsey."

Ramsey was a very popular Confederate veteran who was credited with heroic action at Fort Sumter. After the war he had been spoiled by old soldiers and by his neighbors, who found that he did not object to being regarded as a hero. He was a man of small stature with the amiable indiscretion of occasionally imbibing too freely; but he had an affidavit face, and when speaking of the "irrepressible conflict" he had a tear in his voice. When summoned, he came from the back of the Court House, dressed in an old Confederate uniform. Following the ritual, I asked if he knew the reputation of the defendant for peace and order, and he exclaimed, "Yes, sir. That is Doctor Peeples' Nigger." I explained that "reputation" meant what others said about the defendant, but I had no hope of limiting Matt to saying whether it was "good" or "bad." He continued, "Everybody knows that when Doctor Peeples went to the war, leaving Mrs. Peeples at home, this here man was a little boy and he looked after her. When Sherman's army marched through South Carolina, stragglers following the army came to demand Mrs. Peeples' silver. She was sick in bed and when she refused to tell where the silver was buried, they took hold of that boy; they beat him and threatened to kill him if he did not tell them where to find the silver. He wouldn't talk. Finally they took him out, beat him and tied his hands to a limb of a tree so that his feet were off the ground, but still that boy did not talk. When the soldiers left, Mrs. Peeples got out of bed, took a chair out to the tree and stood on it to cut the rope the boy was hanging by." Then Old Matt turned to the jury and, in a voice choked with emotion, added, "Doctor Peeples always said that boy was the best Nigger in South Carolina."

Within ten minutes the jury found the defendant not guilty. If they had been given the opportunity, they probably would have found me guilty for prosecuting the case. A few days later, while we were fishing, I congratulated Captain Williams on his successful management of this case. He told me he had studied law but decided not to practice. This aroused my curiosity and I asked if he had ever done any serious work. His reply was emphatic. "Oh, no," he said. "The thought of work has always been displeasing to me."

Favorable publicity resulting from my successful prosecution of several important murder cases caused a number of people to urge that I become a candidate for Congress. I was young and ambitious, but this required me to make a vital decision. If I intended to pursue the practice of law with its opportunity for higher income, I should continue as Solicitor, acquiring wider experience; if I preferred to follow a political career with its greater opportunity for public service, it was time to try to go to Congress. There was a general feeling in our section that if a congressman made good he would be continued in office and thus could broaden his knowledge of government and national politics. After considering the question for several weeks and discussing it with older friends, I concluded that I would be happier in public service and that I would make the campaign for election to the House of Representatives.

The representative from the Second Congressional District, in which Aiken is located, was at that time Congressman J. O. Patterson. Though not well known outside the state, he was highly regarded locally and, having served in Congress for six years, he could appeal to the voters on the basis of experience and the advantages of seniority. There was a third candidate, C. W. Garris.

Under the rules of the Democratic party in South Carolina, provision was made for a joint debate by the congressional candidates in all counties of the district. This had been the rule since 1898 and was largely due to the influence of Ben Tillman. When he began his Farmers' Movement, which resulted in his election as Governor, he had the support of only one newspaper, and this a weekly. He had to reach "the people" and he told me that, since he could not provide them with a cock fight, he thought the voters of rural areas would like to hear a debate between him and his opponents. While Tillman described himself as the homeliest man in the state, he was not unaware of his talent for extemporaneous speaking, and the county-to-county campaign meetings he instituted became a rule of the party. With the passing of the years he felt the newspapers were no longer controlled by men who would exclude reports on a candidate they opposed, and in 1912, when he was ailing but still wished to continue after eighteen years in the Senate, he announced that he would not participate in the county-to-county "circus." But neither Tillman nor anyone since has been able to stop the custom, though automobile travel has made it possible to shorten the campaign period by scheduling eighteen meetings instead of forty-six, and radio and television coverage has resulted in reduced attendance.

In 1910 these rural festivals were in full swing. People gathered from all over a county, including women who came for social entertainment rather than from interest in politics. The campaign of that summer turned out to be the most strenuous in the history of the Second District, which then comprised some eight counties and was approximately one hundred and fifty miles in its greatest length. Again it was my lot to traverse this section of South Carolina by horse and buggy and by train. The speeches were often as highly seasoned as the barbecues; at times I wondered which would give out first, my nerves, my money or my stomach.

Patterson's health limited the number of his appearances, but Garris and I fought hard. To save money he and I would join in hiring a buggy to take us to the meetings. As we were friends there was an absence of the bitter, even vitriolic, personal attacks which frequently marked these oratorical contests. In the first primary Garris ran last, leaving Patterson, who led the ticket, to finish the race with me in a second primary. After a short and sharp two weeks' campaign the second primary was held and the "hottest congressional race in years," as it was locally called, came to an end. I won by a majority of fifty-seven votes over Patterson.

Two nights after my victory, on September 21, 1910, some of my supporters held a torchlight parade in Aiken, which was headed by a carriage bearing Maude and me. Illuminated banners were carried in the procession with such slogans as "Fifty-seven Is Enough," and "I love my wife, but oh, you Jimmie!" On a temporary platform erected near the Post Office I made the traditionally short and, I trust, graceful speech of thanks. As I looked out over the faces of the crowd, I was sincerely grateful for the friendship and support of the people of Aiken County throughout the ten years it had been my home. They had indeed been good to me.

# 3 SERVICE IN THE HOUSE

William Howard Taft was still President when I arrived in Washington in March, 1911, to participate in the special session of the Sixty-second Congress, beginning my fourteen years' service in the House. That winter Taft had spent several weeks in Augusta, Georgia, which is just across the river from Aiken, and as congressman-elect I had called on him. At that meeting he had been so thoughtful of the feelings of a young congressman that I always had a warm place in my heart for him.

In historical perspective, those were momentous years in both domestic and foreign affairs, covering the era of President Wilson's "New Freedom," the United States' participation in World War I, and the beginning of our country's adjustment, at first not always successful, to its new role as the strongest power of the Western world. I do not intend to offer any extensive account either of my doings in Congress or of the nation's affairs during that time. My purpose is to share something of the impressions I received, the knowledge I gained, and the friends I made during what was, in essence, a lengthy apprenticeship.

First, the Washington scene itself. Everyone is aware that the city on the Potomac, and the government it houses, have altered considerably in the past half century. In retrospect, some aspects of this transformation strike me particularly. For example, in those days the United States government, enjoying a total income of less than one and a quarter billion dollars, amassed without benefit of income taxes, was served by less than 400,000 civil servants. In his role as Commander in Chief, President Taft led, theoretically, at least, an Army whose total strength was well below an authorized complement of 100,000 men. And the United States Fleet, though second in the world in size, comprised only 380 vessels of all types.

The District of Columbia, with its 330,000 people, still had room for over two hundred farms within its area. Many of the city streets were tree-lined and unpaved, with numerous horse-drawn vehicles. But since the beginning of the century, steady progress had been made in building a center of government at once beautiful and efficient in design; during my first term, for example, there was much talk of new buildings for the various departments. Any year, I suppose, is a good year for a young man to begin a career in Congress. But I confess that Washington in 1911, with all its signs of change and growth, was an exciting place to me.

In national politics, the Democrats were showing signs of strength, the Republicans of weakness. Never before in history had a Republican President called an extra session to promote administration policies when his own party had lost control of the House, but this was President Taft's strategy for passing the Canadian Reciprocal Tariff legislation, refused him by the Republican Senate. The Democrats, and particularly those from the South, were almost united on the question of reducing tariff duties. Harmony had also prevailed at the Democratic caucus I attended in February, which decided unanimously to support for Speaker Champ Clark of Missouri, who had long served in the House and had been the Democratic minority leader for three years.

The Democratic majority determined to change the rules and withdraw from the Speaker the privilege of appointing committees; then in caucus they agreed to give their members of the House Ways and Means Committee power to make Democratic committee assignments. The Republicans put their appointments in the hands of a Policy Committee. These changes were popularly described as a blow against "Cannonism." The reference, of course, was to the old Republican warrior from Illinois, Uncle Joe Cannon, then in his seventy-second year (he was not to retire from Congress for another twelve years), who had exercised powerful influence as Speaker of the House for eight years.

I mention both Champ Clark and Uncle Joe Cannon early in this account of my House days because I came to be on close terms with both and learned much from them.

I well recall the day Clark assumed the speakership. He made a short speech of welcome and advice to the new members, touching on several themes that he discussed with me in greater detail once I knew him. He warned that there would be times when some important measure was pending and congressmen would receive hundreds of letters for or against its passage. The uninitiated would conclude that the people of his district were greatly excited about the issue. But Clark advised members not to be stampeded by this mail, which he styled "propaganda." He said if it were feasible to list the signers of all mail received, it would be found that the same people wrote repeatedly; but that these did not constitute more than 2 per cent of the voters of a district. It was the duty of a congressman, he emphasized, to bear in mind the interest of the other 98 per cent who never communicated with their representative, but expected him to act according to his own best knowledge and judgment.

It did not take long to discover that his was the voice of experience. I found his statement to be true as long as I served in the House and Senate. At times, when it was apparent that hundreds of letters coming to my office were inspired by an individual or a representative of some group, I would answer by asking for more information about his objections and requesting that he tell me the specific parts of the legislation to which he objected. He seldom complied with my request. I gleaned another thought from Clark's remarks which has been in the forefront of my mind ever since: unsolicited advice is a cheap commodity because the supply greatly exceeds the demand.

I learned later that, while respecting the right of the people to petition for objectives in which they are interested, every congressman should remember how easily signatures can be obtained on petitions concerning both national and local matters. Typical perhaps was the attitude of a farmer friend of mine in Aiken County who once told me that he was devoting his time to an effort to defeat his entire county legislative delegation because they had abolished the office of road supervisor, creating instead a five-man commission. This action had been taken, he said, because of a petition. Upon inquiry I found that he had signed the petition himself, and when I expressed surprise he said, "They should have had more sense than to do what I asked. It is their job to decide what is right. They get paid for it. I don't!"

When I began my service in Washington, congressmen, especially from the South, did not enjoy the frequent visitations from constituents which are now such a feature of the legislator's lot. In those early days I usually traveled by train. Even as late as 1916 it was exceedingly difficult to travel to and from Washington by automobile. The roads were mostly unpaved and we usually allowed a full day to get through the Virginia swamps in my Reo automobile. On one occasion in bad weather the journey from Aiken to Washington took four days. Under these conditions, I often felt, the 20 cents a mile given to members of Congress for travel was well earned.

These conditions also affected the travel habits of my constituents, whom I saw but rarely in Washington and who, for obvious reasons, telephoned me infrequently. For some years I could go to my office at nine o'clock, dispose of mail by ten and attend committee meetings until the house met at noon. Usually I remained on the floor without interruption and, consequently, learned what went on. Seldom was I called off to see a supporter or friend of a supporter, which certainly was to my advantage. Congressmen from neighboring cities, and particularly those who had government installations in their district, were more likely to receive callers and had to spend much time in personal service for individual voters.

In the House there was a delegation of some twenty members from the New York City area. Most of them stayed in New York attending to personal business, some of which undoubtedly bore upon the next election since it involved keeping their constituents satisfied. However, one member remained in constant attendance in the House, keeping in touch with the Democratic leader. It was his duty to call the secretary of Tammany Hall when his colleagues were needed for a vote on an important issue, and when this occurred, the entire delegation would be in their seats the next morning. One of them told me that their practice of returning to New York once the session was under way was known and approved by their constituents, who thought they should spend their salaries as well as their time at home. Yet the fact is that uninterrupted attendance not only gives a legislator an opportunity to master the business of government but leads more surely to leadership in the Congress. It was often the case, I noted, that men from small towns—like Claude Kitchin of Scotland Neck, North Carolina; Finis Garrett of Dresden, Tennessee; and John N. Garner of Uvalde, Texas, Democratic leaders in my time—attained prominence in the House, rather than members from the populous industrial areas. That was equally true of Republican congressmen.

Garner, in particular, came from a small town in Texas that barely grew to be a city during his long career in Congress. He didn't receive ten letters a day and answered few of those. He was to be twice Vice President of the United States and a real power in government. Of course, Jack Garner had political talent and he and the others just mentioned were re-elected because of their outstanding ability. But to their colleagues the important fact was that they were always in their places in committee or on the floor of the House.

On the other hand, I learned that if a congressman, instead of attending to public business, spent all his time going to the many government departments scattered over the city of Washington running errands for his constituents, he could not know what was going on at the Capitol. He might qualify to serve as a glorified secretary of a chamber of commerce, but he would never make much of a mark in the Congress.

Let me add that I was certainly not entirely immune from these requests. Most applicants for help seemed to think their request the only one that a representative would receive, not realizing that appeals are not only very frequent but in many instances have to do with matters in no way connected with government. I wish I had kept a special file of some which came to me. I recall being asked to get a bottle of water from the Potomac to be used in dedicating a water development, and some soil from the White House grounds in which a memorial tree could be planted. A minister who had evidently exhausted his own ideas once asked me to collect prayers offered by the chaplains of the two Houses. I did not mind collecting prayers, but I balked when a merchant asked me to collect a bill from a former customer. Probably the most frequent requests received by congressmen come from students who would like the congressman either to write a "paper" for them on some assigned topic or perhaps provide them with arguments that will guarantee them success in debate. These are generally referred to the Superintendent of the Document Room, who sends them speeches on the subject by congressmen.

There are times when to a visitor looking down from the gallery the House of Representatives may appear entirely too disorganized to be an efficient deliberative body. The apparent confusion, casual comings and goings, and informal conferences between members may lead the uninformed spectator to conclude that members do not know what is going on. In the bewildering first days of my service, I felt this way myself, but I soon learned that because of the large membership most of the work on pending legislation is, of necessity, done in committee sessions. There officials of the departments concerned with a bill have been questioned at length, and other interested persons not connected with government but having information to contribute have been heard. Printed reports presenting the majority and minority opinions of the committee have been made available to the House, and members have usually discussed the bill with party colleagues on the committee and have decided how they are going to vote. When the bill is first considered on the floor, there is general debate for whatever length of time the party leaders have agreed upon, the time being equally divided between those for and against the bill. The member in charge of the bill usually explains it, and he allots the remaining time among those favoring the measure. The senior minority member of the committee reporting the bill performs the same service for the opposition. However, a speaker is free to use the time allotted to him not only to comment on the legislation but to talk discursively on other matters. His real audience is frequently his constituents at home. As most of those present have already read the committee report and made up their minds how they will vote, they are not anxious to listen for hours to generalizations on the state of the union and are likely to move about and talk in small groups, partly ignoring the speaker. However, after general debate, when the bill is read for amendment the House quickly comes to order, members giving full attention to learn of any change that is proposed. As speeches are now made under the five-minute rule, something of note must be said in the first few moments, since the audience is not only critical but can be cruel. I say "cruel" because if you are speaking and a congressman seated two feet in front of you turns to talk with his neighbor or, worse, leaves the chamber, cruel is the word for it!

Another feature that adds to the air of disorder is that, compared with the Senate chamber, the House is overcrowded. In my first term, when the membership was 391, each representative had a desk. But as a result of the 1910 census the membership was increased by forty-four and the desks were removed, since there was room only for chairs. I for one was glad when it was later determined before the 1920 census that there should be no further increase in the membership.

Even in a body of 435 a representative can achieve distinction if he possesses unusual ability or unusual personality; if fortunately he has both, he is almost certain to command the respect of his colleagues

of both parties, provided he is diligent in attending committee meetings
and House sessions. At their offices members are besieged by professional lobbyists who present them with "facts" on pending bills. Sometimes these are correct; more often they are not. If a legislator relies
too greatly upon such biased sources, he is apt to be challenged sharply
in debate and find to his intense discomfiture that he is merely expound-
ing the view of some selfish interest. I soon realized that nowhere does
accuracy carry such a premium as on the floor of a legislative body.

Some congressmen feel that they can perpetuate themselves in office
if they can convince their constituents that committee assignments
and seniority, as such, are all-important. Seniority is valuable, but
seniority alone is seldom a reason for keeping a man at any responsible
task, and politics should be no exception. In each Congress there are
members who cannot hope to remain in Washington long enough to
become chairman of an important committee, yet who by reason of
unusual talent and diligence quickly acquire a position of leadership
on the committees to which they are assigned. The rule of seniority
undoubtedly has benefited some men of only average ability who
ordinarily would have found it difficult to be elected chairman of a
committee against their more able colleagues. But though in some
cases it may work to the advantage of mediocrity, the system will
probably survive because no better plan for selecting chairmen has
been suggested that would not involve contests damaging to party
harmony.

I should not give the impression that in my House days I thought
lightly either of seniority or of committee assignments. Speaker Champ
Clark once delivered an address setting forth the advantages of seniority, and it became the habit of every congressman who faced opposition
to his re-election to spread copies of this speech far and wide throughout his district. I am sure that in one campaign I sent out this speech.
It is only natural that incumbents should emphasize the importance
of seniority; the real misfortune is when it becomes a substitute for
character, capacity and courage in congressional service.

In my first term, I drew the Banking and Currency Committee and
the Committee on War Claims. Since I was disappointed by these first
assignments, I discussed the relative importance of various committees
with Uncle Joe Cannon, whom I found to be a delightful person, al-
together different, as I told him, from the "devil with horns" many
Southerners considered him to be. He impressed upon me that the

best committee of all was the Committee on the State of the Union, that is, the entire House sitting as a Committee of the Whole. "If a man will remember he is a member of that committee and stay on the floor when the House is in session, he will learn more about government than in any other way," he told me. Uncle Joe was right; to emphasize this point, the rules provide that when the House is in session, only by its consent can a committee meet.

My dissatisfaction with the Banking and Currency Committee was soon dispelled when I began to know its chairman, Carter Glass. He had been a member of the House for eleven years, during which period he had played the role of an almost silent observer, never making speeches on the floor and seldom uttering a word in a Democratic caucus, though from his contribution in committee his ability was never in doubt.

At the Democratic caucus in 1913 which preceded the passage of the Owen-Glass Act establishing the Federal Reserve System, he first revealed his remarkable effectiveness in debate. The Wilson administration was pledged to a program of banking and currency reform, and when this measure was introduced in June of that year it was confronted by strenuous opposition. The many objections and amendments brought forward in the caucus evidently inspired Glass, for during our tedious debates he made replies as convincing and brilliant as ever a party caucus had heard. His sense of political realities helped keep the main principles of the measure intact, and he continued his militant sponsorship on the floor of the House so that the bill finally became law on Christmas Eve of that year. My admiration for Carter Glass, which was to last until his death, was increased by the remarkable demonstration of political acumen this emotional, testy, yet to me ever kindly old Virginian gave during debate on the Federal Reserve Act.

Every congressman likes to think himself an orator, believing he has been elected largely on the strength of his campaign speeches. To address the House is to put this theory to the test. I had been in Congress about a month before an opportunity arose for me to participate in a debate. It was quite an ordeal for me, as I doubt that there exists anywhere a more exacting audience.

The House was engaged on May 2, 1911, in a hot tariff dispute which centered on the so-called farmers' free list bill. I began by saying, "Tenderfoot that I am, naturally I have been touched . . . by the solicitude and esteem evidenced by the gentlemen on the Republican side of the House, especially those hailing from the New England states, for my good friends the farmers." I then launched into criticism of the Republican stand on tariff for protection's sake rather than as a means of raising revenue. I said to Jim Mann, the minority leader, that if the Democrats proposed the Ten Commandments for adoption, he would so ably criticize them as to cause even partisan Democrats to doubt the wisdom of our course.

Some of my comments bore on conditions in southern cotton mills. New England congressmen claimed that reduced tariff rates, in addition to the competition of southern mills, would destroy their textile industry. There existed then, as now, some northern sensitiveness over the flight of factories southward, just as there is over the flight of cotton cultivation to the western states. In an earlier speech a representative from Pennsylvania had criticized the type of labor employed in southern mills.

I pleaded for an end to sectional strife and the consideration of tariff reduction on its own merits. I ended combatively, citing other Democratic measures, and ventured to predict that "the conduct of the Democratic Party in the House will so justify the confidence of the people, that when the battle of the ballots is fought in November 1912 . . . their majority in the House will be maintained, the Republicans ousted from their control of the Senate and driven from the Executive offices. Democracy will be enthroned and the people rule once more."

My youthful exuberance drew applause—from Democrats—and I sat down well satisfied. With its attack on Republicans and defense of farmers, the speech might well have been regarded as an announcement of my candidacy for re-election!

Shortly after this speech I was conscious enough of my youth to be greatly embarrassed when I fell victim to the childish malady of mumps, then going the rounds among the page boys.

Remembering the strong arguments Democrats made at that time in favor of a tariff "for revenue only," I am struck by the fact that changing conditions frequently alter a point of view. Some years later, during the administration of President Roosevelt, Cordell Hull, as Secretary of State, sponsored the reciprocal trade agreements bill, which the Democratic party forced through Congress, and since then tariff duties have been arranged by treaty between the United States and other countries. However, in recent times there has been a great change in the Democratic party's attitude. It was first evident in the demands of Democratic senators from western states for prohibitive tariff duties on copper and other metals which are mined in their region.

With the industrialization of the South, there have come increasing demands from nearly all southern states for putting higher tariff duties upon many products and even quotas upon imported textile products, particularly from Japan. Circumstances indeed alter political convictions.

In those early days one of my major interests as a representative was the improvement of public roads. A number of bills had already been introduced in Congress looking to a national highway system, but not one had passed or even received serious consideration.

I had the temerity to call a meeting in my office of the ten or twelve members who had previously introduced bills on this subject. I proposed that all pending bills should be abandoned and that a committee be formed to draft a proposal on which we could concentrate. The result was a measure popularly known as the 10-20-30 bill, providing that the federal government pay to state governments annually, for each mile of road used by the rural mail carriers, $10 per mile for dirt roads, $20 for sand-clay roads and $30 for hard-surfaced roads. We thought this the only constitutional way for the federal government to aid in highway improvement.

This proposal was sent to the agricultural committee because its chairman was Frank Lever of my state and we felt he would help us. Lever appointed a subcommittee to study it, but there it remained. When no action was taken, Dorsey Shackleford of Missouri and I circulated a petition, which we managed to get signed by a majority of the House, instructing the agricultural committee to report the bill as an amendment to the agricultural appropriations bill. The committee did not dare disobey the instructions of a majority of the House and the amendment was adopted.

In the Senate it met opposition from Senator John H. Bankhead of Alabama, an advocate of improved highways. However, a compromise was reached with the agreement that a study be ordered and a report made to the next session. As part of the compromise an appropriation of a half million dollars was made as an experiment in the federal-state construction of highways in every state under a matching formula. I secured the $20,000 allotted to my state and had my county match the federal funds to build the first federal-aid sand-clay road in South Carolina.

In the next Congress, Dorsey Shackleford and I started a new proposal, providing for federal aid along the lines of the present Highway Act. We resorted to the same method of getting a petition signed by a majority of the House, but this time asked for the creation of a committee on public roads. We were successful.

I was placed on this committee, which, under the chairmanship of Shackleford, reported and induced the House to pass a comprehensive bill. On this occasion it was supported in the Senate by Senator Bankhead and became known as the Bankhead Act. I felt that at last I had accomplished something in the field of national legislation when President Wilson gave me one of the two pens he had used in signing the bill, saying, "Congressman, in passing this bill we fulfill another platform pledge."

This was interesting, but really it had not been my reason for promoting the bill. I believed it was a proper function of the federal government to contribute to the construction and maintenance of public highways, the roads of a state being used by citizens of other states, and particularly by interstate heavy commercial vehicles, which really destroyed sand-clay roads.

My efforts to put through this legislation convinced me that a member of Congress can accomplish much if he is not so egotistical as to want his own name on every measure he proposes, and is content to entrust it to some person who is in a better position to "father" it. This is particularly true if the other is a senior member whose sponsorship lends prestige to the proposal.

In connection with committee assignments, I was unwittingly the cause of a serious dispute between Claude Kitchin and John Garner over an assignment to the Appropriations Committee. When President Wilson was inaugurated he appointed Congressman Albert S. Burleson Postmaster General, and Burleson's district in Texas elected J. P. Buchanan to fill the House vacancy. Burleson was anxious that Buchanan should take his place on the Appropriations Committee and enlisted the aid of his fellow Texas congressman, Jack Garner, who ranked next to Chairman Kitchin among the Democrats on the Ways and Means Committee, now charged with making committee assignments. Knowing nothing of Buchanan's ambition or of the interest of Garner and

Burleson in promoting it, at the suggestion of Claude Kitchin, who had shown a friendly interest in me, I had written to the Democratic members of the committee, expressing the hope that I might be appointed to the Appropriations Committee, and had received promises of support from a majority of them. After the committee had met, I heard there had been quite a contest for the vacancy I sought, and that Kitchin and Garner had had bitter words over it. Kitchin and I lost out by one vote.

I "spread the word" that when the report was made to the caucus I would challenge its accuracy and read the letters from a majority of the committee promising to name me. Immediately some of the old men on the committee (they must have been at least fifty years old) came to advise me I would destroy my career. I learned that Congressman McGillicuddy, who had written me a letter, was interested at the time in having a good friend appointed postmaster at Bath, Maine. He was told by the Postmaster General that the administration would deeply appreciate his support of Buchanan for the Appropriations Committee. What could the poor man do? He voted against me. I did not challenge the report.

Before the announcement was made, Garner, with characteristic frankness, told me he wanted me to know that there was nothing personal against me in his attitude and that he had led the fight for Buchanan because he was a fellow Texan and also his friend. A little later he did support my appointment to the Appropriations Committee.

Of greater importance than the appointment itself was the bad feeling that existed between Kitchin and Garner because of the contest. Kitchin resented the Postmaster General's using patronage to influence the action of his committee. Thereafter Kitchin and Garner spoke only when public business required it. But several years later, after Kitchin was stricken while speaking in the House, Garner constantly inquired of me about him, and when he had recovered sufficiently to receive visitors, with Kitchin's approval I asked Jack to join me in visiting him. Kitchin was glad to see him and though he was never able to return to the Capitol, he and Garner remained on friendly terms till his death.

Kitchin was one of the finest characters I ever knew. He was a clean man. If in his presence a man started to tell a racy story, Kitchin would leave. The encouraging thing was that his colleagues respected him for it. He was a forceful, eloquent speaker and, as his opponents would testify, dangerous in debate. He had convictions and the courage to defend those convictions. I remember two dramatic episodes connected with him. He was the Democratic leader in April, 1917, when President Wilson delivered to the Congress his message recommending the adoption of a War Resolution. It was obvious that the resolution would be overwhelmingly adopted. But Kitchin was opposed to our entering the war; as Democratic leader he was embarrassed that he could not vote for a course that all but a few of his party supported. Late at night, just before the resolution was to be voted upon, I went to his office outside the House Chamber. There I found his wife and daughters much upset. He told me that, hope and pray as he had, he could not in conscience vote for the resolution, and he felt it his duty to present his views to the House. Then he read to me a statement he intended to make. It was short and simple but impressive. As he read it one of the girls began to cry, which further upset him. Turning to her he said, "Please don't. I am a poor man. I cannot leave you girls wealth, but I do want to leave you the knowledge that your old Dad, while in public life, never voted against his convictions."

Shortly after midnight, following a long day of debate, Kitchin went on the floor and asked to be recognized. Members crowded out of the cloakrooms. He then spoke sadly but firmly. When he had finished, the Republican leader, Jim Mann, was the first to rise and the entire membership stood to applaud in tribute to a courageous man.

I was close to Kitchin at another moment of crisis in his life. He did not write his speeches and seldom made notes. At times, on request, I would sit by him to hand him a paper or on occasion to remind him of some point he wished to make. He was unusually adept at catching a cryptic reminder by only a word. One day when there was an exceedingly hot controversy pending, I was at his side as he was making one of his whirlwind speeches. Suddenly his voice failed and he continued almost inaudibly. From the rear of the House came cries of "Louder, louder!" He had asked me to remind him to make an appeal for unity on the Democratic side, so I said quietly, "Appeal for unity." As he turned to me I saw he was not himself. He murmured, "What?" and slowly sank to the floor. He had suffered a stroke and, though he lived for some time, this was his last appearance in the House.

After his death, a contest arose over who was to succeed him. During his long illness, at his request, Finis J. Garrett of Tennessee had served as Democratic leader, but Garner was ambitious to be elected. Both were strong candidates with devoted supporters. I supported

Garrett, with whom I had worked closely during Kitchin's illness. Some days before the decisive caucus Garrett was in my office and Garner came to see him. He said, "Finis, I have announced to the press my withdrawal and wish to extend to you my best wishes." Garrett, with characteristic dignity, began to express his appreciation, but Jack quickly interrupted, "I want it clearly understood that I am withdrawing only because I know when I am licked." It was an example of the frankness which disarms, and though rivalry between the two had been intense, their relations improved appreciably thereafter.

There were times when more congressmen would be gathered in the Democratic Cloakroom than could be found on the floor of the House. On one occasion I heard Schley Howard of Georgia, who was elected the same year I was, talking with Dorsey Shackleford of Missouri. Shack was another of those who seldom made a speech on the floor but influenced many that were made. Howard said he was going to Atlanta to make a speech and was wondering what he could talk about. Shackleford was not hesitant about suggesting that he oppose the preparedness program which Wilson had just submitted to the Congress; he had it all figured out—how many miles of good roads could be built with the money that would be spent for one battleship, and how many bushels of wheat and bales of cotton could be bought with the total cost of the program.

Howard was a supporter of Wilson, but he fell for it. Upon his return, Howard came over to where Shackleford and I were sitting and reported: "When I got to the Opera House in Atlanta I gave a copy of my speech to a reporter, who went back to his office to write his story rather than stay and hear me speak. I had decided I would first present the President's program and then demolish it. I began, 'My friends, you know that I have been a loyal supporter of Woodrow Wilson.' A fellow in the front row yelled a loud 'Hurrah for Wilson' and was joined by the entire audience.

"I did not like the loud applause, but continued: 'The President does not claim to be infallible, but he has a preparedness program and wants to spend $35 million for one battleship.' Up came the loud-mouthed man in the front row with his 'Hurrah for Wilson,' and again he was only the leader in the chorus that followed. I continued, 'The President also wants to raise the pay of the Army so that he can recruit more men for the war.'

"Once again, and without waiting for the leader, applause broke out, and when that subsided I said, 'And my friends I want you to know that as your congressman I agree with him and shall support his program.' Shack, I put your speech in my pocket and thereafter I simply eulogized Wilson. The Exalted Ruler of the Elks wanted to take me to the club to talk to the 'boys,' but 'another engagement' took me elsewhere. The truth was, I hurried to the newspaper office to kill that speech."

Howard said, "It might have been a good speech for Missouri, but it would have played the devil with me in Georgia." Howard continued to be a supporter of the President.

Membership on the House Appropriations Committee enabled me to have accurate information about the financial needs of the government, and because of my belief in a balanced budget I took a keen interest in fiscal affairs. Under the system that existed when I went to the House, many legislative committees had power to appropriate funds. The frequent result of this was that members who were particularly interested in certain government activities in their districts sought appointment on a committee dealing with the activity, and then were overgenerous in making appropriations.

Several of us worked for years to change the system and finally a new procedure was adopted under the Budget and Accounting Act of 1921, concentrating the power to appropriate in one Appropriations Committee. This act also created a Director of the Budget.

Economy in national expenditures then depended, and still depends to a great extent, on the attitude of the House Appropriations Committee. Members of the Senate Appropriations Committee, busy with the affairs of an entire state, too often followed a policy of accepting whatever the House had appropriated as a basic figure, considering only requests by departments for funds denied by the House. Members of the Appropriations Committee need to be courageous and wary, for they come under considerable pressure—some direct and some indirect. There is a natural tendency for the head of each division of all departments to ask for increased funds every year. After all, a division head believes his duties to be important and he knows that their expansion would increase his personal importance. His estimates are usually accepted by the department's budget officer, who finds the easiest thing is to approve the request and let some other official or the Congress cut it. The Cabinet member accepts the estimate of his subordinates, and only when the estimate reaches the Director of the Budget is it subjected to the scrutiny necessary to check constantly increasing appropriations.

Of the many bills that I managed on the floor for the Committee on Appropriations, I recall with more than usual interest the one I reported at the end of World War I. (I might explain, for the sake of readers not familiar with legislative procedure, that the congressman who reports a bill from a committee manages it on the floor. That means that he requests certain colleagues to defend the controversial provisions, opposes all efforts to amend it, and in general does whatever he can to get the bill passed.) Congress had appropriated vast sums for the fiscal year beginning July 1, 1918, in anticipation of a long war. With the signing of the armistice in November I concluded that if the funds were allowed to remain at the disposal of the various agencies until the end of the fiscal year June 30, pressures would arise to use them on new government projects in order that wartime staffs should not be reduced. Chairman Swagar Sherley of Kentucky left to me the task of drafting a bill which repealed about $15 billion in appropriations. Naturally I received no plaudits from the executive departments concerned, but our action resulted in huge savings to the taxpayers.

While Uncle Joe Cannon, representing the Republican minority, usually voted for economies, there was one occasion when he surprised me. Some months after the armistice a young naval officer asked for an appropriation to enable the Navy to experiment with a device to be dropped at harbor entrances for the purpose of detecting the approach of a submarine. Sherley and I were skeptical about such a visionary idea and in any event, just after the war, thought it high time to practice some economy. Uncle Joe voted for the proposal.

After our meeting I expressed to him my surprise at his vote. He told me that when he was a boy about ten years old, living in Indiana, he heard a congressional candidate ridicule a congressman who had voted for an appropriation of $30,000 to experiment in sending a message by wire from Washington to Baltimore. He added, "Now messages are sent all over the earth and by cable beneath the oceans, and I know that there is nothing the American boy cannot do if given a chance." Uncle Joe was then more than eighty years old, but he had confidence in the American youth.

When "Pitchfork" Ben Tillman died about this time, Cannon was a member of the committee appointed to attend the funeral at the Tillman home in South Carolina, although he was nearing his eighty-second or eighty-third birthday. On his birthday he announced that he would not be a candidate for re-election.

A few days after this announcement, Jake Hardy, who lived in Edgefield County in my congressional district, came to my office in Washington and said he wanted me to arrange for him to talk to Uncle Joe Cannon. I took him over to Cannon's office and first went into the inner office to tell Uncle Joe about his visitor. Old politician that he was, Cannon came out and greeted Hardy like an old friend, telling him how much he had appreciated his courtesies upon his visit to South Carolina, and reminded him of the hot dusty drive to the Tillman home and the funeral. Hardy then said he had read in a newspaper of Cannon's intention to retire from the House and that he had come to beg him not to leave public life. He said, "I am a Democrat and you are an old Republican, but we think alike, and with young fellows like this Senator Beveridge of Indiana going wild, it is your duty to stay here and save this country."

He talked with such earnestness and showed such feeling that Cannon was greatly affected. He thanked his visitor and returned to his private office. When I told him I had had no idea what Hardy was going to say to him, he said, "He's a fine fellow, but he's all wrong. I have seen men stay here when they did not know what was going on. I want to quit now while I still have sense enough to know that for me the curtain has gone down."

Perhaps I have said enough to indicate that service on the House Appropriations Committee can provide some hard political schooling. I remember an incident concerning my friend Martin Madden of Chicago, who for some years was chairman of the Committee. Madden, a Republican of long service and independent convictions, was greatly respected by his colleagues. One day when a bill providing appropriations for the Interior Department was to be considered, Madden advised me that Congressman Cramton of Michigan intended to offer on the House floor an amendment to provide funds for certain expenses of Howard University. This was an educational institution for Negroes in the District of Columbia, which since the War Between the States had been supported in large measure by the Congregational Church.

We both knew that no law existed authorizing appropriations by the government for private educational institutions, and therefore, under the House rules, the amendment would not be in order. Under committee rules it was the duty of Chairman Madden, or the member in charge of the bill, Congressman Cramton, to make a point of order opposing it. The presiding officer of the House would certainly hold that the amendment was not in order. Cramton was offering the amendment for political reasons, and for similar reasons Chairman Madden felt he could not afford to make that point of order. But he thought it right to advise me, as the minority member, of what was to occur so that I could make it. He said he would then request me to withhold the point of order temporarily so that he could make a speech that would please the colored voters, who constituted nearly 50 percent of his constituents.

The prearranged plan was carried out. While admitting there was no law authorizing the appropriation, Madden made a strong appeal for an exception because of the great progress of Negroes in the United States. In turn, I argued that if the rules were violated in this instance, there would be other similar appeals; and if the appropriation was justified, then a law should be passed authorizing the appropriation of funds for Howard University. All of us knew the point of order would be sustained by the presiding officer. It was.

When the bill reached the Senate, where there are few rules, but much Senatorial courtesy, the appropriation was restored, and in the conference between the House and Senate it was agreed to. That too was expected. The result was that I sustained the House rules, Madden made his political speech and was re-elected, Howard University got its money, and next year a law was passed authorizing appropriations for the institution.

After Madden had finished his political speech and the chair had ruled, he approached me and said, "Well, that's over for this year. Let's go back to our committee work." When I expressed some surprise at his performance, he said the colored voters in his district had so increased that when he died or retired no white man would again represent that district. In 1928 he died suddenly in his committee room. The district then elected Congressman dePriest, the first Negro representative since Reconstruction days, and has ever since sent a Negro to the House.

I had been present, not as a delegate but as an observer, at the dramatic political convention of 1912 when Woodrow Wilson won the nomination over Champ Clark, and I soon became a loyal supporter of this great man.

Wilson never seemed to me the cold, austere man he was often pictured. Could it have been that his dignity was mistaken for austerity? I found him gracious and generous, and soon discovered that he had a very human side and often showed a warm desire to help those in public life whom he liked. I remember that an attorney in Washington once interested me in a petition to the President to pardon a young man who had been convicted of embezzlement (wrongly, the lawyer believed), while he was employed in a small bank in Pennsylvania, and sentenced to three years in the penitentiary. The lawyer was interested because he said that in early life he, too, had been the victim of circumstantial evidence.

After reading the affidavits, I found myself believing the young man innocent and I inquired of the district attorney who had prosecuted the case. Because of after-discovered evidence, he also had doubt about the guilt of the prisoner. I sent the file to Joe Tumulty, the President's secretary, who showed it to the President. About a week later Tumulty told me that the President had talked with the Attorney General and had decided to issue the pardon. It was only a few days before Christmas, and the President had told Tumulty to communicate with the authorities at once so that the young man could spend Christmas with his family in Washington!

Despite his idealism, President Wilson was not above being a practical politician. After the outbreak of war in Europe, while he was negotiating with the Central Powers about the rights of Americans to travel on armed merchant ships, Congressman McLemore of Texas introduced a resolution requesting the President to warn Americans not to travel on such vessels.

With a group of five or six Democratic congressmen, I went to see Mr. Wilson in order to inform him of our fear that if the resolution came to a vote, it would pass. He accepted our estimate of the sentiment in the House, but urged that we oppose the resolution wholeheartedly. At Princeton, he added, he had noted that whenever the Tigers were to play Holy Cross they expected to win, and won; when they faced Harvard, they expected to lose—and generally lost. No coach ever made a better pep talk to his team than President Wilson made to us that day, and we returned to the House in fighting spirit. Further, he aided our efforts by appealing directly to the people, and after a week's debate the resolution was overwhelmingly defeated.

One day I went to see the President in company with Senator Ben Tillman of South Carolina. The war was at its height, and criticism of the President was still rife in the Senate. On this occasion I commented on his ability in the midst of all his troubles to play an occasional game of golf and to attend the theater. He said that he liked to go to the vaudeville at Keith's; it helped him to preserve his sense of humor to the extent that he could still appreciate the antics of some members of the Senate. At this, Senator Tillman, who favored forceful speech and indulged in picturesque profanity, expressed his opinion of certain of his colleagues. I thought the Presbyterian Elder would be shocked. President Wilson listened with composure and then said quietly, "Senator, there are times when I envy you your vocabulary."

President Wilson's attitude toward the redoubtable old Ben can be judged by an incident that occurred before the congressional election of 1918. Tillman, who had been in bad health for several years, was nevertheless determined to die in harness and offered himself for re-election. His principal opponent was former Governor Cole L. Blease, who, though then out of office, could be relied upon to wage a forceful campaign. Blease had publicly opposed the United States' entry in the war, attacked the President constantly, and made it plain that, once in the Senate, he would be a thorn in the administration's side. His attitude on war issues, his general aggressiveness and Tillman's relative feebleness, caused concern to many in South Carolina, among them Governor Richard I. Manning, a conservative and a strong supporter of Wilson. He encouraged my House colleague, Frank Lever, who for some years had entertained the ambition to serve in the Senate, to make the race.

Much of this was unknown to me until one afternoon early in June, when I received a message that the President wished to see me. I went to the White House wondering what it was about. He greeted me with, "You must be a most unusual man!" In explanation, he said that when he had asked the Secretary of the Navy, Josephus Daniels, to find out from the Tillman family who was the best person to talk to about Senator Tillman, the Senator's daughter, Lona, had said, "Congressman Byrnes." Similarly, when he had asked the same question of his Postmaster General, Albert S. Burleson, who had served in Congress with Lever, my name had again been mentioned.

The President then told me that in view of Blease's attitude toward the prosecution of the war, the possibility of his coming to the Senate was disturbing. He added, "It has been suggested to me that I offer Tillman an appointment on some commission, like the Canadian Boundary Commission, which would require very little exertion and yet assure him security. Mr. Lever will then be free to make the race. How would Senator Tillman react to such a suggestion?"

I told the President that I had heard of this possibility; but that Tillman was a proud man, and I was confident such a suggestion would crush him. I reminded him that while he was Governor of New Jersey and was severely criticized by some Democratic leaders, including Henry Watterson and George Harvey, Senator Tillman had defended him, and gave my opinion that it would be better to let the voters of South Carolina decide the question than for the President to hurt such a loyal friend. President Wilson interrupted me to say, "What you say is true and is fresh in my mind. If Tillman does not leave the Senate until I take him out, he will go out feet first."

After my visit to the White House, I felt that both the Senator and Lever should know what had happened. Neither was offended. In talking to Lever I said, "The President did say he hoped you and Tillman would remain friends." About a year before, in my presence, Lever had told Tillman that though he had been urged to enter the Senate race, he did not intend doing so. I now reminded Lever of this and said, "The old Senator has a good memory. He may recall your statement and it may affect your friendly relations."

Lever agreed and I arranged a conference between them. Later, Lever told me he reminded Tillman of the earlier conversation and said he was prepared to withdraw if Tillman held him to his statement. Lever broke into hearty laughter when he quoted Tillman as saying, "You have a right to change your mind; go ahead and run against me, and I'll beat the hell out of you."

Tillman no doubt impressed Lever, because a few days after this President Wilson wrote a letter to Lever publicly requesting him to remain in the House, and as a result he withdrew from the Senate contest. Senator Tillman did not live to make the race—he died about six weeks later. A third candidate, N. B. Dial, was elected.

I also benefited from the President's political kindness. This same year, 1918, was the only one in which it seemed that serious opposition had developed against me in my district. There were three competitors,

G. L. Toole, an Aiken lawyer and veteran member of the state legislature, T. G. Croft of Aiken, and George Evans of Edgefield. All were
strong candidates.

For five years I had been a consistent supporter of the President
on important issues and had voted for the War Resolution. When the
General Staff of the Army presented a draft bill, which was endorsed
by the President, I voted for an amendment to permit volunteering
while the draft machinery was being prepared. The amendment was
defeated. I then voted for the bill.

Strangely enough, while I was writing this narrative, a friend gave
me a letter that I had sent nearly forty years ago to a constituent. After
giving my reasons for voting for the volunteer amendment, I said,
"If in order to stay in public life I must sacrifice my independence and
vote against my conscientious convictions in a matter of this kind, I
don't want to stay."

My independence favorably impressed my constituent, but caused
my rivals to believe that they had an issue on which to oppose me, and
they charged that the President would be happy should I be defeated.
The President, as a rule, did not interfere in primary contests. It
therefore added interest to the election when I received, on the very
eve of election day, a letter reading as follows:

THE WHITE HOUSE
August 27, 1918

MY DEAR MR. BYRNES:

I would be very much obliged to you if you would at some early date
drop in to see me at the White House in order that I may discuss with you
some phases of the new appropriations bill.

You have always rendered such effective service to the administration and
government on the Committee on Appropriations, I am anxious to seek
your advice.

Yours sincerely
WOODROW WILSON.

In this way the President, without overt interference in a party
contest, sought to help my cause. When the ballots were counted, I
received many more votes than the combined vote against me and
had no further opposition as long as I remained in the House.

Immediately after the election I returned to Washington to see the
President. We did have some discussion about the appropriations bill

then being prepared, but, in fact, we both had something else in mind!
And the generosity of his congratulations was heartwarming.

Two months later, in October, 1918, when the war was in its last
stages, Carter Glass, Congressman Richard S. Whaley of Charleston,
and I, at our own expense, paid a visit to France. Our principal mission
was to visit the Army supply services, but afterward we went to Pershing's headquarters on the American front. General Pershing had an
officer take us to see Verdun. The Germans had not shelled that particular point for several weeks, but while we were there shells began
to raise clouds of dust among the ruined buildings. They fell too close
for comfort or safety, and since, as Glass remarked, there was nothing
more inglorious than the death of three civilians on a battlefield, we
hastily retreated.

Upon our return to Paris we talked with Admiral Sims and later with
Colonel House, learning from House that representatives of the Allies
were meeting in Paris to draft the terms of the armistice. Admiral Sims
severely criticized the Army supply services under General Harbord
and General Johnson Hagood, regretting that its failures had forced the
armistice on us. In order to recheck our own estimation that it had
functioned effectively, we returned to Tours to make further inquiries.
It was a tiresome early morning trip, over 150 miles by train, but our
journey was worth while because our early impressions were confirmed. In January, 1920, when Admiral Sims' charges brought on a
Senate committee investigation, both Carter Glass and I were able to
testify in favor of the Army, based on the records we had seen at Tours.

From France we crossed the Channel and on the eleventh of November were in Edinburgh, where we visited the Grand Fleet, then
at anchor in the Firth of Forth. The commanding officer of the flagship
was on deck with us showing us his command when he was approached
by a young officer with a message. When he had read it, he took several
steps before he paused and then said quietly, "I am sure you will be
interested to learn that the terms of the armistice came into force at
eleven o'clock." He offered no other comment or explanation, but
when we arrived at the flagship of the United States Fleet, to be greeted
by Admiral Hugh Rodman, a Kentuckian, we found no such effort at
self-control. Shore leave instructions were being hastily issued and in a
short time we could see the sailors swarming down the ladders of the
other ships into small boats headed for shore.

When we returned to the heart of Edinburgh, pandemonium had

been let loose. Sailors, our own very much in evidence, and girls from the munition factories, as well as the usually staid citizens, were celebrating madly. Next day, by invitation of the Lord Mayor, we marched with the city officials to the Cathedral service. The kilted Black Watch Regiment in ceremonial array made it a scene never to be forgotten. The day following I left my two friends and sailed from Liverpool for the United States.

As our ship approached New York, a news bulletin was received announcing the resignation of William Gibbs McAdoo, Secretary of the Treasury. There was press speculation that Glass, who was chairman of the House Banking and Currency Committee, was favored for the post but that the President had been advised he was in ill health. As I had been with Glass daily, I knew that fears about his health were groundless. The day after I returned I telephoned Joe Tumulty, who made an engagement for me to see his chief the next day. I found President Wilson interested in my statement about Glass and in favor of his appointment, which was announced a day or two later.

After this I gave the President my impressions of some of our war leaders in Europe. I told him I had been particularly impressed by what General Bliss, our representative on the Supreme Council, had said to me in Paris. In his view all the human selfishness that had been temporarily repressed during the war was reasserting itself, and he was heartsick because of the attitude of many of his colleagues. I then emphasized Bliss' belief that the only hope for a return to idealism was for the President himself to attend the Peace Conference and with his great prestige in Europe appeal personally for support for his program.

President Wilson said that for some months he had relied on Bliss' reports and recently had received the same advice from him. He did not wish to attend the Conference and would go only if he concluded there was no other way to redeem his pledge that the war had been fought to end all wars. The President added that he greatly regretted his inability to speak the French language, for he was confident that if he could he speak directly to the people of France, particularly the women, he would muster great support for his peace efforts.

In the days that followed, when I heard him criticized for going to Versailles, when it was said he wanted to be made president of a world organization, my mind always went back to his altruistic statements that day. What happened later—the defeat of his League of

Nations and his illness—is history.

The President's long illness, I am sure, was responsible for what some people considered an unkind act to Joe Tumulty. In the winter of 1920 the National Democratic Club of New York City invited the President to attend its annual dinner. Each year the banquet was attended by the national party leaders and the President would send a message. On this occasion, when Tumulty arrived at the banquet hall, he was told by the master of ceremonies that the President had not even acknowledged the invitation. Tumulty, to help his chief, hastily wrote a message extending the President's best wishes to the club and its members, signing it "Woodrow Wilson."

A few days later The New York Times editorially commented that the message was not phrased in the usual Wilsonian English. The President resented this criticism and from his sickbed wrote The Times that he had sent no message to the Democratic Club banquet.

That evening Tumulty gave a dinner to a friend of the President who was visiting Washington. Finis Garrett, Jack Garner and I were among the guests. After dinner, as the jovial Tumulty rose to pay tribute to the guest of honor, Charlie Michelson, the Director of Public Relations for the Democratic Committee, facetiously demanded to know whether the statement he was about to make had been authorized by the President.

When the laughter subsided, the greatly perturbed Tumulty said: "I do not blame you for laughing, but I want you to know that I am not angry with my chief. He is a very sick man, and while he is sick nothing he can say to me or about me will lessen my devotion for him. I recall my financial straits when he became Governor of New Jersey and appointed me his secretary. Then he brought me to Washington and gave me an opportunity to enjoy for eight more years an intimate association with a man of great mind and great heart. The superior opportunities my children enjoy are due to him, and if in my life I do anything worth while, all the pleasure that comes to me will be due to Woodrow Wilson."

The guests who had laughed were quiet now and there were tears in some eyes as they applauded this expression of gratitude. A cold man does not inspire such loyalty.

In President Wilson's fight for the League of Nations he had no abler or more loyal supporter than Senator John Sharp Williams. Williams was one of the scholars of the Senate and, having spent several years in Europe when a young man, was deeply interested in foreign affairs. When he announced his voluntary retirement from the Senate, he brought a feeling of sadness to members of both Senate and House. He was quoted as saying that after spending so many years in the two Houses of Congress, he would miss his old friends, but he would rather "be a dog in Mississippi baying at the moon than spend the rest of his days in Washington."

Tumulty, who shared with Pat Harrison and me a deep admiration for this colorful friend, suggested that his colleagues give a dinner for Williams on the evening before his departure. Tumulty extended the invitation, but the reply was disappointing. Williams said he was going to have his last dinner in Washington with an old friend, the former bartender at the Hancock, at one time a famous place on Pennsylvania Avenue near Fourteenth Street, where statesmen and would-be statesmen frequently stopped for late afternoon refreshments. Williams said he had often stopped there on his way home, and this bartender friend saw to it that he was given a private room where his wants were looked after amply—but not too well—so that he was always able to reach home in good standing with his family. He said the retired bartender and his wife had invited him to dinner, and he wanted to spend his last evening with these plain but loyal friends.

Williams was gifted in the art of repartee. One day Senator Heflin complained that on the previous afternoon he had been speaking in the park near the Washington Monument when a plane had flown overhead several times, moving close enough to the ground to disturb his audience. Heflin introduced a bill to regulate flying over the District of Columbia. Senator Williams objected, saying, "We have regulated everything on earth and now he wants to regulate things above the earth." He added that "if the young man disturbed Senator Heflin's meeting, it was a scientific disturbance of the air—something that never would be caused by the Senator's speech." Reflecting upon Williams' habit of taking a drink Heflin replied, "At least when I was speaking, I had all of my faculties with me." Said Williams, "Well, what difference would that make?"

The day President Wilson's successor was inaugurated was a day of sadness for him and his friends. Wilson was able to accompany President-elect Harding to the Capitol, where, according to custom, he was seated in an office adjoining the Senate Chamber, surrounded by members of the Cabinet, ready to approve any legislation completed in the closing minutes of the session. He had told Harding he would not be able to accompany him to the platform for the inaugural address, and shortly before twelve left for his home on S Street. We all knew that emotionally as well as physically he had been subjected to a trying ordeal that morning. Shortly after he left the Capitol, Carter Glass, Cordell Hull, Pat Harrison and I went to his home. We expected only to see Mrs. Wilson, but were received by her and the President.

After his months of illness and the severe strain of that morning he was a pathetic figure, but with pride and courage he sought to appear cheerful. As we talked, some women who had gathered in the street opposite his door began to sing "Onward, Christian Soldiers" and other hymns. When we left, we stopped to express our appreciation, and as we spoke to them the President came to an open window and waved to the faithful group. I had not joined in the singing, but I found it hard not to join in the tears of those assembled.

The election that had sent Harding to the White House had of course been preceded by the usual political conventions. In 1920 the Democrats had met in San Francisco, and on this occasion I had attended as a delegate. I was a friend of Attorney General A. Mitchell Palmer, who hoped to be the nominee, and I intended to help him if possible. Because several friends in my district wished to go as district representatives, I decided to seek election as a delegate at large from the state. After I arrived at the state convention in Columbia, I found that others shared my ambition; and when our national committeeman invited me to serve as temporary chairman and make the keynote address, I realized that this flattering proposal, if accepted, would injure my candidacy for delegate at large. I therefore declined the honor and was pleased, when the delegates at large were voted on, to receive the second highest vote cast.

So far as I know, the convention at San Francisco was the first national convention at which the loud-speaker system was extensively used. The apparatus of that time left much to be desired, the voices coming from it having a thin metallic sound and frequently dying away. I can still see the look of contempt with which William Jennings Bryan thrust it aside when he took the platform to speak. He soon demonstrated in penetrating but beautifully modulated tones that it was a useless device for him.

The contrast between the Great Commoner and Woodrow Wilson

interested me: both were dedicated idealists and men of integrity but, in most of their personal characteristics, worlds apart. Wilson spoke in a low voice with calmness and precision; Bryan was oratorical. I remember Wilson's telling me a story that revealed something of them both. When Bryan was his Secretary of State, he said, he feared his general loquaciousness in Cabinet meetings. Wilson found, however, that if he listened attentively to Bryan, who spoke first, and congratulated him warmly on his presentation when he had finished, the Secretary was likely to lose interest in the affairs of other departments shortly thereafter and ask permission to withdraw.

At San Francisco I had my first opportunity directly or indirectly to further the political fortunes of Franklin D. Roosevelt, whom I had met briefly at the Baltimore convention in 1912, but had known more intimately while he was Assistant Secretary of the Navy. On many occasions he had appeared before my subcommittee of the Appropriations Committee, presenting the Navy's request for funds. He was always familiar with his facts and figures, and then, as in later years, was a good salesman for the Navy.

Early in the convention it was apparent that my friend Mitchell Palmer had no chance, and the presidential contest narrowed down to a struggle between McAdoo and Cox, the latter having the support of the powerful New York delegation, led by Charlie Murphy of Tammany. At one point, when the name of Woodrow Wilson was mentioned and delegates began to parade, Roosevelt, well aware that he was going against the majority of his delegation, showed his independence by grasping the New York banner and, after a scuffle, taking it into the parade.

After Cox obtained the nomination, the question of the Vice Presidency arose. It seemed to me that it would be advantageous to have Roosevelt as Cox's running mate, not only because of the size of the New York vote, but because as an independent Democrat, who would not hesitate to oppose Tammany, Roosevelt would appeal to the independent voters. I therefore ventured to call on Charlie Murphy, who had an odd little office under the speaker's platform where he held "consultations." As I was going in, I recall meeting David Lawrence, who told me I was not the first on such a mission; he wished me success.

Murphy was evasive, though he said he was open-minded. He said several Southerners had called on him urging that Roosevelt be nominated. Some hours later he announced that the New York delegation would support FDR, who then was nominated by acclamation. Without Murphy's support it certainly would have been a hot fight, and there was doubt that FDR could win without his own delegation's support. However, 1920 was not Roosevelt's year, nor indeed that of any Democrat.

During the campaign I made many speeches for the party. At the request of Carter Glass, I went to Clarksville, in the Virginia district represented by Congressman Slemp. I found at the hotel Congressman Fordney of Michigan, an old war horse of the Republican party, who was to speak that afternoon. He suggested that he would attend my meeting at eleven o'clock if I would listen to him at three. A young lawyer who introduced me spoke for an hour and five minutes, but he certainly didn't need that much time to enumerate the accomplishments of a young congressman. Feeling that something was necessary to get my audience in a good humor, I said I felt so much at home that before leaving the hotel I had wagered with a friend that I could guess the politics of the people I met on the street; that I correctly guessed one man to be a Democrat, but when I asked the next man if he was a Republican, he said, "No, I just had the smallpox." The Democrats laughed. When Fordney winked, I should have expected trouble.

At the afternoon meeting I sat where Fordney had sat during the morning. He told his audience that the trouble with the speaker from South Carolina earlier that day was purely climatic. He said, "In northern Michigan, which is my state, it is cold and nearly everybody is Republican; here in Virginia, where it is warmer, you will find more Democrats; go to South Carolina, and you will find nearly all are Democrats; go on down to hell, and you'll find nothing but Democrats!"

Harding was elected in a landslide. With his election, the Democrats lost control of the House. It was a new experience for me to be in the minority—and what a minority! My recollection is that we had but one Democratic congressman from a western State—John Evans of Montana. With the exception of the congressmen from New York City and Boston, the Democratic party in the House was a southern party. Political writers predicted that the party would disappear. The small minority, however, provided intelligent, constructive opposition. While we had less responsibility, we had more work to do. On the Appropriations Committee there were so few Democrats that I served on three subcommittees, and we constantly attacked the majority for their mistakes and their extravagances. But with all the work, we had a lot of fun!

While I had known Harding when he was in the Senate, I had no occasion to see him after he became President. He was a very handsome man with a good nature, but the office of President is no place for one with only good looks and good nature. He was imposed upon by his friends in and out of the Cabinet. When the Teapot Dome oil scandal broke, I voted for the investigation. Later, when Doheny and others were indicted, he and several others were represented in court by my cousin, Frank J. Hogan. I had not seen much of Frank in the years immediately preceding, but when I met him one day, I referred to his employment and inquired about his poor clients. He was in good form and replied with a statement doubtless shared by most lawyers, "Jim, the best client for a lawyer to have is a rich man what am scared."

Upon Harding's death, Calvin Coolidge became President and I saw more of him and Mrs. Coolidge. Mrs. Byrnes was then the president of the Congressional Club, composed of the wives and daughters of members; after standing by the President during a reception, she said she did not know whether he was as stingy with his money as represented, but she could testify he was a miser with words. Certainly this New England trait did not detract from his sterling qualities or make him less attractive to me.

In early 1924 I began to feel it was time for me to decide whether I intended to remain in politics and be a candidate for the Senate or whether I should return to the practice of law. I weighed my chances of election carefully, for I knew that my rather slender financial resources would be gone at the end of the senatorial race.

This will indicate that, though I was certainly no richer by my many years of service in the House, fortunately I was free of obligations. If a man is interested primarily in making money, he should not go into government service, for there he cannot make it honestly; and if he is willing to make it dishonestly, the sooner he is out the better. It has been my thought that in public life the opportunity to render service is the supreme reward. We had always lived within our means in Washington and did not find that social activity made a great drain on our income, our preferred form of entertaining being small dinner parties with our friends.

By April I had made my decision to enter the Senate race. The question may be asked why I did not prefer to remain in the House. The answer is that I was realistic enough to know that there was no opportunity for me to attain official leadership, there being many men of greater seniority, ability and popularity with the members. Nor could I hope to become chairman of the Appropriations Committee, of which I was still a member, because there were four or five Democrats on it with longer service. A member who has some ability and energy but no official position may attain a place of influence, but his exercise of such influence may become a constant source of irritation to the official leadership. This inevitably impairs the friendly relationships that make congressional service attractive. In the Senate, because of the smaller membership, its constitutional authority in certain phases of foreign affairs, and in other ways, there is greater opportunity for service. Also —and this was important to me—if I were to enter the Senate race and fail, I could return to the practice of law while I was still young enough to make a new career. Later, this would be more difficult. These considerations, in addition to the promptings of many friends in my home state, led me to enter the 1924 Senate contest.

In the first primary there were four candidates, including the incumbent, N. B. Dial. The result of the first primary left me in the field facing the formidable Cole L. Blease, who had served two terms as Governor and earlier had made an unsuccessful bid for the Senate. He led me by about 17,000 votes, and the question was whether in the two weeks before the second primary I could induce the 30,000 anti-Blease voters who had voted for Dial to support me.

My opponent had been known in previous campaigns for his vituperative arguments, but now he employed different methods. He was even prayerful, urging that a return to family prayer would do more than armies to preserve peace. He always could command the unswerving allegiance of many farmers and most textile workers as well as of many others who admired his audacity and his forensic ability. While Governor, he had built up a personal organization which assured him of the highest vote in any contest in which he had more than one opponent.

On the afternoon prior to the election on Tuesday, thousands of circulars that purported to endorse my candidacy were distributed throughout the state, and particularly in the areas in which the Ku Klux Klan was strong and active. The circular was signed by about ten persons and stated substantially that in my boyhood I had attended the

Sunday school of a Roman Catholic church in Charleston and had served as an altar boy; that the signers wished to testify to my "high Christian ideals"; and finally that they declared me worthy of "the highest American honors."

It was a blatant effort to arouse the religious prejudice of anti-Catholic voters. I could recall only two or three of the persons whose names were signed to the circular, and those I had known only casually in my boyhood and had not seen for more than twenty-five years. Upon inquiry that night, I learned that they were my bitter political opponents. On the following day I suffered my only defeat in an election, losing to Blease by approximately 2,200 out of 200,000 votes.

Many people attributed my defeat to the circulars, but of this no one can be certain. It is true that six years later, in my second Senate campaign, numerous voters told me they had opposed me in 1924 on this account but now were supporting me because they disapproved of such tactics. However, I saw no point in making an inquiry into who instigated and perpetrated the trick, because as far as I was concerned I was defeated and the election had passed into history. I preferred to look to the future.

It was with sincere regret that I left the House. During my fourteen years there, because of the constant change in membership every two years, I estimated my service had brought me in touch with at least 2,000 members. Coming as they did from 435 districts, they constituted a cross-section of the American people. Among them were many my wife and I regarded as intimate friends, and for the membership as a whole I had great respect. Of the large number who served in that period, I recall only two who were suspected by their colleagues of lacking financial integrity. The rest were honest, sober men and their conduct reflected credit upon the people they represented.

Just before the expiration of my service in the House, in March, 1925, Sam J. Nicholls, who had ably represented South Carolina from the Fourth Congressional District in Congress for six years, and his law partner, C. C. Wyche, my long-time friend (and now U. S. District Judge in South Carolina), invited me to join them in the practice of law in Spartanburg. It meant leaving my home in Aiken with all its cherished associations; but having lived there for so long, devoting much of my time to advising friends about their legal problems, I knew that if I opened an Aiken law office, while I would be kept busy, I would seldom be able to charge a fee. The fact is, as my Spartanburg partners were soon to discover, I never did know how to set a fee, and there, as well as in my later partnership, this very necessary task has been left to others.

After becoming a member of this law firm, as a result of my early experience as a practicing attorney, I found life as a trial lawyer most congenial and my partners very considerate. At Christmas, 1925, when I had been with them for only nine months, it was with amazement and satisfaction that I learned I had made much more money in that time than ever before in a like period.

Members of our law firm devoted little time to politics, either national or state, until about two weeks before an election, when we began taking a serious interest. So at this time my political activity was spasmodic. In the presidential campaign year of 1928, I did not attend the national convention at Houston which nominated Al Smith. For the first time in many years the Republican party made an active campaign in the southern states for its candidate, Herbert Hoover. There was much opposition to Smith in the Solid South, his Democratic critics usually giving as their reason for opposing him his views on prohibition, but in many instances their opposition was due to religious bigotry. I traveled to several states to make speeches for the Democratic candidate and was glad that South Carolina eventually gave him more than 90 per cent of its votes.

In the fall of 1929, with thousands of other South Carolinians, I went to Columbia to attend the State Fair and the traditional "Big Thursday" football classic between Clemson College and the University of South Carolina. When our party left the stadium, I bought an afternoon newspaper. Startling headlines told us that there had been a sharp break in all markets that morning and indicated that further declines might follow. They did. This was the beginning of the Great Depression.

In the South, as in the West, for some years entirely too many small state banks had been opened in agricultural areas where there was always a demand for credit. Often when a farmer seeking more credit was denied advances by his bank, he would undertake to organize another bank; accordingly, his kin, his friends and acquaintances, and almost invariably his congressman were given the privilege of being associated with his venture. Much to my later regret, I had been offered and had accepted several such opportunities. These banks were among the first to close and caused me to pay 100 per cent stock liability.

None of our people starved, but the price of commodities continued to fall and unemployment figures to rise. As fear for the future spread, the average citizen began to think seriously about the economic policies of the United States and of the views and abilities of their representatives in Washington. Some businessmen who did not admire Senator Blease, and many others who had opposed him for years, began to urge me to be a candidate for the Senate in 1930. I had spent six years in Spartanburg; I was happy practicing law, and was surprised when I found myself seriously considering these requests.

In retrospect, I suppose, what really brought me back into public life was that politics had gotten into my blood. After fourteen exciting years in the House, even the life of a trial lawyer seemed tame. I also believe my return was due in great degree to the fact that Cole Blease was the only man who had defeated me in a campaign and I wanted a chance to reverse the verdict.

In all events, June 17, 1930, saw me once again embarking on the state campaign. Again there was a third candidate, Leon W. Harris, a lawyer of high character, forceful and courageous. During the next ten weeks I visited every county, speaking from one to five times daily. Mrs. Byrnes had as grueling a time as I, but she insisted on doing the driving. In the last week of August the first primary was held. Senator Blease again led me by some 18,000 votes, but the anti-Blease voters were not so divided as in 1924. Moreover, Mr. Harris, who had been eliminated, announced that he would vote for me in the runoff. I therefore approached the second primary in a state of cautious optimism, and visited places where in the first primary I was weak.

One such place was a cotton mill town in York County where in the first primary I had received only a few votes. With some friends, I went to the community park where the meeting was to be held, and found only a small group waiting. Gradually the audience increased. Knowing it was hostile territory, I was surprised and encouraged when a man introduced himself as the pastor of a local church and asked the privilege of introducing me. I gladly consented and when the lights in the park had been turned on and a fair-sized crowd gathered, we both climbed into a truck which was to serve as the platform.

The preacher began by telling the audience how honored he was to introduce a candidate for the United States Senate. But, he continued, "Unfortunately for him, he is opposing our friend, Coley Blease, the greatest statesman South Carolina has ever known." He then launched into a lengthy recital of the qualifications of Mr. Blease and of his wonderful record as Governor and senator. He ended by warning his listeners that they could expect me to criticize Senator Blease, and said that at the conclusion of my remarks he would distribute literature setting forth Blease's record which would refute all my criticisms. He closed without mentioning my name.

For a moment I was overwhelmed. Recovering, I told them my name and said that throughout the campaign, in joint debate with Mr. Blease, I had refrained from any personal criticism of him and would not break this rule in his absence; moreover, I would always cherish the fair and flattering introduction of the pastor. I was extravagant in expressing appreciation of the many compliments paid me by the chairman. It was comforting to note, the day after the election, that the general spirit of fair play which exists among most voters caused me to receive at this particular box many more votes than in the first primary.

A short time after the election I received a letter of congratulation from the preacher. He must have thought my words of appreciation of his introduction sincere, because he enclosed his note for $250 and requested me to send him a check for that amount, as he was in financial straits. His letter, like one written by Saint Paul to the Ephesians, to this day remains unanswered.

In the runoff I was nominated as the Democratic candidate by a majority of approximately 5,000 votes, and since I had no Republican opponent, this meant my election in November. A further stage in my career, that of United States senator, lay before me.

# Part II

---

## THE SENATE

# 4  THE DEMOCRATS TAKE OVER

My first session in the Senate commenced in December, 1931. Having served in the House of Representatives, I did not feel like a complete stranger and, having often seen the Senate organize at the opening of a session, the procedure was not new to me.

According to custom, the new senator is escorted to the front by his senior colleague, and that morning Senator E. D. Smith walked with me down the aisle to be presented to Vice President Curtis, who administered the oath. The senators who greeted me helped to put me at ease, because among them were close friends who had served with me in the House and who had preceded me to the Senate. There were Joe Robinson of Arkansas, the Democratic leader, Carter Glass of Virginia, Alben Barkley of Kentucky, Pat Harrison of Mississippi, Bennett Clark of Missouri, Kenneth McKellar of Tennessee and Carl Hayden of Arizona, who is the only member of the group who is still serving in the Senate. On the Republican side I counted as friends Wallace White of Maine and George Norris of Nebraska, who had been old House colleagues. Cordell Hull and John H. Bankhead were sworn in at the same time.

Harrison had a dinner for me that evening and this gave me a chance to get better acquainted with senators I had known only casually.

As a rule the Secretary of the Senate, or the secretary to the minority party in the Senate, informs the newly elected senator to which seat he has been assigned, gives him information about the staff he can employ, and sees that he has a copy of the rules of the Senate. I did not have to be told that at each desk there was a snuffbox for the convenience of the members, though I am sure no senator during the previous twenty-

59

five years had used the snuff provided. It was equally unnecessary for him to tell me that there was a barbershop in the basement of the Capitol. The barber was rather insistent that I visit the shop and see the shaving mug, with my name in gold, which had been provided for my use. This too was a tradition from an earlier day. I never used the services of the barbershop, thinking I should not make the taxpayers pay for that personal service and doubting too the efficiency of a political barber.

A new senator is assigned to committees by the Steering Committee, whose chairman is the party leader. It is usual for a senator to make known his committee preferences, but it is difficult for the freshman to get one of the three or four preferred assignments, for a vacancy on any major committee is quickly filled by some senior member. Some preference is usually given to a man who has had service in the House. Because of this, and with the help of my friends on the Steering Committee, I was placed on both the Appropriations Committee and the Banking and Currency, as well as given an assignment to a less important group—the Audit and Control Committee. Two years later, when the Democrats took control of the Senate, Senator Glass, as chairman of the Appropriations Committee, made me chairman of the subcommittee which had charge of naval appropriations and appointed me to the deficiency subcommittee, which had charge of deficiency appropriations for all departments. I was also made chairman of the Audit and Control Committee.

House experience had taught me that if a new member of either House or Senate expects to stay awhile and accomplish anything, he is wise to tread softly, to become familiar with the rules and, more important, with his colleagues.

On one of the first occasions that I addressed the Senate, I drew great encouragement from Henry F. Ashurst of Arizona, one of the scholarly senators. He kept nodding his head and seemed not only interested in what I was saying, but in sympathy with it. Later, however, I saw him do it on so many occasions to so many other senators that I realized it was just evidence of his good nature.

Frequently, he had in his lap the book that is on the desk of each senator and that contains the *Congressional Record* for the seven or eight preceding days. One day I noticed Ashurst, whose desk was on the middle aisle, nodding sympathetically to a speaker but immediately returning his gaze to the *Record*. Approaching his desk from the rear,

I saw that in his bound *Record* he had a copy of *The New Yorker*. I asked him if, when he was through, he would lend me his copy of the *Record*, saying that it looked more interesting than mine.

In organizing my office I had expert advice from my sister, Leonore Byrnes Fuller, who had made a study of the Civil Service laws and regulations. She took leave of absence, without pay, from her job and came to my office, where for six months she was very helpful to me and my constituents.

Attention was focused on political matters in the months that followed my entrance into the Senate. Business conditions continued to deteriorate each day, despite President Hoover's predictions and his efforts to restore confidence. The Democrats charged that he and his administration were entirely responsible for the deepening depression. The general discontent naturally caused Democrats to believe that the approaching presidential election might bring an end to their twelve years in the political wilderness.

There was considerable interest in Franklin D. Roosevelt's chances of leading the party to victory. He was serving his second term as Governor of New York and had made a good impression on the country since his return to public life. In November, 1928, I had written him a congratulatory note in which I said, "Your election is the only comfort I have received out of the voting last Tuesday. Recalling your splendid administration in the Navy Department, I am confident that you will be successful as Governor, and I shall watch with keen interest your career." I added, "It gave me great pleasure in the San Francisco Convention to urge your nomination for Vice President, and I am now only anxious to have the opportunity to urge your nomination for the Presidency."

In 1931 I still believed that because of his record and because his state had the largest vote in the Electoral College, he was the strongest candidate the Democrats could nominate, and in that emergency the best qualified. This opinion I frequently expressed, and when in October, 1931, one of his New York friends inquired about my attitude toward his nomination, I sent him a copy of my 1928 letter, saying that I had not changed my views. Thereafter I was to receive many communications from Mr. Roosevelt, and in January, 1932, I accepted an invitation to visit him at Albany. We discussed the national political situation as well as that in my own state, and when in March Mr. Roosevelt's representative, James A. Farley, paid a visit to South

Carolina, on my recommendation he called on Claude N. Sapp, our state chairman, who was already working to help his candidate.

At our state convention in May there was some division of sentiment, owing in part to the fact that in 1930 Roosevelt had favored repeal of the Eighteenth Amendment. Despite some opposition on this subject, it was clear that a majority of our convention favored the Governor of New York. In a letter and telephone conversation Roosevelt expressed to me the hope that the South Carolina delegation might be instructed to support him. I told him that since our state had traditionally refrained from instructing delegates, it would be unwise to press the matter. Instead, when the time came, I urged adoption of a resolution endorsing Roosevelt, the course followed in the case of President Wilson. A few of the eighteen delegates finally selected to go to Chicago favored Governor Ritchie of Maryland or Newton D. Baker; but under a resolution that we adopted binding the delegates to vote under the unit rule, I was able to tell Governor Roosevelt, on our adjournment, that he could rely upon South Carolina's eighteen votes.

Just after the adjournment of the convention I was called to the telephone. My wife, then in Washington, advised me that my mother, who was living there with my sister Leo, had suffered another stroke and was in serious condition. Before many hours had passed, I was at her bedside. While she did not die until the following day, she was not able to speak to me.

The National Convention opened on June 27. It was soon apparent, despite Farley's optimism, that the New York Governor could not secure two thirds of the votes against the combined strength of Smith, Garner, Ritchie and numerous favorite sons. It seemed that we might have a repetition of the disastrous situation in New York in 1924, when the convention was deadlocked for a hundred ballots and feeling between the opposing forces became so bitter that it was impossible for the party to elect the outstanding candidate, John W. Davis. At this point some of Roosevelt's lieutenants began urging a change in party rules to provide for nomination by a simple majority. As at a later convention in 1936, I was strongly opposed to changing the rules during the convention, though I shall have more to say about this later. Fortunately, in 1932 Governor Roosevelt instructed his friends to abandon this particular effort. After a close vote to elect a permanent chairman and the adoption of a platform including repeal of the Eighteenth

Amendment, we proceeded to the roll call on the nomination. At about eight o'clock on the morning of July 1, after three roll calls, including one on adjourning, and an all-night session of intense political activity, the convention was still deadlocked, with Roosevelt lacking more than eighty votes to clinch the nomination. Moreover, in some delegations there was great unrest. Mississippi was seated just behind us. Its twenty votes were kept in line for Roosevelt only by the unit rule, for the delegation was split 10½ to 9½. Further, one delegate had threatened to change on the third ballot. If Mississippi switched to Al Smith, others might follow. After the second ballot Senator Pat Harrison of Mississippi, a strong Roosevelt supporter, had left the hall for his hotel, relying on the statement of leaders that there would be no further balloting that morning. But the convention voted against adjournment; another roll call was ordered. Senator Hubert Stephens, acting as chairman of the Mississippi delegation, seated just behind me, was promptly surrounded by delegates who wanted the delegation again polled. Stephens asked me to join the group. I predicted with confidence there would be no important change and argued that after twenty-four hours in session we should adjourn and do a little thinking. The delegate who threatened to change his vote agreed to vote once more for Roosevelt, and said that if he didn't get the two thirds, he would then change. My prediction proved correct, there was no material change, and we adjourned.

After the welcome adjournment, instead of going to my hotel, I hastened over to rouse Pat Harrison. As he left his bed to meet with his delegation, I tumbled into bed in his room. Two hours later he came back to report that Mississippi was still holding. However, during the day, victory for Roosevelt was assured by Jack Garner's release of the Texas delegation. Garner had remained in Washington, refusing to speak to anyone on the telephone from Chicago but Sam Rayburn. But they knew when to trade. Garner's friends agreed to withdraw his name and support Roosevelt, whose friends agreed, in return, to support Garner for Vice President. This also would bring to Roosevelt most of California's delegates, who had been supporting Garner. As soon as this was known, favorite-son candidates withdrew, delegations rushed to the band wagon, and Roosevelt and Garner were named. The next morning we went to work on the campaign.

A few days before the Convention, Bernard Baruch had asked me if I could support Newton D. Baker, who had been Secretary of War in

Woodrow Wilson's Cabinet. I told him I could not; that I shared his admiration for Baker, but was committed to Governor Roosevelt. He thought if there should be a deadlock, Baker might have a chance.

Baruch was not a delegate but he attended the convention, and at the Roosevelt headquarters his attitude was known. The morning following the nomination, Baruch telephoned me at Roosevelt headquarters and said he intended to support the candidate. At my request he came to headquarters. On July 12, just after the convention, I wrote to Governor Roosevelt informing him of that visit: "He [Baruch] wanted to make a suggestion or two as to your speech [of acceptance] and I took him to Louie Howe's room. I knew Howe was busy but thought it important that we should get Mr. Baruch interested in your campaign. . . . My reason for writing now is to suggest that when you have an opportunity you invite him to come to see you to discuss the situation. I am sure he would appreciate it. . . . I told him that on the only occasion I had seen you in some years, at your home in New York, you had referred to him as one of your dearest friends and he replied he reciprocated that personal friendship. I think if you can see him you can enlist his active support which will be most valuable in this campaign." I also told him Baruch suggested that an Advisory Committee be appointed, having upon it "some men of the type of Owen D. Young." I do not know that Governor Roosevelt invited Mr. Baruch to visit him at that time, but I know that Mr. Baruch actively supported him and was a generous contributor to the campaign fund.

I was unable to accept an invitation to accompany the Governor on his early campaign trips, but some two weeks before the election I joined his party and, with Senator Pittman of Nevada, assisted Raymond Moley, the original presidential Brain Truster and speech writer. Moley did most of the writing after consulting us about substance. Toward the end of the long itinerary, Roosevelt had made so many more speeches than originally planned that he had exhausted his material—and Moley, too. When Atlanta was added to the list, Pittman and I rapidly drafted a memorandum on the agricultural situation and forestry, which the Governor improved and enjoyed delivering, for forestry was particularly dear to his heart. The following day we were faced with the need to prepare en route a major address for Baltimore that night. But the train made so many stops in Virginia and the candidate so many platform appearances that he had no opportunity to discuss the speech with us before we reached Washington in the late afternoon. Here Jack Garner and several others boarded the train for conferences, and it was only when we were actually on the way to Baltimore that we finally got busy with our discussion and drafting. This was the speech in which the "Four Horsemen" of the Republican leadership were named as "Destruction," "Delay," "Deceit," and "Despair." Later that evening the Governor unofficially dedicated the text to his own "Four Horsemen," giving autographed copies to his three "ghosts" and requiring us to sign our names on his copy. I still have mine.

Many of the newspapermen who had been on the campaign tour lived in Washington and were now anxious to get home. They therefore hastened to file the advance text, and few remained to hear the speech delivered. In the manuscript I had prefaced criticism of the administration by remarking that the Republicans had been "in charge of the executive and legislative branches of the Government for twelve years."

During delivery of the speech, inspired no doubt by the enthusiasm of the crowd, Mr. Roosevelt interpolated "and, I might add for good measure, the Supreme Court as well." Those press men who had gone home were soon routed out by calls from their editors for more information about the candidate's "attack on the judiciary." Since the radio had carried the remark to the most distant newspaper offices in the country, there was naturally some confusion over the episode. The following morning in New York, when I went into the President's car, he quickly said, "I know what you are going to say before you say it! What I said last night about the judiciary is true, and whatever is in a man's heart is apt to come to his tongue—I shall not make any explanations or apology for it!"

The Governor was staying at his mother's home on 65th Street. He was kept busy meeting a constant stream of visitors, mostly from outside the state, while Moley and I worked continuously at Moley's office at Columbia University, preparing memoranda for more speeches. The important address at the Brooklyn Academy of Music was not finished until time for us to start for the meeting. Throngs lined the streets in the vicinity of the packed meeting hall. I rode with the Governor, who was greeted by a smiling Congressman Driscoll, carrying a flag, to escort us to the stage, happy that this speech of the Presidential candidate was being made in his district. There was some drama in the fact that Al Smith would be present to meet Roosevelt for the first time since their struggle over the nomination, though he had in the last two weeks campaigned for the ticket in Massachusetts and New Jersey. When we arrived back stage, Governor Smith was not present, but shortly he arrived, walked over to where Roosevelt was sitting, and said cheerily, "Frank, all the world's a stage and tonight you and I are the actors. I would like to escort you to the stage." Roosevelt responded in like vein and, taking Smith's arm, walked onto the stage with him to the delight of every Democrat present—and there were many, because every foot of space in the hall was taken.

For me the climax of the campaign was the Madison Square Garden speech. The candidate needed little help with this—it was all his own, and he felt quite at home with the huge crowd. Outside, the police estimated, fifty thousand listened, parked around the amplifiers. I did not know how the rest of the country was reacting, but after that week in New York I was convinced that Roosevelt would carry New York State. My confidence hardly matched that of the candidate. A few nights before the election I was with him at his home when his close friend and former law partner, Basil O'Connor, paid him a visit. O'Connor asked him about his chances the following Tuesday, and I was amazed at the confidence which Roosevelt displayed in reply. When O'Connor expressed doubt about Connecticut, Roosevelt bet him a dollar he would carry it. Typically, at lunch on the Saturday before election he told his secretary, Missy LeHand, that her biggest file after the next Wednesday would be one marked "Unsolicited Advice." His confidence in his election was fully justified, and his prediction about his files proved correct.

Immediately after the election I went to Washington for conferences with party leaders. During the months that followed, the President-elect made plans for his Cabinet. Some of the men he was considering he discussed with me. When he mentioned Senator Hull for Secretary of State, Glass for the Treasury, and Walsh for his Attorney General, I told him my only objection was that he was taking from the Senate too many of the ablest men, whose support would be needed in the difficult days ahead. Yet I knew it was important to have men in administrative positions who had spent years studying the problems of our government. As is known, Carter Glass declined the proffered Treasury appointment. First Mr. Roosevelt had his personal physician, Admiral Cary Grayson, and me talk to Glass, who felt his wife's wretched health would make it impossible for her to undertake the social responsibilities required of a Cabinet member's wife. Later, at the request of the President, I tried again, taking Ray Moley with me. Glass told us his wife had agreed that he should accept but that there were tears in her eyes when she did so, and he felt he owed it to her to decline.

As long as he hoped Glass would accept the Treasury post, the President made no decision about the Secretary of the Navy, the post that Senator Swanson of Virginia wanted. The President could not appoint the two Virginia senators to the Cabinet. When we told the President of Glass' decision, he said he would appoint Swanson to the Navy post. Swanson knew the Navy and loved it.

In passing, let me say that while the public knew Admiral Grayson as the personal physician to both Presidents Wilson and Roosevelt, it was not generally realized that both in their time relied on him for political counsel. He had the gift of understanding people. During Wilson's long illness, they became very close. This in turn brought Grayson into friendly association with the then Assistant Secretary of the Navy, FDR. When Roosevelt was selecting his Cabinet, I knew he consulted Grayson about several appointments, but Grayson never admitted being a presidential adviser. The Admiral's home was one of the few private residences in Washington where President Roosevelt liked to relax with a few congenial friends. The public never knew it. Admiral Ross McIntire succeeded Grayson as personal physician; he too advised the President on more than health matters, but not to the degree that the more politically minded Grayson did.

Another appointment Roosevelt and I discussed was that of Director of the Budget. I recommended Lewis W. Douglas of Arizona, whom I knew from his work in the House on the Economy Committee to be one of the ablest and most courageous men in Washington. The President accepted the suggestion and Douglas was appointed. I was also asked about the selection of a Secretary of Commerce. Daniel C. Roper, during the Wilson administration, had been Commissioner of Internal Revenue. In the preconvention days he had advocated Roosevelt's nomination, and during the campaign had been helpful in many sections of the country because of his reputation as a consistent prohibitionist and teetotaler while Roosevelt was advocating repeal. Though two or three other names received serious consideration, the President finally decided on Roper and asked me to notify him of his selection.

In November I was invited to visit the President-elect at Warm

Springs and spend Thanksgiving with him. While it was partly a social visit, the main purpose was to make plans for the legislative program, and we discussed, in addition to Ray Moley's ideas for the railroad rehabilitation plan, the reorganization of the government departments and reduction in expenditures.

The President was always interested in the people around him, and one evening he told us about having had as dinner guests Jack Cohen, editor and publisher of the Atlanta *Journal*, and Clark Howell, the editor and publisher of the *Constitution*. The two distinguished southern journalists were engaged in fierce business competition but were devoted to the President, and he felt he should try to get his two friends together. He felt he had succeeded to a degree, and so far as I know there was a permanent reconciliation.

The President told me that Huey Long was coming to Warm Springs to see him. He said he always addressed him as "Kingfish" and, despite the opinion of some senators that he was difficult to get along with, he believed he would be one of his active supporters. I had doubts about how long his support would last, and the fact is that before a year elapsed Huey was quite personal in his attacks upon the President. However, he did not lack respect for the talent of FDR as a salesman.

Once four or five of us were in the cloakroom discussing features of a pending measure we did not like and considering the advisability of going to see the President about it. Long, always restless, had been walking up and down the cloakroom; he passed by us once or twice and finally stopped to say, "Gentlemen, you haven't asked me for advice, but I could not help hearing your discussion. I want to suggest that if you do go to consult that gentleman in the White House, you will come away carrying a package."

I was hardly back in Washington when a newspaper published the rumor that the President was interested in having as majority leader someone closer to him than Senator Robinson, who had been the Vice Presidential candidate with Al Smith four years before, and that Robinson was to be convinced "diplomatically" that he should allow me to assume the leadership of the Senate. I was really worried. Joe Robinson was my friend. I had no desire to displace him. I had been in the Senate but a short time and wanted only to improve my opportunities for service. There was nothing more calculated to impair my position than to have my colleagues suspect that I was even acquiescing in a move by the President to interfere with the Senate leadership. I hastened to issue a statement that I was not and would never be a candidate for Robinson's place. I then wrote Robinson, sending him a copy of the statement and assuring him of my support. Shortly after this, Robinson moved my election to the Steering Committee. We were to remain close friends and collaborators until his sudden death in 1937.

I was, of course, aware that newspaper articles dubbing anyone "the fair-haired boy" of the coming administration and "the President's favorite senator" were harmful in the Senate, inviting friction and causing rivalries, and might endanger the extensive legislative program contemplated. In that program I was deeply interested.

It is difficult for young people of this day to appreciate the sufferings of the people of that day. Even those of mature years enjoying the prosperity of this period find it difficult to project their minds back and recall the conditions that existed as we approached the end of 1932. Factories were being closed daily, throwing thousands of workers out of employment; their savings were withdrawn from banks and soon exhausted. With the purchasing power of the people reduced, merchants went into bankruptcy.

In the big cities of the country bread lines increased, and I recall seeing in a Chicago newspaper a picture of men seeking food in a garbage can. In rural areas conditions were not much better. The prices of all commodities were far below the cost of production. A large percentage of our farms were then mortgaged, and as these mortgages were foreclosed, some farmers in the Midwest threatened to shoot the judges who ordered their farms to be sold.

Small state banks first began to close, then larger ones, then national banks. As the people started runs on banks to withdraw funds, several states enacted laws authorizing banks to require thirty or sixty days notice of withdrawal. In some states they called it a moratorium on withdrawals. At the request of bankers in the District of Columbia, where several banks were subjected to runs by depositors, I sponsored a moratorium measure for the District which was quickly enacted by the Congress. The Great Depression not only meant loss of property; it meant loss of life, for there were many suicides.

In our efforts to find a remedy for this situation, we had no guideposts. I recalled that when I went to the House of Representatives I had firm convictions about federal-state relations and the wisdom of preserving local governments, the necessity of maintaining a balanced budget, and like subjects; but when we entered World War I in 1917,

I recognized that, in a war emergency, principles as well as policies had to be temporarily subordinated to the necessity of some experimentation in order to preserve the government itself. The economic crisis now demanded a similar attitude.

In December I had begun working on economy measures such as those incorporated in the Post Office and Treasury bill, so that after March 4 the Chief Executive would find himself vested with sufficient authority to reorganize, consolidate, and, where necessary, abolish government agencies. I felt the emergency situation now called for an unusual concentration of power in the White House, however temporary that concentration might be.

Before Mr. Roosevelt arrived in Washington, he was busy planning every aspect of his activities during his first days there. I remember he telephoned me that on the morning of his inauguration he wished to attend church, inviting those who were to be in his Cabinet to join him and his family. He asked me about the steps at the Washington Cathedral. I knew these might be difficult for him and suggested that St. John's Episcopal Church, just across from the White House, might be better. He was familiar with it, and had someone make the necessary arrangements. He arrived in the city on a cold, rainy Thursday night and went to his suite at the Mayflower Hotel. Washington was completely packed, not only with sightseers, but with everybody, it seemed to me, who had even a remote claim on the future administration. The change after twelve years meant a turnover in jobs, and the depression ensured that these jobs were at a tremendous premium.

The morning of the day Mr. Roosevelt was to arrive, Ogden Mills, the retiring Secretary of Treasury, asked me to come to his office. He told me that each hour the banking situation was growing worse. While we talked, messages bearing news of further bank closings came to him from the Federal Reserve Board. In the course of our conversation, Mills telephoned to Winthrop Aldrich, president of the Chase National Bank in New York, asking him to take the first available train to Washington. Mr. Aldrich said he had been down the previous day and was reluctant to return. Mills said: "It is imperative that you come, and if you have in your organization a good man, even if he knows nothing about banking but has a lively imagination, bring him too." Aldrich replied that he was planning to take a trip to Bermuda. At this, the Secretary commented, "If you go, don't get a round trip ticket—when you're ready to return, there'll be nothing worth returning to." Aldrich came to Washington that afternoon.

I had known Mills in the House; he was extremely able and conservative in his views. I never thought he would make such statements, but I felt he was right. Hoover and Mills had tried every orthodox procedure approved by bankers to stem the deflation, and had failed. It was time to try the imaginative and unorthodox.

Later that afternoon Mills again got in touch with me, asking that I meet him at the Treasury immediately after dinner. He knew Mr. Roosevelt was due at his hotel about nine that night. When I met Mills, he requested me to ask Governor Roosevelt whether he would join President Hoover in a statement substantially to the effect that there was no reason for the panic then spreading among the people; that the country was basically sound; and that if the people would have confidence in government, a solution for the banking troubles could be found. When I reached Governor Roosevelt's suite, he was surrounded by prominent men in the field of politics from all sections of the country. Just as soon as I could, I asked him to go with Cordell Hull and me to an adjoining room, where I told him of my conversation that evening with Secretary Mills.

Governor Roosevelt very promptly said that he would not join Mr. Hoover in such a pronouncement. Mr. Hoover, he said, had made so many statements about prosperity being "just around the corner" that he had lost the confidence of the people. If President Hoover did not know what to do, he (Roosevelt) did, and just as soon as he had taken the oath of office, he would do it.

From this decisive statement it was clear that FDR was determined not to deal with the outgoing administration in general, and with Ogden Mills in particular. His feeling against Mills—"little Oggie," as he called him—was marked, for he not only regarded him as Mr. Hoover's principal lieutenant but resented the personal attacks the Secretary had made on him during the campaign.

In any event, I told Mills of the Governor's reply and, when he indicated a desire to transmit another request, told him I preferred not to act further as intermediary, that it would accomplish nothing, and that in the Governor's suite then was Mr. Woodin, who was to be his Secretary of the Treasury.

The next day was another Black Friday. With the bank failures in Pennsylvania and Massachusetts, the tally of financial disaster was almost complete. Yet as the news of these new closures reached a rain-soaked Capitol, thousands were pouring into Washington to celebrate a change of government and honor a new leader. Among the crowds excitement rose as many hundreds of visitors learned that the banks "at home" had closed, and realized their inability to cash checks for hotel expenses, return transportation, and the celebrations planned by some of the more fortunate. In any other land, I am sure, there would be rumblings of revolt. But those I saw and talked to the next day, Inauguration Day, were beginning to face a bleak future hopefully. What lent them their courage? Surely much of their optimism came with the words of the President in his Inaugural Address—"The only thing we have to fear is fear itself."

## 5  NEW DEAL DAYS

Even before the echoes of the music on Pennsylvania Avenue died,
the President was busy conferring with his leaders about the immediate
steps to take. He had decided to order the temporary closing of any
bank still open and wanted to discuss how such an emergency proclamation could be drafted. It was indicative of the seriousness of the
situation that not one of these men, who usually differed on important
political issues, expressed dissent. Other subjects were barely mentioned, since all realized that the banking problem was the crucial one.
Informally the President stated his intention to move for the guarantee-
ing of bank deposits, but he agreed that this could wait. The next day
he acted. Plans for a special session of Congress were announced and
the bank-closing proclamation issued.

From the beginning of those whirlwind "Hundred Days," it was
quite clear that the President intended to lead, and that he set great
store on continuous and, if possible, favorable publicity about the
various projects afoot. Some days after he became President, he asked
me to come to the White House in the afternoon. After discussing a
number of matters, he said he was determined not to be criticized for
giving interviews to favorite correspondents, nor did he intend to have
a newspaperman acting as "unofficial" White House spokesman, as
Hoover had. He proposed to inaugurate the practice of holding press
conferences to which all correspondents would be invited, and asked
me to remain for the conference he was about to hold. I can see him
now, leaning back in his chair, pretending to enjoy a slow puff on a
cigarette in his long holder, but really playing for time. A question
about the banking situation was followed by one about agricultural

73

prices and several inquiries about political appointments. The reporters quickly jumped from domestic to foreign affairs, and the President had to be fast on his mental feet. When the newsmen were gone, he asked what I thought of it. His hand was trembling and he was wet with perspiration. I answered that it was fine for the reporters, but I feared the effect on him. He said he recognized the hazards; that it would be only a short time before "my foot will slip and I will make a damaging 'off the cuff' remark." But I saw he liked the conference and found it immensely stimulating. I think that he found in these verbal challenges a substitute for the competitive sports in which he could no longer take part. He started something that gave to the press a power it enjoyed in no other land; and no other President, whatever his inclinations, will find it possible to end the custom of meeting the press in this way. If he is wise he will not try, because it gives a President a wonderful opportunity to enlist support of the public for his programs.

The key words of the administration's first weeks were in fact "solvency" and "economy." Accordingly, when Congress assembled in special session, the President had an Emergency Banking Act ready for consideration.

The night of March 8 the President called a group of congressional leaders to the White House and made known the principal features of the banking bill on which for several days Glass, Moley and I had been working, along with several House members. Among other things, this bill provided that banks would reopen only under license by the Treasury; those deemed to be sound would be opened immediately; those about which there was any question would be operated by conservators until it was determined that they were completely solvent; hopelessly insolvent banks would be kept closed and liquidated. The bill was introduced in the Senate the next morning and passed with only seven dissenting votes. In the House, after thirty minutes debate it was passed by acclamation, and at eight o'clock that night was signed by the President.

After clearance by the Comptroller of the Currency, many banks began to function again. But Treasury financing faced a problem. The Treasury had a deficit of some $2 billion, and this was increasing at the rate of $5 million a day. In view of today's public debt, some might call this infinitesimal. But it must be recalled that most banks had gone through the wringer, and officials, facing angry depositors, were slow to purchase government securities. A nation had to be convinced that its government was aware of the problems and had a plan to combat the spiraling crisis within the limitations of a balanced budget.

That night other congressional leaders from the Appropriations Committee went to the White House, where the President outlined the economy measure.

The next day, Friday, March 11, the President sent to the Hill a "surprise" and comprehensive economy measure—"To maintain the credit of the United States Government." As a member of the Senate Economy Committee, I had worked on details of this measure for some time together with Cliff Woodrum of the House Appropriations Committee and Lew Douglas, the newly appointed Director of the Budget. We now aimed at a cut of not less than 25 per cent of current expenditures for the year ending June 30, 1933, as well as of expenditures projected for the fiscal year commencing July 1, 1933. Legislation is in order on an appropriation bill only when a motion is adopted to suspend the rule prohibiting it. Seriousness of the times made it possible for me to secure unanimous consent for consideration of our amendment proposing a new law. This gave the President greater power to consolidate and reorganize federal agencies. It cut more than $100 million from salaries of government employees, including a cut from $10,000 to $8,500 in congressional salaries. Because of the curtailment of veterans' benefits, the bill provoked a storm in Congress that required all the parliamentary skill we could command. After four days the measure went through. During this rough passage I thought of the words I had used in a speech on government finances late in January of that year: "The people must come to realize that government has no money except that which is taken from their own pockets; that Uncle Sam is not Santa Claus and the Treasury not a Christmas tree; that the efficiency of a representative in Congress should be measured not by his ability to secure funds from the Treasury but by his ability to defeat the efforts of those who seek to secure funds from the Treasury." Unfortunately, in exercising the discretion granted to fix the amount of compensation for various disabilities, the Veterans Administration cut some benefits too deeply and made the whole proposal very unpopular.

Later in the same session of Congress, when the appropriations bill for the independent government agencies and offices was introduced, providing funds at the reduced rate authorized by the Economy Act, the controversy over the cuts flared up again. The veterans' organizations had mobilized to reverse the defeat in the Economy Act. In a statement President Roosevelt said he thought the service-connected cuts were deeper than intended and promised to review those cases, and he suspended the plan to close some regional offices of the Veterans Administration until that situation was reviewed. The President agreed to limit pension cuts to war-disabled veterans to 25 per cent and to leave on the rolls 150,000 veterans whose disabilities were presumed to have originated in the war. The House stood by his compromise. In the Senate an amendment repealing more of the cuts was adopted. The House rejected the Senate's amendment. Shortly after midnight the Senate agreed with the House version, nine Democrats who had previously voted against our cuts changing to support the President. The Bill was adopted 45 to 36.

In March, 1934, economies in the independent offices bill again aroused a controversy. An amendment was added, not only restoring increased allowances for veterans, but authorizing the restoration of the pay cuts for federal employees, including salaries of members of Congress, which had been reduced in 1933. Lew Douglas, Cliff Woodrum and I recommended that the President veto the bill. After much deliberation he exercised his veto. We did all we could to sustain that veto, but failed.

It was a resounding defeat for Mr. Roosevelt and for us. In my opinion it entirely changed the President's attitude toward economy measures. He evidently concluded that whatever may have been the wish of the Congress in 1933, it was no longer willing to support him in his efforts to economize. Then, too, new advisers to the President had come on the scene, most of whom believed in a liberal spending policy. The action of the Congress convinced the President, who was no follower. He immediately became the leader of those who were advocating liberal spending.

While these economy measures were being shunted back and forth, legislation of great importance had been considered. The Agricultural Adjustment Act, which for the first time sought to control agricultural surpluses by curtailing production and paying farmers for land not cultivated, had provoked controversy in the Congress and in the country. All agreed upon the necessity for increasing the prices of agricultural commodities, but no two seemed to agree on how this end could be accomplished.

The peril was that the general feeling of crisis would result in legislative programs that were not merely bold and experimental but downright reckless and unpredictable in their effects. While this farm relief bill was before the Senate, Senator Wheeler, who believed strongly in the free coinage of silver, introduced an amendment that would have revived the old sixteen-to-one idea of Bryan and the Silver Democrats. He was a plausible advocate for any cause. His proposal was defeated by only eleven votes, with nineteen absent senators. At once I knew we were in trouble, for it was plain that many members who had voted against this proposal would be willing to support some other move toward inflation, should one be offered. Their chance appeared immediately in the form of an amendment by Senator Thomas of Oklahoma which was quite as radical as Wheeler's. My worst fears were confirmed when a close friend, John Bankhead of Alabama, told me that he and several others, who had voted against the Wheeler amendment, felt Thomas' ideas should be given a trial. Senator John Townsend of Delaware, a staunch Republican and a conservative banker, also spoke to me about the attitude of some Republican senators from the agricultural states who had voted against Bryanism but who were now prepared to support Thomas. I noted that even he did not sound too determined in opposition himself.

Since Ray Moley had been in the gallery on previous days keeping in touch with developments, I asked him to accompany me to the White House to inform the President of the situation. Together we thoroughly canvassed every possibility and at length Mr. Roosevelt drew up a memorandum which he asked us to draft in the form of an amendment. That evening, with Senator Key Pittman of Nevada, we prepared a rough draft which that night Moley took to the President for any changes he might suggest. Meanwhile, since the Thomas amendment was due for consideration at twelve the next day, I was given the task of approaching its author and seeing that he kept an open mind. I asked him to go with me to see the President, who did an excellent sales job—in fact, so good that Thomas said he would be glad to substitute most of our draft for his own. Moley, Pittman and I then began the job of final drafting. When Thomas finally offered the amendment to the agricultural bill, there was strong opposition, but the Senate approved the amendment and the bill by a good majority. Later it passed the House by an overwhelming vote.

The night of its passage I explained in a radio talk that the object of the amendment was to increase price levels by directing the Treasury to enter into agreements with the Federal Reserve Board and the Federal Reserve Banks under which those banks would purchase $3 billion of government obligations. This should result in putting $3 billion more into circulation, and as this currency found its way into the banks it could be counted as reserves and thus make it possible for commercial banks to obtain additional credit. The Federal Reserve Board was to prevent undue expansion, and to accomplish this had the power to sell all or part of the $2 billion of government securities it held. The amendment further authorized the President to fix the weight of the gold dollar up to 50 per cent if, after investigation, he found this necessary to protect our foreign commerce against the effect of depreciated currencies abroad.

This was not orthodox currency legislation, but, in the emergency, conditions were not orthodox. The bankers were especially critical, but no one offered a substitute. The President did not have to use the extraordinary powers granted. After passage of this bill with the Thomas currency amendment, farm prices rose and with them the value of farm land. This in turn benefited the banks, which held more than $500 million of farm mortgages. The measure contributed materially to ending a condition that had destroyed both the farmers' values and their morale. Nor should it be forgotten that we had put through the most conservative proposal for inflation which the Congress would accept at the time, a factor generally ignored by critics both inside and outside the administration.

While the agricultural bill was under consideration, I was greatly distressed to learn that Father Coughlin, the radio priest from Michigan, who was widely known for his inflationary proposals, had arrived in Washington and announced his support of the Thomas amendment. This I feared would cost us the votes of several moderates. Almost immediately I was told by a Senate page that Senator Thomas was in Senator Pittman's office on the first floor of the Capitol, waiting to have his photograph taken with Father Coughlin and me. For political reasons, I had no wish to be photographed just at that time with Father Coughlin. I could picture headlines crediting him with drafting the Thomas amendment, but I could not offend Thomas. For about an hour I successfully evaded the pages who were following my trail. Finally Senator Thomas himself caught up with me, and I had to say I would come in a few minutes. I remember that I started down the back stairs in order to gain a moment longer to think. It did not do any good. As I reached the first floor, I encountered Father Coughlin walking toward the door for which I was headed. In desperation, I said, "Wait! You'd better not go in there. There's a photographer who will want to take your picture—that will be embarrassing to a priest." He replied, "Not at all; we have been waiting an hour for just that purpose."

After we were inside the office I suggested to Pittman that since he and I were only latecomers to the program, Senator Thomas and Father Coughlin should hold the center of the stage and we would stand on the sides. It was fortunate! After the picture was taken and I was on my way back to the Senate, the photographer, a good friend named Hyman Greenberg, said, "Senator, you did not look very happy." I said, "For political reasons, I am not happy." About twenty minutes later I was called to the telephone. Greenberg was on the line offering an apology to me and Senator Pittman because in developing the film our two figures by some mischance had been eliminated. I forgave him.

I recall another instance, with a less happy outcome, that showed me it was wise to be friendly with the photographers. One of the members of the Unemployment and Relief Committee, of which I was chairman, was Senator James J. Davis of Pennsylvania. We were holding extensive hearings, which sometimes got boring because every senator on the committee wanted information on some phase of relief. But Jim Davis had been Secretary of Labor in Hoover's Cabinet and was expected to be interested. After lunch one day, when he was nodding in his chair, I saw a photographer aiming his camera at him. Asleep, Davis was not the same handsome man we knew when he was interestedly examining a witness. I began to talk in a loud voice, shuffling my feet and pushing back my chair with a great noise as though I were crowded for space. In spite of all the commotion I could stir up, Jim slept on and the photographer got his shot, which was published by an unfriendly newspaper under the heading "Our Sleeping Senator." Jim told me that no editorial in that newspaper could have hurt him, but he was ruined politically by that picture.

It may be worth while to stress the mental attitude of our people in the spring and summer of 1933. There are many present-day critics of the measures then enacted who took a very different view at the time. Indeed, I spent part of each day seeing captains of industry who were clamoring for legislation providing government controls to stabilize or save the banks, the market, foreign or domestic trade, and the like.

Willingness to experiment and to receive assistance from the government was general because so many had lost faith and hope.

This attitude was illustrated by a comment of Walter P. Chrysler, who, like many other businessmen, saw only bankruptcy ahead. We met one night shortly after the inauguration when he was trying to find out what the government would do or could do to stop the depression. He told me that he had no hope of regaining even a portion of his losses. With wry humor he said that in the good old days he had bought himself a very comfortable tent for fishing trips and was in hopes that his creditors would leave him this particular asset. He was going to pitch it near a stream and fish and use his worthless stock certificates to line the sides of the tent!

We established the Farm Credit Administration, and within a year it was lending at an average daily rate of $5 million. This saved the foreclosure of many farm homes. The Banking and Currency Committee also reported the Home Owners Loan Act, the purpose of which was to save mortgaged homes, wherever located, from foreclosure.

There was another unusual bill: the National Industrial Recovery Act. General Hugh Johnson was credited with having written the first draft of this proposal. Certainly he was the power behind the President and later was to administer the act. In view of its history it is surprising that the proposal was first advocated by the United States Chamber of Commerce and later was sponsored by the liberal Senator Robert Wagner. Its purpose was declared to be the establishment of government "partnership" with industry. Business advocated it because it provided for industrial agreements free from fear of antitrust prosecution. However, it had something for everybody. Labor was pleased because every employer had to comply with maximum hours and minimum wages and working conditions approved by the President. It gave the President extraordinary control over industry during the emergency and authorized him to spend more than $3 billion on public works.

I had nothing to do with drafting either the National Industrial Recovery Act or the Agricultural Adjustment Act and was not on the committees reporting those bills. I did assist with the drafting and the passage of the bill creating the Securities and Exchange Commission. That was not emergency legislation. For some years there had been a need to end the abuses in the manipulation of securities by groups of financiers. By combining their resources they squeezed out small investors and amassed fortunes.

The railroads were the principal targets of the big speculators and investment bankers. Ray Moley and Sam Rayburn directed the drafting of the Railroad Rehabilitation Act, and when it reached the Senate I pressed for its enactment. Prior to enactment of this measure, whenever a railroad was in financial trouble and a receiver appointed, speculators and bankers got everything but the spikes and the crossties. This legislation gave some relief to our transportation systems, without which we could not have become the arsenal of democracy ten years later.

On June 16 the special session adjourned. Certainly the President had fulfilled his promise of action. Many had doubts about the future as a result of the methods employed, but the masses of the people, gradually recovering from the suffering of the depression, were hopeful—and happy.

A few days after the Congress adjourned I attended a summer Gridiron party at the Chevy Chase Club. During the evening Marvin McIntyre, one of the President's secretaries, told me that Ray Moley was leaving that night for the World Economic Conference, which had been in session in London since June 12. He was going as a special envoy of the President. I had come to think a lot of Moley and, believing that he was making a mistake, I left the party with McIntyre for Moley's hotel, where I found him packing for the trip. I told him he could serve the President best by remaining at his side to confer with him about instructions to be sent to the delegation that was already representing us at the conference; that if it should be announced that he was leaving for the conference as a special envoy of the President, the delegations from other governments would ignore our delegation and its effectiveness would be impaired. He was sufficiently interested to say that the next morning he would fly to see the President, who was in New England at the time. Evidently the President did not agree, because the following day Moley left for London.

Our delegation there was composed of Secretary Hull, Senators Pittman and Couzens, Congressman McReynolds, Governor James M. Cox and Ralph W. Morrison, a Texas banker. Moley did everything possible to avoid creating the impression that he was superseding the delegation, but he was not successful. Hull, writing some years later, said that Prime Minister MacDonald telephoned him, asking that he send Moley to see him, adding as an afterthought, "if you care to come along, do so." In an effort to avoid conflict, Moley had announced that he would confine his interest to an effort to stabilize the currency, a subject under the primary jurisdiction of the Treasury, not the Department of State. After many conferences he arrived at an agreement that he confidently believed the President would approve. However, without first informing Moley, the President issued a statement strongly disapproving the agreement.

It is almost certain that the conference would not have accomplished anything, even if Moley had never gone to London, but the President's action made it absolutely certain. The British particularly resented it. Moley loyally tried to justify the President's statement, but MacDonald charged the President with responsibility for the failure of the conference. Hull continued for a week to discuss reciprocal trade agreements, but the conference adjourned without any accomplishments.

At the request of the President, Secretary Hull immediately after the inauguration had appointed Moley an Assistant Secretary of State, not with the idea of having him perform any departmental duties, but to let him have an office just opposite the White House so that the President could quickly get in touch with him. I do not know what transpired between the President and Moley when the President sent him to London, nor do I know what occurred when he returned. At the time, the press erroneously reported that the episode caused Secretary Hull to ask for the resignation of Moley as Assistant Secretary. However, written evidence shows that as early as April, 1933, Mrs. Mary Rumsey had told the President that she and her brother, Averell Harriman, and Vincent Astor wished to acquire a magazine and that Moley had agreed to become its editor. The President approved the idea but did not want Moley to leave the administration.

In June, Astor arranged to start the weekly magazine *Today*, with Moley as editor, and he induced President Roosevelt to agree to accept Moley's resignation. Secretary Hull issued a press statement denying that he had requested the resignation or had suggested it to the President. The President also denied that Hull had made a request that Moley be asked to resign. Certainly, Hull's statement was friendly. Moley's resignation was unfortunate for the President because he had no abler or more loyal supporter in his campaign and in the Hundred Days following his inauguration. Moley's extraordinary ability, his wise and calm counsel, enabled him to perform a great service not only to the President but to the country.

I have said nothing about unemployment relief in my review of legislation passed during the special session. My views of the Federal Emergency Relief Act of May, 1933, and of the National Industrial Recovery Act, which established the Public Works Administration, may well be prefaced by a brief public statement I made to the New England Society of South Carolina in December, 1933. After reciting some of the legislative program passed by the Seventy-third Congress, I stated:

Whether you believe these policies to be idealistic or revolutionary, you have the knowledge that most of them are authorized by Congress only for the period of the emergency. When the emergency passes, they must pass. For permanent prosperity all thoughtful men know we must rely upon private enterprise with only such government regulations as are essential for the protection of individual rights.

Everyone now realizes that in a modern society one of the greatest perils to a country's security and freedom is excessive unemployment. In 1933 the problem was to help our citizens find jobs without destroying either their self-respect or their political independence. With this hope the Public Works Administration was established and put under the control of the Secretary of the Interior, Harold Ickes.

The more direct relief activities were placed under Harry Hopkins, who believed that work relief was preferable to the dole and rushed into existence the Civil Works Administration. It was not well organized and was abandoned after six months.

Another effort was made in early 1935 to put the unemployed on "useful projects" through the Works Projects Administration. The projects were selected by local authorities. By this organization millions were employed at only a subsistence wage and as a result of a "means" test. Many of the projects benefited various communities and millions of self-respecting citizens were spared the humiliation of accepting charity. Before long, however, it was apparent that its sponsors believed their agency, or something like it, must have a permanent place in our national life. To this I was strongly opposed, believing that every citizen is obligated to support the government, not that the government must support every citizen.

As economic conditions improved, I urged upon the President the importance of beginning to reduce the appropriations for direct relief and of starting "to plan for WPA more projects that are permanent and essential." With respect to the 3,500,000 unemployed on the relief rolls, I urged that local officials were better qualified than a federal agency to pass on those who genuinely needed assistance. I knew that Harry Hopkins had come to realize the great power that lay in the disbursement of these hundreds of millions of dollars. City and county officials knew that they could win popularity by having the United States government foot the bill for the improvement and main-tenance of streets and buildings instead of taxing their constituents. It was an unhealthy situation, but Hopkins opposed any reduction, either because of the demands made on him or because of his desire to retain his power. Power intoxicates men. The man intoxicated by alcohol can get over it next day, but if intoxicated by power he will never get over it.

It was difficult for us all because every congressman and every senator was besieged daily by powerful political influences in his state, begging for more spending for everything from fire engine houses to college libraries, and for more money for direct relief.

Then in 1935 we enacted the social security law and the Unemploy-ment Compensation Act. The record shows that many Republicans as well as Democrats in both Houses voted for these measures. As eco-nomic conditions have improved, many who favored these bills changed their minds, but no political party and no candidate for the Presidency has advocated their repeal. It was my hope that these two permanent laws would make it easier to abolish WPA and direct relief.

But, as I have indicated, the establishment of WPA had spawned fresh problems. The strength of the political influence brought to bear in connection with its activities frightened me. It was a factor in the elections in every state. Pressures were exerted on Congress not only by state, county and city officials, but even by the presidents of univer-sities and colleges—some of whose graduates were members of the Senate—who seized the opportunity to have the federal government build football stadiums and libraries at no cost to the colleges.

One feature of the public works job was the almost permanent disagreement between Ickes and Hopkins. Ickes' projects paid pre-vailing wages and there was no "means" test for employment, but it was not surprising that there were jealousies and dissension between them, for often there was no sharp dividing line of authority. In 1934 a project in my own state caused the President to discuss their quarrel with me. South Carolina had asked for aid to construct what later was

mes F. Byrnes.                                                    (*Tom Nebbia*)

The author at about ten years of age.

James F. Byrnes and his mother, Elizabeth E. Byrnes, in 1930.

Leaving a White House conference on neutrality legislation, September, 1939. (Left to right) Vice-President John N. Garner, Senator Byrnes, Congressman Sam Rayburn and Senator Sherman Minton.

(*United Press International*)

Mr. Byrnes receives the congratulations of President Roosevelt after taking oath as Associate Justice of the U.S. Supreme Court. With them, Carter Glass and Mrs. Byrnes.　　　　　　(*United Press International*)

The U.S. Supreme Court, 1941. From left to right (sitting), Justices Stanley Reed, Owen J. Roberts, Chief Justice Harlan F. Stone, Justices Hugo L. Black, Felix Frankfurter; (standing) James F. Byrnes, William O. Douglas, Frank Murphy, Robert H. Jackson.　　　(*Fabian Bachrach*)

A scene at the 1944 Democratic National Convention.

With the late General George S. Patton, Jr., before a World War II monument in France, 1944.

With Generals Eisenhower, Marshall and Bradley in France, 1944.     (*U.S. Army*)

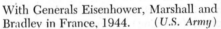

...ing sworn in as Secretary
...State, July, 1945. Mrs.
...onore Byrnes Fuller on
...treme left, Mrs. Byrnes
...nter and Justice Richard
...Whaley administering the
...th. Members of the Cabi-
...t and the Congress in the
...ckground. (*Wide World*)

...dding Foreign Minister
...orges Bidault good-by
...er Council of Foreign
...inisters meeting in Paris,
...46. Mr. Molotov left, Mr.
...vin right.
...*xploitation Photographique*)

...st time Soviets "took a
...lk" from the Security
...uncil, March, 1946. (Left
...right) Empty seat of An-
...ei Gromyko, Sir Alexander
...dogan (Great Britain),
...lward R. Stettinius, Jr.,
...cretary of State Byrnes,
...*.* Col. William Roy Hodg-
...n (Australia), Dr. Pedro
...ao Velloso (Brazil) and
...vgve Lie.
...*nited Press International*)

Attending the opera during th
1946 meeting of the Council c
Foreign Ministers in New Yorl
Second row, left to right, M
Molotov, Mr. Vishinsky, M
Byrnes, Mr. Bevin; front row, un
identified woman, Mrs. Byrne.
Mrs. Bevin and Mrs. Worthing
ton Miner (Mr. Byrnes' niece)

Secretary of State Byrnes speal
ing from the floor during th
Paris Peace Conference, Sep
tember, 1946.      (*Gjon Mil*

vernor and Mrs. James F. Byrnes, at Governor's House, Columbia, S.C.
(*National Geographic Society*)

The crowd listening to Governor Byrnes' inaugural address, Columbia, Sou
Carolina, January, 1951.                           (*Munn-Teal Photographe*

Orphan students, being educated by proceeds from Mr. Byrnes' writin
gathered at the Governor's House, June, 1954.           (*Jimmy Price Stud*

known as the Santee-Cooper power development and had requested my assistance. For a hundred years engineers had recommended this development, which had been started under private enterprise but had been abandoned a few years before the depression. I was sympathetic; for though I believed that power projects should normally be developed by private utilities, I also believed that when private capital could not or would not develop a necessary project, government might step in.

Revenue bonds were to be issued for the amount the state borrowed from Public Works Administration, but Works Progress Administration was to assign to the job common laborers who asked for employment relief in the area. However, the use of both agencies required the co-operation of Ickes and Hopkins. Laughing, the President told me that if I succeeded in getting their agreement on this, or on anything else, he would consider me for a high diplomatic post. But my relations with the two men were very pleasant. I did not have the trouble he anticipated, and in time the Santee-Cooper project became a reality. The state authority has met its obligations as required by the federal government.

In these years relief spending was one of the paramount issues. It did not end with the first Hundred Days, nor even with the first four years. In 1937 the President and I differed over economy measures and in particular over a cut of $500 million which I proposed in relief appropriations. This economy proposal I described in a broadcast at the time, in which I urged the administration to go further in its effort to achieve solvency than the various cuts suggested by Mr. Roosevelt in his budget message of April 20. I asked that the relief appropriation be cut by one third and a further 10 per cent reduction be made in all ordinary expenditures of the government except those to meet fixed charges. It was also desirable, I said, for Congress to require local communities to pay up to half the cost of their relief projects. All this would save up to a billion dollars.

I reminded the radio audience that I had hitherto voted for every relief measure. I continued, "If today the same conditions existed as in 1933 I would vote for the same appropriations. But the same conditions do not exist. The emergency has passed." I wanted to keep my promise that when it passed, these emergency measures would lapse.

I pointed out that some of our recent tax levies had failed to produce the expected revenues, and that a government, like an individual, must deny itself many desirable things in order to live within its means. I ended by warning that the Congress had a duty to see that the budget was balanced and that this duty should not be shifted to the President.

I heard that the President was disturbed about my attitude. I therefore wrote him a letter, explaining my plan in full. He was leaving Washington for New Orleans, where he was to board a ship for a brief vacation. On April 28 he sent me a letter indicating his general dissatisfaction at my position, and concluding, "I did not know you had any plan except what I have read from time to time in the newspapers. I am, of course, ready at all times to discuss matters of this kind at your convenience." The letter originally ended stiffly with "Very sincerely yours"; but when signing it, the President had run his pen through these words, substituting "As ever yours, FDR." This was a characteristic action, the kind of thing he habitually did that made it difficult to get mad with him.

In June my economy proposal was defeated in committee, but a second amendment of mine, requiring local governments to make contributions of 50 per cent, where possible, was adopted. Hopkins spent over two hours protesting against this to my committee. The outcome was a lunch with President Roosevelt during which he insisted that it was not yet time to aim at such drastic measures. I could not agree and continued my efforts.

This was a different Roosevelt from the one who in 1933 had urged economy and whose policies I had strongly supported. FDR had come to like making financial awards. Hopkins, studying the President as no one else did, recognized this trait and capitalized on it. If mayors like Kelly of Chicago, Frank Hague of Jersey City or Dave Lawrence of Pittsburgh urged a project for WPA money, Hopkins would reject it if he thought it unwise. But if he thought it meritorious he would offer encouragement, saying, however, that because WPA funds were short, he wanted the mayor himself to present his cause to the President. The mayor, knowing the grant of funds would help him in the next election, would earnestly plead for his project. The President finally would say he was convinced and approve the allotment Hopkins had already decided to approve. When the mayor got home, he could truthfully tell how he had won his case after a hard fight. This help to the mayors tied the big cities to the President politically. Where prior to the depression a political machine like Tammany of New York depended upon municipal help for funds to care for the needy faithful, it now looked to the federal treasury, though it had to divide the credit for aid with the President of the United States.

However, as far as my economy bill was concerned, political pressures were too strong for me; it was plain that my requirement of a contribution by local governments could not command a majority vote on the floor of the Senate unless the figure was lowered to 25 per cent. I finally accepted this compromise, urged upon me by Senator Robinson.

Again in December, 1938, I renewed my fight to curb the PWA and to put an end to WPA. In an address to the Southern Society of New York, I demanded further cuts in emergency expenditures and the adoption of a more permanent and economical relief program for unemployment. When I returned to Washington, the President invited me to lunch. As I entered the door, he greeted me by singing "Oh, where is my wandering boy?" During lunch, he argued for the continued support of Works Progress Administration, and I frankly told him I was going to do everything possible to bring about its liquidation, relying upon social security and unemployment insurance, which were then in operation in twenty-three states, for more permanent relief. We agreed to disagree!

A month later the President asked for $875 million for WPA, saying that was the least amount that would enable it to function. Our committee reduced the appropriation to $725 million. The President and Mr. Hopkins made personal appeals to some senators for support. Senator Barkley, the Democratic leader, made a strong fight for the full amount. Senator Alva Adams of Colorado and I took the position that if we did not make the cut now, we would never liquidate WPA. We won by a vote of forty-seven to forty-six. That was the beginning of the end of WPA.

Three weeks later the committee, of which I was chairman, filed a report proposing a co-ordinated system of relief, based primarily on extended and improved unemployment insurance benefits; on increased aid for the aged, the blind, and dependent children; and on a consolidated public work program, handled by a Department of Public Works.

During the depression it was inevitable that there should be an investigation of banking and investment houses. In the midst of the rush of emergency legislation late in May, 1933, the Senate began a full-scale inquiry into the House of Morgan. It was the second investigation of that banking house during my congressional service. In my first term I had been present in December, 1912, as a member of the House Banking and Currency Committee when J. P. Morgan, Sr., testified before the Pujo Committee. The story of the two-day cross-examination of the elder Morgan is well known. I recall an exchange between Morgan and counsel for the committee which occurred when counsel questioned whether Morgan had made a certain large loan on what appeared to be very small collateral. The old man answered that his statement was quite true and that he could remember on one occasion making a loan of a million dollars without any collateral. Experience told him the debtor possessed the capacity to pay and the character that made payment certain. "But" he added, "you would not understand that."

It was interesting more than twenty years later to hear the younger Morgan testify. Unfortunately he was subjected to what he rightly regarded as an indignity when a midget suddenly hopped up on his knee during a committee session and was photographed. This incident produced one of Carter Glass' fiercest outbursts of rage. Believing that Counsel Pecora, or at least some member of his staff, had known in advance of the publicity stunt, he began to attack him bitterly. The hearing was about to dissolve into complete disorder when I quickly moved to adjourn. When I announced that we would resume the inquiry later, Glass strode from the room grumbling loudly about the Senate committee hearing being turned into a circus.

Investigation of the Morgan company was a manifestation of the general increase of radical sentiment brought about by the depression. But in fact it helped focus attention on the need for some reasonable control of banking and stock exchange activity. An example of legislation of this type was the Glass-Steagall Act of June, 1934, which insured individual bank deposits. As a member of the committee I worked with Senator Vandenberg of Michigan to help pass this bill. He was not a friend of the New Deal or of the President, who was also interested, but the oddity of the combination did not strike any of us at the time. Van took a special interest in the bill because of the great losses suffered by the people of his state from the closing of banks in the days immediately before Roosevelt's inauguration.

The next year a senatorial committee began another type of investigation which was to have long range and even dangerous consequences. In April, 1934, a resolution was passed calling for an inquiry by the Munitions Investigating Committee into the manufacture of, and traffic in, arms. Sponsors of the resolution claimed that because of the vast profits made in World War I by suppliers of arms and ammunition, manufacturers of munitions had a vested interest in war and in fact were responsible for our entry into the European conflict. As chairman of the Committee to Audit and Control Contingent Expenses, I did not oppose the investigation when the Democrats on the committee told me that they would elect Senator George of Georgia as its chairman. Unfortunately, on the day they first met, Senator George and Senator Clark of Missouri arrived late and found that Senator Bone of Washington, a Democrat, had joined the Republicans present in electing Senator Gerald P. Nye of North Dakota.

Nye at that time was a sincere isolationist. He took speedy advantage of his position to make sensational headlines. His staff called the du Ponts and others "merchants of death." His counsel was Stephen Raushenbush of Pennsylvania, who later secured from executive departments several bright young radical-thinking lawyers, including Nat Witt, J. J. Raushenbush and Alger Hiss. Hiss at that time was employed in the Department of Agriculture.

Most of the committee's activity I followed through the press, my interest being occasionally heightened by the fact that its work was costing a lot of money. The extreme liberals in the executive departments were always ready to help such investigations, and sometimes the Senate Audit and Control Committee had to curtail their activities. In the munitions investigation I learned that the Investigating Committee quickly exhausted the small appropriation my committee allotted, but managed to run for a while longer on $65,000 of WPA funds which had been appropriated for the employment of persons to administer relief work. This caused Senator Glass to say that the United States Senate was not on relief and that he objected to its being the recipient of WPA money.

Much of the work of the Nye Committee was done by counsel and his staff, for the chairman was occupied with his senatorial duties. Senator Nye did, however, constantly make speeches throughout the country on the wickedness of the arms trade. He was a good speaker. He told me that public interest was so great that he was paid generously for his appearances. Moreover, his speeches on this theme were printed in the *Congressional Record*, distributed widely and a generous supply of them held in the Senate Document Room.

Often when schools assigned to students a topic on isolationism or on our role in World War I for debate and study, requests for suitable material would reach members of the House and Senate. The letters would be referred to the document clerk, who would send out some of Nye's speeches, there being no other speeches on the subject. Also the committee itself was used as a forum to develop pacifist propaganda, much of which reached the colleges and high schools and influenced the thinking of our young people. No one attempted to answer Nye, others in public life being too busy fighting the depression.

This went on for nearly two years. One day in 1935 I read that the committee's counsel had charged that the income tax return of Bernard Baruch for 1918 had mysteriously disappeared from the Treasury. I telephoned to members of the committee, saying that I wished to appear before them. Few of the senators attended regularly, and I wanted them to know of my intention to testify. Most of them were present when I entered the committee room. I spoke of B. M.'s record in the war—of how I had known him in 1918 when I was a member of the Deficiency Appropriations Committee of the House and he was chairman of the War Industries Board; that on one occasion, when money was urgently needed to send a commission to England on a matter affecting war purchases, Congress was not in session so Mr. Baruch himself footed the $85,000 bill. I also told how at the end of hostilities he had advanced transportation expenses to all the women employees of the War Industries Board to return home when that organization had come to an abrupt end. I described it as outrageous to suggest that such a man would conspire with an employee of the Treasury to remove his tax return for 1918 in order to destroy evidence of profit-making.

There was general approval by the committee, including Senator Nye, who took the opportunity to disclaim any criticism of Baruch's war record. It was a good illustration of how employees of an investigating committee can abuse their great power if unchecked. On this occasion, fortunately, hysterical accusations were checked. But the over-all effect of the committee's activities was to exaggerate isolationist and pacifist tendencies and to encourage a cynical attitude towards defense needs at a time when the totalitarian states of Europe were gathering their strength.

The Audit and Control Committee was comprised of only five senators. In practical operation my colleagues ordinarily left it to Senator

Townsend, a Republican from Delaware, and me to decide whether the Senate should provide funds to conduct an investigation, and, if so, what amount we should make available. In exercising this responsibility I came to appreciate that a congressional investigation could be either helpful or extremely harmful. It was never intended that a Senate committee should serve as a grand jury on wheels, running over the country seeking the perpetrators of some crime who properly should be punished by the courts. Every resolution of investigation specifically states that the investigation is to secure information upon which to base legislation. During the last half century time and again a senatorial inquiry has developed information about matters that would not have been discovered by a grand jury and that resulted in the enactment of remedial legislation.

The abuse of this great power can often be laid to counsel employed to conduct the work of the committee. The successful lawyer will not leave his office and his home and spend months in Washington for the relatively small compensation. Consequently the committee chairman seeking counsel is frequently forced to choose between a lawyer who, because of lack of ability, has little practice to lose or some man of real ability whose zeal for the cause makes him uninterested in the compensation. The latter is likely to be a dangerous man because, as counsel, he will be entrusted with the power to summon citizens to Washington and to submit them to cross-examination. He may be more interested in promoting his prejudices than in securing information, and the citizen may be denied a fair opportunity to defend himself.

Holding these views, I insisted that a senator sponsoring a resolution of investigation should agree to conduct the investigation himself instead of leaving it to a lawyer. To further this end our committee would limit the funds for the investigation.

A worth-while investigation was that conducted by Senator Truman during the war. It is interesting how this inquiry started. President Roosevelt telephoned me that the Secretaries of War and Navy were disturbed because they had been informed that the House would probably adopt a resolution, introduced by Congressman Eugene Cox of Georgia, to investigate the awarding of contracts by the armed services. What particularly worried the Secretaries was that Cox had been offended by an official of the War Department, and they feared that as chairman of the committee he would require many key men to leave their work to testify, causing delays in the defense programs.

I knew Eugene Cox and told the President the Army's appraisal of him was not correct, but the President was so afraid something would hamper the services that I decided to report one of the several resolutions pending before my committee, knowing that if this was done the House would not authorize another investigation. When I looked through the several resolutions before my committee, I found one introduced by Senator Truman and immediately asked him what had prompted his resolution. He told me that a contractor in Missouri alleged that the War Department awarded its contracts only to the big contracting organizations, on the theory that they alone were equipped for quick construction. He said that he thought his constituent was right, but that the armed services were opposed to his resolution and he had no idea it would be reported. I knew he had been a supporter of the administration, so within an hour I secured unanimous consent for the consideration and passage of the resolution. With Senator Barkley and the Republican leader, we suggested to the Vice President a splendid committee, with Truman as chairman.

The House did not act on Congressman Cox's resolution. The Truman Committee employed as counsel Hugh Fulton of New York, who was a good lawyer, and under the direction of Senator Truman he conducted a constructive investigation. The amount appropriated for the original resolution was based solely on the thought of investigating the complaints of the Missouri contractor about awarding contracts. Fulton spent little time on that subject, but made a constructive inquiry into all expenditures of the armed services.

It was interesting that the little contractor in Missouri and Congressman Cox of Georgia started a chain of events that had much to do with the nomination of Senator Truman for Vice President. Later, as President, Truman appointed to the Supreme Court a member of his committee, Senator Burton of Ohio. That can happen in politics!

While I was Director of War Mobilization, I received a request to appear before a Senate committee. When I reached the committee room, I found waiting there Donald Nelson, chairman of the War Production Board, and Paul McNutt, chairman of the War Manpower Commission. There were two young lawyers present, but no senator. McNutt and Nelson told me that they had been waiting for an hour. After a further short wait, one of the young men said that the chairman and members of the committee were very busy and would be delayed, but he would start the inquiry; some of the members should arrive before long. He requested me to take the witness chair.

Holding the views I have set forth, I told him that I would wait until the senators arrived. He then left the room—I presumed to get a senator. Senator Thomas of Utah soon came; and after the lawyer had talked with him, the Senator asked me a few questions, saying, however, that he knew very little about the inquiry. When I had answered the questions, I talked to Senator Thomas personally and he expressed regret that I had been taken from my duties.

As I left, McNutt told me that it seemed he spent a good part of each day in committee hearings. Of course, he and Nelson were afraid not to respond to a request that was signed by the chairman of a committee. McNutt said that I, as a former senator, could refuse to submit to examination by the young men, but that they would have to respond. It confirmed my view of the inconvenience department officials and ordinary citizens, too, can be made to suffer if a responsible member of a committee—Senate or House—fails to stay in active charge of an inquiry.

It is inevitable that at times there should be abuse of the investigatory power in a minor way. I recall one committee that continued an investigation of wildlife for a number of years. Each time its funds were exhausted and a new appropriation requested, I would try to reduce the amount, suspecting that the senators in their good nature were simply providing employment for a committee clerk they liked. I never knew the explanation of that clerk's hold upon them until one night I attended a small dinner given by a member of the committee, where I was greatly entertained by the sleight-of-hand tricks of a gentleman whom I finally recognized as the clerk of the committee. It was easy then to see why that investigation could never be finished.

The year 1936 brought not only a national election, but my second and, as it happened, last race for the Senate. Early in June Mrs. Byrnes and I began the familiar round of campaign meetings at which all candidates appeared throughout all the counties of the state. I had two opponents, Thomas P. Stoney, a very able lawyer and former mayor of Charleston, and William Curry Harllee, an ex-colonel of the Marine Corps. Mr. Stoney was an aggressive candidate and a forceful speaker, but my re-election was not in doubt. Though my wife conscientiously took notes at every meeting, I followed the tactic of never referring to my opponents by name and of not listening to their speeches. When I finished talking, I would leave the stand and meet with my friends in the community, some of whom I had not seen for several years. I was not unaware that some of my friends would leave when I left.

My own victory was so complete as to be humbling. I received 87 per cent of the vote, and led in every precinct except one at Warren's Cross Roads. I have never visited this place, but Warren's Cross Roads is fixed in my memory.

Our speaking campaign in South Carolina had been interrupted for two weeks by the Democratic National Convention in Philadelphia. Before it opened I went with Senator Wagner to the White House to discuss the platform. The President told us he was anxious for the proceedings to be as brief as possible, and that he himself would not appear until the fifth day to make his acceptance speech. By this time Al Smith, John W. Davis and other outstanding Democrats were in active opposition to Roosevelt, and Landon, the Republican candidate, promised to make a strong campaign. At the President's suggestion I asked my delegation to appoint me to the Platform Committee. When many varied groups had been given the opportunity to express their views, we went into executive session. There were many controversial proposals, some mild, some militant, resulting in our sitting into the early morning hours.

While we were in this meeting delegate Burnet R. Maybank, then mayor of Charleston, who had been assigned to the Rules Committee, came to see me. He said that a motion to abrogate the two-thirds rule was pending in his committee, and from the apparent support, including the backing of the President, he feared it would be adopted. Together we went back to his committee to try to mobilize support against it, but there was no encouragement.

Prior to the convention, the President had mentioned to me that he favored a change in the two-thirds rule. I told him I was opposed to the change, not only because traditionally we had followed the two-thirds rule, but because I thought that if a man should be nominated by a bare majority of the delegates, it would show such division of sentiment that in the short time before the election it would be difficult for the candidate to heal the breach and lead the party to victory. Further, the Democratic National Convention, unlike the Republican Convention, was rapidly coming under the domination of the big city bosses. For instance, in New York, New Jersey, Pennsylvania, Massachusetts and Illinois, the Democratic party is controlled by the bosses of the big cities, who name most of the delegates to a national convention. At that convention they control so large a percentage of the total votes that if they agree on a candidate it takes relatively few bandwagon delegates to give their man the necessary 51 per cent. I reminded him that at Baltimore he had supported Wilson, who would have lost the nomination to Clark but for the two-thirds rule. The big-city political machines were for Clark, but now, because of relief appropriations and organized labor, the city bosses were securely in the President's corner.

The leader of the fight to change the rule was my colleague, Bennett Champ Clark. Never have I known a man so dedicated to his father's memory. I was devoted to him. When we could not agree on a subject, we did not discuss it. The defeat of the elder Clark at the 1912 Baltimore convention after he had gotten a majority caused Bennett to pursue his goal with all the energy of an avenging fury. The night he reported the repeal resolution to this convention, the chairman put the question and so quickly announced adoption that delegates had no opportunity to voice opposition. I have no doubt, from the action of the Rules Committee (upon which there was a member from each state) in recommending the change by a large majority, that the result would have been the same, but the method was a warning to the delegates of the way a chairman can railroad decisions.

# 6  END OF THE HONEYMOON

---

The November election was a Democratic landslide, resulting not only in Roosevelt's re-election but in large Democratic majorities in both House and Senate. This did not mean, however, that every Roosevelt proposal would find prompt acceptance in Congress. On domestic and foreign issues there were differences among Democrats. These differences were shortly to be aggravated by the President's moves, early in the following year, to reorganize the Supreme Court, and Bennett Clark, who had agreed with the President at the convention, fought his Court plan.

Most of the so-called New Deal bills had been designed to meet emergency situations. Most of them were drafted by the Attorney General and his assistants and introduced at the request of the President, who properly received credit or blame for the results. Members of the Congress realized that under the panic conditions then existing it was not feasible to hold extensive hearings during which the constitutionality of a proposal might be carefully examined. With the daily clamor of a distressed people for prompt action, legislators had been content to accept the legal opinions of the Attorney General on the legality of the various proposals. I admit that was my attitude. It was not difficult because of my confidence in Robert H. Jackson, later Justice Jackson.

Beginning in June, 1935—when it dealt with NRA—the Supreme Court proceeded to declare unconstitutional several statutes in the President's legislative program. It scrapped the Railroad Retirement Act, the Frazier-Lemke Farm Bankruptcy Act, the "Hot Oil" Act, the Guffey-Snyder Bituminous Coal Act and, in January, 1936, the Agricultural Adjustment Act, most of them by a vote of five to four. Six months

96

later, just before the national conventions, by another five-to-four decision the Supreme Court invalidated the New York minimum wage law, casting doubt on the validity of similar legislation in other states.

With the four conservative justices consistently against the administration, it was clear that unless Chief Justice Hughes and Justice Roberts voted with their colleagues Stone, Brandeis and Cardozo, no important legislation enacted since March 4, 1933, would be upheld. All this made the people, and President Roosevelt, Court-conscious.

We now know that after the overwhelming vote of confidence he had received, the President began to plan legislation, not only to replace the invalidated measures, but to reorganize the Court itself. But at the time I had no hint of it.

For some time I had been strongly of the view that several members of the Court had consistently shown a disposition to base decisions on personal philosophies and political opinions rather than on interpretation and analysis of the Constitution and statutes. Nor was I alone in the Senate in this belief. The view was rather general among my colleagues, for it was reported that in private conversation several of the justices had voiced serious criticisms of administration policies in a very partisan spirit. These criticisms soon became quite widely known in Washington.

Nevertheless, I was surprised to learn of the President's Court plan from the majority leader, Senator Robinson, when he returned from the White House on February 5 and told a few of us that at twelve o'clock the President would send a message to the Congress urging a Court reform program. Neither Robinson nor Ashurst, chairman of the Judiciary Committee, had had any previous intimation of the President's intention. Ironically enough, the proposal to add an additional justice for each one who declined to retire at seventy was a modification of a plan for legal reform made in 1913 by Justice McReynolds, then Wilson's Attorney General. He was now well over the age limit and a vigorous critic of the New Deal.

I was not disturbed by the argument that Congress did not possess the right to change the number of justices, because on several occasions in our history it had done just that.

I did not like some provisions of the bill or the President's procedure; but because of my belief that the Court was legislating by a majority of five and had to be restrained in some way, I announced that I would vote for the bill.

Opposition flared up on all sides. In the Senate some of the President's most loyal supporters felt they should not support these proposals. Very soon I concluded the bill could not be passed and I suggested to the President that he consider the wisdom of compromise. He was adamant and allowed the struggle to grow fiercer. After Senator Hatch offered a compromise plan, I again went to the President, advising him to accept a partial victory. By that time the issues had been confused by the Court's sudden change, when it sustained several statutes whose constitutionality had been challenged, and by the retirement of Justice Van Devanter. However, I was unable to convince the President, who continued to press for passage of the bill.

Then one hot day in July, Joe Robinson, who had been struggling for weeks to line up a majority, was called from the air-cooled Senate chamber into the hot hallway. A few minutes after his return he told me that on stepping outside he had felt faint and had been forced to sit down for a moment. His condition troubled him, and he left the Senate earlier than usual that afternoon. He was alone in Washington, as Mrs. Robinson was at their home in Little Rock. The next morning he was found dead in his apartment. On the floor near him was a book which he evidently had been reading when stricken. It was soon clear that the chances of the Supreme Court bill had died with him. Robinson alone could have marshaled the support of three or four senators who were his close friends, who were not committed and whose votes were absolutely essential for success.

Vice President Garner had absented himself from Washington for some weeks, during which time I tried to keep him advised. He was at Senator Robinson's funeral, and upon our return I asked if he did not believe the time had come for him to canvass the opinions of the several senators whose positions were in doubt but who, it was believed, would oppose the Court bill. He had already done this and, having assured himself of their intention to vote against the bill, he went to the President. With his usual candor he told Mr. Roosevelt that the votes were lacking for anything like his original proposal. The President became convinced that his Court bill was buried with Robinson.

The tragedy of Robinson's death caused a further rift in the Senate, growing out of the selection of a new leader. I was urged to be a candidate for the place and there was a revival of the newspaper stories which had forecast that Robinson would go to the Supreme Court and that I would succeed him. I announced I was not a candidate. At this point, however, two good friends of mine, Alben Barkley of Kentucky and Pat Harrison of Mississippi, made known their availability. I was forced to make a choice between two friends. I decided on Harrison and, as usual, did not remain passive. Harrison began consulting me.

At his request I went to see the President and reminded him of Harrison's enthusiastic support in Roosevelt's various campaigns and of his notable support as chairman of the Senate Finance Committee. I said Harrison did not request his assistance, but did ask for his neutrality. I recall saying that I thought the Chief Executive should not interfere with Democratic senators in their choice of a leader, and that if he did enter this family dispute he would not emerge unscathed. The President said he had not taken and would not take part.

The next morning a letter the President had written to Barkley was made public. I do not know whether it was written before or after our conversation. It began "My dear Alben" and designated him "Acting majority leader of the Senate." The text dealt with the need to continue the fight for an undiluted Court bill. It did not mention the leadership contest, but to the Senate and the press it gave the impression that the President preferred Barkley to Harrison, who had expressed himself freely as being in favor of some compromise of the Court bill. Later, something Steve Early said to me made it even clearer that Mr. Roosevelt favored Barkley, and very soon Harry Hopkins was actively engaged in trying to elect him. Harrison and I knew the minds of the Democratic senators and found it fairly easy to count noses—in fact, as the day of the election approached, there were few Democratic senators whose position seemed to us in doubt.

I had asked one supporter of Harrison, Senator Dieterich of Illinois, to second his nomination. Dieterich agreed and talked over his speech with Harrison. Unfortunately the election was postponed for a few days. The evening before it took place, Dieterich told us that what he called "pressures" from Mayor Kelly of Chicago made it impossible for him to carry out his promise. I admired his candor. It was reasonable to assume that Harry Hopkins, whose control of WPA funds could seriously affect Mayor Kelly, had asked him to appeal to Dieterich, and that he, being dependent upon Kelly for re-election, could not resist.

Because of such pressures, when the caucus of Democratic senators met, I moved that the vote be taken by secret ballot. As the votes were counted, each contestant had twenty-seven votes when the final one remained to be counted—and it was for Barkley! I am sure my disappointment was as great as Harrison's, for our estimate, after taking into account the loss of Dieterich, had given us a majority of one. Someone had switched.

Immediately after the vote was taken I went to my office, just a short distance from the Conference Room. Without any prearrangement at least a dozen Harrison supporters followed and held a political post-mortem. Taking the list of Democratic senators, we began to check off those who had promised to support Harrison and to guess which one had not. As one name was reached about halfway down the list, the men present looked at each other and agreed it was useless to read further. Walter George said, "Jim, why did you count him?" I said, "Pat Harrison told me he was the first senator who asked him to be a candidate and that he would answer for that vote." My visitors left agreeing on one thing—Pat was too trusting. A year or so later I heard the senator in question say at a luncheon given to him by Barkley that he had in fact changed his position and voted for Barkley. The unanimity with which twelve senators had picked him as the defector indicates that a legislator may fool his constituents, but seldom can fool his colleagues. Incidentally, it wasn't Barkley who got him to change his vote; it was Hopkins. This contest in no way affected my friendly relations with Senator Barkley.

Some of the heat engendered in this contest was probably due to the President's Court fight. However, the two contestants were popular senators and the post an important one. The majority leader greatly influences party policy, for among other things he decides the order in which bills on the calendar shall be considered, a power that may mean life or death to a bill in the closing days of a session. As leader, he also is chairman of the Steering Committee and influences the assignment of senators to committees.

During the Court fight, the President followed some advisers who entirely misjudged the general sentiment of the country. Having obtained an overwhelming vote of confidence from the electorate in 1936, Mr. Roosevelt was disappointed by his inability to control Democratic senators. But it was folly to be tempted into using the power of his office to try to purge men who were independent thinkers, especially after the party had been shaken up by the mixed reaction to the Court plan. One of the first to bear the brunt of presidential attack was Senator Gillette of Iowa. He was an excellent legislator and had supported the President on a majority of important issues. However, in the 1938 Democratic primary, Mr. Roosevelt singled out for his assistance a congressman whom he considered to have been more in accord with his policies. Gillette was well liked in the Senate, and his friends resented this. I was one, for I knew the many occasions when I had sought his help for administration proposals and obtained it. I did what I could to contribute to his renomination and was happy when he was returned.

Truman of Missouri, like Gillette, had voted with the President on most of his controversial legislation; but this was not enough. Mr. Roosevelt entered the Missouri contest and tried to nominate Governor Stark. At the request of Senator Truman, I went to the President and urged that he remain neutral. The President told me that while he did not know much about Mr. Truman, Governor Stark was an intimate friend, was very progressive, and would make a great senator.

This led to a discussion of the demerits of other members whom the President called "conservatives." I urged him not to try to control the legislative branch of the government, pointing out that Senators represented their states and not the President; that the senators in question were generally voting the views of the people who elected them and would return them to the Senate. I said that the voters would resent interference by an outsider even though he was President. I did not convince the President that he should abandon his interference, but I left no doubt in his mind that I would do everything in my power to help my friends who were marked to fall under the ax.

In a few instances I was able to provide some indirect financial assistance for those in political distress, including Senator Millard Tydings and Guy Gillette of Iowa. Also, after Senator Truman had talked with me about his situation, saying that he lacked money to pay for radio time, I persuaded Mr. Baruch to contribute $4,000 to his campaign fund.

There came a time when the Big Purge moved nearer home. In the midst of the primary contests for the Senate, the President went on a fishing trip to Florida. He was expected to return to Washington in the middle of August. It was rumored that he would stop in Georgia and South Carolina to urge the defeat of Senators Walter F. George and Ellison D. Smith. Marvin McIntyre, one of the presidential secretaries, told me of this in a telephone conversation, saying he thought it was unwise and asking if I could do anything to stop the President. Surprisingly enough, Harry Hopkins also telephoned me, making substantially the same request. He asked that I send him a telegram to Pensacola, Florida, which he could show to Mr. Roosevelt after he landed. Hopkins was very friendly with the mayor of Charleston, Burnet R. Maybank, who was a candidate for Governor; and he asked me to state in the telegram what I had told him of the adverse effect interference by the President would have on Maybank's chances.

My telegram was a long one. Senator Smith had two opponents, Governor Johnston and State Senator Edgar Brown. I gave my opinion that if Mr. Roosevelt stopped in South Carolina and urged Johnston's election, it would cost Smith some votes but do much more harm to Brown, who, like Johnston, was running as a presidential supporter. If Brown was eliminated in the first primary, then in the second primary contest Johnston would have to get Brown's votes in order to win, and if left alone he could probably do this. But if the President interfered, and the voters felt that Brown had been unfairly dealt with, many of his followers would vote for Smith; thus the President probably would help to defeat the man he wanted elected.

As to the governorship, I explained that Maybank faced seven opponents. He had daily boasted of the President's good will; therefore, if Mr. Roosevelt came to the state and did not mention Maybank favorably, it would hurt him. On the other hand, if he did mention him, the other candidates would almost certainly unite against Maybank. All this I told Hopkins in my wire, mentioning, however, that he, Hopkins, had asked for my views. I added that I had stated publicly that I was not actively supporting any one of the three candidates for senator, and hoped I could continue that course.

Mr. Roosevelt did, of course, descend on Georgia, and it is political history that in the presence of Senator George the President said he regarded Georgia as his second-home state; that if entitled to vote, he would vote against George, who had opposed many of his proposals.

The statement he made, coming from a Democratic President in an overwhelmingly Democratic state, was a powerful appeal. When he finished and turned from the mike, he spoke to Senator George, who said calmly and with dignity, "Mr. President, I accept your challenge."

I only regretted I could do so little to help George. But despite everything the federal government could do, George won. Shortly after, Senator Ed Smith of South Carolina, himself a survivor of the purge, said that in talking to George he remarked, "Roosevelt is his own worst enemy," to which George replied, "Not as long as I am alive." But time is a great healer and Walter George showed no evidence of such feeling. Through the years "Miss Lucy" and Walter, "Miss Maude" and I, had dinner together on most Sunday nights, and never once did he mention to me Roosevelt's attempt to defeat him.

On the purge trip, when the President's train reached Greenville, at the request of citizens of that city, I went to greet him. While his chief was taking a bath, McIntyre talked to me. He expressed regret at the Georgia incident and said he hoped the same error would not be made in South Carolina. A few minutes later I went with him into the President's car. He was enthusiastic about his fishing trip, and when I asked him what he would say to the many thousands gathered around the train, he replied, "I'll tell them about my fishing." "Wonderful," I replied, "we can all agree on fishing." I am sure that at the moment he fully intended to talk only of fishing.

McIntyre and I went out and watched and listened from the adjoining track just beside the car platform. When the applause from about 15,000 people died down, the President spoke of his fishing trip for a few moments and then said, "I have had a hard trip and do not have time to make a speech. Later I am coming back to meet with you and talk with you." The crowd roared with approval, and the President then continued, "I like the way you look. You don't impress me as being people willing to work for fifty cents a day, as one of your senators has said." Smith's political opponents were claiming that he had made this statement, though the Senator had denied it, and the *Congressional Record* confirmed his statement that he had used the words only as an illustration of a point, not as a fact.

As the crowd cheered, McIntyre jumped to a step and pulled the bell cord, signaling the train to start, but the damage had been done. Up to this time the contest had been close. Governor Olin D. Johnston was popular and had a strong personal organization. "Cotton" Ed was a very colorful character who had never had an organization, but relied principally upon his record of fighting for the farmers of the nation and upon his ability as a campaign speaker. Brown had supported Roosevelt and had a strong following. The President's visit changed the character of the contest. Because Johnston had been invited to ride on the President's train, it was recognized that he was favored. But the candidates were actually forgotten by many. There was a hot argument over whether the President had misrepresented Senator Smith—and more important, whether he should try to influence a contest between three Democrats. Brown was hurt most. He withdrew, and most of his supporters joined the Smith forces. Many who had intended to vote for Johnston resented the President's interference in a Democratic primary and turned to Smith, giving him a majority of nearly 50,000. If the purge was a failure generally, it was totally unsuccessful in at least two southern states where outside interference in an election is hotly resented.

The first time I saw the President after the election he said, "Well, you beat me in that election down there." I replied, "It may be of some interest to you, Mr. President, to know that the eighteen delegates who were at the Chicago convention when you were nominated in 1932 voted against your interference." The President said, "We'll forget it!" and he quickly went on to talk about a matter pending in the Senate in which he was interested.

Essential to the existence of our form of government is compliance with the constitutional mandate that the three branches of our government shall be kept separate. The President's power to appoint judges may, in some cases where the President's political prestige is involved, lessen the independence of the judiciary, but this is offset in part by the independence that comes from the right of a judge to hold office during good behavior. If, however, a President can defeat senators of his own party who disagree with him and secure the election of others who do agree with him, he will completely control the Congress and that division of powers that the framers of the Constitution intended to insure freedom from a dictatorship will disappear.

In the banking crisis Ogden Mills had asked Winthrop Aldrich to bring someone to Washington with some "imagination." The extreme liberals who were advising the President now had too much imagination. At that particular time I think I performed a service for President Roosevelt as well as the country by often opposing their radical ideas. Frequently the President would ask what I thought the Congress would do about a proposal that had been suggested by one of these advisers. Whenever he prefaced the proposal with the statement, "I am the same kind of Democrat as you and Hull," I knew a "hot one" was coming.

Some of these people tried to sell me their pet schemes, and in my conversations with them I found they were just as unreasonable as the diehard reactionaries who had opposed such reforms as the revised banking laws, regulation of the Securities and Exchange Commission and the Railroad Rehabilitation Act.

In those days we still had many topsoil roads—arched center with ditches on each side. In rough weather the motorist tried hard to avoid the ditches by staying in the middle of the road. I thought of myself in the Senate as a conservative liberal trying to restrain the extremists of the right and the left. But being a moderate is like being a peacemaker—you are blessed out by both sides.

Early in 1937 I had participated in bringing about a joint committee on reorganization and proposed that Senator Robinson act as chairman. On his death, I took his place and continued the extensive hearings which were necessary to meet all the varied points of view and objections. However, the President's attitude toward the Court and his failure to act on the sit-down strikes, to say nothing of the "lump-sum" relief funds so favored by Hopkins, did not make it easy to win support for his reorganization policies. We therefore adjourned in August without taking action.

In January, 1938, I introduced a revised version. I knew it was sound, but such was the decline of the President's influence over Congress that its merits were largely ignored. It aroused the President's critics. Father Coughlin, for example, charged that it would make Mr. Roosevelt a "financial dictator"; and when, on the eve of Senate action on the measure in March, he appealed to his radio listeners to send telegrams of protest to members, Western Union offices were flooded with over 75,000 messages. Quite a few were directed to me personally, for I had met Coughlin's Sunday afternoon broadcast with one of my own.

Before the Senate voted, the bitterness aroused almost exceeded the importance of the legislation. We had beaten off various amendments, including one to exempt the Veterans Administration from the provisions of the bill which was defeated by only one vote. There had been other similar close votes, and in the case of the Corps of Army Engineers, the most powerful lobbying organization of all, I was forced to give way and exempt it from the bill. Despite other last-minute attempts to alter the bill, it passed the Senate by seven votes. But as I feared, a week later, on April 8, it was defeated in the House by five votes. This was one of the worst blows the President had yet received from the Congress. I need not stress my own disappointment.

When Congress reconvened in December, we started again. To everyone who would listen I pointed out that for twenty-five years proposals had been made to reorganize the executive branch, and here was the opportunity to effect a change with congressional safeguards.

The fight by Ickes for the transfer of the Forestry Service from Agriculture to Interior was one of the hardest and meanest. While it was on, Henry Wallace called at my office, saying, "I want to ask your advice about an insulting letter written me by Ickes." I was in the midst of writing a humorous speech which I was to deliver that night to the Alfalfa Club, and was not feeling very serious. I told him I had a friend, Major J. Calvin (Deacon) Hemphill, who had been editor of the Charleston *News and Courier*. Hemphill boasted of his judicial temperament and illustrated his point by telling me that one night when he was very busy a man burst into his office and excitedly said, "Major, what would you do if a man called you [mentioning an unmentionable name]?" Said Hemphill, "What are the facts?"

Wallace, feeling far more disturbed about his own insult, said, "If you want the facts, just read this letter," and he handed to me a four-page letter from Harold Ickes. Without profanity, it was as insulting as any letter I ever read, questioning the integrity of Wallace, and all because of the Forestry feud. I said, "the only suggestion I can make is that you either tear up the letter and pretend you never saw it or, when you next see Ickes, punch him and hope you will be separated before harm is done to either; you certainly cannot win a name-calling contest with Ickes." I never heard of any fisticuffs.

But it seemed that because I was chairman of the reorganization committee I had become the father-confessor in this dispute, and Ickes came to see me, using strong language as he charged that the President had promised him that the Forestry Service would be transferred to his department. I suggested that if the President was guilty as charged, and he felt so bitter toward him, it was up to Ickes to resign.

I heard also from the third party to the feud. The President subsequently talked to me about it, telling me that Ickes had resigned at least three times, but he just ignored his resignations. "They are here in this drawer," said the President, pointing to his desk, "and I am thinking seriously of writing a form letter of acceptance, just leaving the name blank. When a prima donna comes in to present his resignation, I'll say, 'Just wait a few minutes,' and have Grace fill in the name."

While that fight was on I was so bombarded by department lobbyists that I could hardly work in my office, and was accurately quoted by a newspaper correspondent as saying, "The President will have to stop the executive agencies from lobbying for exemption from my bill. I am having enough trouble beating Burt Wheeler's amendments and I cannot take on the whole government in another fight." The quotation reflects, I think, my general weariness—I am sure the President was doing his best, though it was an impossible task. Finally, on April 3, the Administrative Reorganization Act of 1939 was passed. To indicate how the President kept up with Senate proceedings, even before I reached my office he had telephoned Miss Connor, saying that he wasn't calling to speak to me but he simply wanted through her to send me congratulations; that I must be too tired to talk to anybody right then. When I got the message, I concluded the President too had noted my general weariness.

One of the things that bothered me in this controversy was that the opposition on the Democratic side was led by men whom I numbered among my dearest friends—Harry Byrd of Virginia, Ed Burke of Nebraska, and Burt Wheeler of Montana. But early in congressional life men learn not to let differences about issues affect their personal relations. They realize there is always a tomorrow; on that day there will be an entirely different issue, and the opponents of today may be the allies of tomorrow. When we voted upon the reorganization bill and left the Senate Chamber, Harry Byrd was one of the first to congratulate me. That is one of the reasons he is respected and loved.

Under the powers granted him, the President merged some agencies, promoting efficiency and saving some money, but the results fell short of my hopes, confirming my belief that the nearest earthly approach to immortality is a government bureau. In justice to the President it must be said that while he was trying to implement the provisions of the bill, developments in Europe and the imminent threat of a world war made it impossible to devote the necessary time to the task of executive reorganization. Imperfect as the structure was, its revision had to wait for a time when the life of the country was not threatened.

# 7 ALL POSSIBLE AID SHORT OF WAR

Developments overseas that affected the security of the United States now began to rival and finally to outstrip domestic issues in importance. Late in August, 1937, I sailed from New York, with Mrs. Byrnes and Senator and Mrs. Adams of Colorado, as a delegate to the Inter-Parliamentary Union in Paris. As I was at the time chairman of the Senate Committee on Unemployment and Relief, I arranged to visit several other European states in order to see how they handled their unemployment problems. France we found in the throes of a bitter struggle between capital and labor. Leon Blum's Popular Front government, driven into extreme socialism by its Communist membership, had increased all wages but could do nothing to halt the ever increasing cost of living. French labor seemed to be interested only in how little it could do and how much it could get for that little. Many of the shops closed for a three-day week end, and absenteeism and strikes were rife in all branches of industry and particularly, it seemed, in those essential to national defense. It was natural that upon going eastward into Germany we found ourselves constantly making comparisons. Even more impressive than the lack of stoppages and idleness under the Nazis was the drive to achieve military as well as economic strength.

This last point was brought home to me when we attended the annual Party Congress at Nuremberg. Our guide was a representative of the German Foreign Office who had met us on the *Europa* and had extended us the invitation. Twelve thousand crack troops, representing the various units of the new German Army, executed elaborate maneuvers before a hundred thousand awed spectators while overhead four

108

hundred war planes gave further proof of Germany's preparedness. The climax of the spectacle was the Führer's drive around the stadium as, standing in his automobile, he received a frenzied reception from the massed onlookers. It was a singularly impressive and frightening demonstration of the realities of the European situation.

During our stay in Berlin we heard constant talk of preparations for war and witnessed the first general blackout practice against air raids. Senator Adams and I also took advantage of an opportunity to visit one of the labor camps for the Hitler Youth near Nuremberg, the equivalent of our own Civilian Conservation Corps. Early in our depression President Roosevelt had talked to me of his hopes for the success and usefulness of this particular project. He was most anxious that these camps should give idle youths healthy and useful employment and, by bringing young men from different parts of the country into contact with one another, help minimize sectional differences. Most observers would agree, I believe, that the camps did in fact perform a useful civic as well as economic function. At all events my conversations with the President on this subject heightened my interest in what Nazi Germany was doing along similar lines.

Because our visit to the youth camp had been hurriedly arranged, we arrived in the absence of the commanding officer. Yet everything was as much in order as if the Führer himself had been expected, and the young men we saw behaved like thoroughly disciplined army recruits—which of course they were. Our guide spoke of the benefits to the country of promoting an organization in which boys from every class and every corner of Germany could learn to work together. His sentiments were not dissimilar from those expressed to me by President Roosevelt. What made the end product so different was the fanatical hero worship of the Leader and the encouragement of militarism which figured so largely in the German camps and was conspicuously absent in our program.

The sights and sounds of the Nuremberg rally, the contrasting disunity in France and the deep pacifism, the peace parades and peace meetings that we later observed in England, gave me concern. It was plain that Hitler at least was not afraid of talking war and arming while the European democracies were proclaiming their love of peace; the spirit of their peoples seemed completely opposed to a crusade against the dictatorships which would involve bloodshedding.

Nor was our own nation willing to face the prospect of involvement in a world struggle against the Axis. Shortly after my arrival home in Washington, I reported to the President what we had seen and heard and told him I thought we must give immediate attention to improving our defense program. He was already convinced of the aggressive designs of the dictators and, by the time I saw him, had delivered his address at Chicago in which he referred to the necessity of a quarantine system to keep the warlike nations under control. He had deliberately chosen a center of isolationist sentiment for this pronouncement. It immediately aroused strong criticism, not only from the professional isolationists, but also from those bent on preserving our strict neutrality. The President was disappointed by the general lack of favorable response, and by the noticeable lack of enthusiasm when shortly thereafter he submitted to Congress estimates for increased military appropriations. In this, members undoubtedly reflected the temper of the people, and there was no disposition to rescind the three Neutrality Acts, the last and most comprehensive of which had been passed in May of that year.

By this time Italy had conquered Ethiopia, Japanese aggression against China was ancient history, and in Spain a civil war was raging which might engulf both our potential European allies and enemies. Then in March, 1938, came the Munich agreements. By the end of that year the President was convinced that Hitler would shortly be ready to risk general war, and he began to seek means to modify the 1937 Neutrality Act by removing the mandatory feature of the embargo on arms and armaments. However, he did not want to get too far ahead of public opinion, and though there was hot discussion over neutrality from January, 1939, onward, it was not until late May that Secretary Hull submitted to both Houses of Congress the administration proposals for a more flexible law. Debate continued to rage in and out of Congress, and on July 11 the Senate Foreign Relations Committee voted twelve to eleven to postpone further consideration of the bill before adjournment. This was a keen disappointment to Roosevelt and Hull, who had to be content with an understanding that neutrality legislation would be the first order of business when Congress reconvened in November.

It was about this time that the President suggested that he would like Senator Glass and me to secure assignment to the Foreign Relations Committee. We both were on the Steering Committee, which had charge of assignments; and since there were vacancies on the

Foreign Relations Committee, as soon as our request was made known to the chairman, he arranged the appointments.

I have indicated that the Congress, after postponing neutrality legislation, adjourned and waited. Hitler did not! On September 1 his attack on Poland added the word "blitz" to our vocabulary. In accordance with the existing law, the President proclaimed our neutrality, invoking the arms embargo. A few days later he telephoned me in South Carolina that he intended to call a special session of the Congress for September 21 to consider repeal. He wanted me with certain others to come to Washington in advance and discuss the situation with him. Accordingly, Hull; Garner; Speaker Bankhead; Senators Barkley and McNary, the respective Democratic and Republican leaders in the Senate; and the House leaders, Sam Rayburn and Joe Martin, met in his office. To stress the bipartisan nature of the group, Governor Alf Landon, titular leader of the Republican party, and Colonel Frank Knox, his 1936 running mate, were also invited. Senator Pittman, chairman of the Foreign Relations Committee, Vermont's Senator Warren Austin, Senator Minton, and Congressman Bloom and Mapes were also present.

Before asking for bipartisan action, the President gave us all the information he had received on the last-minute negotiations between the warring nations before war had begun. He was conciliatory and persuasive. In fact, his attitude and purpose were aptly described by Messrs. Alsop and Kintner, who wrote in their *American White Paper*, "Now he is preparing to compose his ancient quarrel with Congress," referring, of course, to the differences growing out of both the Court fight and the purge. For completeness I might add the remainder of the quotation, which stated in somewhat journalistic terms that Mr. Roosevelt was inviting me, "the Democratic moderate . . . to share in the Senate management of the embargo repeal, and promising not to infringe on the cherished but somewhat dubious independence of the legislative branch."

I needed no prompting to join in this fight because I believed it essential that the action be taken at once. Knowing that the bill could not be passed without a real battle for the approval both of Congress and of the nation, upon the request of the President I devoted my time to this cause to the exclusion of everything else. For five weeks debate was hot both in committee and on the floor of the Senate. One newspaper stated that the issue was of more importance than any similar controversy "since the fight over the League," and certainly we went at it with all the determination of a Wilson or of a Lodge.

It was helpful that on this occasion no one could truthfully charge that the White House was seeking to influence the decision. The President had told me that he was willing to leave the outcome entirely in the Senate's hands, and during this crucial period I heard of no act or statement at variance with this. Toward the end I received a grand compliment from Richard L. Stout in the *Christian Science Monitor*, who prophesied that the administration would win "its big fight." He thought that one reason was my activity on the Senate floor, where, he said, I was "Jimmie" to at least half of the members. He was flattering enough to add that I symbolized that unity of my party on the international issues "which had brought even Governor Alfred E. Smith and Senator Glass of Virginia out in support of the New Deal program."

On the eve of the vote I gave the press a statement predicting that there would be "sixty-five votes for the repeal and that the isolationists would not muster a maximum of thirty-one votes." Senator Nye challenged the accuracy of this. The actual figures were sixty-three to thirty.

In the interim between the Senate and House votes, I spoke on the Herald Tribune Forum, explaining why the law needed revision. I pointed out that it prohibited the sale of arms to belligerents, but not iron, steel, cotton, and other raw materials which enter into the manufacture of munitions. These war materials at that time could actually be delivered by American ships to belligerent ports. It was now proposed to substitute legislation that would permit us to sell our farm and factory products within the United States for cash, leaving the transportation to the purchaser. Further, American vessels, American citizens, and American property would no longer be able to enter a zone of war. These arguments made sense to the average citizen, and after favorable House action the bill became law on November 4.

During that winter of 1939-40 many of my colleagues were deceived by the absence of fighting in Europe; and though we had completed extensive hearings on the need for additional naval appropriations, I felt we would not get the battleships and cruisers the Navy was asking for if the entire bill was brought up immediately. So while I saw to it that some funds were appropriated for the Navy, I held back on the construction sections of the program in order to avoid having the bill wrecked by amendments. Later, when Hitler overran one country after another, I brought in a comprehensive naval bill, which was approved by the Senate in short order.

I have already mentioned that Frank Knox, the Republican editor of the Chicago *Daily News*, had attended our September White House meeting on repeal of the Embargo Act. Now, immediately before the Republican convention in June, the President took a further step to encourage the idea of bipartisanship by appointing Knox Secretary of the Navy, and another Republican, Henry Stimson, as Secretary of War. At our White House meeting Knox had assured the President of his full co-operation on preparedness and had so impressed him with his interest and drive that I was not surprised when Mr. Roosevelt asked me how I thought the Senate would receive his nomination.

At the same time he asked me what the feeling would be about Stimson. I had known Mr. Stimson for some time and admired him, and had no doubt he would be confirmed. However, before answering in regard to Knox, I first wanted to talk with some influential Democrats in the Senate. In a short time I was able to report that though a few of them disapproved of the appointment, they would support the President. One of the key men was Senator Scott Lucas of Illinois, who said at once that he favored Knox. A few days later, after he had talked over the matter with Mayor Ed Kelly of Chicago, he told me that Kelly urged him to vote for confirmation, this despite the fact that Knox's newspaper there had consistently attacked Kelly's regime. This attitude was very encouraging because it demonstrated that in the national interest even the boss of a political machine could disregard politics.

The invasion of Norway the previous month had preceded the launching of a full-scale attack on the Low Countries and France. After Dunkirk, in response to an appeal from Prime Minister Churchill, the War Department was authorized to release to Great Britain many millions of outdated stocks of arms, munitions, and even aircraft. The fall of France and the great air battles over southern England in the autumn of 1940 brought British fortunes to a low ebb. With invasion hourly expected, the British demand for war matériel was greater than ever. Yet dollar resources were running out and war orders placed here were badly delayed. To a close few, the President disclosed the frank estimates of Britain's peril made to him by Winston Churchill at the time. It was frightening.

In August, after the fall of France, the Army Chief of Staff, General

George C. Marshall, appeared to testify before our Appropriations Committee. During a recess he discussed with me the problems caused by his lack of authority to promote younger officers of exceptional ability. He said that he had asked for legislation empowering him to do this, but that the bill had been pigeonholed by Chairman May of the House Military Affairs Committee, largely because of pressures brought to bear by officers considered inefficient by the General Staff. Of course, with the chairman of the House committee out of sympathy, General Marshall was justifiably pessimistic, and I determined to try to help him.

Under the rules of the Senate, legislation cannot be added to an appropriations bill in Committee. But, with a suspension of the rules, it can be offered when the bill is brought to the floor of the Senate. At my request General Marshall had one of his staff draft an amendment which looked harmless enough, but which would give him the authority he required. It read, "In time of war or national emergency determined by the President, any officer of the Regular Army may be appointed to higher temporary grade without vacating his permanent appointment." When the appropriations bill was on the Senate floor and all pending amendments were disposed of, I offered my amendment. I was prepared to explain the emergency requiring the amendment, but no questions were asked and its was adopted unanimously.

The bill now went to a joint conference with members of the House Appropriations Committee and not May's Military Affairs Committee. By personal visits to the House conferees in which I explained the proposal, I enlisted their co-operation, and the conference report, including the amendment, was adopted in both Houses. I was told by a friend on the House Appropriations Committee that it was some days before May learned through one of the Army officers affected that he had himself voted for a bill containing the "blocked" legislation. Before the end of the year thousands of needed promotions of young officers had been made. General Marshall later told me that this device had enabled him to promote General Eisenhower over 366 senior officers. Others promoted as a result of it were General Mark Clark, George S. Patton, George C. Kenney and Carl Spaatz. In Congress nothing just happens—somebody must make it happen!

Meanwhile Mr. Roosevelt's efforts to get a Selective Service Act through Congress were meeting determined opposition. This was not surprising just two months before an election, but the opposition was successfully overcome by mid-September. Two weeks earlier, acting under his powers as Commander in Chief, he had concluded the defense agreement with the British government known as the "bases-for-destroyers" deal. It was to be expected that the November election would reflect popular endorsement or disapproval of these audacious moves, and indicate whether the administration could go further in its efforts to give aid to the Allies "short of war."

The electorate gave its answer emphatically. Mr. Roosevelt's triumph fortified his resolution to continue to build American strength while giving all possible aid to the Allies. He asserted the need for this in his annual message to Congress on January 6, 1941, outlining at the same time a "Lend Lease" plan to assist any nation resisting aggression. Where the idea of Lend Lease originated is something of a mystery. The President often said it was his own idea, and I believe that as finally proposed it was. However, there is evidence that the seed of the idea came from the Treasury Department lawyers, who had discovered a statute of 1892 which authorized the Secretary of War "to lease property not required for the public use." This seems to have led to the notion that the War Department might furnish a quantity of war materials overseas. But because a lease would involve specific provisions that might prove embarrassing, any scheme had to include lending as well. In the late fall of 1940, Mr. Roosevelt had gone on a short cruise and was undoubtedly turning the question over in his mind at that time. After his return he tried out his ideas at a press conference before submitting his message to Congress. His general argument was that it was better for us to furnish weapons for our friends to use on foreign soil than to wait and have them used at home, with loss of American lives and property. He used the simple illustration of lending a garden hose to help a friendly neighbor put out a fire, without stopping to bargain over terms for its use. This attitude of enlightened selfishness had a very general appeal and influenced many people to express approval to their congressmen.

At the President's request, I took an active part in managing the Lend Lease bill during the debate in Congress.

While it was still being considered, and the result in doubt, Lord Halifax arrived to serve as British Ambassador. A day or two after his arrival in Washington he came to see me, telling me that as the new British Ambassador he had been invited to address the Pilgrim Society of New York and that he had accepted the invitation. But, he said, after reading the press reports of the Lend Lease debate, and some criticisms of Britain, he wanted my opinion about his making a speech at this time. When I told him I thought that he should not speak until the bill had been acted upon, he asked if I would talk with Speaker Rayburn to get his view of the sentiment in the House. I telephoned to Sam, who concurred, "even if Lord Halifax must have lumbago." Later that morning Halifax sent to me by a page a note saying he would take steps to postpone his visit to New York. He asked me to tell Speaker Rayburn of his decision, adding, "I think, as he suggested, I may have to invoke lumbago to my aid." In his memoirs, Lord Halifax says the speech was never delivered. In this, as in all other matters where I had dealings with this Ambassador, he showed a keen appreciation of sentiment in this country.

The debate over Lend Lease continued for three weeks while the isolationist group remained adamant; but when on March 8, 1941, it passed the Senate, the voting was sixty to thirty-one in favor. This was a much larger majority than we had anticipated in January and did not differ significantly from the final vote on the repeal of the neutrality law. It is no exaggeration to say that this was the beginning of the end of the dictators, though some years of toil and bloodshed lay ahead.

In the midst of these months of concentrated effort and anxiety, the country, Congress, and the administration had to turn their attention to the purely domestic excitement of a presidential election. My own involvement began in June, when Mr. Roosevelt asked me to help Senator Wagner with the various drafts of the platform that had been submitted to him as chairman of the committee. The President was particularly interested in the wording of the declaration on foreign affairs, for the European situation was exceptionally grave and he was already thinking about the defense policies it might be necessary for him to propose during a third term.

Then in July, about ten days before the Democratic National Convention at Chicago, he invited me to dinner. As the other guests were Ed Flynn, national committeeman of New York; Ed Kelly, mayor of Chicago; Frank Walker (later to be Postmaster General and chairman of the Democratic National Committee); and Harry Hopkins, I knew it was a purely political occasion. After dinner, the conversation centered on plans for the coming election. The President referred to the pressures on him to become a candidate for a third term and to the grave misgivings that the possibility had raised both in his own mind and in the minds of some party leaders. He said he disliked to break with precedent and seek a third term, but the fact remained that he had failed to develop anyone else in the party who, in his opinion, could win. Elaborating further, he mentioned the names of two potential candidates, Jim Farley and Jack Garner, expressing his friendship for them but also his doubts of their ability to be elected. Under the circumstances, he said, he found himself perplexed about whether he should permit the use of his name, and he asked for the opinions of his guests.

Notwithstanding the earnestness with which he spoke, I must say that I found it hard to credit him with sincerity. As far back as January he had talked to me in the same vein and I had agreed that he would have to be a candidate. I felt committed to him. Now I was sure that he believed himself to be the only Democrat who could be elected, but at the same time I thought that he had perhaps become a little frightened about the third-term issue and wanted to be "persuaded" to make the race. Of course that was not difficult, and the group told him it was his duty to run. I remember saying that whatever doubts he now had, certainly it was too late for him to build up any alternative candidate and that, having failed to do this, he could not announce at this late date that he was "not available." Moreover, I reminded him that recently he had virtually drafted men like William Knudsen of General Motors into government service because the danger of war was so great and his retirement now to Hyde Park would be contrary to the spirit of his appeal to others. He professed to be impressed, and later he incorporated this particular argument in his radio speech of acceptance, when he said: "Lying awake, as I have, on many nights, I have asked myself whether I have the right, as Commander in Chief of the Army and Navy, to call on men and women to serve their country or train themselves to serve, and, at the same time, decline to serve my country in my own personal capacity, if I am called upon to do so by the people of my country." In any event, after a general discussion, during which the President expressed some doubt about whether he could be elected because of the widespread feeling against a third term, he said he would make the race.

He then raised the question of his running mate, Jack Garner having announced that he positively would not accept the nomination that year. Again the President discussed several possibilities, but cited objections to all of them, and concluded by saying that he thought I should be nominated. I was quick to reply that I was not a candidate. I said I did not believe that the party was yet ready to accept any man from the Deep South, either for the Presidency or Vice Presidency. Mr. Flynn said he thought I was right, adding that, to be frank, he had already expressed the view that it would not be wise to nominate me because, having been baptized in the Roman Catholic Church, I had later become a member of a Protestant Church. The President said he knew that some people were doubtful about the wisdom of nominating me because of my religious history, but that he did not agree. (I did not then know what the President told me the following day: that Flynn was a White House guest and before the dinner had expressed the same view to the President.) The President went on to say that he did not think my nomination would cost the ticket any votes, and he told of a candidate for lieutenant governor of New York —Charles Poletti—who, it was alleged, had a similar history. When political opponents attacked Poletti on this score, the President said, the Catholic Democrats generally supported him, either because they did not care about his religious affiliations or because they wanted to prove that they were not prejudiced. Many Republicans also voted for him in order to register disapproval of such tactics. As a result he ran ahead of the ticket! Walker and Kelly both said that they were Catholics and disagreed with Flynn; Hopkins agreed with FDR. To me the discussion was embarrassing and with emphasis I said that I was determined not to let my name be presented.

Whether right or wrong, I was sincere in the belief in 1940 that the time had not yet arrived when a loyal Southerner could be named for either President or Vice President without the loss of some northern votes. In my opinion the third-term fight would be a close one, and if Mr. Roosevelt should be defeated many would attribute his failure not to the real cause but to the fact that a South Carolinian had been selected as his running mate. It would then be many years before a national convention would again nominate a Southerner for either office. Further, I regarded a man's religious views as a purely private matter and even if FDR was right, I did not want my religious history made the subject of national political discussion.

Some years later a biographer of former President Truman, Jonathan Daniels, published an article in *Look* magazine which touched on this nomination. In it he quoted FDR as saying in 1940: "My second choice was Jimmie Byrnes but I talked with Archbishop Spellman and others in the church and they said that the feeling against a renegade Catholic would be such that any Catholics in doubt would resolve the difference between us—and so at the last minute it was Wallace." Shortly after the article appeared, I received the following letter from the Archbishop:

August 28, 1950

DEAR JIMMY:

My attention has been called to an article in *Look* Magazine, "How Truman Got to be President," by Jonathan Daniels of the Raleigh, North Carolina, *News and Observer*. No such opinion as that ascribed to me was ever conveyed by me to the President. I am writing to Mr. Daniels and *Look* Magazine asking that it be corrected and that they publish this denial with the same prominence as was given the original article.

With very best wishes and kindest regards, I am

Very sincerely yours,
F. CARDINAL SPELLMAN
*Archbishop of New York*

In acknowledging His Eminence's letter, I said that I was confident he had made no such statement, but had not written him about it because I did not want him to feel that he should request a correction. I also added for his information: "After the Convention in 1940 the President requested me to accept the position of National Chairman, Mr. Farley having resigned. In that conversation he referred to a rumor that he had asked your advice about my nomination and you had opposed it, and he stated that it was untrue."

At Archbishop Spellman's request, *Look* published his correction and also the statement contained in my letter to him. This episode, I think, demonstrates how sometimes history can inadvertently be manufactured as well as made!

Returning to my recollections of the President's dinner party, I suggested to the group that they agree to name Cordell Hull as Vice President. I regarded him the most capable candidate, and he came from Tennessee, a state not regarded as Deep South and far more doubtful than my own. (It voted for Eisenhower in 1952 and 1956.) Mr. Roosevelt thought well of the idea, but the group as a whole reached no definite decision. The following afternoon the President told me that he had talked with Hull, who had personal reasons for declining, which he did without equivocation.

Though newspaper reports that I was being considered persisted, I had definitely eliminated myself, and when I went to the convention I devoted my entire time to the platform. I served on the Platform Committee at Mr. Roosevelt's request. Previously, on June 24, the Republican party had put itself on record as "firmly opposed to involving the nation in a foreign war." Burt Wheeler of Montana, Pat

McCarran of Nevada and David Walsh of Massachusetts, who were also on the committee, wanted us to write a similar and equally unequivocal plank. Some other members shared their views, but the President was opposed to it, I knew, and so was I. The committee bypassed that section of the platform to give us a chance to confer, and the three senators and I withdrew. The only place we could find to talk was a room marked "Ladies Rest Room." Once inside, we locked the door.

McCarran said that if their proposal was rejected, many delegates would leave the convention. After long argument I agreed to their wording, provided they would add, "except in case of attack." When I read this amendment to the President over the telephone, he wrote in those five words on his own copy, which he had before him, and said he wanted to consult Hull. But perhaps the full story is best told by giving extracts from a letter I wrote to FDR on March 28, 1944, when another convention was approaching and similar problems were in the air:

DEAR MR. PRESIDENT:

Recently there have appeared in the press statements that in 1940 you favored a declaration in the Democratic platform that the United States would not send armed forces to fight across the seas. I was a member of the Platform Committee. I discussed with you the language of the platform and I know these statements misrepresented your position.

There was presented, for consideration of the committee, a draft of the platform which Chairman Wagner said included contributions from many people. That draft was dated July 9 [1940]. It provided:

The American people are determined that war, raging in Europe, Asia, and Africa, shall not come to America.

The direction and aim of our foreign policy has been, and will continue to be, the defense of our own land.

We will not participate in foreign wars.

We will not send troops to fight in lands across the seas. . . .

I do not know who suggested the above language. I disapproved of it and so did others. Some men urged a stronger declaration against intervention in the war in any way whatsoever. Others urged the adoption of language pledging intervention in the war. . . .

Early on the morning of July 16 [1940], I talked to you over the telephone. You were greatly disturbed by the press reports of the attitude of some members of the Platform Committee, and I advised you in detail of the situation and of several suggestions that had been made to change the draft to accord more nearly with your views.

While the committee proceeded with the consideration of other parts of the platform, I spent the entire morning trying to bring about an agreement on this plank. Most of that time was spent in conference with Senator Wheeler and Senator Walsh of Massachusetts. Those gentlemen from time to time would confer with others on the committee who shared their views. The committee had completed its consideration of the platform before we were able to reach an agreement on this national defense plank. They adjourned for lunch. We continued in conference.

I then spoke to you on the telephone, advising you that we could reach an agreement on the language which was finally adopted in the platform, reading as follows:

> We will not participate in foreign wars, and we will not send our army, naval or air forces to fight in foreign lands outside of the Americas, *except in case of attack.*

Secretary Hull was with you. I expressed the opinion that this was the best declaration upon which we could reach an agreement, and that I thought it was in accord with your views. You stated that the addition of the words "except in case of attack" made it satisfactory to you and to Mr. Hull. I recall stating that we certainly did not have in contemplation going to war except in case of attack, and you agreed that was your view.

My agreement was really with Senator Walsh. Senator Wheeler had gone to lunch but Senator Walsh stated he felt confident Senator Wheeler would agree. Shortly afterward the committee reconvened, and the plank was presented. Senator Walsh expressed his agreement and his confidence that Senator Wheeler, from statements previously made by him, would agree. The paragraph was adopted.

Sincerely yours,
JAMES F. BYRNES

After I talked to the President about the platform, to my surprise he told me he had not made arrangements for anyone to make a speech nominating him. Senator Lister Hill had told him, he said, that Alabama would either nominate him or yield to New York for that purpose. The President asked me to request Hill to nominate him, and say that he preferred a simple statement that "Alabama places in nomination the name of Franklin D. Roosevelt." The President seemed sincere in wanting a short speech, and I emphasized this view in delivering the message to Senator Hill, who said he would respect his wish.

Lister was not given to long speeches, but he was enthusiastic about the President and let it be known in a speech of twenty minutes—it was a good speech. But for a while I was afraid he was going to talk too long, and told Ed Kelly a story about Shiloh Baptist Church in Aiken County, South Carolina, which, in looking for a new minister, invited a young man to preach a "trial" sermon. He was the guest of Quilla Seigler, the wealthiest farmer among the membership. The young preacher felt that Seigler would influence the action of the deacons, so it was not surprising that when he had finished his message, he said, "The congregation will bow their heads while Brother Seigler leads us in prayer." In that field Seigler had had no experience, but he bowed his head and, thinking fast, pulled the coat of Jim Fulmer, who was sitting just in front of him, and said, "Five dollars if you'll pray." Old Quilla, telling me about it, said, "Fulmer started off in high gear and I soon knew I had overpaid him—it would have been better if I had asked for a two-dollar prayer."

After Lister finished, a long demonstration in the convention hall gave me time to telephone to the President about another angle of the proceedings, and he made no complaint about the length of the nominating speech.

Many months before the convention, James A. Farley had announced that he would be a candidate. He had been campaign manager for Roosevelt in 1932, and chairman of the national Democratic party as well as Postmaster General for eight years. I do not know what caused the rift in the personal relations of Roosevelt and Farley. I heard that until about six months before the convention, Farley was under the impression that Roosevelt would not seek a third term; consequently he became a candidate and assured his supporters that he was "in to the finish." Whatever the facts may be, when the President finally announced his candidacy Jim realized he had no chance of winning, but he remained in the race. Late the evening of July 16 there occurred the enthusiastic, if not entirely spontaneous, demonstration for Mr. Roosevelt. He was drafted, as he desired. I was made chairman of the Notification Committee to inform the President officially of his nomination. The next morning the committee retired to a room off the main auditorium where there was a telephone in a corner. I was soon talking to the President at the White House and, in the presence of the committee, told him of the instructions we had received. It was not news to him, but the formalities were observed. When this was finished, the President told me that Hopkins had been conferring with labor leaders, especially Philip Murray of the C.I.O. and William Green of the A.F. of L., and had reported that they all favored Wallace's nomination for Vice President. I expressed doubt about the wisdom of nominating Wallace and once more urged Hull or Barkley. The President said that he had again talked with Hull, who still refused to be considered, and he thought that as Wallace had the support of labor and of the farmers, he would be better than Barkley. As the President would not be dissuaded, I reluctantly said that I would support Wallace and requested the President to hold on while I conveyed his decision to the committee. The members of the committee, which included staunch friends from many states, were not enthusiastic but agreed to go along with the President's choice.

After reporting back to the President I went to my room, worn out by the long hours in conference with the Platform Committee. My rest was cut very short, because some of the delegates were immediately up in arms when they learned of Mr. Roosevelt's preference for Wallace. Speaker Bankhead, who had been a more or less active candidate, began to receive additional pledges of support. Paul McNutt was being urged to get into the race. Delegates from various states urged me to let my name be placed in nomination, and I was kept busy refusing. Senator Harrison came to the platform where I was, saying that at the request of several delegates he was going to nominate me. When I told him that I would immediately decline and say I was committed to Wallace, he said he would not embarrass me. By the time the convention was called to order that evening, the insurrection against Wallace was so great that I telephoned the President again to inform him that there would be several nominations and a real fight. He said he had already received similar reports. He was seriously offended, declaring that traditionally the nominee for Vice President had been named by the nominee for President; and that if there was such a lack of confidence in him that Wallace was rejected, he would not accept the nomination for President. He added that I could so inform the delegates.

When Bankhead and McNutt were nominated, each received a rousing ovation, but Wallace met with boos as well as cheers. While seconding speeches were being made, I went to the floor to visit delegation leaders and I repeated Mr. Roosevelt's statement to many of them who opposed Wallace. Despite this, there was doubt about the outcome until the roll call was halfway completed. When I was sure of the outcome, I started to leave the hall to notify the President that he could relax, that Wallace would be named. Passing by Mr. Wallace on my way out, I told him not to worry; that he would certainly be nominated. He asked if I thought he should make a speech of thanks to the delegates. I replied that he had witnessed the temper of the delegates and reminded him that the proceedings were being broadcast to millions by radio; that if the galleries should again boo him as they had when his name was presented, it would be very unfortunate. He took my advice to let well enough alone and did not ask for recognition.

In the midst of my efforts to persuade rebellious delegates to vote for Wallace, at a moment when I seriously feared the outcome, I got a chance to smile when a delegate who was evidently not one of the Wallace supporters stopped me. I had tried twice to ignore his call, but now, in a voice loud enough for many to hear, he said, "Hi, Jimmy, what's your mileage now?"

Immediately after the convention Farley resigned as national chairman. In common with many others, I was sorry to see Jim Farley leave public life. Whenever he was discussed by senators, congressmen, or other political leaders, one was certain to hear, "Well, Jim Farley may disagree with you, but he'll tell you the truth and if he makes a promise he'll carry through." In politics or business, that reputation is priceless. The President sent for me and urged me to take over Farley's job. Declining firmly, I reminded him that I was still a member of the Senate and that my duties there must come first. To counter his insistence, I proposed Joseph P. Kennedy, then serving as Ambassador to Great Britain. The President telephoned to him in London, but Kennedy declined. It was after these refusals that the President approached Ed Flynn, who accepted the post.

This was not the last I heard of Joe Kennedy in the 1940 campaign. On a Sunday, about ten days before the election, the President telephoned me that Kennedy was arriving in New York that afternoon, and that it was rumored he would announce his support of Willkie. Apparently the Ambassador was dissatisfied about something, and the President had thought it well to send a message asking him and Mrs. Kennedy to dine at the White House that evening. He invited Mrs.

Byrnes and me to join them, asking that I wire Joe not to issue a statement about the political campaign until he had seen the President. I sent the message, and that evening Maude and I attended the dinner, at which the President's secretary, Miss Marguerite LeHand, affectionately known as "Missy," was hostess.

Kennedy brought Mr. Roosevelt a personal message from Chamberlain, the former British Premier, who was still working as best he could, though his physical condition was described as hopeless. Before dinner Joe gave us an extremely interesting picture of war conditions and the economic situation in Great Britain. After dinner the President gave him an opportunity to talk about his work as Ambassador. Kennedy is not a bashful man. He is a forceful talker, and in his vocabulary are many words not found in dictionaries. He used some of them in his denunciation of the State Department and of the treatment accorded him. I wondered what the President possibly could say in its defense. To my surprise, he did not try. He understood entirely, he said, how Kennedy felt; as a matter of fact, he thought that Kennedy's views were charitable, and it was only because of the war that he, Roosevelt, had put up with similar treatment. He was determined that after the election there would be some real housecleaning, so that friends of his, like Joe, would never again be subjected to such outrageous treatment. As the President went on, I thought Kennedy was even beginning to feel a touch of sympathy for the State Department boys. In any event, once his complaint had been made and approved, Kennedy became more cordial and the President asked him to make a radio speech advocating his re-election. The moment Kennedy agreed, Miss LeHand telephoned the National Committee and arranged for radio time the following Wednesday night.

Showman that Joe Kennedy is, he tried to keep the press representatives in doubt about whether he would announce support of Roosevelt or Willkie. As part of this plan, he asked me to tell the committee that he would personally pay for the time on the national radio hookup and would speak under the auspices of his wife Rose and their children. On Wednesday night he made a most effective speech, arguing for the President's re-election.

One incident of the campaign and its sequel may be briefly mentioned, for it illustrates the President's resourcefulness in dealing with political problems. Among other states, I visited Missouri, where Senator Bennett Clark was seeking re-election, and I also went to help Sherman Minton of Indiana, who was having a hard contest. While I was in Indianapolis, Clark telephoned me, saying that there was considerable feeling among the doctors at a regional meeting of the American Medical Association in Chicago because it was reported that the President had committed himself to a program of socialized medicine. I learned from Minton also that some of his friends in the medical profession had heard the same story and were considering offering a resolution expressing regret at Mr. Roosevelt's attitude. I felt all this was serious enough for me to telephone the President, only to learn from him that he had made no such commitment; he said that in a speech to the Red Cross at Bethesda, Maryland, next day he would make his position clear. He had his secretary wire me a copy of his statement, which I passed on to Clark and Minton.

The sequel came the next year after the President's decisive victory and while he was preparing his message to Congress. He requested me to come to his office, where Secretary of the Treasury Morgenthau was urging him to include in the message a section on a government health plan. I caught my cue and presented as forcibly as I could the arguments against this, reminding the President of his words to the Red Cross meeting at Bethesda in October. I concluded by pointing out that he badly needed congressional support for many other controversial proposals, and suggested that I telephone from his desk to Congressman Doughton, chairman of the House Ways and Means Committee, and Senator George, chairman of the Senate Finance Committee, who would have charge of the proposed legislation, asking if they would favor the proposal. Morgenthau was quick to say that such a call would be useless because I knew both these important committee chairmen would oppose it. At this the President entered the conversation. "Henry," he said, "if you really believe that, certainly you would not wish me to start a losing battle with the Congress, especially in view of my declaration on the subject." The President's purpose had been accomplished and I retired.

Before leaving the 1940 campaign, let me add this bizarre footnote. In its closing days some of the President's friends were greatly disturbed by the threatened publication of certain letters indicating that his running mate was deeply interested in the doctrine of theosophy. Mr. Wallace had corresponded with a lady on this subject, and she had sold them. They were now in the hands of an unfriendly newspaper publisher. The letters were so visionary that publication was delayed because their authenticity was in doubt.

Upon the President's return from Cleveland, where he had been given a great reception, he was told by Steve Early that some of his friends were making an effort to purchase the letters. Mr. Roosevelt was in a waggish humor. When he learned that the woman had been an employee in the Department of Agriculture, the President, knowing well Henry's deserved reputation as a moral, chaste man, mischievously asked if there was any evidence that Henry had ever registered with her at a hotel. Steve quickly said "no," everyone realized Mr. Wallace's relations with her were purely intellectual. The President, with apparent seriousness, shook his head and replied, "Too bad. The American people understand romance and would forgive Henry for it. They do not understand theosophy and I fear they would never forgive him for that." In fact, the President was so stimulated by his Cleveland reception that he was certain people were going to vote for him regardless of what Mr. Wallace said or did. Nevertheless, I know the letters were bought—by whom I do not know—for a few years later Harry Hopkins told me he had them in his locked files in the White House.

Wendell Willkie had waged a vigorous campaign. The Democratic National Committee had reserved thirty minutes of radio time, beginning at eleven o'clock on the night before the election. The President asked Cordell Hull, Dorothy Thompson and me to use half this time. He had learned that the Republicans had reserved thirty minutes immediately following his time and that they would have on their program Wendell Willkie, General Hugh Johnson and Joe Louis. Johnson could hit as hard in debate as Louis could in a ring. President Roosevelt said that this trio would expect a severe attack from us and he wanted us to throw them off balance by making speeches devoid of criticism; he wanted "a program that will be patriotic—even prayerful."

From the four speeches one would not have guessed that they were closing a hot political campaign. "Peace on earth, good will to men" was our theme, and the President wound up the program without a partisan word, closing with the Lord's Prayer. Listeners who were tired of hearing charges and countercharges for more than a month agreed that the program left the President's opponents no excuse for the critical speeches they had prepared.

The third-term issue, as everyone now knows, proved a bugaboo, and with FDR firmly in the saddle for another four years, it was a pleasure to be able to concentrate again on the work of the Senate.

A few days before Roosevelt's third inauguration, Jack Garner, getting ready to leave Washington, asked me to lunch with him. I expressed regret that I had another engagement. I kept my engagement to lunch with the President at his desk. When we had almost finished eating, and without notice to the President, "Pa" Watson walked into the room with Vice President Garner. Old Jack's bushy eyebrows arched even higher than usual, and as he approached the desk he said, "Jimmie, I see now why you wouldn't eat my grub!" I left so that he could say good-by to the President.

On the day of the inauguration, as soon as I could get away from the White House, Maude and I went to Garner's office to bid him good-by. To my surprise his friends were so absorbed in the celebration that I found Jack alone—Mrs. Garner, as was her custom, had gone ahead to open the house in Uvalde. We stayed until Bascom Timmons, a Texas newspaper correspondent and one of Jack's dearest friends, came and told me he was going to take him to the train.

I told Jack that I hoped before long he would find some excuse to return to Washington and we could get together, but he said with emphasis, "Jimmie if you ever see me again, you will have to come to Uvalde." He meant it. I have not heard of his being far from Uvalde.

Little did I realize that my days in the Senate were numbered. It is true that during the months of the Court fight, newspaper writers, speculating about the possible successors to the justices whose retirement would be forced by the bill, had sometimes mentioned my name. This was flattering, because most lawyers would welcome the opportunity to serve on the Supreme Court, but I did not give the matter any serious thought. I cannot say exactly when the idea that I might really be appointed first occurred to me, but I suspect it was after the retirement of Justice Butler in 1939. Some days after that occurred, Governor and Mrs. A. Harry Moore of New Jersey visited us in Spartanburg. The Governor told me he had written to the President suggesting that I be appointed to the Butler vacancy. While I appreciated Moore's kind interest, I did not think his suggestion wise from the President's point of view. By tradition, the President was expected to appoint justices from different sections of the country. There was another tradition, the origin of which I do not know, that at least one member of the Court should be a Roman Catholic. Butler was a member of that Church and was from Minnesota. I wrote the President:

I told Harry that if I were President I would appoint as a successor to Justice Butler some man possessing the qualifications of a judge who resided in the West and who is a member of the Catholic Church.

While Governor Moore's intentions were good, I believe, for the reasons I stated to him, that his advice was unwise and I do not want you to think it was offered upon my suggestion or with my knowledge.

In reply I received from the President the following letter: "All the same Harry Moore was right in his suggestion and I had, of course, thought of it and approved it before. The only fly in the ointment is the one you mention, for I, too, think that for various reasons the appointee should be from the West and should be a Catholic."

Bernie Baruch told me that he, too, had suggested my appointment to the President, and there were one or two others who had also proposed it. In every instance the President had not objected to the idea, but had said he would dislike to have me leave the Senate.

Over a year later, in January, 1941, I was in a meeting of the Senate Foreign Relations Committee when Pat Harrison came up and said that he and Barkley wanted to talk to me. We stepped into the clerk's office, and Pat told me that Justice McReynolds had retired and that they and Carter Glass were going to ask the President to appoint me.

Afterward Glass gave me an account of the interview with Mr. Roosevelt. Glass had not supported the President on domestic issues, but he had on all foreign issues, and though the President called him "the old rebel," he liked him. Carter said that when he made the request, the President answered, "Of course, I will appoint him," adding, "He is just as much my friend as yours—I wanted him to be my running mate in 1940." He continued, "My only regret in appointing him is that I need him so much in the Senate." To this my old friend replied, "Don't worry about that, Mr. President, Jimmy has done my work for years, and now I'll do his." As he finished his recital, there were tears in his eyes. I felt very humble because it seemed he loved me almost as much as I loved him.

On June 12, the senior senator from Virginia requested unanimous consent that my nomination be confirmed by the Senate without being referred to committee, as required by the rules. This was a courtesy to a senator. It was seconded by my friend Senator Van Nuys, the chairman of the Judiciary Committee. At the same time Robert Jackson was also nominated for associate justice and Harlan F. Stone as Chief Justice, succeeding Charles Evans Hughes. These two nominations were promptly reported by the committee and confirmed.

However, my duties in the Upper Chamber were not quite at an end. During the long fight for the reorganization bill, Senator Pittman had proposed to exempt the Forestry Service from its provisions because he feared Harold Ickes might persuade the President to transfer that bureau to his control as Secretary of the Department of Interior. I feared his move would be adopted, and I knew that if this exemption was made the door would be open wide for other exemptions. I appealed to Pittman to withdraw his amendment, promising to have the President tell him that Forestry would not be transferred. He would agree only if I could get a letter to that effect, because he was afraid that Ickes would get the President to make the transfer. I got the letter and Pittman supported the bill. After the bill was passed, as Pittman had foreseen, Ickes never ceased his efforts to get charge of the Forestry Service. When he asked me to help him, I told him of the President's promise to Pittman, to which I had been a party, and that I would oppose any effort to transfer that bureau. Ickes abandoned his idea until 1941, when the President's authority to make such a transfer was about to expire. He then returned to the President, presenting a plan for legislation extending these powers, saying that this would be new legislation and that the President would not be bound by his previous statement to Pittman, who had died some months before. All this I learned when the President sent me Ickes' letter with a memorandum attached. It read:

June 23, 1941

*Personal, Private, Confidential, Restricted and Secret!*
Memorandum for—
   Mr. Justice James F. Byrnes
   U.S.S.C.-Elect
   Help! Help! What would you say if you were in my place? Help me before you join the upper classes!

F. D. R.

I thereupon wrote the President a letter which I knew he would show to Ickes:

Referring to your inquiry as to whether I could introduce and put through the Senate the reorganization bill, I regret that I cannot do so.

As I told you ten days ago, I have been terribly embarrassed by remaining in the Senate after my nomination was confirmed. After talking with you, I announced that the day Senator Barkley returned to the Senate, I would resign. Barkley is expected to return on Monday. It will be impossible for me to announce that I have changed my plans and will remain in the Senate to lead a fight on the reorganization bill. If the bill were to be considered next week, I would feel that I could not participate in the fight. As a matter of fact, the Senate will on Monday begin taking a recess for three days at a time and continue for approximately ten days.

I was then acting as Senate leader in the absence of Barkley, who was ill. As soon as he was able to return to duty I was free to take the oath of office as associate justice, which I did on July 7, 1941. The day following, the Clerk of the Senate read to my Senate colleagues the following brief letter:

Hon. Henry Wallace
United States Senate                                    July 8, 1941
Dear Mr. Vice President,

I have today submitted to the Governor of South Carolina my resignation as United States Senator.

Respectfully,
James F. Byrnes

# Part III

## THE SUPREME COURT

## 9  ON THE BENCH

When I became chairman of a senatorial committee I was assigned as a committee room the old robing room of the Supreme Court in the Capitol, a short distance from the Senate Chamber. It was a beautiful office, with a fine old crystal chandelier which had originally graced the White House. There Theodore Roosevelt had found its tinkling prisms distracting and had ordered its removal. On the wall the celebrated painting by Copley of Henry Laurens in the Tower of London added to a South Carolinian's pride of occupancy. I was always happy in this room.

The robing room was one of three large rooms that comprised all the space, other than the Court Room, allotted by the Congress to the Supreme Court of the United States until 1935. Then the justices moved into the veritable palace of white marble on First Street just across the Capitol Plaza. My transfer from the familiar Capitol Building, around which for over twenty years my Washington activities had centered, to the splendors of the new Supreme Court Building represented a great change. The classic structure, and in particular its core, the Court Room itself, reflected a dignified strength and even aloofness far removed from the organized confusion of the Hill. The justices are seated upon a dais; in front of them is a desk the full width of the dais; and behind them are red velvet curtains, which the public may think are a part of the decorative scheme, but which in fact have a utilitarian purpose, for they are hung principally to improve the acoustics.

Many visitors throng the public areas of the building, but the justices are assured of complete privacy. Even their arrivals and departures are private, for they may drive into a basement garage where

135

a private elevator takes them to their suites behind great bronze doors to the rear of the Court Room. Each justice has a suite of three offices, one of which is used by his law clerk, another by his secretary; the quarters of the Chief Justice are somewhat larger than the rest. The offices are furnished in American oak with open fireplaces, and as an additional luxury each suite has a shower bath. I was told that Justice McReynolds used to have a fire in his fireplace, often eating his lunch before it, but I never heard of others making use of theirs. The shower certainly seemed an extravagance.

There is a large conference room where the members assemble before each court session or for deliberation. They lunch together in a room on the second floor; guests are not invited. Each justice has his messenger serve him a lunch brought from the dining room on the first floor, which is open to the public, or from some other nearby restaurant. Chief Justice Stone, I remember, was a lover of cheese and often his lunch consisted of a "collection" of cheeses brought from his home. Discussion at lunch was stimulating and entertaining, with only one subject barred—the work of the Court.

According to political writers, the Court of which I was a member was one of the youngest—the average age being around fifty-seven— and one of the friendliest. I never had time to check these calculations of the ages of my colleagues, but I can testify to their general good humor. Contrary to popular impression, justices are very human, and during my service, at least, they were very sociable. I recall a dinner at my home for the justices and their wives, when their spirited singing of old songs prompted me to comment that there was more harmony in their singing than in their decisions.

Few agree on the training a lawyer should have before being appointed to the Court. While Secretary of State, upon the only occasion President Truman asked me to recommend someone for appointment, I suggested the selection of one of the Judges then serving on the Circuit Court of Appeals. However, I do not believe that all members of the Court should come from the lower United States courts, because a man who serves on the bench for years necessarily becomes, to a degree, isolated from the people. He may become narrowed in his thinking. I believe it wise to have upon the Court one or two lawyers who have served in the Congress and had training in drafting laws, and who should therefore appreciate that it is the function of the Congress, not the Court, to do the legislating for the country. Further, in selecting a judge for either the Supreme Court or a court of lesser jurisdiction, it does not seem wise to have only men whose legal experience has been confined to representing the United States government. In recent years there have been many appointments from the Department of Justice. This is as unwise as it would be to select lawyers whose experience has been confined to representing corporate interests. Nowadays a large percentage of litigation involves the government, and it may be difficult for such a judge entirely to divest himself of the belief that the government is always right. To my mind, a well-balanced Court would be one whose members have had varied legal but predominantly judicial experience, and would include one or two with experience on state courts.

The Supreme Court usually acts on appeals from a lower federal court or from a state supreme court, or through petitions for certiorari, which means that the Court has before it the fullest records of a case in order that it may determine whether a hearing should be granted. After such a petition is considered, if four justices believe a hearing should be granted, the case will be placed on the calendar.

There is one term of court annually, commencing on the first Monday in October and lasting until the final week in May. During this period, sessions are not continuous but last about two weeks, with a free period intervening. While I served, conferences were held at twelve noon on Saturday, though since then the time has been changed to eleven o'clock each Friday. When arguments have been heard, cases are usually decided at that week's conference, which, in order to assure complete secrecy, is attended only by the justices themselves.

When members gather for a conference or for a session of court, it has been the custom for more than half a century that upon entering the room each should shake hands with all his colleagues, who are referred to as "brethren." On my first day I regarded this as rather superfluous, for I had greeted each of the brethren elsewhere that morning. Later there were times when it reminded me of the usual instruction of the referee in the prize ring, "Shake hands, go to your corner and come out fighting." But I soon realized that it was a useful reminder of the courtesy and mutual respect that the justices seek to preserve no matter how heated their debates. As a rule, conferences continued for five or six hours, the Chief Justice seated at the head of the table, his senior colleague opposite him. The Chief Justice presents

the issues of each case and expresses his opinion first. He is followed
by the justices in order of seniority, and at the conclusion a vote is
taken. At this time it is the junior justice who votes first. It has been
said that this arrangement was adopted to avoid any question of senior
members influencing their juniors. This explanation did not impress
me, for surely any justice, having already expressed his views, would
ordinarily vote in harmony with them.

During periods of recess the justices are occupied with writing
opinions. That task is assigned to a member by the Chief Justice, provided the decision is unanimous or the Chief Justice has voted with
the majority. When the Chief Justice is with the minority, the task
of assigning the writing of the opinion falls to the senior justice among
the majority. The Court has the services of its own printers, and
elaborate precautions are taken in this department also to insure essential secrecy. The author of an opinion circulates the proof to the
other justices in order that each may approve it as an appropriate expression of the Court's view of the case. If a justice is impressed with
the opinion, frequently he will amplify the customary "I agree." In fact,
when recently I looked over some of my opinions, with the notations
by the justices, I was considerably amused. One notation is "Neat and
complete. I verily believe that you say more by saying less—and what
you say is truly good." Another, and this is from the Chief Justice,
"I agree. It makes the stump speech of your opponent seem quite unnecessary." A decision will not be announced until the language used is
agreed upon by all the concurring justices. Thus it is evident that the
opinion in a case represents not only the view of the author but also
that of the majority of the Court responsible for the decision. If there
is dissent, the senior justice of the minority either writes the dissenting
view himself or designates a colleague to prepare it. This too is circulated and perhaps changed several times in order to meet the views
of other dissenters. Any one of the justices may contribute a separate
dissenting opinion if he desires to.

Up to the time I left the Court it was the custom for each justice to
read his opinion in open court. If there were separate concurring
opinions and dissenting opinions in one or more cases, the reading of
opinions would consume several hours. There was no reason for the
custom because on Opinion Day the Clerk of Court made printed
copies available to all interested parties. However, since it always had
been done, the decision was, then, that it always should be done.

Beyond his right to assign the writing of opinions, the Chief Justice has no greater authority than other members of the Court. Officially he administers the Court's affairs, but in practice he delegates most of such duties to the Marshal and Clerk of Court. I had close contacts with Thomas E. Waggaman, the Court Marshal, and Elsmore Cropley, the Clerk, and as the months went by my respect and admiration for these two public servants grew. On my first day in the unfamiliar surroundings of the Supreme Court Building, Mr. Waggaman called at my office to offer assistance. He always spoke in the subdued tones generally adopted by attendants at a funeral, in contrast to the tone of voice of the justices and particularly of members of the Senate, where talk was frequently loud and long. I soon found myself changing to a lower key whenever I talked with Waggaman.

Each justice has a personal law clerk. Some of the justices select a clerk from among the honor graduates of the university law schools, upon the recommendation of the dean. These posts are prized because of the valuable experience to be gained, but as a rule a clerk remains only a year or two, since he is anxious to get started in his profession. It is his job to read the briefs and arguments submitted by the litigants and to write a memorandum setting forth the issues and citing court decisions relative to the case under consideration. The effectiveness of the clerk depends upon the conciseness and the fairness with which he presents the facts of the case and the legal authorities he cites. Since the Court works under pressure, this preliminary work is of great importance to the justice.

Justices differ, as do the clerks; consequently the relations between the several justices and their clerks differ. If a justice industriously reviews the memoranda and personally studies the cases cited, all is well. Otherwise, he may find himself influenced too much by the opinions of his clerk. In my own case, I selected James E. Doyle of Madison, Wisconsin, who was employed at the time in the Department of Justice. Jim was an exceedingly capable lawyer whom I could trust to present a memorandum of the facts and the law without seeking to smuggle into it his own views and prejudices.

During the hot and humid summer months in 1941 after I had resigned from the Senate, my wife and I were busy house hunting in Washington; for since I confidently expected to spend the rest of my working days on the Court, I had sold our Spartanburg home. As luck would have it, the only house we both liked had also caught the eye of another new associate justice, Bob Jackson, who secured it before we could. We therefore retained our familiar apartment in the Shoreham Hotel. Here I spent considerable time studying the petitions for certiorari which were filed with the Court in anticipation of its coming term. I was accustoming myself to a completely new life, new associations and new duties, with, as I have said, an expectation of permanency.

I had known all the members of the Court before my appointment; most of them I knew intimately, and they quickly made me feel at home. I was agreeably surprised that it was not very difficult for me to adjust my thinking to this new field. In the Senate I had enjoyed the friendship of senators on the Republican side because they knew I had no violent prejudices. The truth is, I had schooled myself to consider the point of view of the other man.

In thinking of the role of the Supreme Court, I felt strongly that its function was to interpret the laws and not to make laws; that where there was doubt about the meaning of the language of a statute, the Court should seek to ascertain the intent of the legislature by referring to the reports of the legislative committees and the statements made at the time by those in charge of the bill; and that a judge should not substitute his personal views for the intent of the Congress and the President who approved the bill.

While I believed it to be the supreme test of judicial statesmanship to preserve the balance between the powers of the federal government and the powers of the states, I realized that the preservation of that balance was difficult and called for the exercise of wise discretion, free of personal prejudices. It is commonplace that the Constitution expresses great principles in language that permits the application of those principles to entirely new conditions. This is perhaps most clearly demonstrated in the application of the Commerce Clause to methods of transportation and communication hardly dreamed of in the days of the Founding Fathers. This philosophy was to be subjected to severe tests in the cases decided by the Court during my service, but I tried to adhere to it.

Of the fifteen or sixteen decisions announced by me, several were of more than routine interest. The first opinion I wrote was that of

*Edwards* v. *The State of California*.[1] Following the depression, thousands of people migrated to that state—not entirely because of the mild climate, but because of its liberal allowances for relief. In this situation the state legislature enacted a law making it a misdemeanor for anyone to bring, or assist in bringing, into California a nonresident, knowing him to be indigent. In December, 1939, Edwards, who lived in Marysville, California, went to Texas in order to bring back with him his wife's unemployed brother. Edwards was subsequently prosecuted and, upon admitting the facts, was convicted and sentenced to six months' imprisonment. On appeal, the state supreme court had affirmed the lower court.

When this case came to the United States Supreme Court, a majority decided to reverse the state court. We differed, however, about whether the Court's opinion should be based on the Commerce Clause of the Constitution or on the ground that the right to move freely from one state to another is an incident of national citizenship. Writing the opinion, I based reversal on the Commerce Clause, which had been frequently construed by the Court as protecting the interstate travel of persons as well as commodities. The social phenomenon of large-scale migration of citizens did not admit of diverse treatment by the several states; for if one state could deny admission to a person regarded as indigent, others would surely adopt retaliatory measures.

In another case from Texas,[2] I wrote an opinion in which the Court reversed the judgment of the state court that the defendant was guilty of "murder without malice." The appellant was an ignorant Negro who, it was charged, in an altercation with a white man, had grabbed him by the throat, choked him to death, and then fled. The Negro had been sentenced to three years' imprisonment. Here the record disclosed a clear case of an extorted confession. It also occurred to me, from my knowledge of Texas, that the jury must have entertained some doubt about the defendant's guilt, else the verdict would never have been "murder without malice," nor would any judge have imposed so light a sentence. The Supreme Court reversed the state court and subsequently the petitioner was acquitted.

Other cases were not so easy of solution.

While on the Court I felt a dissenting opinion should not be written unless a justice felt strongly on the subject. The value of dissent was, however, demonstrated in a case brought by the Wages and Hours

[1] 314 U. S. 160.
[2] *The State of Texas* v. *Ward*, 316 U. S. 547.

Division of the United States Department of Labor against the A. H. Belo Corporation.[3] This company published the Dallas *Morning News* and also owned a radio station there. The question involved was a complicated one—it suffices that it concerned an effort of the Department to prevent the corporation from paying a certain wage scale which was allegedly in violation of the Fair Labor Standards Act.

In our conference the Court divided five to four in sustaining the Department's position, the majority including Justice Robert Jackson, who, though absent, had asked to be so recorded. It fell to me to write the dissenting opinion for the minority, and Justice Reed wrote the majority opinion. When the two opinions were circulated, Justice Jackson visited me and said that after reading the dissent he regretted not having been present when the decision was reached. After some discussion he decided that his first thoughts about the case were erroneous, and he notified Justice Reed that he wished to change his vote. Bob Jackson had that sort of courage. Subsequently, Justice Reed and I met and made the changes necessary to make mine the majority opinion and his the dissenting opinion.

My belief that it is the duty of a judge to declare what is the law and not what he thinks the law should be was severely tested in the case of the United States against the International Brotherhood of Teamsters *et al.*[4] This arose from the following circumstances. Quantities of merchandise regularly entered New York from other states in trucks owned by farmers or by various companies, driven by their own employees. Members of the Teamsters' Union insisted on their right to drive the vehicles within the state or at least to unload them. When truckers balked at using union drivers, there were some instances of violence to force them to do so or to pay a fixed charge representing the day's hire of a union member. There was adequate state law to punish such acts of violence or extortion, but, instead, the union men had been prosecuted and convicted in the United States District Court under what is known as the "Anti-Racketeering Act" of 1934. The Court of Appeals for the Second Circuit, in an opinion written by Judge Learned Hand, one of the ablest judges ever to have served on any court in the United States, reversed these convictions on the ground that the district judge had inaccurately interpreted the language of the

[3] *Walling, Admr.* v. *A. H. Belo Corp.*, 316 U. S. 624.
[4] 315 U. S. 521.

act. With five other members of the Supreme Court, I voted to sustain that decision of the Court of Appeals. When given the task of writing the opinion, I did not welcome the assignment, for I heartily disapproved the action of the union drivers. But Justice Black and I had been members of the Senate at the time the Anti-Racketeering Act was passed, and we knew the act was not intended to apply to the facts of this case.

In the opinion, I emphasized that where there was doubt about the proper interpretation of a statute, the Court should look to the legislative intent. Referring to the *Congressional Record*, I showed that Congress did not pass the bill until it had been redrafted by the Department of Justice, following conferences with the president of the American Federation of Labor, and after a proviso had been added "preserving the rights of bona fide labor organizations." Even so, the House would not consider it until Attorney General Cummings wrote a letter stating that the bill was approved by the Federation of Labor and that it would apply only to activities affecting interstate commerce in connection "with price fixing and economic extortion directed by professional gangsters." Before the bill received the President's signature, Senator Copeland, on behalf of the Senate committee, had submitted to the Senate a report saying that the essential purpose of the legislation was to "close gaps in existing federal laws and to render more difficult the activities of predatory criminal gangs of the Kelly and Dillinger types." At the time I talked with Copeland, who said that the report was made for the deliberate purpose of preventing any future misunderstanding of the intent of the Congress. The accuracy of his statement of the intention of the Congress was not questioned.

On the evening before the Court conference at which the majority opinion was finally agreed upon, Chief Justice Stone, the sole dissenter, told me that after reading the opinion I had submitted, he was thinking of changing his position. The next morning he said that though he had some doubts because of the evidence bearing on the intent of Congress, the conduct of the union truckers was so outrageous that he was going to resolve his doubts against them and write a dissent. Because of my great admiration for him as a judge and affection for him personally, I regretted his decision, but I knew our course was in accord with his own philosophy. This view was confirmed a few years later when, just before he was mortally stricken while on the bench, he declared in an opinion, "It is not the function of this Court to disregard the will of the Congress in the exercise of its constitutional power."

The opinion in the teamster case hinted that if Congress wished to broaden the application of the law, it should legislate to that effect. Congressman Hobbs of Alabama, an able member of the House Judiciary Committee, introduced a bill repealing the provision of the law exempting labor activities, but a year later told me it was impossible to get Congress seriously to consider his bill, its opponents contending that the evils complained of were already punishable or could be made punishable by state laws. Nor has Congress acted since, which seems to be ample evidence that the Court correctly interpreted the intent of the Congress.

Our first President, and later Thomas Jefferson, warned against the Court's arrogating to itself the power to make laws. Time and again the Court itself has disclaimed possessing legislative authority, and just as often has exercised it. In recent years there have been so many such instances that sharp criticism has been leveled against the Court. However, the decision in the case of *Trop.* v. *Dulles,* decided March 31, 1958, gives encouragement that at least four members of the present Court still realize there is a limitation upon their powers. In a dissenting opinion by Justice Frankfurter, concurred in by Justices Burton, Clark and Harlan, these Justices declared:

All power is, in Madison's phrase, "of an encroaching nature." Judicial power is not immune against this human weakness. It also must be on guard against encroaching beyond its proper bounds, and not less so since the only restraint upon it is self-restraint. . . . It is not easy to stand aloof and allow want of wisdom to prevail, to disregard one's own strongly held view of what is wise in the conduct of affairs. But it is not the business of this Court to pronounce policy. It must observe a fastidious regard for limitations on its own power, and this precludes the Court's giving effect to its own notions of what is wise or politic. That self-restraint is of the essence in the observance of the judicial oath, for the Constitution has not authorized the judges to sit in judgment on the wisdom of what Congress and the Executive branch do.

Further encouragement to those who still believe in the Constitution is derived from the recent lectures of the distinguished jurist, Learned Hand (now retired), published in March, 1958, under the title *The Bill of Rights*. Judge Hand, in referring to the exercise of legislative power by the Court, said:

Moreover, it certainly does not accord with the underlying presuppositions of popular government to vest in a chamber, unaccountable to anyone but itself, the power to suppress social experiments which it does not approve. Nothing, I submit, could warrant such a censorship except a code of paramount law that not only measured the scope of legislative authority but regulated how it should be exercised.

Particularly disturbing to the people of all sections of the land has been the series of decisions impairing the power of the Congress and the legislatures of the states to discover or to punish persons charged with subversive activities, such as the case of *Pennsylvania* v. *Nelson*, where the Supreme Court set aside the laws of seventeen states providing punishment for conspiracy to overthrow the government; the Slochower case, reversing the New York courts, which upheld a state law authorizing the discharge of a teacher who refused to tell a Congressional committee whether he had been a Communist; the Watkins case, holding that where a congressional committee was investigating subversive activities, the defendant had the right to require the committee to state the specific purpose of the investigation and prove to the Court that the question the defendant refused to answer was relevant to the purpose of the investigation; and also the Jencks case, where the Court decided the government must furnish, upon request of a defendant, the FBI files about the testimony of witnesses for the government. There were other somewhat similar cases and most of them by five-to-four decisions.

The abuse of the power of judicial review and the assumption of the power of a third branch of the Congress cause many people who have deep respect for the Supreme Court to fear that it will no longer enjoy the confidence of the country unless the Congress curbs it by exercising its own constitutional authority to regulate the appellate jurisdiction of the Court.

Once aroused, the people of the United States will not be willing to transfer all the lawmaking powers of the President and the Congress, who are elected by the people, to five justices who are not elected by the people and who can be removed only by impeachment by two thirds of the Senate.

Personally, I have regarded the Court as the defender of the Constitution against action by the executive or the Congress in violation of that instrument, and I think it exceedingly unfortunate that the people now have to appeal to the Congress and the executive to defend the Constitution against the usurpation of legislative power by the Supreme Court.

# 10 EXTRACURRICULAR ACTIVITIES

The morning after the Japanese attack on Sunday, December 7, 1941, the Supreme Court met to hear arguments in the case of *The United States* v. *Bethlehem Ship Building Company,* growing out of contracts for ships built by that company during World War I. As I listened to the arguments, my mind kept turning not only to "the law's delays" but to the irony of our considering a case arising out of the construction of ships twenty years ago, when so many of our naval vessels had been destroyed only the day before.

When I called on the President the next morning at his invitation, he was in bed surrounded by documents and newspapers. His appearance shocked me. As he told of developments since Sunday afternoon, he was more nervous than I had ever seen him. We continued our discussion as he dressed and wheeled himself into the bathroom to shave. I sat on the only seat in the room. He was worried about the steps to be taken immediately to put the nation on a full war footing, saying we were not prepared either militarily or psychologically for the ordeal confronting us.

When he asked my help with certain legislation and I promised assistance, I mentioned my thoughts while listening to the Bethlehem case. Jokingly, I told him that I had once thought him wrong in urging mandatory retirement of Supreme Court justices at the age of seventy; now it seemed preferable that in time of war only men over seventy should be allowed to serve on the Court. More seriously, I reminded him that after twenty-four years of service in Congress, nearly all of it on appropriations committees studying the work of the departments, I had acquired a lot of information about the government that might

147

enable me in wartime to perform greater service than upon the Court; and if he ever concluded I could be of more value elsewhere, I hoped he would call upon me.

He did not delay in doing so. Within a week he told me that Attorney General Biddle had been asked to confer with me on all the emergency war legislation and executive orders to be issued. I was asked to help expedite the legislation. This arrangement was later succinctly described by Francis Biddle when he reported to the President, "All defense legislation is being cleared by the departments and then through Jimmy Byrnes, who takes care of it on the Hill."

When we had completed drafting the First War Powers Act, I conferred over the telephone with Senator Barkley, Speaker Rayburn and others. They wanted to be certain the departments did not slip into emergency legislation pet projects to which the Congress was opposed. When I assured them that every item was essential for the emergency, they had the bill quickly passed. Soon I found myself giving several hours a day as well as many evenings to conferences and calls about these extracurricular affairs.

After a while some of my activities and contacts with officials outside the Court work became known publicly. There was no question of my resignation at this time, but I discussed my activities with Chief Justice Stone, who applauded my efforts to aid in the emergency. He suggested relieving me temporarily of the task of writing opinions and for a short while did lessen my work in this respect.

At this time there was little precedent for an associate justice's performing any service for the executive branch. In 1913, when Congress created a commission to investigate second-class mail rates, Justice Hughes had served as chairman, at the request of President Taft. Later in the Second World War, Justice Owen J. Roberts was appointed to inquire into the Pearl Harbor disaster and Justice Jackson to serve at the Nuremberg Trials of war criminals. But these were still early days, and after some thought Mr. Roosevelt and I both agreed that it was better for me to say nothing—and simply act.

Early in January, with requests for new legislation pouring in, Attorney General Biddle, his assistant Oscar Cox, and I worked over the Second War Powers Act. The scope of our conferences may be judged by the résumé of its leading titles in the memorandum that accompanied our final draft to the White House:

1. It empowers the Interstate Commerce Commission to have equivalent authority over motor carriers as it now has over other carriers.
2. It provides a simpler method of acquisition of real property.
3. It provides sanctions for enforcing priority orders.
4. It authorizes the Federal Reserve Bank to purchase government securities other than on the open market.
5. It empowers the Secretary of Commerce, under certain conditions, to waive navigation inspection laws.
6. It strikes out the Taber Amendment from the Act authorizing the requisitioning of war materials, which amendment exempted tools and machinery in going concerns.
7. It amends the Hatch Act so as to eliminate part-time employees who serve on nominal compensation.
8. It provides compensation for air raids, and for fire wardens working under OCD, in accordance with Mayor La Guardia's suggestion.
9. It extends the time under which vessels of Canadian registry may transport iron ore on the Great Lakes for the duration of war.
10. It provides that soldiers, sailors, and marines may mail letters free of postage.
11. It makes aliens enlisting in the armed forces eligible for naturalization.

Our strategy here was to present Congress with an omnibus bill, hoping that the popular proposals, such as the one on free mail for the armed forces, would win support for the more controversial ones. With the close co-operation of Senator Barkley and Speaker Sam Rayburn, and with the support of Judiciary Committees of both Houses, which had charge of the bill, this important measure passed Congress in record time.

It was about this time that Hopkins telephoned, asking my views about the demands being voiced daily by the press and the public for the appointment of a czar with full authority to merge the activities of several organizations then controlling war production. I told him such demands were also being urged by Senator Taft as well as other senators, and that it was important to bring an end to the chaos and confusion then existing. He told me that the President and Winston Churchill, who was then visiting at the White House, were going to Hyde Park and that he was to be there for a few days, and asked that I send him a memorandum on the subject which he could give to the President. I promptly sent him a memorandum urging the appointment of an individual to head procurement who might be assisted by a board, but stressed that one person should be given the power and held responsible for the program. The memorandum continued:

The President can name a man—for convenience call him Hopkins—and charge him with the duty of supervising and expediting procurement. When the President has decided upon an increased program, he should submit it to Hopkins instead of to a committee. . . . If because of a deficiency in the supply of steel, there is a controversy between Army and Navy and civilian services as to the amount to be allotted for their respective needs, Hopkins should decide that controversy. Having decided it, he should keep behind each service . . . so that the President can get from him at any moment the status of the program. . . . You say, "All right—find the man." . . . If you now have in the organization a man who has served his apprenticeship, who has some appreciation of the problems of the Procurement Divisions of the Army, Navy and other services, and who has the ability to make other men work, appoint him, instead of bringing in another new man. . . . Pick the best man you now have on the team and let the heathen rage.

On Monday morning, a week later, General Watson told me that the President wanted me to call on him at 11:45. I concluded it was about my memorandum, but I had hardly hung up the telephone when another call came from the White House. This time it was Hopkins, who had seen the engagement list; learning the President was to see me upstairs, he asked me to stop by his room first. When I arrived, Hopkins told me that at Hyde Park he had tried to discuss with the President the subject set forth in my memorandum, but Mr. Roosevelt still seemed reluctant to come to grips with the problem and had seemed irritated when it was suggested. As a result, Hopkins had not given him my memorandum. He reiterated his agreement with my views and said he hoped I would present it to the President.

When I saw the President and after he had discussed an entirely different matter, I produced the memorandum and asked that he read it. As he read he made some notes. When he had finished he said he had been considering the appointment of a commission, but possibly my suggestion was better. Noting the recommendation that there should be no reversal by him of any decision made by the procurement head, he wrote on a pad, "whose decision shall be final," remarking, "That, of course, is essential." I emphasized, and he agreed, that the man selected could serve only as long as he was known to have the President's complete confidence. He then said that if he had to make the appointment that morning, he would name Donald Nelson, who had favorably impressed him the previous evening during a discussion Nelson had had with Lord Beaverbrook and Jesse Jones about the rubber problem. I told the President I had no recommendation, but did urge speedy action. Hurrying off, I arrived at the Court a little late, the only time I was guilty of tardiness.

During the day Hopkins telephoned that the recommendation had definitely been accepted, and Pa Watson made another appointment for me to see the President the next morning. On this occasion I found Budget Director Harold Smith waiting for me. He said the President had sent my memorandum to him the previous day. Hopkins joined us when we went in to talk with the President. Smith endorsed my proposal and said that something of the kind should have been done months before. We then discussed a draft of the necessary executive order and a press announcement. Hopkins was for issuing both immediately to avoid unofficial leaks, but Mr. Roosevelt insisted that nothing be done until he told Vice President Wallace, whose chairmanship of the Economic Defense Board would be abolished.

As it happened, Wendell Willkie called on the President that afternoon. I could understand the President's liking this man and was not surprised that they talked at such length that Mr. Roosevelt's schedule was quite disrupted. Consequently, when I arrived late in the afternoon to see a final draft of the order, I found that the consultation with Mr. Wallace was not over. About six o'clock, however, the statement was finally released and a War Production Board, under the chairmanship of Donald Nelson, came into being.

My frequent visits to see the President immediately preceding the issuance of the order had inspired the publication by the Associated Press of a rumor that Mr. Roosevelt might "borrow Justice Byrnes temporarily to aid in revamping the production organization." This story I denied, for I had no intention of undertaking the task.

Following the establishment of WPB, requests for my intervention with legislative leaders grew fewer, though the President continued to call on me for suggestions. There was, for example, the case of the Office of Alien Property Custodian. One Sunday morning I was invited to the White House to discuss what the President called "a difficult decision." Under an act of Congress of May 17, 1940, the Treasury

Department had frozen alien property amounting to approximately $7 billion. Several important alien-owned corporations housed Treasury officials acting as "observers," but effectively controlling operations. At the same time the Alien Property Custodian in the Department of Justice held approximately $4 million and a number of claims in process of liquidation. After our entry into the war, the President was authorized to take over the property of all enemy aliens, which would add billions of dollars to the sums already in custody.

Mr. Roosevelt and I had been in Washington in 1918 and were familiar with the scandals arising out of the seizure of such properties in World War I, which had as a sequel the imprisonment of the then custodian. The President wished to avoid a repetition of this episode, and also wished to avoid any criticism that his administration would treat harshly aliens who had spent most of their lives in this country but had never been naturalized. He laughed when I told him that I would prefer to see the Alien Property Office located on the Triangle on Pennsylvania Avenue in front of the District Building with its walls made of glass so that its employees and the lobbyists would be always under the eyes of the public.

When he asked me to suggest a man to put in charge, I said Leo T. Crowley, chairman of the Federal Deposit Insurance Corporation. He had proved to be an efficient administrator, had the respect of leaders in the world of business and finance, and his relations with the Congress were excellent. The President said, "I have been thinking of the same man, but don't like to move him from his present post. Can we work out some plan giving him both offices?"

This task was not a light one, since both the Attorney General and Secretary Morgenthau thought they should be in charge. My file contains a lot of memoranda covering proposals and counterproposals, and there were many personal conferences. The complexity of the situation may be judged by this note from the President:

MEMORANDUM FOR JIMMY BYRNES:
I feel I cannot make a final decision on this until next week for obvious reasons.

Meantime, could you examine the possibility of making Crowley Alien Property Custodian—in the Attorney General's Office—with full responsibility, but giving him two assistants—one in the State Department, on the International angle, with relatively little to do; and another in the Treasury

Department, the latter maintaining supervision over the assets which are now or would hereafter be run through Treasury machinery?

My reply was that it was not wise for the President to "scatter among several agencies the power and responsibility placed in him by Congress." It was illogical, I thought, to put the Department of Justice in charge of the physical property of an alien corporation and the Treasury in charge of its bank deposits: "All alien property coming under the President's control should be under one custodian who should be given full power and held responsible. If it is deemed advisable for the Treasury to retain control of the seven billion dollars of frozen assets, I would give the Secretary of the Treasury all other alien property and hold *him* responsible."

The struggle still continued, and on February 17 I again wrote to the President: "Referring to our Sunday conversation, I attach a suggested order carrying out the idea of an independent organization. Paragraph three embodies the course . . . of leaving in the Treasury the assets and business enterprises now under its control until the Custodian calls for the transfer. This is satisfactory to Crowley. It would make possible the gradual absorption of the Treasury organization into that of the Custodian."

Eventually persistence and, I believe, common sense won, and it was with true pride that I watched the office effectively managed during the next few years. Certainly it was an improvement on our World War I record in this field.

When the Court adjourned for the summer, I remained in Washington. It was my hope that I could soon leave for South Carolina and my cottage on Sullivan's Island, near Charleston, but many vexing problems were still unsettled. For one thing, Donald Nelson of the WPB was already deeply involved in a struggle with the War and Navy Departments over the extent to which the services should control the economy and, in fact, act independently of his agency in all matters of vital interest to them.

Meanwhile the inflationary situation threatened to grow much worse. I know the President received much advice, including my own, on the need to establish ceilings on wages, prices and rents. Back when the war started in September, 1939, I thought Congress should act on this matter. Now a bill to give the President such authority was pending in Congress, but he hesitated to make a special appeal for it because he knew it was exceedingly controversial and he feared it might delay the enactment of other essential measures. When he finally did ask the Congress to act on it, pressure groups successfully resisted its passage.

I was told that, at the President's request, Sam Rosenman was in consultation with various agency heads whose tasks would be affected by price legislation. Rosenman told me the department heads were divided and that he was urging the President to issue an executive order without waiting for action by the Congress. It was my opinion that would be unwise. Rosenman drafted several different orders and finally completed one which he gave to the President to take with him to Hyde Park, where he was to spend a few days before making a Labor Day speech. The newspapers speculated that in his speech the President would announce the signing of an order creating a stabilization czar, but they guessed wrong.

I was at my island home when Louise Hackmeister, the efficient assistant handling the President's personal telephone calls, located me. The President said he was afraid that the Congress might delay acting for some months and asked my reaction to Rosenman's proposal. I advised him strongly against this course, because the regulation of wages, prices and rents would affect everyone, and even with Congressional authority it would be a difficult task. I urged that another effort be made to secure the necessary legislation, and he agreed to do this. That same afternoon Secretary Ickes telephoned, saying he had heard that the President was considering the issuance of an executive order without congressional authority, and asked that I call the President and insist upon congressional action. The "Old Curmudgeon" was delighted when I told him of my earlier conversation with the President and of his decision to make another appeal to the Congress.

Within two or three days the President sent another message to Congress and also made a Fireside Chat over the radio, telling the people of the necessity for prompt action. The Congress passed the bill, which was signed by the President on October 2. By that time I had returned to Washington for the fall term of the Court. The President asked me to come to see him the following morning. It was a bedside talk, with the breakfast tray pushed aside and newspapers and documents scattered over the covers. Sitting in bed with several pillows at his back, he usually planned his day and saw some callers;

in this atmosphere he always seemed to me more relaxed than when he was at his office. But it was not just another talk for me. This one resulted in my resignation from the Supreme Court.

After greeting me, the President said he wanted me to take leave of absence from the Court and accept the appointment of Director of Economic Stabilization, saying he knew I was familiar in a general way with the proposed executive order. In addition to the duties outlined by his order, he said, there were many other things he would wish me to do. Because I wanted him first to know my view about a "leave of absence," I said that no one could grant such leave, that it was my own responsibility; but that I would like to know what he meant by "other things" so that I would have a clear idea of the scope of my duties.

The President said he would not have time to devote to the prosecution of the war on the military front and the diplomatic problems daily arising, and at the same time to supervise domestic affairs; that he wanted me to relieve him of the problems on the home front and the jurisdictional disputes which increased with the creation of every new agency. He said, "In these jurisdictional disputes I want you to act as a judge and I will let it be known that your decision is my decision, and that there is no appeal. For all practical purposes you will be assistant President." He told me he wanted me to have offices in the White House because this would emphasize the unique status of the post.

When the President had outlined the scope of the duties, I told him that the day after Pearl Harbor I had offered to serve wherever he thought I could best serve in time of war; that I would accept the appointment; and that because I did not think it would be proper for me to remain on the Court, I would resign at once.

(Miss Margaret Coit in her book *Mr. Baruch* wrote that Hopkins, without any direction of the President, talked to me about accepting this appointment. Her information was erroneous. Hopkins preserved his intimate relationship with the President by never arrogating unto himself such authority. I cannot imagine Hopkins assuming to appoint an assistant President when it would have required that man to resign from the Supreme Court.)

It was not easy to leave the Court, with its opportunity for service, its prestige and security—the work I liked and the associates for whom I had a genuine affection. But in time of war my duty was plain.

Within an hour I had returned to the White House with a letter for the President, which in my handwriting took but two lines:

DEAR MR. PRESIDENT:
I hereby resign the office of Associate Justice of the Supreme Court.

Within a short time I had an official reply:

DEAR JIMMY:
I hereby officially accept your resignation of the office of Associate Justice of the Supreme Court of the United States.

At the same time, officially and personally as well, I extend to you my deep appreciation in leaving the Supreme Court in order to assume a position of highest importance to the carrying on of the war.

In one sense, this is an act of great personal sacrifice on your part, but I know you are happy in undertaking a task which affects every individual and every family throughout the Nation during the war, and will assist the well-being of us all in the days after victory has come to our beloved country.

Sincerely and affectionately,
FRANKLIN DELANO ROOSEVELT

I immediately notified the Chief Justice and to my gratification received from him a letter signed by all the members of the Court. It said: "All of us part with you reluctantly and with regret. We are reconciled to your going only by the realization that you are moved by a sense of duty to render service of public importance in a time of great national emergency."

Within a few hours of the public announcement, former Chief Justice Charles Evans Hughes sent me by a messenger a warm letter of good wishes, recalling that he and I were the only members to resign from that body in more than one hundred years. *

That afternoon I had another conference with the President. We agreed that while originating policies and resolving conflicts, in no way should we attempt to develop another operating agency; it was clear that the small offices in the White House would emphasize again that I was to act as a judge and not a contestant. This the President had urged in explaining his desire to appoint me.

In announcing to the press the appointment, he again expressed this view when he said, "This position calls primarily for judicial consideration. The organization will therefore be small because administra-

* The Chief Justice, writing hurriedly, overlooked John Hessin Clarke, who resigned in 1922.

tive action will be carried out by the existing agencies." When I spoke to the press the same day, I summed up my responsibilities by saying, "Control of prices necessarily involves many departments, and inevitably conflicts will arise. My duty will be to hear the differences, resolve the conflicts, and relieve the President of that determination." I also remarked that my office would be in the left wing of the White House—but there was to be no political or economic significance attached to my location there!

Fifteen months before, when my appointment to the Court had been announced, David Lawrence, who had been my friend since the days of Woodrow Wilson, expressed regret that the President should have filled the vacancy from the Senate instead of making a selection from the judiciary, and wrote: "Senator Byrnes' experience is wholly legislative. An old friend of the President, he has been invaluable to him in getting legislation through the Senate. But he has sometimes opposed administration legislative proposals. He has never been regarded as a New Dealer in the sense, for example, that Justice Black, the other Court appointee from the Senate, has been so regarded."

So I was pleased when upon my resignation, in commenting on my decision in the teamsters' case, Mr. Lawrence pointed out that "Justice Byrnes applied the statute just as he found it, irrespective of how he personally might have felt about the union activity . . . and that is typical of his deep sense of justice." And he reversed his former statement by saying, "It is to be hoped that the President will go to the Senate again for his selection."

# Part IV

---

# THE WHITE HOUSE

# 11  THE WAR ON THE HOME FRONT

When on Monday morning, October 5, 1942, Donald Russell, my assistant, and Miss Connor accompanied me to the nearly completed wing of the White House, they said the offices had been correctly described by the President as "very small."

I was already familiar with the size and appearance of the rooms we were to occupy, but the faces of Russell and Miss Connor clearly indicated surprise. Lumber and debris were scattered everywhere, the walls were white and completely lacking in trimmings, the floors bare, and there was not a stick of furniture. One had the feeling of "moving out" rather than moving in to what one might imagine offices in the White House to be. Austerity was in fact to be our lot throughout the war, for this new wing was not finally completed until after we had left in 1945. After a week or two, with the lumber removed from the entrance and some pictures and rugs brought in, we became reasonably comfortable, though crowded. The Washington press, familiar with the mushrooming of government agencies, could not believe that the space assigned would continue to house all my staff. But it did, though we had to put up a temporary partition to make a cubbyhole office for Miss Connor and, as a last resort, install our news ticker in the men's room.

Russell, one of my small staff of five, had closed his law office at the beginning of the war and had come to Washington to engage in war work. Knowing that Under Secretary of War Patterson needed capable lawyers with a knowledge of business practices whom he could use in the renegotiation of war contracts, I had sent Russell to see him and in a few days he was at work at the War Department. Now, like

161

Bob Patterson, I found myself needing the services of a man with Russell's qualifications, and had drafted him to serve as my assistant.

We had been in our offices only a few days when the President, without notice, came over to call. I was out at the time, but upon my return a few minutes later I found my staff quite excited. They were not accustomed to receiving the President. They reported that after going through the offices and the conference room, he said, "Tell Jimmy I want him to get some pictures for his walls; Ickes ought to be able to furnish him some of those done by the WPA artists during the depression." He was not the only one to complain of the lack of elegance in our office *décor*. Even the economy-minded Jesse Jones was sharp in his complaints that we should have more "plush" in our offices.

Things have changed since the early days when this additional working wing was first added to the White House. One feature I know is gone. The wing had been built about two or three feet lower than the main building, and a ramp was constructed sloping toward my office so that the President's chair might be easily wheeled down when he wished to visit the offices or to use that exit.

When he introduced me to the press as Director of Economic Stabilization, the President was generous enough to say that he was certain I would be fair to everyone. The reception of the news by the country was extremely favorable. But the plaudits with which the appointment was greeted did not deceive me. I expected the going to be rough and my popularity to be short-lived.

I looked back to the White House conference in September, 1939, when the President had decided to call a special session of Congress because of Hitler's attack on Poland. During our discussion of the consequences of repealing the Neutrality Act and of adopting a "cash-and-carry" policy, I had argued with my Senatorial colleagues at the conference that the action we were contemplating would necessitate some across-the-board control of prices, rents, wages and services. But the consensus was against any such step—we were not at war, it was said, and the people would not stand for it. However, in no other way could we have lessened the perils of the inflation which confronted us later. By the summer of 1942, prices had climbed month after month until the cost-of-living index reported an increase of 17 per cent over the September, 1939, figure. All this time Congress had hesitated to authorize government controls, fearing that to peg wages and prices would curb purchasing power, lower living standards, and legalize inequities. Particularly troublesome in this last connection was the fact that excessive demands for men and materials as well as for accommodations in defense-plant areas had pushed up prices in some localities and some industries far in excess of the general level.

Now Congress had been forced to act, the President had issued his executive order, and at this rather late day it remained for me to attempt to make the control policy work. I expected to be saying "no" to a great many people for a long time, and I was not mistaken. In six months I had more acquaintances and fewer friends than ever before. W. H. Lawrence of *The New York Times* estimated the extent of my task in a friendly article published a day or two after my appointment: "It is generally agreed in the best informed Washington circles that the inexorable demands of war . . . will make it possible to check, not prevent, prices rising. Those who are closest in the picture estimate that living costs may advance another 9 per cent during the next year. . . . If the advance can be held, after four years of war, to roughly 25 per cent, it will still be an accomplishment in economic history of the first magnitude."

Though I may be anticipating a little, let me state here that from October 15, 1942, when OES really began operating, until April, 1943, when we drafted and the President issued the famous Hold-the-Line order, the cost of living advanced 4.3 per cent. From then until April, 1945, first under my administration and later that of Judge Vinson, who administered the order with firmness, it went up only 3.2 per cent. It was in the twenty-two months after Vinson's retirement and the abandonment of Hold-the-Line that it spiraled upward 20.2 per cent, surpassing the figure estimated in Mr. Lawrence's article as a minimum advance possible.

At the time of my appointment the President had issued an executive order freezing all wages, salaries, prices, profits and rents, with certain exceptions. This had been prepared by Harold Smith, Director of the Budget, and was of course based on the new powers given to the President by the anti-inflation law. Within twenty-four hours we began to use the wide powers granted OES. It was announced that the Agriculture Department would limit loan rates on wheat and corn to 85 per cent of parity instead of allowing them to rise to the legal level of 90 per cent. The object was to hold down feed prices and encourage a stable price for poultry and eggs.

On the same day I held a conference with the National War Labor Board on a general wage policy. Hitherto the Board had dealt only with labor employed on war contracts, but now its powers were extended to cover employees in all industry. At the end of the meeting I announced that the Board would adhere to the "Little Steel" wage stabilization policy. This permitted increases to industrial workers in approved cases of not more than 15 per cent to compensate for the rise in living costs during the period between January 1, 1941, and May, 1942. The arrangement had been generally acceptable to a majority of employers and employees; but as the cost-of-living index had jumped 2 per cent in the previous six months, considerable pressure was now being put upon the Board for a greater increase. I hoped that my announcement from the White House of this decision on wage policy would indicate presidential approval and strengthen the Board's resolution.

Wages under $5,000 could be increased if permission was granted by the War Labor Board. But no salaries between that figure and the maximum of $25,000 could be increased unless my office had been shown that the increment was due to the recipient's assuming a different and more responsible assignment. In connection with the salary question, I recall a visit from Wayne Coy, Deputy Budget Director, about my own compensation. The day following my appointment, he showed me an order prepared, he said, at the request of the President and for his signature, fixing my salary at $20,000. I told him that since I was to enforce the ceiling on wages and salaries of others, it would be helpful if I took a reduction from this figure, which was what I had received as a member of the Supreme Court, and fixed my salary at $10,000, the amount then paid to members of Congress. At our next meeting the President mentioned the subject, suggesting a salary of not less than $15,000, the compensation then received by Cabinet members. As he expected me to attend Cabinet meetings and to settle controversies between Cabinet officers, he felt I should receive the same salary. Afterward I was grateful for his insistence, as it became apparent in reviewing my finances that a cut to $10,000 would have seriously impaired my ability to meet the income taxes due for that year on my salary of $20,000 as a Supreme Court justice, since no withholding tax was then required.

With regard to rents, it had been decided to extend controls to all rental property throughout the country. I approached Congressman

Steagall of the House Banking and Currency Committee, who had been in charge of the original bill covering housing in defense areas, and offered to testify at the necessary committee hearings. On October 14 the bill we sought was passed unanimously and went to the Senate, where again I testified at the committee hearings, calling attention to a press statement that some rents in New York City had been increased by 200 per cent, and that there were instances elsewhere of men in uniform being charged up to $18 per night for temporary accommodations. The next day no less than four New York realty boards protested that I had done their city "irreparable injury" and had been badly "misinformed." I was not convinced. The bill was passed.

The executive order setting up OES had mentioned creation of a stabilization board "with which the Director shall advise and consult." The week the Steagall bill went through Congress I held the first meeting of the Board. Besides myself as chairman it consisted of the Secretaries of the Treasury, Morgenthau; Agriculture, Wickard; Commerce, Ickes; and Labor, Perkins; the chairman of the board of the Federal Reserve System; the Budget Director, Harold Smith; the Price Administrator, Leon Henderson; and the chairman of the War Labor Board. A day or so after the executive order was issued, the President at my suggestion had named additional members who would represent management, labor and farming interests. These were, respectively, Eric Johnston of the U.S. Chamber of Commerce and Ralph E. Flanders, now senator from Vermont; William Green, A.F. of L., and Philip Murray, C.I.O.; and James G. Patten of the Farmers' Union with Edward A. O'Neal of the Farm Bureau Federation. Thus the groups from which the greatest resistance was to be expected found themselves represented.

My thought in arranging this was not only that their counsel would be of value but that it was better to have them inside as consultants than outside as critics. From the outset, however, it was made plain that while advice was welcome, the responsibility for decision was mine. After I had outlined the powers conferred upon the Director of OES, I pointed out that while in normal times our economy was based on personal incentive and on the profit system, we had now to give more attention to keeping prices down than profits up. "We will make mistakes, but in war inaction is the greatest of mistakes," I pointed out.

It was shortly apparent that this group was too large to accomplish much. The members who contributed most were the representatives of the so-called special interests. In addition to seeing quickly which of our proposed policies they could agree upon, I benefited from the free and open discussion of their particular problems.

The evident intent of the Congress in passing the stabilization law had been to authorize the President—or his deputy in these matters—to prevent any further rise in costs. This usually required a flat refusal to consider any additions whatever to wages and prices. At the same time instances arose when the primary goal of all—speedy and total victory—required increased production and could only be served by making exceptions. Exercise of the discretion on this point left to me by the President was one of my most difficult tasks. Every interested person or group expected the Director of Economic Stabilization to understand that while they favored holding the line, his or their case was "different."

As it was clear that the question of food prices would continue to be an issue, and that it was bound up with the supply of labor available for farm work, I knew we needed drastic changes not only in the war food program but in the existing arrangements for controlling manpower. As early as October 16 I had invited Secretary Wickard to begin preparing a plan to regulate farm wages—in this case, of course, looking to their general improvement in order to increase food production. I submitted to the President a detailed memorandum urging the appointment of a Food Administrator in the Agriculture Department.

Mr. Roosevelt waited until December 6 before issuing an executive order giving the Secretary of Agriculture control, not only over the production of all foods and of fats, cotton, wool and tobacco, but over their allocation and distribution to our civilians, to the millions in war service, and to our overseas Allies. The Secretary was to work principally with the chairman of WPB in determining allocations, and with the Price Administrator, Leon Henderson in extending a rationing system for commodities in short supply. This was as simple as the administrative machinery could be made under the circumstances, and the day after it was issued the President authorized me to act as his representative in enforcing the executive order.

The demands of our Allies for food supplies were so pressing that some shortages at home were inevitable. Many of these troubles were exaggerated by the fact that the drafting of agricultural workers into the armed services made it difficult to increase production. There was much discussion in Congress and in the press of the role the Army might play in helping to harvest seasonal crops where unskilled labor could be utilized. But, in addition to a shortage of adequate farm machinery and workers, the main problem lay in the attractiveness of the higher industrial wage scales. In seeking farm help the farmer could not compete with industrial wages, especially since he had a ceiling on the commodities he was selling. Accordingly, after a policy meeting of the Stabilization Board on November 13, I announced that existing wage ceilings on agricultural wages would be temporarily lifted and that Secretary Wickard would make a survey to determine the actual effects of subsequent rises in farm wages under $2,400 per year. The Department of Agriculture would consult with the War Labor Board or with OPA on any rise in wages for farm workers that might cause the cost-of-living level to go up, and such increases would not finally be granted until my office had given specific approval.

Later, in March, 1943, a separate War Food Administration was set up within the Department of Agriculture. To head this I recommended the appointment of Chester C. Davis of St. Louis. Davis, an energetic administrator, resigned after only three months because of disagreement over departmental policies and the extent of his own authority over prices and rationing.

When he resigned in July I turned to Marvin Jones of Texas to replace him. Judge Jones had been on temporary duty in my office since January, advising on policies affecting agriculture. He had been chairman of the Agricultural Committee of the House for many years before going to the Court of Claims, and was well known to the farmers of the nation. As Food Administrator he not only handled the continuing problems of inadequate machinery and labor supplies but did much work on the rationing problem.

We did not ration simply to exercise administrative authority. We recognized that it was a hardship. When in August, 1944, Judge Jones told me we had sufficient stockpiles of food to allow the removal of certain canned foods from the rationed list, we hastened to announce the freeing of these items. This brought Jones the first public commendation he had received since assuming his unwelcome task, which he performed with distinction until July, 1945.

It was of course quite apparent by the beginning of 1943 that hoarding and black marketeering were a menace to the economy. As an instance of our campaign against these twin evils I cite the decision to ration shoes which was made in February of that year. Our information showed that for the last six months of 1942 one out of every ten pairs of shoes made in the United States were for the armed forces, and that when our Army invaded North Africa every soldier carried three pairs of shoes with him. The requirements for the armed forces so reduced the supply available for civilians that rationing was necessary, but obviously hoarding would begin rapidly if word of our plan leaked out. Therefore, on a Sunday afternoon when the stores were closed, I released the OPA order suspending the sale of shoes for two days. This also gave merchants an opportunity to familiarize themselves with the regulations for limiting purchases.

On this same day, in a nationwide broadcast, I announced that the President had ordered a forty-eight-hour minimum work week for all full-time workers in areas where there were labor shortages. I took the occasion to warn the public that the standard of living must be further depressed and that other steps were contemplated to prevent wages and prices from rising. The reason for these additional sacrifices on the home front, I explained, was that our war plans for 1943 called "for a very substantial increase in our war production," required "the enlistment of additional millions into our armed forces," and contemplated, "within a measurable period of time, the invasion of Europe—a military campaign which will involve casualties such as this nation has never before endured." I also referred to the fact that the War Labor Board had that day announced its refusal to approve an increase above the Little Steel formula to over 180,000 employees of the big meat-packing companies. This was a warning to other labor organizations that they should expect like treatment.

I also reported that farm incomes were at the highest level in history and that any changes in the farm parity formula would be opposed by my office. I repeated that the War Labor Board and the Office of Price Administration had been directed that any action on price rises must be cleared by my office, and finally I called on absentee workers in farm and dairy occupations either to return to the land or be deprived of their draft deferments.

This speech was generally referred to in the press as the "work or fight" program. Less than a week later, on February 13, in addressing the Newspaper Editors in Washington, I urged them to join the battle against the black marketeers, closing with the statement that the time had come "to stop fighting each other and start fighting the enemy."

The hope I expressed that we might stop fighting each other was related in some measure to my efforts to settle amicably and privately disputes between various Cabinet members, "czars" and other highly placed—and high-powered—officials. Much of my time after October, 1942, had been devoted to hearing details of their disagreements, reconciling differences, and, whenever possible, preventing the warring parties from rushing to the press with their quarrels.

In almost every case these were not quarrels over trifles but represented genuine and serious differences of opinion. Sometimes the contenders were permanent members of the President's team; more often they were the temporary and greatly valued aides whom the government had recruited in time of crisis. Each of these men had been something of a dictator, accustomed to fixing policies and seeing them executed. He was confronted in government service with the need to make compromises with other executives, which often was difficult for him.

When, for example, all materials were in short supply, the head of an operating agency, believing his department to be the most essential, felt he had to fight to secure what he needed or be held responsible for delays. It was no easy task to reconcile these disagreements, whatever their source.

One of the first was the rubber dispute. The problem of adequate rubber supplies for both military and civilian use had been reviewed as early as August, 1942, by a three-man board consisting of Bernard Baruch, James B. Conant of Harvard and Karl T. Compton of M.I.T. A month later Donald Nelson, chairman of the War Production Board, appointed William M. Jeffers, president of the Union Pacific Railroad, director of the entire rubber program with instructions, among other things, to implement the findings of this board.

Jeffers was an able and aggressive man—a two-fisted fighter. Very soon friction developed between him and the services over their share of the available supplies and those allocated for civilian use. The climax of the dispute came after the first week of January, 1943, when I called Jeffers to meet in the White House with Secretary of War Stimson, McNutt, Nelson and others. There was a very heated discussion. In strong language Jeffers pictured the needs of the civilian population, asserting that people could not be expected to produce food on the farms or weapons in the factories if their needs were ignored. He said that his knowledge of the laboring man was not academic—he carried a union card in his pocket—and that he was also at home with the farmers, having often eaten in their kitchens while on his tours of inspection.

Secretary Stimson was equally forceful in presenting the urgent demands of the armed forces. He countered Mr. Jeffers' remarks by saying coolly, "I do not carry a union card and I prefer to eat in the dining room. But I still think I know something of the willingness of the civilian to make sacrifices for the war effort."

Two younger officials also attended this hearing: Under Secretary Forrestal of the Navy and Under Secretary of War Patterson. They earnestly supported Stimson's claims, whenever they could, against Mr. Jeffers. Forrestal, in the midst of an argument, turned to an unassuming gentleman who had seated himself—not at the conference table but in a corner of the room—and said, "Mr. Searls, what would you say about the percentage I have proposed for allotment for military purposes?" The stranger suggested a figure somewhat less than that contended for by Forrestal, but also less than Jeffers wanted. Forrestal expressed surprise but declared himself willing to accept his judgment. To my amazement, Patterson also concurred.

When the conference adjourned I returned to my office and told Miss Connor to get in touch with this Fred Searls, who I learned was one of the many able businessmen serving with the War Production Board, and ask if he would come to see me immediately. When we met, I told him that someone whose opinion caused men like Forrestal and Patterson to alter their position was unusual. I asked him if he would feel free to give me the benefit of his independent judgment, regardless of any opinion held by Director Nelson. Searls replied that he was in government service only because our country was at war—he had two sons in the armed forces—and if I believed his judgment to be of any value, it would certainly be expressed without regard to the views of others. Had I known him then as I was to know him later, I would not have asked the question.

I then asked him, in the light of the arguments he had heard, to dictate his ideas of a fair allocation of rubber priorities. He did so, and after discussion I concluded his proposal was wise. A few hours later I reported to the President the differences which the conference had revealed and suggested Searls' solution. The President, who was to leave in an hour for Casablanca, said he would be entirely satisfied with any decision I reached and would stand by whatever I did. However, being first of all a Navy man, as he was wheeled out of his office, he could not resist stopping at the door to say, "But Jimmy, don't forget the Navy."

When I announced the Searls program of priorities for rubber instead of the program originally proposed by Mr. Nelson, it met with general approval, in which Nelson joined. In consequence of this experience, using the power vested in me by the OES executive order, I drafted Fred Searls, who became "an ever present help." Able, loyal and patriotic, he refused to accept any salary or reimbursement for expenses. He saved the taxpayers millions of dollars. As a geologist he had traveled in many lands, and never hesitated to leave his home and his business to travel to distant parts of the world to help solve war problems and later, when I was Secretary of State, to help secure military bases abroad. Except that he is president of the Newmont Mining Corporation, little is known of him; he consistently avoided publicity of any kind.

It was about this time that an unfortunate disagreement developed between Donald M. Nelson, chairman of the War Production Board, who had been a vice president of Sears, Roebuck & Company, and Charles E. Wilson, chairman of the Production Executive Committee of that Board. He had been president of the General Electric Company. This dispute split WPB into two factions and finally reached the stage at which Mr. Wilson presented his resignation to the President. In declining to accept it, Mr. Roosevelt asked me to try to end the quarrel.

My first step was to induce Wilson to withdraw his resignation. He agreed to do this, but by his attitude I felt that he was making only a temporary compromise. An outstanding executive in the business world, he was restive because he felt the authority allowed him was too limited for the accomplishment of his goals. To some extent also his difference with Mr. Nelson arose from an uncertain division of powers. Wilson, in doubt as to how far he could act independently, was convinced that he could do justice neither to the Board nor to himself. He also believed that stories in the press criticizing him had originated with Nelson; this Nelson denied.

Rumors of Wilson's resignation continued to appear in the press, until he gave me a second letter of resignation, asking that I pass it on to the President. Still hoping to avoid losing this capable executive, I asked him and Nelson to come to my office to discuss their problems.

Nelson professed to be surprised to hear of Wilson's decision to resign. He stated that he held Wilson in such high regard that should the resignation be accepted, he would resign and there would be two top positions in WPB to be filled. From Wilson's expression I felt that he doubted the sincerity of Nelson's protestations, but Nelson was earnest and the two men appeared to reach some accord at this meeting. However, I was not surprised when their troubles continued, and grew worse.

Meanwhile, from the Congress there were growing complaints about Nelson. The Truman Committee investigating military expenditures was particularly critical of him, and there was apparently much support for a bill introduced by Senator Pepper in January, 1943, creating a new agency to replace the strife-torn WPB. The President was so disturbed that he told me he felt he must make a change and was considering sending Nelson on a mission abroad and appointing Wilson as his successor.

On February 5 I wrote and handed to the President a letter referring to our talk. I began my letter by saying that much as I admired Wilson's ability, I feared that if he were appointed to head WPB in place of Nelson, the faction associated with the retiring Director would be bitterly resentful. This would be of minor importance in peacetime, but it was vital now to restore harmony in the production field. As an alternative I recommended the appointment of B. M. Baruch, stating the case as follows:

You would be taking no chances. He knows that organization better than anybody in it. For the past year he has spent four or five days each week in Washington, and the heads of the various divisions have taken their problems to him. Without any power he has accomplished miracles in straightening out controversies and in securing the co-operation of manufacturers. Mr. Wilson, Mr. Eberstadt, and every other leader in the organization would welcome the appointment of Baruch.

You and I know his appointment would be welcomed by the Congress. Mr. Hill telephoned me today that the agitation for the Pepper bill was due entirely to their belief that War Production Board was not performing; Truman is of the same opinion. They believe the appointment of a strong man would kill the Pepper bill. When they say "strong man" they do not mention Baruch, but I know they would throw up their hats for his appointment. The press would welcome it. . . .

Last but not least, he is loyal to you. For a year he has worked as hard as if he were on the payroll and had the honor of an appointment from you. You would be appointing not only the best man for the place, but appointing one of your best friends.

The last paragraph was written because I did not understand why the President had failed to use Mr. Baruch in some important war job. When the President read that concluding paragraph, he looked up and said he was very fond of B. M. and expressed respect for his ability. However, as he discussed the suggestion, I saw he feared that Mr. Baruch, if appointed, would make statements to the press about many problems, and President Roosevelt did not want advice —publicly. An argument I presented was that in World War I, Mr. Baruch had proved a good team worker. Finally the President told me to prepare a letter offering B. M. the appointment. To my mind, this meant the solution of the WPB problem, and at the same time it would use the valuable services of my friend.

I returned to my office, where we kept a supply of the President's green letterheads, which he used for his more personal letters, and drafted the letter of appointment. To avoid a leak, it was not dictated to the stenographer who ordinarily took my letters, but was written in the "inner office" with instructions that the copy was to be placed in the locked files. The original and one copy I promptly took to the President. I wanted to have it signed that afternoon, fearing that if the President told Hopkins that night of the proposed change, he might be dissuaded by Hopkins, who Baruch thought was unfriendly to him. Roosevelt signed the letter, and knowing Baruch was in Washington, I took it to his hotel. It made a strong appeal for his services:

For a long time I have been calling upon your assistance in questions affecting our war production. You have given unsparingly of your time and energy and your advice has been exceedingly valuable. I know that you have preferred to serve in an advisory capacity and have been disinclined to accept an appointment that would require you to devote all your time to an administrative position. However, I deem it wise to make a change in the direction of war production and I am coming back to the elder statesman for assistance. I want to appoint you as Chairman of War Production Board with power to direct the activities of the organization.

With your knowledge of the subject and your knowledge of the organization, I am sure you can arrange so that it will not require you to work day and night. I would not want you to do that, but I am confident you will accept because of your willingness to make any sacrifice you believe will aid in the prosecution of the war.

When he read the letter, Mr. Baruch said he was leaving for New York that night and on the following day would let me know whether he could accept the appointment. I was disappointed. For many months he had been telling me of his discussions with Nelson and Wilson about WPB problems that he felt he might solve. Even though the appointment meant assuming responsibility, I thought the opportunity to serve in this important post, which called for his attendance at Cabinet meetings, would please him. However, when he insisted that he could not decide immediately, I did not press him.

The next day B. M. telephoned that he was sick and that his physician had ordered him to bed. He was ill for about a week; when I next saw him after his return to Washington, he told me that he had been to see the President, but that FDR must have changed his mind because he had made no reference to the appointment and Baruch would not mention it first. I suggested that the President's cordial letter called for an answer, but he did not respond. Those were hectic days, and I often was baffled by events, but at no time do I recall an experience more bewildering to me than this incident.

By this time it was evident that for some reason the President did not want to appoint Baruch, and equally apparent that Baruch did not want to assume the responsibility of the office, so it was up to me to find another solution for the WPB difficulties. However, this was not easy and the WPB war continued.

President Roosevelt's forty-eight-hour-week order, to which I have referred, was put into effect immediately by the chairman of the

War Manpower Commission, Paul V. McNutt. He had held this position since early December of the previous year. For some time before his appointment it had been clear that real control had to be exercised over the country's labor force, and that the Selective Service System should also be supervised by the Commission.

The President was loath to delegate powers in this field, and the sweeping reforms which his executive order of December 5, 1942, instituted came only just in time. One of the valuable provisions of the order was that men over thirty-eight would no longer be inducted and that those of that age already in the services might be discharged at their request to take jobs in essential industries or in agriculture, in which, as I have indicated, there was a chronic labor shortage. We now urged county war boards, which were composed mostly of farmers, to seek out suitable registrants between the ages of thirty-eight and forty-five and get them into food—and particularly dairy—production. We also found that over five hundred conscientious objectors could be used in dairy farming; and that among the two million men who had been classified as 4F on account of disability, there were more than six thousand experienced dairy workers. This was an important addition to the working force at the time.

We also received valuable service from the land army of workers brought to the United States from Mexico and from the Bahamas and Jamaica. In the spring of 1943, when plans were being worked out to supervise the recruitment and use of this labor force, it seemed to me that officials of the Department of Agriculture were not moving as quickly as they might. I therefore moved in, telephoning to Mr. Samuel Ze Murray, president of the United Fruit Company, who of course was very familiar with West Indian conditions, asking him to come to Washington. After telling him of our problem, I asked if he could suggest a capable man who would take charge of bringing qualified farm workers to the United States. He said quite simply that he would like to do it himself. When I expressed surprise, he told me that his son had been killed in the Pacific in February, and he wanted to perform this service in his memory. Mr. Ze Murray thereupon took charge, and helped to relieve a critical situation in agriculture, particularly along the Atlantic seaboard. He later did other valuable work for the Agriculture Department.

Early in March, 1943, when we were beginning to make the stabili-

zation machinery work, Sam Rosenman suggested to the President
the formation of a commission, to be known as the "Clearance Committee"—a sort of "super war cabinet" which would consist of B. M.
Baruch, Admiral William D. Leahy, Harry Hopkins, Mr. Rosenman
himself, and me as chairman. Mr. Roosevelt asked for my opinion.
However, he did not seem to have clearly in mind what authority
the group would have or what its exact duties would be. He asked
me to talk it over with Rosenman. After doing so, it seemed to me it
would be just another committee overlapping in scope existing administrative machinery. I therefore wrote the President that any
advantage to be gained from such a group would only come from its
meeting with him for informal discussions:

This has never been tried. If tried, we could determine whether it could
accomplish anything of value. If it were found to be of value, you could then
consider formally creating a committee and publicizing it. This would be far
better than formally creating and publicizing the committee and later finding
that it served no useful purpose. . . .
I think no matter what you called the Committee, the Press and the public
would call it a War Cabinet. They will wonder why Army, Navy, Shipping,
Manpower and Production are not represented.
If the Committee is going to determine policies, they will be asked to
appear before Congressional Committees. . . .
Having stated my views, I want to say with sincerity that if you think
otherwise and ask me to serve on the Committee, I shall do everything in
my power to prove that you were right and that I am wrong in the views
I have expressed.

In his reply of March 9 the President, while accepting the suggestion that we meet informally with him, agreed that the note of
caution I had sounded was justified. The time of meeting was fixed
for each Thursday at eleven o'clock. The group met only about half
a dozen times to consider manpower problems, but without the President's attendance, which may have accounted for the lack of enthusiasm. In any event, as I feared, the move accomplished nothing and
was soon forgotten.

The struggle by groups for selfish advantage still continued, and
by early April I had to induce the President to sign a comprehensive
executive order, which came to be unpopularly known as the "Hold-

the-Line" order. It drastically affected the special interests of many. For example, workers were now prohibited from changing their jobs for higher paying jobs unless the war effort was aided thereby; and there was to be no increase of rates to common carriers and public utilities. Many exemptions previously authorized were abolished, and Price Administration and Food Administration were directed to move to reduce excessively high prices and to authorize no further increases except to the minimum extent the law required. The War Labor Board was to redouble its efforts to conform to the Little Steel formula.

On April 9, the morning after the order was issued, the President received request after request from senators and congressmen, as well as from the leaders of organized labor, who wanted personal conferences with him. He declined to see them, and simply directed Pa Watson, his appointments secretary, to pass them on to me. My whole day was devoted to hearing pleas from former colleagues in Congress who came to protest in behalf of their constituents, and from representatives of the Farm Bureau Federation and the Farmers' Union, as well as from William Green of the A.F. of L. and Philip Murray of the C.I.O.

This was the only time I knew the patient and persuasive Murray to lose his temper and bang on my desk to emphasize his point. The rank and file of the labor organizations looked to their leadership to obtain for them an annual increase in wages or benefits of some kind. In wartime, as the cost of living rose, they were insistent in their demands for more pay. I could only assure Murray that I knew the situation was difficult, but only firm action in September, 1939, could have prevented the present inequities.

The following day he again appeared in my office. In the interval he had insisted on seeing the President, who had told him he must come back to me. It was like this man to preface his remarks by an apology for having lost his temper. He said I must remember that in his world, leadership was attained by fighting every inch of the way; that at the heels of a labor leader there were always ambitious men who to advance themselves would encourage their followers to make unreasonable demands; and that it was in these circumstances that he had developed his aggressiveness.

He then told me of some of his struggles to develop the C.I.O., and said that while he wanted to do all he could to help the President, I should understand his position; some of the members of his organization of steelworkers in Pennsylvania were neighbors of coal miners who boasted that John L. Lewis got what he wanted but that Murray was doing nothing for his men. It was clear to me that Murray feared he would be hurt badly if the miners were exempted in any way from the Hold-the-Line order. On the whole, I cannot describe our meeting as satisfactory, but I felt that I knew him better. Certainly, I liked him better.

In the same Hold-the-Line order the President extended the price ceilings to certain fruits and vegetables not previously covered. Following Murray came my good friend Charles McNary, the Republican leader of the Senate; after congratulating me enthusiastically on the order, he requested me to see representatives of the strawberry growers of Oregon! They would be badly hurt if the order was immediately enforced. They did not want it to apply until after they marketed their berries. He approved the order "in general," but urged that "the Oregon strawberry growers are in a different situation from others." I had to say that there could be no exemption.

I quickly realized that I was the professional "no" man, and was concerned lest having to say no to all the requests of former colleagues would so antagonize them as to destroy my ability to render any service when important legislative matters were pending. And there were many times when I was called on to lend a hand. For instance, soon after this the President told me that the conferees of the Senate and House who were considering a tax bill providing for a withholding levy of 20 per cent were hopelessly deadlocked, and asked me if I would try to bring about an agreement. I immediately saw Congressman Robert Doughton, chairman of the House Ways and Means Committee; and after several talks with him and with Senators George, Walsh, and Bennett Clark, induced them to agree on a compromise of the existing differences, provided the President would approve the bill.

I told the President of the agreement, and said, "Will you authorize me to tell these gentlemen you will approve the compromise?" When he said he would, I said, "Mr. President, I understand from these senators and congressmen that Secretary Morgenthau probably would not favor the compromise." He replied, "Maybe not, but I want it settled. Henry is in New York, and if you can get the agreement by the conferees and have it announced this afternoon while the

Secretary is away, I will be spared a bedroom visit of complaint to-morrow morning."

It was about this time, I think, that Churchill came to Washington to discuss plans for the Normandy invasion. One evening while he was here the President invited me to have dinner with him and the Prime Minister, and we discussed our postwar plans. Among other things I mentioned my hope that gradually we could reduce Federal income taxes and strive to put a limit of 50% upon the amount of income taxes to be taken from a man's earnings. This amount, I said, plus the taxes of state, county and city governments, should be a sufficient "take" from the people, the majority of whom I believed would regard fifty-fifty as a fair division. Churchill wanted to talk further on this subject and asked me to come to his room the next morning. Knowing he would sleep late I waited until the morning was practically gone and telephoned him around twelve o'clock. He asked that I come around. I found him not only unorthodox but un-dressed. Even his zipper suit would have improved his looks. But he was enthusiastic about his hope that after the war he could bring about a reduction of taxes in Britain.

For some months, whenever a strike had threatened, the War Labor Board had been successful in its efforts to bring about a settlement. However, after the firm stand taken in the Hold-the-Line order, several strikes occurred in April. In the case of the plastics workers at the plant of the Celanese Corporation of America, when the President appealed for a return to work, within a few hours the workers were back on the job. The same was not true of the bituminous coal miners, who demanded a new contract which would include a $2-a-day wage increase and provide for an $8-a-day basic wage underground, travel pay and unionization of minor bosses. The operators of the mines con-tended that this would violate the Little Steel formula, since two years previously the miners had received an increase exceeding the per-centage authorized for all workers. By the last week in April, as the deadlock continued, the Labor Board estimated that 150 mines had shut down and 70,000 men were idle. All appeals from the Secretary of Labor were ignored and the secretary of the miners' organization took the position that the Labor Board was "malignant in its preju-dices" against the mine workers.

When things had reached an impasse, the Board reported to the President by letter, which the chairman asked that I deliver on its behalf. After we had discussed the situation, the President addressed a telegram to John L. Lewis and to Thomas Kennedy, secretary of the United Mine Workers. It asked them to resume work immediately while submitting their case to the War Labor Board for final determination. Mr. Roosevelt called attention to the fact that the Labor Board had appointed a panel to hear the case; on it sat Morris L. Cooke, representing the public, Walter White, representing the operators, and David B. Robertson of the Brotherhood of Locomotive Firemen and Enginemen, representing labor. It too had been ignored, and the miners were striking not only against the owners but against the government itself, in time of war. He warned that if work was not resumed by Saturday morning at ten o'clock, he would use all his power to protect the nation's interest.

When the miners failed to respond by the deadline Saturday morning, the President signed an order directing Secretary of the Interior Ickes to take immediate possession of all mines producing coal in which a strike "has occurred or is threatened." My staff prepared a news statement to be issued by the President. In it he repeated his call to the miners to return to work and promised that an examination of their case would be made in the light of the facts disclosed by an investigation of the cost of living which was then being made in the mining areas. Also the government would see that prosecutions were begun in cases where prices had been allowed to exceed those set in the recent executive order. He added that he proposed to talk to the miners of the nation on Sunday evening at ten o'clock.

The rest of the day Ben Cohen, then a member of my staff, and Robert Sherwood gathered material for the President's talk. On Sunday morning, when I read my newspapers I was pleased to see that the strikers were receiving little encouragement from the press. Midday Sunday, Secretary of Interior Ickes talked to me, expressing the opinion that Lewis would not want to challenge the government and that the miners would be ordered back to work. But I still continued to work throughout the afternoon with the President, preparing the address. About half an hour before the time scheduled for him to go on the air, when the speech was completed and mimeographed for distribution, Ickes called me to say that Lewis had agreed to order the miners back within two days. I hurried over to the President's room with the news. The President decided to go ahead with the broadcast and only a few necessary changes were made.

My staff meanwhile had gone home. During the afternoon a newscaster had mentioned over the radio that it was my birthday, and I casually said to someone sitting by me that it was a devil of a way to spend a wedding anniversary and birthday, to say nothing of the Lord's Day! When our work was done I found that the President had sent a car to my hotel to bring Mrs. Byrnes to the White House and had announced to his staff that after he had given the radio speech there would be a party for us.

It was a pleasant occasion. The guests were those who had been working on the broadcast: Grace Tully, Harry Hopkins, Robert Sherwood, and Steve Early. The strike having been called off, the President was in a happy mood. He led in singing "Happy Birthday" and then he and I sang "When I Grow Too Old to Dream." The star of the evening, however, was Robert Sherwood. I can see him now—more than six and a half feet tall and less than 170 pounds—proving his versatility by dancing and imitating even the flapping of wings as he sang "When the Red, Red Robin Comes Bob, Bob, Bobbin' Along."

For several days preceding the President's demand upon the miners, members of Congress had been considering the introduction of antistrike legislation, and Senator Connally had asked me what I thought the President's reaction would be to such a bill. The morning following the radio talk I told Connally, "Last night I spoke to the President about your bill and he said that, having appealed to the miners to return to work today and being informed that Lewis had ordered the men back to work on Tuesday, he did not want to propose the introduction of antistrike legislation or to express an opinion about it." Connally replied that he agreed and thought it wise for the President to "lay off the subject entirely, leaving us to do as we please."

On May 2, the day of the President's broadcast, the mines were in the hands of Secretary Ickes, who supposedly had a two-week truce period to work out a new contract with Lewis. The position of the War Labor Board, which I endorsed, was that the miners' demands for increased wages should be treated like those of all other employees, but Lewis' actions after the seizure made it plain that he had no intention of adhering to this policy. At first, Ickes was hopeful that he would be able to bring about a settlement that did not violate the stabilization regulations. However, he found that the miners stood by their traditional position—no contract, no work—and that the contract must include increased wages and portal-to-portal pay. Increased pay without increased production is inflationary.

Miss Perkins, too, talked to Lewis in the hope she could bring about a solution. Of course, like Ickes, but unlike me, she did not have the responsibility of trying to hold the line on wages without making exemptions for particular groups. One day, after a strenuous conference on the subject, I went down the hall to my office, thinking she had gone in the other direction. As I went through my secretary's office, she asked how things went. Being tired and a little edgy, I said, "Fannie Perkins has ants in her pants." Miss Connor's expression betrayed her discomfort, and I turned to look with dismay into the face of the Secretary of Labor. In my embarrassment I stepped aside and with a bow motioned her into my office, all the while groping desperately for some phrase to help me appear nonchalant. Of course, there was no explanation or excuse to fit the occasion and I feared my apology would not lessen the offense. But, bless her heart, Fannie appeared to enjoy my confusion!

This is not the place to detail the record of the long months until November, when Ickes met Lewis and agreed on a contract that gave the miners an increase but something less than Lewis demanded. People may criticize Lewis' methods, but they will not question his unusual talents. During this period official and unofficial strikes continued, including four general walkouts, at times involving over half a million coal workers; steel output was lowered, unrest over wages demands spread to rubber and engineering plants, and Congress enacted the Smith-Connally Anti-Strike Act.

The Ickes-Lewis agreement of November did not end the coal troubles, which continued until well into 1944. Nor was it any easier to deal with the owners, who feared that continued operation of the industry by the government constituted a threat to their properties. They complained repeatedly to President Roosevelt, who would refer to me the questions raised. I wrote to them once that "the government desires to return the mines to their owners as soon as this can be done without increasing the risk of interrupting mine operation," and assured them that the mines had not been taken over, as they alleged, to punish the operators! But I realized that in the complex situation then existing, this assurance would give them little satisfaction.

In what I write about the coal strikes, the railroad strikes, and other controversies, it must be remembered that I am not writing a detailed history of these controversies. Nor am I attempting to set forth the viewpoints of all the disputants. I am only recording what I saw from my post and my participation in these events.

Our troubles over coal were only off to a good start when Prime Minister Churchill arrived in Washington on May 11, 1943, to hold his fifth wartime conference with the President. Plans for future offensives were much in the air, which meant that Roosevelt would be continuously and increasingly preoccupied with military and foreign affairs. It was also plain to what degree the success of their plans would depend on the effective use of our total productive capacity. In short, the subject of war mobilization was still one for extensive debate, and there was much support in the Congress for the creation of an Office of War Mobilization. To this end the Toland-Kilgore-Pepper bill had already been introduced in the House.

This would have set up a new administrative agency with formal control over the work of some fourteen existing agencies. It would create, I felt, an office that was cumbersome in its structure and over-formalized in its executive procedures, which would prevent the Director from using the degree of initiative and adaptability that my experience in OES had demonstrated was essential to any office of the sort. It was therefore clear to me that if an OWM was to be established —and I thought this advisable—it should be done by executive order, and should represent a delegation of presidential powers that would invest it with an unquestioned status in the making of policy. I felt that this was the moment to approach the President on the question.

At the same time my wholehearted endeavors to make stabilization work were beginning, in my view, to impair my usefulness as the President's assistant in other vital matters on the home front. In a letter that I wrote to the President on May 14, I began by saying that "Theoretically the Stabilization Office is limited to a determination of policies and to the determination of wages and prices when such matters are in controversy." In practice, however, I went on, the Director had been forced not only to keep in touch with department officials in deciding working methods of rationing, price fixing and the like, but in some instances to take the initiative in making effective arrangements to carry out stabilization policies. Our original thought, I pointed out, was that the director should sit as sort of an appellate court, reaching his decisions on the basis of memoranda submitted to him by the administrative agencies. This course was not possible in practice.

Senators and congressmen with whom I had been associated for years understandably insisted on seeing me in person, as did the labor leaders. "In each case these people," I wrote, "have a natural desire for an opportunity to present their case to the official having the final decision," and my refusals to accommodate them were liable to impair good relations between the President and them. I continued: "I have presented to me daily by the departments and by members of Congress matters of far greater importance to you than the price of potatoes and beans. I feel that I can render you a greater service by trying to assist in such matters. The effort to do these things and then hear the claimants for increased wages and prices is an impossible task." This led to my conclusion:

I am convinced that you should appoint as Stabilization Director some person who would have no other duties, whose relations with the Congress are not such as to demand so much of his time, and whose relations with you are not such as to have you held responsible for his decisions. If the Director had his office in the Federal Reserve Building and was not helping with the coal strike and other problems forced on the White House, the public would not hold you any more responsible for his decisions than the decisions of the heads of other agencies. It would disassociate from the White House the official whose duty it is to constantly say "no" to farmers, wage earners, and the people generally.

After receiving my letter, the President telephoned inviting me to lunch with him Monday; he told me that hitherto he had had no idea of the problems of my office and that my story had spoiled his weekend. We discussed these problems fully on Monday, and I also presented my ideas on the need to create an Office of War Mobilization.

He asked that an order be prepared incorporating my ideas. Ben Cohen and Donald Russell worked with Wayne Coy of the Budget Bureau and drafted the proposed executive order, after which it was submitted to the President on May 22. In my brief submission memorandum I mentioned that the title used to describe the office was that proposed in Senator Kilgore's bill and had also been suggested by the Toland House committee. The order was duly signed and released on May 27.

I suggested as my successor in OES Judge Fred M. Vinson. The

President liked the suggestion and immediately asked that I try to reach him by telephone. Vinson was then on the U.S. Court of Appeals for the District of Columbia. When we were connected, I told him of my own new duties and stated that the President had authorized me to say that he wanted Fred Vinson as Stabilization Director. Without hesitation he said, "If you could resign from the Supreme Court, there is no reason why I should not leave the Court of Appeals." Having known Fred for fifteen years, I was not surprised. When I told the President of his answer, he telephoned Vinson expressing his appreciation.

The appointment was well received, particularly by his old colleagues in the House, where he had served for over twelve years. It took him but a few days to clear up his affairs at the court, and to set up his office in the Federal Reserve Bank Building. For me this was a very pleasant arrangement since our close friendship, dating from my congresisonal days, was renewed, and almost every afternoon Vinson came to the White House to discuss our mutual problems.

# 12 "ASSISTANT PRESIDENT"

The order establishing the Office of War Mobilization and appointing me Director, couched deliberately in general terms, conferred on me greater authority than a President had ever previously delegated, and a new range of duties. Essentially, it gave me, under the President, power to originate policies and lay out programs that would co-ordinate the work of all the war agencies and federal departments in any way connected with the production, procurement, transportation and distribution of both civilian and military supplies; moreover, it gave me the power to see that these decisions were carried out.

As I began, from the same desk and office, to tackle the tasks of this mobilization program, I was convinced that it was even more important than before that my decisions should carry full presidential support, and be final. To this end, I instructed my staff not to go to other offices for consultation, telling them that problems from operating agencies must be brought to us. Nor did I enlarge my staff. This now consisted of Ben Cohen, our legal adviser; Fred Searls, whose qualifications I have previously described; Donald Russell, assistant to the Director; Walter Brown, who handled research and press relations; and Sam Lubell, research assistant. Miss Cassie Connor, administrative assistant and confidential secretary, completed our permanent team; all other assistants were procured for special tasks on a part-time basis. The modest size of our staff and quarters effectively demonstrated our resolve not to compete with other agencies.

One of the goals of the War Mobilizer in his efforts to "develop unified programs" was to "eliminate interdepartmental friction." Here the device of an advisory committee, provided for in the President's order, had its uses. Consisting at the outset of Secretaries Stimson and Knox, Fred Vinson of OES, Donald Nelson of WPB, and Harry Hopkins, who bore the title of chairman of the Munitions Assignments Board (later Marvin Jones, the Food Administrator, was to join us), it was a clearing house for controversial issues and a forum for ideas. President Roosevelt presided over several of our meetings, which at first were fairly frequent but after a while were discontinued.

My first act of a long-range nature was to call on all agencies engaged in the war effort to review their procurement programs realistically and objectively. I first asked Secretary Stimson to set up a review board in the War Department at General Staff level, and persuaded Colonel Frederick Pope of the American Cyanamid Company to act as my personal representative on it. Within a day or so similar requests went out to the Navy, to the War Shipping Commission, and to other leading agencies, including Lend Lease.

The crux of this matter lay in the response of the services. I wanted them to co-operate from the outset and was prepared for the brief flurries of dissatisfaction that occurred at first. For example, I had persuaded the distinguished naval architect, William Francis Gibbs, who is known as the designer not only of some of our finest combat ships but of our largest and most luxurious liner, the *United States,* to represent OWM on the naval procurement review board. Some of the admirals took the position that this would involve revealing maritime secrets to an unauthorized person, an attitude shared to some extent in their turn by the Army authorities. But when I proposed to submit the issue to the Chief Executive, the opposition was withdrawn and other agencies fell into line behind the services. In this work I enlisted the services of Franz Schneider of the Newmont Mining Corporation, who had worked extensively with the problems of war shipping, to represent us on that review commission. Later, when manpower problems grew particularly pressing, I was able to induce B. M. Baruch to join us as my representative on the War Manpower Commission. No one of this "all-star team" would accept compensation.

At my request, the President also arranged for the establishment within the Joint Chiefs of Staff organization of a Joint Production Survey Committee. This was to advise the Joint Chiefs on changes in procurement programs in the light of war developments and changing military strategy. This particular committee consisted entirely of military personnel, accountable only to the Joint Chiefs. However, my representative, Fred Searls, attended its meetings and followed its work closely. At the request of the Joint Chiefs, I attended a number of their luncheon meetings and I may add that I experienced none of the lack of co-operation about which I had previously heard complaints.

During the period this review work was underway, I met almost daily with the men designated to represent me on the special committees which the agencies had set up. It was characteristic of my organization that politics was never discussed, and it was many weeks before I learned that three of the seven were registered Republicans and a fourth called himself an independent Republican. That the work they undertook was essential can be shown by an extract from a helpful letter I received from John M. Carmody, one of the Maritime Commissioners, who wrote on July 5 endorsing our program: ". . . we take less than ten minutes to approve contracts for nearly a billion dollars for slow ships, for delivery starting January, 1944, and ending December, 1944. I think it is high time an objective review of our program is made along the lines of your letter . . . it is inevitable in so extraordinary a war that programs get out of balance . . . this review of our program and the total war supply program . . . will save billions of dollars and contribute greatly to production and manpower and price stabilization."

These activities increased my already high regard for the Under Secretaries of War and Navy, Bob Patterson and Jim Forrestal. Never have I known two more competent or unselfish men in public life. I have a letter from Forrestal, voluntarily written to OWM some two months after our review had begun, stating that in his department the total value of deliberate cutbacks which had not been compensated for by increasing other programs, amounted on that date to $2,855,-470,000.

Similarly on November 15 Under Secretary Patterson reported that the total Army reductions during the previous eight months—the life of OWM—totaled approximately $7 billion. Not only did these downward revisions save dollars but, more important in wartime, they helped us to avoid nonessential construction and diverted manpower and material into needed channels. Forrestal suggested to me as the war progressed that we should continue to press for re-examination of building programs, so that "we would not be putting materials, men and money into vessels and equipment that we shall not use."

This became something of an issue over a year later when Forrestal, who had been Secretary of the Navy since May, 1944, was asked by Admiral King to secure the President's approval of an additional construction program of eighty-four combat ships. I learned that the day after the request was made, President Roosevelt authorized his naval aide to inform Forrestal that he had not had time for detailed study of the recommendation, "but said you could inform the Budget Bureau that he favored the construction and authorizes you to take it up with the Budget."

It was true that as a result of our sudden reverses in the last German offensive, the Battle of the Bulge, there did exist at the time of King's request considerable doubt whether the war would end as early as had been hoped. But Harold Smith, the Budget Director, told the President that he thought the construction program entirely superfluous. Mr. Roosevelt rejected this advice. After Smith told me about it, I asked Fred Searls to write an analysis of the Navy's proposal. This convinced me of the soundness of Smith's opposition and I took it to the President with a request that he hold matters up pending a more detailed study.

I then got in touch immediately with Jim Forrestal. It seemed to me, I told him, that the tonnage planned might be of some value in the war against Japan, should that conflict last through 1947, but I doubted that it would be essential. I also approached Admiral King, who told me that he had submitted a detailed program only to show what would have to be done in case further ship construction should be decided upon.

Then Forrestal, with the frankness he always displayed, said that the real author of the eightly-four-combat-ship construction was Carl Vinson, chairman of the House Naval Affairs Committee. Vinson is one of the ablest members of the House of Representatives, and has specialized in naval affairs throughout his long service. His only weakness, if it is one, is his unbounded devotion to the Navy. He seemed to have yielded, in this instance, to the pressures brought by congressmen interested in the country's navy yards. Vinson had fought so hard for the Navy during its lean years that Forrestal, while conceding that the program was perhaps not essential, wanted a good explanation to give him. I therefore wrote the President:

When the Budget first protested against the program your statement was, "I am inclined to agree with the Navy." You did not make a positive decision.

In view of the expenditure of manpower and material at this time; the fact that many of the ships will not be completed until the end of 1947; that it will require some months to put them in commission; and of the number of enlisted men required to man these ships, I hope you will advise the Secretary that the program should be canceled.

Of course, I did not fail to let the President know the background facts, and the next day he decided against the program. Forrestal then proposed a compromise providing for construction of twelve vessels of a different type and more urgently needed. This was approved, with a saving of approximately one and a half billion dollars. Further, when Vinson was invited to see me and we reviewed the situation amicably together, Carl was entirely satisfied.

Though the President had been ill for some days, when I told him that we should discuss the Navy's procurement review program, he asked that I come to his private sitting room. I was not hesitant about bringing up this subject, even when he was confined to his room, because he was always willing to be interrupted by matters affecting the Navy. His occupation when I arrived wonderfully illustrates his methods—in the absence of his secretary. Seated on the divan with him was his cousin, Miss Margaret Suckley. Between them was a pile of papers that had been sent up from his office during his illness. On the floor there were four separate piles of papers.

I said, "What are you doing?"

The President said, "I am sorting these documents and letters according to my idea of their importance." That pile (pointing) I call A, which means *very* important. The next pile is B, which is important; C means not so urgent; and D—that last pile—somebody else can attend to."

When I expressed wonderment at the simplicity of his system, he said that if the people in his office would let his papers alone, he would always know what was in each stack of papers, but someone was always insisting on his being more orderly.

The procurement review program was satisfactorily under way by the summer of 1943, but we were still beset with troubles over manpower and strikes.

One day when we were discussing the strike problem, the President asked me whether I thought it would be helpful if he should appoint some man as Secretary of Labor. He had real affection for Miss

Perkins, as I did, but he never lost sight of political values; in this case he was looking ahead, he said, to the effect continued labor troubles might have on the next election. He was vulnerable. Having fought for several years for the power to merge independent agencies in the established departments of the government, within two years he had established one independent agency, the Manpower Commission, to handle manpower problems, and another, the War Labor Board, to handle wages and salaries. Both should have been in the Department of Labor. There was considerable talk that if this policy was continued, the Labor Department would find itself doing nothing but collecting statistics.

I told the President that Miss Perkins was doing as good a job as could be done by any woman, but that her job was one for a tough, two-fisted man at any time, and now it was almost impossible. He said he had long been holding a letter of resignation from Miss Perkins, which she had insisted he was to accept whenever he wished to. He added, "With her, it is no mere gesture. Fannie Perkins means what she says." I said that doubtless the appointment of a man would help at this particular time, and he said, "All right, Jimmy, you get the man." I was stumped for a few moments and then thought of a former official of the A.F. of L. who at the time was a consultant in the War Department. The President knew him but thought he would not be a wise choice, since a man from either one of the great labor organizations would offend the other group. I left promising to think about it.

The next day I went back with an idea: appoint Miss Perkins head of a bureau having jurisdiction over education, relief programs, health and the Children's Bureau; transfer Ickes to the Department of Labor, placing War Manpower duties in that department; and make McNutt Secretary of the Interior. Presenting my idea, I said, "Harold Ickes is a good administrator, a liberal, friendly to organized labor, and tough enough to call himself America's Number One Curmudgeon. McNutt is likewise a good administrator and he knows the West" (which always seemed to me a requirement for the Interior Department). "Miss Perkins would be happy in the field assigned to her and she has had years of experience as a department administrator."

The President said, "Jimmie, that sounds like Tinker to Evers to Chance," referring to the three infielders of the Chicago Cubs who had become famous for their double plays. He liked the plan so much I felt it would be approved—but that was late Friday afternoon. I did not know with whom he discussed it, but Monday morning he told me he had changed his mind. Then I learned that on Sunday afternoon Philip Murray had been to the White House. Whether the President sent for Phil or someone with whom FDR talked told Murray of the plan, and thus sent him hurrying to the President, I still do not know. In any event, the attempted double play didn't work and Perkins, McNutt and Ickes held their bases.

In the summer of 1943 every day was exciting and frequently anything but pleasant. There was, for example, the feud involving Vice President Wallace, who had become head of the Board of Economic Warfare, and Jesse Jones, chairman of the Reconstruction Finance Corporation. One or another of the many corporations under the control of Jones' RFC was in constant conflict with Wallace's agency, and because of the prominence of both men their chronic and acrimonious differences brought the administration much unfavorable publicity. For a long time I hoped that they would declare an armistice, but the enmity existing between their assistants made it impossible.

On June 29, 1943, Wallace sent to the Senate Appropriations Committee a statement alleging that Jones had blocked certain Economic Warfare contracts. Charging his colleague with "harmful misrepresentation," he followed up with such phrases as "obstructionist tactics" and "hamstringing bureaucracy." Jones volleyed back that the Vice President was "full of malice and misstatements" and called for a congressional investigation. It was under these circumstances that the two men met, by invitation, in my office the afternoon of June 30. Before the hour of the meeting my secretary reported that a large group of newspaper reporters had gathered at the closed gates of the East Wing entrance to the White House grounds, there to await their prey.

It was evident that one of the principals had let leak news of the meeting, and since each knew that he would meet a barrage of questions upon leaving, I felt there was little chance of accomplishing a reconciliation. Wallace arrived first. When Jones entered the room Wallace greeted him politely, but Jones, apparently to avoid shaking hands with him, simply took a seat without even approaching me with his usual friendly gesture. Wallace was cool but Jones was hot, and I feared he might physically attack the V.P. We talked for an hour but made no progress. In fact, within an hour after they had left, Wallace issued another statement to the press containing further charges. Soon over our news wires a counterstatement came in from Jones, calling it a "dastardly attack."

I hope I shall not be charged with having been unduly pessimistic when I wrote next day to the President:

I am satisfied that there is no way of reconciling the differences between Mr. Wallace and Mr. Jones. Since last December there have been several times when I believed that they had settled their differences. They lived in peace but for a short time.

Last night in my office they agreed that under the arrangement that now exists they could get along if both organizations really tried to do so. The statements issued by them shortly afterward only confirmed the opinion that the present arrangement cannot continue.

I suggested to the President that he act immediately, withdrawing authority from both Wallace and Jones and creating a new organization that would unify the policies and functions of the several agencies concerned with foreign economic affairs. It might be called the Office of Economic Warfare and would replace the Board, which would be abolished. As director of the agency, I recommended Leo T. Crowley. Under this sweeping reorganization his office would also perform the duties of certain subsidiary corporations of the RFC, the U.S. Commercial Corporation, the Rubber Development Corporation, and the Export-Import Bank. After some discussion the President agreed, and on July 15 he issued the necessary executive order.

At Mr. Roosevelt's request I also prepared a letter for him to send to both Wallace and Jones. In it he said: "I am sure the unfortunate controversy and acrimonious public debate which has been carried on between you in the public press concerning the administration of foreign economic matters, make it necessary in the public interest to transfer these matters to other hands. . . . I am sure that the American people understand that both of you have attempted to do your duty as you have seen it; but we must go forward without any further public debate as to matters which are now academic so far as winning the war is presently concerned."

At the same time, in the hope of ending what was called by some the "Washington War," I prepared for the President's signature another letter, addressed to the heads of all agencies and departments of government:

I realize the nervous strain under which government officials are working in war time but I cannot overlook any further violations of my instructions. . . . If when you have a disagreement with another agency as to fact or policy, instead of submitting it to me or submitting it to the Director of War Mobilization for settlement under the terms of the Order creating that office, you feel you should submit it to the press, I ask that when you release the statement for publication you send to me a letter of resignation.

The last week in July, 1943, the President told me he was tired and was going to take his staff on a fishing trip for a week. He said he knew I had been having a hard time settling feuds and "holding the line"— and he wanted me to try a fishing line. I thought it a mistake for both of us to be away even if it was midsummer, but the President said he would be in touch with the White House—and, well, fishing is one temptation I find it hard to resist. The party included his secretaries, Grace Tully and Dorothy Brady, as well as Pa Watson, Steve Early, Ross McIntire, Admiral Leahy and Admiral Brown.

I think the Canadian Minister had sold the President on going to Manitoulin Island in Georgian Bay with his report of fine bass fishing. The President's two private cars were shifted to a sidetrack close to the water's edge. It was a very secluded spot. There were two fishing boats with competent guides. The first day Grace went with the President and me, and Dorothy went with the other group. It was the first time I ever saw the President enjoy real fishing. On week end trips on the Potomac the naval officers in charge of his boat never took the trouble to locate the fishing drops in advance. These Canadian guides knew their business and we had good fishing. The second day the ladies declined to go, saying that they believed the men might have still better luck without them, and that they were going to drive around the countryside instead.

We organized a pool, to which every fisherman contributed a dollar. At the end of the day the money was divided between the man who caught most fish and the one who caught the largest. Reaching a decision on the biggest fish provoked much argument.

The zest with which FDR went at whatever he did, from negotiating with Stalin to working on his stamps, and the enjoyment he was able to draw from whatever pleasure the moment turned up were surely God-given qualities, and just as certainly enabled him to carry the enormous burdens of the Presidency.

I recall, for example, the first of the several week ends my wife and I spent with him at Shangri-la, his retreat in the Catoctin Hills of Maryland. The camp consisted of several small cabins for his staff and a larger one for himself and his guests; it was part of what had once been a summer camp for young people and was now a training center for General William ("Wild Bill") Donovan's OSS boys. Before this trip, the President said, he and Mrs. Roosevelt had spent only one day there, and had had a picnic lunch. On this occasion, however, he had sent ahead the Filipino mess boys from the presidential yacht, who took with them not only food but a number of prints and pictures to be hung in the house. After lunch, while we were out walking, the President got in his wheel chair and with the help of his valet put up his pictures and prints—the President himself meticulously selecting the exact spot where he wanted each picture placed. The next morning he slept late and after breakfast, with Fala sitting by his chair on the porch where he had a beautiful view of the valley, he spent two hours working absorbedly on his stamp collection.

I think it was on this trip that General Donovan, Director of the Office of Strategic Services, was also a guest. During the course of the week end he took Mrs. Byrnes and me over to see his training camp, which was under the direction of a remarkable character, a former Police Chief of Shanghai. When we arrived, the Chief had his men running along a narrow board about fifty feet from the ground; it was supposed to represent a housetop. If they slipped, they fell into a net. After watching this and similar stunts, we went into a house where, accompanied by one of the recruits, we walked through a hall about four feet wide and dark as melted midnight. Suddenly the floor beneath us dropped about six or eight inches and in a split second there appeared ahead of us the figure of Togo. While off balance the recruit fired from the hip, hitting the papier-mâché Togo in the head. Then in short order Hitler appeared and was got rid of the same way, and the recruit earned a rating for good marksmanship. It was circus stuff; as we followed through the performance, I concluded the recruits should come from Ringling's Big Top. The President had not been able to accompany us, but I knew this was something that would appeal to his love of adventure, so we took the Police Chief back to the house to meet the President, who was vastly entertained by his repertoire of stunts and stories, and by his assortment of trick weapons.

On week-end trips on the Potomac or to Shangri-la, the President always took along papers requiring his attention, but, as I have said, he would find time to relax. He liked to sing and had a good baritone. One week end when we had sung, for the second or third time, his favorite "Home on the Range" and all the World War I songs we knew, such as "There's a Long, Long Trail," like most people of 1917-1919 vintage we began to deplore the fact that no catchy songs had been written during the current war.

Shortly after this, the President said he wanted me to go with him to the National Theater, where a show was to be staged by men of the armed forces; he understood it would feature a new war song by Irving Berlin.

We entered the theater through a side door after the lights were out and went to a box where the President was carefully screened and carefully protected by Secret Service men. The boys put on a good show and we heard for the first time "This Is the Army, Mr. Jones." It was a good marching song, but we did not thereafter try to sing it.

We left before the show ended, and the presence of the Commander in Chief was known to very few until after he was back in the White House.

Upon our return from the Canadian fishing trip we found that the President's action in the Wallace-Jones disagreement had not ended the "Washington War." It was only a short time before the long-smoldering differences in the State Department came to a head. It was known around Washington that relations between Cordell Hull and his Under Secretary of State, Sumner Welles, had gone beyond mere disagreement on policy matters. There was no longer any cordiality between them and they only spoke to each other when departmental matters made it necessary. Their offices joined, which added to the unpleasantness.

One afternoon the President called me to his office and said that Hull was insisting upon Welles' removal because another "element" had come into the picture critical of Welles, which had been mentioned in some newspaper columns. This was not my first knowledge of the quarrel, because for some weeks Hull had been calling me at intervals, begging that I talk to the President about his troubles. I knew the President had unusual respect and affection for Hull, but I knew, too, that he had known Welles since his boyhood and respected his ability. I hesitated to become involved with the President and his two friends. Therefore, after he set forth all the facts, I told him that he alone could make this decision; but I did suggest that if he acceded to Hull's demand, certainly he should send Welles on some mission abroad, as he had done in another case.

Within a day or two Averell Harriman came over to my office to tell me how strongly Hull felt. Harriman had barely left the room when Hull called again, and this time he was even more urgent. I took shorthand notes of what he had to say and passed those notes on to the President in a memorandum which began, "Harriman has talked to me and since Averell left, Hull has telephoned!" The memorandum left no doubt that Hull was going to continue to insist upon some action.

When the President told me he had decided to go along with Hull and wanted a suggestion, I realized that this vacancy in the State Department would make possible a remedy for a bad situation abroad. For some time I had been overwhelmed with complaints from the armed forces and the State Department representatives overseas about the confusion in the duplication of our economic activities there. A conference with the heads of interested agencies accomplished nothing. The only remedy seemed to be the merging of all agencies engaged in foreign economics into one agency to be known as the Foreign Economic Administration.

My idea I set out in a memorandum, suggesting that he appoint as Under Secretary of State Edward R. Stettinius, who had been directing Lend Lease; appoint Leo Crowley, who was Director of Economic Warfare, to be the Director of the new agency, knowing that Hull and Crowley would work together well; and make Herbert Lehman, who was handling Foreign Relief and Rehabilitation Operations, "a special assistant to you with directions to organize immediately the United Nations Relief Administration, which is due to meet on November 9. That is what you originally had in mind he should do." This I pointed out would create a single agency and put an end to the intolerable situation abroad, where several agencies were competing to lend, lease or give away something.

I never knew whether the President offered the assignment abroad to Welles. I do know that, two days after my memorandum to him, the President acted, signing an executive order merging these agencies, and announcing the resignation of Mr. Welles, the appointment of Stettinius and the new appointments for Crowley and Lehman.

Characteristically, the President, disliking to give a friend bad news, turned to me when he had signed the order and approved the press release and said, "Now, Jimmie, I am doing this with the understanding you will personally explain it to Herbert." Again I had to be the bearer of unwelcome tidings, but Governor Lehman, who had a deep affection for FDR, readily appreciated the necessity for his transfer and so my task on this occasion was not a difficult one.

No less serious than the coal strikes was the worsening railroad situation. The heads of the railroad brotherhoods, in common with other labor leaders, had entered into the "no-strike" agreement for the duration. Nevertheless, in the fall of 1943 we were faced with a general stoppage of railroad service unless their demands for wage increases were met. Historically the railway leaders regarded their situation as entirely apart from all other workers. There was a statute providing for a mediation board to decide their disputes with the carriers, and some of them had the notion that the stabilization law did not apply to them.

It is true that the railwaymen, like some others, deserved some sympathy when they saw other employees in essential war industries working overtime and receiving additional pay. They compared their lot with these fortunate workers, not with that of the men at the front, and felt sorry for themselves. At the same time my successor in OES, Judge Vinson, after a full examination of their case, held that the maximum allowable wage increase under the Little Steel formula was four cents an hour.

The result was a protest to the President in late October, demanding that he use his discretion to make, on their behalf, wage adjustments "to aid in the effective prosecution of the war or to correct gross inequities." A vote to strike was taken, but action was temporarily deferred until the leadership could make personal application to the President. They had become accustomed to President Roosevelt's acting as arbiter of their wage disputes.

However, Mr. Roosevelt was en route to Teheran via Cairo for his first conference with Stalin and Churchill; in his absence the leaders of the nonoperating employees got Senator Truman to introduce a bill to require the carriers to pay the increases they wanted. Judge Vinson submitted to the Senate a statement of his reasons for declining to approve increases of over four cents an hour, and

Senator Josiah Bailey of North Carolina made a courageous speech citing the danger of the Congress enacting a law to fix the wages of employees of railway companies or of any industry. If wages could be raised by act of Congress, he said, they could also be reduced by the same body. But the power of the railway organizations was never better demonstrated than when the vote was taken: only five senators voted against the measure—Byrd of Virginia, Bailey of North Carolina, Ellender of Louisiana, and Vandenberg and Ferguson of Michigan. The bill went to the House.

As the anniversary of Pearl Harbor was at hand, I used the occasion for a radio appeal, saying in part: "*No* group has a right to hold a political pistol at the head of Congress or of any administrative agency and say they will strike. Any group which threatens to strike in wartime unless the executive or legislative branch of the government meets its demands is using a political pistol. The government must say to any such group, Lay that pistol down."

The words of a song that was very popular at that time, but is probably forgotten today, "Pistol packin' mama, lay that pistol down," had inspired my phrase, and one of my friends among the railway employee leaders told me that reference had hurt them more than any of the serious arguments in my speech.

Throughout much of our history the Senate has been rightly regarded as more conservative than the House; but since the adoption of the Sixteenth Amendment to the Constitution, providing for the direct election of senators, careful observers have noted gradual lessening of conservative thinking in the Senate. In this case the Senate passed almost unanimously a bill that the House committee would not seriously consider. The House recognized the evil precedent it would establish, pointed out it would substitute political bargaining for collective bargaining, and pigeonholed it. Some leaders of the railway employees also saw the dangers to collective bargaining and did not press it. The subserviency of the Senate in this matter evidently caused them to fear their own power.

On the day the President returned from Teheran a delegation asked him to see representatives of employees and employers. Before he received them, Judge Vinson and I submitted a memorandum to him, making it clear that the crux of the matter was whether the yardstick to measure wage increases of railway employees should be different from that applied to all other occupations.

At the request of the President, Vinson and I were present when the representatives of the employees and carriers arrived. To my surprise, the President criticized the employees for threatening to strike. He made a stirring statement, picturing our soldiers whom he had just seen on the battlefields of Europe, and stressing the effect of strikes and threats of strikes on the morale of these men. He was disappointed to find these employees fighting for increased pay while millions of other men were fighting for their country. He then asked the disputants to go into the Cabinet room and adjust their differences within the stabilization law. There was no settlement. The next day negotiations were resumed in my conference room in the East Wing, but they were not successful either.

The President then asked the representatives of the employees and the carriers whether they would agree to his arbitrating the issues. The carriers agreed, but the representatives of the employees stated that they could not. On Christmas Eve, Al Whitney, president of the Brotherhood of Railway Trainmen, and Al Johnston, president of the Brotherhood of Locomotive Enginemen, informed me that, regardless of the position of others, they were calling off the strike as far as their two organizations were concerned and agreeing to let the President arbitrate. In a letter to me, Whitney paid tribute to the President as a friend of labor and said: "I feel I would be an ingrate and unpatriotic were I to doubt his integrity in this crisis and decline to permit him as Commander in Chief of our Armed Forces to arbitrate the differences existing between the railroads and the employees that I represent." To his credit, Al Johnston took a similar position. At five o'clock on Christmas Eve the strike order for those two unions was rescinded, but the other organizations left theirs in force until the following Thursday.

As we approached the deadline, I asked Secretary of War Stimson to come to my office. He brought with him General Somervell, commanding the Army Service Forces of the War Department. We prepared and the President signed an executive order directing the Secretary of War to take over the railroads that night at seven o'clock. The press release, prepared in my office, quoted the President as saying: "I cannot wait until the last moment to take action to see that the supplies to our fighting men are not interrupted. . . . If any employees of the railroads now strike, they will be striking against the government of the United States."

While Secretary Stimson was in my office, he agreed to commission in the Army, for the operation of the railroads, the president of the Pennsylvania Railroad, M. W. Clement; Ernest Norris, president of the Southern Railway; and the two leaders of the brotherhoods who had co-operated in rescinding their strike orders, Al Whitney and Al Johnston.

The effect of these railroad difficulties was to be seen in the usually calm General Marshall, our Chief of Staff, with whom I talked on New Year's Eve. He said he was sleepless with worry and that the strike had dashed his hopes that there would be a collapse in the Balkans which might have encouraged us to break through into that area. He said German propaganda experts were telling the captive states that we were having so much internal strife that the Army was having to take over the railroads, and that our condition was such that we were nearing internal collapse and would soon ask for a negotiated peace.

He was so disturbed, he said, that he had debated whether or not it was his duty to go on the radio, give his opinion and then resign. As one who felt as keenly as he did the necessity of getting supplies to our fighting front and like him knew of our battle needs, I shared his frustration and dismay. The story of his near resignation, in a modified form, leaked from the War Department early in January.

By January 18 we were advised that the Carriers Conference Committee and the organizations of firemen, conductors and switchmen had at last reached an agreement, ratifying a graduated scale increase as recommended by the Special Emergency Board and acceptable to Judge Vinson, the Stabilization Director. An agreement was also reached by the nonoperating brotherhoods which was approved by Vinson. When this took place Secretary Stimson returned the roads to the owners.

The coal and rail strikes during World War II brought home to me how completely our government is at the mercy of the leadership of key unions. It is impossible for our nation to wage a global conflict without coal and without a sure means of freight transportation. Even at the outset of the atomic age, when new sources of power and means of transportation threaten the old, it will be a long time before this situation alters materially. In peacetime, Congress will hesitate to pass legislation making it possible to conscript labor, should war come. Yet our experience showed plainly how far, in the absence of such a law, the United States government had to go to meet the demands of these powerful organizations and how we had to rely on the reasonableness of the individuals who directed their affairs. Nor is it easy to see how the government can ever enforce wage controls effectively against other workers while admitting its impotence to deal with the vital areas of coal mining and transportation.

While these strikes were keeping me busy during the fall months, President Roosevelt was abroad having his own problems in an entirely different field.

His journey to Teheran had been preceded by preliminary meetings with Churchill and Chiang-Kai-shek outside Cairo. The first of these sessions took place on November 23, 1943. The Chinese leader had been pleading for an offensive which would break the Japanese encirclement of China. He wanted a strong campaign in Burma with an amphibious attack against the Andaman Islands, to be called Operation Buccaneer. Roosevelt promised assistance, much to the dismay of Churchill, who feared that the drain on the supply of landing and tank-landing craft would hamper operations in Italy, and might seriously hurt the proposed invasion of the French mainland planned for May, 1944.

President Roosevelt and the United States Chiefs of Staff were also absorbed in the question of who would command the Normandy operation and whether there should be appointed a Supreme Commander over all the allied forces against Germany, both in the Mediterranean and northern European areas. Some of these preoccupations are reflected in the President's letter of November 23, 1943, written after the preliminary meeting at Cairo. (See following page.)

On the same day this letter was written I received the following secret message from the Chief Executive through the White House Map Room and communications center:

Extremely important and urgent that I know at once whether the present schedules for production and completion of landing craft can be increased during January, February, March, April and May. On the assumption that landing craft takes precedence over all other munitions of war, will you let me know how many additional landing craft by types can be delivered during the months of January, February, March, April and May. List each month separately. Call conference of all interested departments. Very urgent.

Signed ROOSEVELT

**THE WHITE HOUSE**
**WASHINGTON**

November 23, 1943.

*Private*

Dear Jimmy,

We are safely at Cairo and the meetings have started. The Generalissimo is here also.

All goes well, but there are so many new angles cropping up that I think the return date will have to be postponed until about the middle of December.

Of course, you must let me know if you think that my presence in Washington is seriously required. I see no such reason at the present time as everything seems to be going well.

I am delighted that Wilson is not leaving yet. Tell him for me that I hope he will surely stay until the turn of the year.

Keep up the good work. Every good wish,

F.D.R.

The Honorable James F. Byrnes,
The White House,
Washington, D.C.

I immediately got in touch with our own specialists, and before long William Francis Gibbs and Franz Schneider, together with Fred Searls, were assembled in my office. After a brief planning session they got busy with the several officials in charge of ship construction, working into the night so that the required information could be assembled. The next morning I held a conference of the "interested parties" in the Cabinet Room and that day, with their help and that of our specialists, I was able to give the President the Bureau of Ships' detailed predictions of deliveries of the six principal types of landing craft in six months' time.

My cablegram was lengthy but specific and the figures were based, as I indicated, on the assumption that landing craft production would take precedence over all other munitions, including key items for Russia. Now, as I look at the totals for each month in the copy before me, it appears a mere list of numbers—but at the time every detail was of some consequence in world affairs. I had also to inform the President that if the order for landing craft priority was given, there would inevitably follow a slowing down of our output of Army trucks, naval shipping and high octane gasoline, and that we would have to get started at once if the changes were to be made.

After forty-eight hours, when no reply had reached us, I felt I should send the President a further cable: "Increased landing craft program submitted Wednesday possible only if we immediately issue directive giving priority over all programs any kind. Wire whether I shall have Nelson issue directive."

Before the day was out I was forced to take preliminary steps without awaiting instructions and cabled him: "Horne says unless priorities for landing craft over all other programs authorized today deliveries referred to Wednesday's message would be delayed. I have advised Nelson to grant such priorities. Please wire if this is your wish. My opinion is that figures of agencies overcautious and you could count on 15 per cent above those figures." I added the encouraging note at the end because I knew from experience how cautious these particular officials were in their estimates. The next day I was able to send further information:

William Francis Gibbs advises me that if immediately authorized, forty to fifty additional ships nearly identical with LCIL but having speed of twelve knots probably can be delivered within specified time by converting Army cargo vessels under contract in Gulf intended for duty in MacArthur theater. Could probably start deliveries within sixty days. If these ships are held not suitable for all functions of LCIL they can at least be substituted for noncombat duty of LCIL and LST, releasing the latter. If you approve wire me authority to proceed.

On November 28, by which time the President and his party were already in Teheran, messages began to reach Washington in reply to mine. The first, from Harry Hopkins, read: "Extensive studies of various problems required before decision can be reached. In meantime you should proceed as before the question of increase in landing craft was raised." This seemed to me to foreshadow the abandonment of the plans for the extra amphibious operation, a supposition confirmed by a cable from Mr. Roosevelt: "The increase in critical types of landing craft proposed in your message of 25 November, coupled with unstated effect on other critical programs, does not become effective soon enough to justify change in present construction programs."

It is now a matter of record that Mr. Churchill discussed "points of difference" with the President, until after midnight. The principal difference was over the amphibious landing craft promised to Chiang. It was this problem that occasioned the inquiry about available ships.

In his desire to help Chiang in the proposed offensive, the President had the support of Marshall and King, who feared that if Operation Buccaneer was canceled, Chiang might not allow Chinese forces to take part in the Burma campaign, and the President was reluctant to abandon it. At the same time he did not want to cripple the campaign in Italy or to endanger the planned invasion of France. Finally, after considering the production schedule I had given him, he sent Churchill a message on December 5, just before leaving Teheran: "Buccaneer is off." Churchill's heart was in the European campaign and this message made him a happy man!

At the first Cabinet meeting after the President's return we listened to an exceedingly entertaining report on his trip and of some of the highlights of the conference. The threatened railroad strike and our concern over manpower did not affect his good spirits and he took delight in telling how, to his surprise, Stalin had revealed a real sense of humor, provoking Mr. Churchill into arguments in order to hear his impassioned defense of the Empire. I was able to give him some encouraging news: the crisis over high octane gasoline was lessening. In September the Petroleum Administrator had reported that the whole program to build additional plants was being slowed down by a lack of fittings and valves for the refining machinery, as well as by a lack of skilled workers, but by the middle of December substantial progress had been made. It was important because it was useless to expedite aircraft production if, when the planes were built, there was no fuel to keep them in the air.

The strikes in the coal fields and the threatened strike by the railroad men had led to demands for industrial conscription. In late December, after Mr. Roosevelt's return, and while the railroad situation was still difficult, both Secretaries Stimson and Knox discussed with me their view that a national service law was necessary. A few days later, together with their respective Under Secretaries and with the chairman of the Maritime Commission and his vice chairman, they submitted to the President a formal recommendation that the crucial manpower situation could only be met by the prompt enactment of a national service law. Although it was known that there was intense opposition in Congress and within the unions to the drafting of men except for duty with the armed forces, they wished him to recommend the controversial legislation.

I was under the impression that Mr. Roosevelt, who was well aware of the probable reaction, would shy away from any such legislation. However, in his message to Congress of January 11 he called for a national service law "to prevent strikes" and make available for essential war service "every able-bodied adult in the nation."

As far as I know, he had not discussed his intention to make this statement with any one of the agencies responsible for manpower— certainly he had not mentioned it to me, though I had seen him daily in connection with the railroad strike. A hint that it might be in the air had come the previous day when Secretary Stimson telephoned me, asking if such a recommendation would be made. My answer was that I knew nothing about it. The speech had barely been read before Stimson called me to say that although he was in favor of it, he was hurt that I had not been frank with him. I had difficulty convincing him that I was not aware of the President's intentions.

Others converged on me, including the President's unofficial liaison officer with the labor leaders, Anna Rosenberg, who evidently believed me responsible; she too was hurt because only a few days previously she had been told by the President that there would be no such recommendation. Next came Paul McNutt, who, unlike Anna, was enraged because he was taken by surprise at what was being done in his own "shop"—why, he demanded, had the chairman of the Manpower Commission not been consulted? I could only suggest he ask the President.

Later Mrs. Rosenberg complained directly to Mr. Roosevelt, who told her he had purposely not consulted anyone because he did not want to be bothered by conflicting advice after he had made up his mind. To this she replied, "Now, boss, little Anna could not have changed your mind. The truth is, you have never definitely decided what is best." She also reported to me that she asked him if he really expected the proposal to get through Congress. He said he did not, and in this he was correct.

I did not talk to the President about his recommendation to Congress, and therefore never knew exactly what prompted it. However, recalling his conference with the leaders of the railroad workers after his return from Teheran, and the earnestness with which he described to them the sufferings of the men on the battlefields, I will always believe he was influenced by that strike, which forced him to take over the railroads of the country.

I have made it plain that our program to increase war production was only getting into full stride by the summer of 1943. Yet as early as October of that year, long before the Teheran Conference with its extensive plans, I had called a meeting of all appropriate agency heads to "work out a uniform program of aiding discharged veterans; disposing of surplus war stocks and plants and terminating contracts." We had failed to prepare adequately for war. I wanted no failure to prepare for peace. It was obvious that the different departments could not have varying policies for the termination of contracts, and when I talked to the President about it, he asked me to establish a unit in my office to co-ordinate these policies. I did so promptly.

I asked Bernard Baruch and John M. Hancock, a Lehman Brothers partner and long-time associate of Baruch, to head up this demobilization unit, confirming my verbal understanding with "B. M." in the following memorandum, dated November 5:

Referring to your memorandum of the 4th, in this matter the President requested me to establish a unit in this office for the purpose of handling the problems of demobilization. I want you to head that unit. . . .

I think you should feel free to talk to the public, the press or the Congress at any time as to your findings. I think however, that as to matters involving basic policies where a formal statement is to be made, it should be first submitted to me in order that we may make certain it is not in conflict with any plan of the President or any plan that I may have in mind. Unless it is a statement of policy that you regard as of vital importance, I would not expect you to submit it. . . .

The President having asked me to take charge of the problem, I cannot divest myself of full responsibility. The only way I could entirely divest myself of responsibility would be to advise the President it could not be done in my office and ask him to establish a separate agency. He believed that it was not wise at this time to separate the problems arising out of the revision of our war mobilization plans. Because I concurred, I agreed to assume the task.

If you agree to head the demobilization unit, I would expect you to go about the task in your own way, with your own staff, making your decisions and announcing them, unless the decision was one of basic policy, or one affecting in a substantial way the continuing war programs, in which case I would expect you to first advise me of it.

If I disagreed with the policy, you and I would discuss it and because we have never yet failed to agree on important matters, I have no idea we would have a disagreement. If we unfortunately did, the final responsibility being mine, I would have to make the final decision.

On receipt of this memorandum, Mr. Baruch embarked upon his study, with the assistance of several able associates. From October, 1943, until he and John Hancock had completed their work in February of the next year, we conferred many times on the problems that large-scale demobilization and reconversion would inevitably bring.

I approved most of their report, disagreeing principally with recommendations that would perpetuate my office, and sent the document to the President the next day. At that time I reviewed the progress of our mobilization programs to date, pointing out that our shipping programs were well in hand: that "You need have no further fears" about future supplies of high octane gasoline; that the rubber director had stated that though his program "had hurdles ahead, it will come through." Emphasizing that the west coast manpower plan had relieved the situation there, and that from now on it should improve generally, I concluded that our production programs were proceeding satisfactorily.

I then referred to our successful efforts to adjust some procurement programs for the Army, which, I said, "cause me confidently to predict that the savings for this fiscal year will be in excess of the $28,000,000,000 heretofore reported." I added that the Navy, though it had fewer contracts than the Army, had canceled as many as it could. I also reminded Mr. Roosevelt of the effective work of Judge Vinson's Office of Economic Stabilization in determining wage and price policies.

My conclusion was that the Office of War Mobilization, as originally envisaged, was nearing the end of its usefulness:

There is no program of mobilization now developed by this office which could not be developed by the War Production Board. There is no question of policy now on veterans' questions determined by this office which could not be determined by the Committee I have described.

Therefore, I believe the time has come to abolish this office.

My recommendation to abolish OWM was no empty gesture. But it was characteristic of the involvement of the President in strategic and military affairs at this time that I received no direct reply to this suggestion. I was disappointed when a day or so later Mr. Roosevelt returned the Baruch report with a typewritten slip: "Return to J. F. B., FDR," without any indication of what he thought of it. My impression that he had not yet studied the report carefully was reinforced by a press story in which he was quoted as saying he had had time to read only half of it.

Late in January, 1944, while the report was still being written, I had told the President that from my conversations with Baruch I knew he would suggest three ways of disposing of surplus property; consumer goods by the Procurement Division of the Treasury Department; defense plants through the Defense Plants Corporation, then controlling such installations; and finally raw materials by a new agency to be created by the Reconstruction Finance Corporation.

I told Mr. Roosevelt that I agreed with the suggestion and that the last task would need the services of someone with wide business experience; that the best man we could get would be Will Clayton, formerly of Houston, who had been serving with Jesse Jones in the Commerce Department; Clayton had given me his resignation, but I believed that he could be kept in Washington if he was offered an independent position. This proved correct and on February 21 his appointment to head the new Surplus Property Administration, created by executive order two days previously, was announced.

The same press release also stated that General Hines would take charge of the Retraining and Re-employment Administration, which would handle veterans' affairs. In line with my letter to the President, though both these specialized agencies co-operated closely with OWM, they were given separate staffs, and I was to keep a watchful eye over their activities.

The reception given by the public to the reconversion plans brought home to me the fact that many of our citizens were more concerned with what would happen after our anticipated victory than with the effort and sacrifice still needed to ensure it. In September, 1943, I had intervened in a dispute between the service departments and the Office of War Information over the release of photographs portraying the grimmer side of war. I thoroughly agreed with Director Elmer Davis that it was necessary for the public to be made familiar with the miseries as well as the glamour of military operations. The spring of 1944, with the invasion of France pending and a national election in the offing, was a time of challenge but also of distraction. "Business as usual, only more so," seemed to be growing in popularity as a slogan.

This was understandable. From this date on the temper and mood of the people at home were constantly affected by news from the battle fronts. The report of the advances of our armed forces caused many men, in most of whom there is some human selfishness, to plan for the quickest possible return to production of peacetime goods and many workers to think of transferring to their old jobs before the veterans returned—just another evidence of larceny of the soul! When our combat forces suffered a setback, there was a temporary postponement of peacetime plans. The Battle of the Bulge, for example, slowed down planning for reconversion for a time.

In the first week of February, 1944, I was faced with the task of adjusting a controversy between the President himself and Senator Barkley, the majority leader of the Senate, a controversy to which I or my staff may have contributed. A tax bill was pending that the President felt he could not approve. I heard that he had been much impressed by the arguments of Judge Vinson in favor of a veto. Vinson was then Director of Economic Stabilization and was very frequently consulted on revenue legislation; he was splendidly qualified for this by reason of his long service on the House Ways and Means Committee. He and his assistant, Edward Pritchard, came to my office one day and left a memorandum for the proposed veto message. I did not see it then, since I was out of the city that day.

After my return the President forwarded me a letter from Morgenthau recommending that the bill be vetoed. In response to this a member of my staff prepared a memorandum stating that while I had originally thought a veto unwise, the Secretary's letter had led me to conclude that he and Judge Vinson were right. This memorandum was attached to Vinson's and sent to the President. Barkley later said that he talked with the President, urging him not to veto the bill, but some days later the President sent a veto message to Congress. Barkley was offended by the President's action. He particularly objected to the bill's being described as providing relief "not for the needy but for the greedy," In his book, *That Reminds Me,* he wrote that he was told the phrase was coined by a member of my staff. I do not recall it, but it is entirely possible, because I did not pay much attention to the memorandum that was written to accompany Vinson's. And if a member of my staff did it, I am responsible. On the other hand Grace Tully, one of the President's secretaries, says in her book *F.D.R., My Boss* that the President himself coined the "greedy not needy" phrase.

After the message had been read in the Senate, Steve Early came to my office quite excited, saying that Mr. Roosevelt, who was in Hyde Park at the time, should be informed that Barkley was announcing his intention to resign as majority leader. I immediately telephoned, telling the President that nothing could be more unfortunate than ill feeling between him and the majority leader, particularly in view of the personal friendship which had long existed between them. I said that I did not know whether he had warned Barkley of his intention to veto the bill; but that regardless of what had occurred, he should now assure Barkley that no reflection upon him or any other member of the Senate was intended.

At first he demurred; in fact, I must record that in our preliminary exchanges he said, "The thing for you to do is to forget about it and just don't give a damn." However, as I continued to press for a reconciliation, the President finally said if I would write a letter along the lines I had suggested to him, he would agree to send it. He did not know at that time that Barkley, in his speech criticizing the veto message, had commented that Mr. Roosevelt's experience with timber was limited to the sale of Christmas trees. When he learned of it, he was greatly offended, for he prided himself on his knowledge of forestry.

I dictated a letter, my own copy of which has upon it this notation made by my secretary, Miss Connor:

February 23, 1944

Letter written by JFB and submitted to the President for approval by telephone. (President in Hyde Park.) The President made a few minor changes and telephoned them to JFB. Letter turned over to Mr. Early to be put in form of telegram and delivered by him to Mr. Barkley.

The message expressed the hope that Barkley would not persist in his intention to resign; but in case he did, that the senators would immediately and unanimously re-elect him. It contained what I really felt, ending with this statement on the President's behalf: "With the many serious problems confronting us, it is inevitable that at times you should differ with your colleagues and differ with me. I am sure that your differing with your colleagues does not lessen their confidence in you as leader. Certainly your differing with me does not affect my confidence in your leadership or in any degree lessen my respect and affection for you personally." The last sentence, as my intimate friends will recognize, is one which I have frequently used during my political life.

That afternoon on my way home I stopped by Barkley's apartment and urged him not to decline the leadership, as I felt his colleagues would re-elect him on the following day. I knew his patriotism and his forgiving disposition and I recall telling him that I too had differences with the President, but that while the country was at war men occupying important positions like our own should overlook those differences.

The following day Senator Barkley was re-elected majority leader and graciously wrote the President expressing appreciation of the letter which I had prepared and the President had authorized to be sent. So far as I know, the most cordial relations thereafter existed between those two friends.

In June of 1944 our armies had taken the offensive both in Italy and in France, encouraging further the hopes of the optimists for a speedy termination of the war. Members of both political parties began to take an increased interest in reconversion and veterans' affairs, and several bills were introduced. Among these, one sponsored by Senators George and Kilgore sought "to provide a national program for demobilization and postwar adjustment," and hearings began on it in the Senate Military Affairs Committee. The chairman and the authors of the bill had asked that I appear. It was clear that Congress would insist on determining the character and function of the reconversion program and was not going to leave its direction to agencies created by executive order.

I had very definite views on the problems the committee sought to solve, but these did not encompass any post for myself after hostilities had ceased. Further, because of my often-repeated statement that the nearest approach to immortality is a government bureau, I wished to encourage the abolition of mushroom agencies which wartime needs had produced. I therefore prepared with care a statement to be used before the committee on June 12, forwarding a copy to the President for his information. In it I said, in part, "In changing from peace to war, it was necessary to create a number of agencies. When peace comes these agencies should go." Then I recommended that the Congress should not establish a new agency; that my office should be abolished and its functions and the functions proposed in the bill be given to the War Production Board, setting forth the reason that that agency would have to continue for some time.

Within three hours after the advance copy of my statement was sent to the President, the following note was brought to me:

This is an excellent suggestion—but at the same time, a very bad one. Perhaps that part of your work which you speak of can logically be turned over to WPB—except you and a few people in your office whom I cannot possibly get along without. In other words, your memorandum is constructive but, at the same time, destructive.

As you know, you are indispensable on the handling and the actual settling of scores of problems which are constantly arising. You have been called "The Assistant President" and the appellation comes close to the truth.

Therefore, please put your mind to work to keep your work—or the better part of it—in that category.

Since the writer of this memorandum had created the Office of War Mobilization by executive order and was emphatic in his views that it should continue, my statement to the committee on Monday morning was somewhat changed. But in order to make my own position clear, I said that while I realized that the bill would not pass within the week before the summer adjournment, I knew the big task after the recess would be to continue work on demobilization measures. "Should the bill then pass, I do not want to be immodest and assume that the President would offer me the appointment to the office the bill creates; but if because I am now Director of War Mobilization, he should wish to do so, I feel that at that time the mobilization problem would be such that I could decline to accept and I would so decline. I make this statement so you will know that any opinion I express about the bill is not influenced by a personal interest in the office it would create."

This clear statement of my resolve not to remain in any permanent office charged with postwar adjustments did not attract attention in the press, though it had been noted by the President. It was important to me that, having spent time and effort reducing the number of government agencies in peacetime, my final efforts should have the same aim. At least my desire to leave public office and the White House should indicate that I was not a candidate for the office of Vice President at that time.

Within a few days Congress adjourned. This was but a month before the Democratic convention was to open in Chicago. Meanwhile, some of Mr. Roosevelt's Republican critics were attacking him on the ground of old age, and he was also reported to be a sick man. It happened that it was necessary at that time for him to appoint delegates to a certain international conference, among them two senators, one from each political party. Barkley, the Democratic leader, asked him to name the ranking Democrat of the appropriate committee, and Senator White recommended the ranking Republican. Though he understood that Senator White was following the seniority rule in this, the President reacted violently to his choice. I was asked to produce a solution, but, as I told him in a full page of argument, if he did not follow precedent he would find other Republicans declining to serve and would create a large issue out of a little appointment. "My thought is," I concluded, "that it would be bad to start an international conference with a party fight."

In answer the President wrote:

I have your memorandum about _____. This is one of the things which in a cumulative capacity hurts the reputation of the House and the Senate. People as a whole, when they hear things like this, do not give a damn about custom, prestige or anything except capacity. _____ certainly has not got the capacity.

If this were not an election year I would go ahead and offer the place to the best available Republican and let them make an issue out of it. I feel that I am spineless and almost weak-minded in yielding up the right of it, but I hereby do so for the sake of some wrongheaded thought of avoiding a party fight.

So go ahead and tell _____ I am a shellfish and hereby yield in this fool situation—incidentally not for the first time.

I leave the reader to judge whether this reply was that of a sick man who had lost his grip on affairs!

It is a remarkable fact—one which we Americans took for granted but which caused other nations to marvel—that amid all the strains and perils of global war, our country could devote its energy and interest to that recurrent upheaval known as a presidential election—to say nothing of the other contests for federal and state offices. From the beginning of the year 1944, both Democrats and Republicans were engaged publicly and behind the scenes in making preparations for the conventions, most of the interest centering, of course, on the choice of candidates for President and Vice President.

As later events demonstrated, the choices made by the convention of the Democratic party were especially fateful ones, for President Roosevelt died only a few months after his inauguration. Since his death many have interested themselves in the considerations and pressures that may determine the choice of a vice-presidential candidate, and the fact that President Eisenhower's health was an election issue in 1956 has re-emphasized the need for the public to give greater attention to the method by which a running mate is selected. With this in mind, I have felt it pertinent to relate, in fuller detail than I ordinarily might have, what I know personally of the background and the sequence of events leading to the choice of Mr. Wallace in 1940, and of Mr. Truman four years later.

The 1940 convention I have already described. In 1944 it was clear that the nomination was Mr. Roosevelt's for the asking. It had been equally apparent to me for some time that he was determined to be his party's nominee again in order that he might finish the war and address himself to the tasks of peace. In view of his twelve hard years,

216

and the tragic sequel to his election for a fourth term, it may be asked whether those of us who knew him well and saw him almost daily did not have some question about his physical fitness for the ordeal of another term.

To this I can only give my opinion at the time. On several occasions late in 1943 the President did look tired and overwrought, but we were all familiar with his remarkable capacity to "bounce back." This expression reminds me of a phrase often used by his personal physician, Dr. Ross McIntire, who had him under daily observation: "That man is like a rubber ball." I now realize that we were perhaps too close to Mr. Roosevelt to note the deterioration observed by those who saw him less frequently. Even a few days before his death, when I telephoned him at Warm Springs and he told me he felt much better, I thought from his voice and the pungency with which he expressed his views that he had again bounced back. This may help to explain why, little more than a year before this, his friends had not questioned the wisdom of his decision to run again.

I have said there was little doubt about the President's intentions. The question of who would be on the ticket with him was quite undecided. Wallace's renomination was opposed by Bob Hannegan, National Chairman, and by Ed Flynn, the New York City boss, who continued to have more influence with the President than any other political leader.

During the months of March to June, 1942, Flynn had been embarrassed by some unwelcome publicity in the New York press over the so-called paving block incident, involving the removal of paving blocks from New York City to his country home. Some time afterward, when I was in Mr. Roosevelt's office, he had asked me how I thought the Senate would react should he name Flynn Ambassador to China.

My reply was in the form of a question: "What qualifications does he have for that particular assignment?"

The President said, "None. But he wants it, and I am anxious to do something for him."

What lay behind his suggestion, I assumed, was a desire to restore Flynn's prestige. But at that time events were especially critical in the Far East. Moreover, many of the church organizations, which long had collected small change from Sunday-school children to carry on missionary activities in China, would take a particular interest in the choice of an Ambassador. How would they react to the appointment of a political boss of New York City? I had no ill will toward Flynn but I told the President I thought a majority of the Senate would feel about it just as I did, and I recommended that he appoint him to Cuba or some other post. He said that was also his opinion. However, he would ask his "missus" to talk to Madame Chiang Kai-shek, who was to come to the United States for medical consultation early in December; and if, as he expected, Madame Chiang objected, it would give him a reason for not proceeding. What Flynn was told I do not know, but the appointment did not go to him.

Shortly afterward, the President told me Flynn would be sent as Ambassador to Australia. I was then serving in the White House as Economic Stabilizer. When that appointment went to the Senate in January, 1943, there was a storm of objection. The paving block incident was rehashed in the Senate and press. Democrats and Republicans announced their intentions of voting against his confirmation and some of the President's most loyal supporters feared that a vote in Flynn's favor would have dire political consequences for them. At the request of Senator Barkley, then the majority leader, I met one Sunday afternoon with about a dozen senators; Frank Walker, the chairman of the Democratic National Committee; and Mr. Flynn. A vote on Flynn's nomination was scheduled for Monday. The situation in the Senate was discussed frankly. Leslie Biffle, Secretary of the Senate, had a poll of the senators that showed the appointment would not be confirmed. I joined several senators in urging Flynn to consider whether, when he could not win, he wished to force his friends in the Senate to cast a vote that they thought might be very damaging to them.

The group's feeling was so unanimous that finally Flynn decided to ask the President to withdraw his name. He did not seem to be offended with me. On the contrary, at his request I went with him to Frank Walker's apartment and repeated to Charlie Michelson, the public relations director of the Democratic party, the wording that I had suggested for Flynn's letter of withdrawal.

Within the hour Mr. Michelson had drafted the letter. The President had been away, but returned to the White House about nine o'clock. When Early and I showed him Flynn's letter, he was happy to get out of that losing fight and quickly approved an announcement, prepared by Early, that the nomination would be withdrawn. I did not have time to give more thought to the incident, but have since had reason to wonder whether Flynn held me responsible for his disappointments.

After Harry Hopkins returned from the Teheran Conference in December of 1943, he came to my office and told me that during the trip home the President had talked about how well I had managed things during his absence and had expressed the hope that I could be nominated for Vice President. My reply was that I had not changed the views I had expressed in 1940 and I did not wish to be considered. I meant it. Since 1940, I said, as Economic Stabilizer and as Director of War Mobilization, I had been called upon to decide for the President some of the most difficult economic and political questions confronting the administration. Every time you decide a controversial question, you make enemies, and my "Hold-the-Line" campaign had certainly not been popular in labor circles. Hopkins replied that the President was strong in his opinion and intended to talk to me about the matter.

Hopkins' technique was not new to me. Harry was no purveyor of unwelcome news; but if the President made an observation that he thought would be pleasantly received, he would relay it, proving not only his friendly interest in you but his very confidential relation with the President. It was human and understandable. Nevertheless, Mr. Roosevelt did not bring up the subject with me at that time, and certainly I did not mention it to him.

However, in the early spring of the following year a number of friends who had discussed the coming convention with the President told me that Mr. Roosevelt thought that Mr. Wallace should not be nominated again and had spoken of my being named. Then one day Frank Walker, the Postmaster General, telephoned to me, asking me to ride home with him. On the way he told me he was satisfied that Mr. Wallace could not be nominated and that I should be. When I reminded him of the position I had taken four years earlier, he said I should not be influenced at all by Ed Flynn's opinion; that everyone now knew he was all wrong. I repeated emphatically that I did not want to be considered.

On June 13, in the late afternoon, Bob Hannegan spent two hours with me. Much of the time he spent trying to convince me that I should be the candidate for Vice President, and the remainder of the time I spent telling him that he was very kind, but mistaken. I repeated that I favored Cordell Hull. Hannegan said he had told the President that Wallace could not be nominated but that I could, and the ticket would win. To this the President had observed that he had wanted me in 1940 and would rather have me on the ticket in 1944 than anyone else. Hannegan added that General Watson, who was present during the conversation, had interrupted to tell the President that he too was much in favor of "that ticket." Watson later confirmed all this to me.

The next day the President asked me to come to his office and said, "Bob and I have decided on you as permanent chairman of the convention." I hastened to say that I did not want to serve in that capacity. He told me that they had decided that the temporary chairman should be either Senator Kerr of Oklahoma, Governor Broughton of North Carolina, or Senator Jackson of Indiana, but that he was eliminating both Broughton and Jackson because "they talk through their noses." He then told me how Joe Robinson had been nominated for Vice President at Houston in 1928. After Al Smith had been nominated for President, Roosevelt had suggested Senator Robinson, but Smith did not know him and was not enthusiastic; whereupon Roosevelt had told Smith that Robinson had done a wonderful job presiding over the convention and was the logical man for second place on the ticket, and Smith had finally agreed. The President now said, "History will repeat itself."

In this connection, he said that Robinson, when nominated for Vice President, had asked Pat Harrison to preside thereafter. He then told me how, shortly before adjournment, the famous telegram had been received from Al Smith stating that he wished the delegates to know that he favored the repeal of the Eighteenth Amendment. Roosevelt and Harrison feared that when the telegram was read to the convention it would promptly start a fight on the floor, and that the debate might disclose such a division of sentiment that it would do great harm to the party. They decided Harrison should read it rapidly, and immediately a delegate would move to adjourn. Notwithstanding the rapid reading, some delegates were quick to catch the meaning and were on their feet demanding recognition. Harrison recognized a delegate who he knew would move to adjourn and, with the same speed with which he had read the message, he put the question on adjournment. Many delegates yelled "No," but with a bang of the gavel he declared "Motion carried and the convention adjourned."

Some days after this conversation with the President, Maude and I went with him to Shangri-la. He took with him a lot of work, but he managed to find time to talk about campaign strategy. He said he would do little campaigning until the last ten days before the election, and he felt so confident of his election that he mentioned plans for his fourth term, discussing the use of Army camps after the war for military training centers. He again said that he and Hannegan were sticking to their decision that I should be permanent chairman of the convention and a candidate for Vice President. It was obvious to me that his earlier talk about Robinson's being nominated while he was permanent chairman at the Houston convention had been intended to influence me; and while I did not think much of the plan, I did conclude that he was sincere in wanting me for his running mate and I found myself beginning to think about it seriously.

Two weeks later, I began to receive indications of opposition rather than of support. On July 6, Mrs. Anna Rosenberg, a member of the War Mobilization Advisory Board who worked closely with the leaders of organized labor, saw the President immediately after Ed Flynn had called on him. Previously she had told me that the President had spoken favorably to her of my nomination. But on this day she came by my office to say that Mr. Roosevelt had told her that Flynn objected to me as a nominee, arguing that the Negroes of New York State would vote against the ticket because I was from the South. Partial confirmation of her statement came next day from Hannegan, who told me that the President, after his talk with Flynn, was not so enthusiastic about my nomination as he had been. He was now listing as potential candidates Winant, Douglas, Barkley, Truman, and "from the South, Byrnes," and he was inviting Hannegan, Ed Kelly, Ed Flynn, and Frank Walker to dinner on Tuesday, July 11, to discuss the situation. I was not to be invited, since my own status would be under discussion. Incidentally this was the day the President announced that, in view of Hannegan's assurance that a majority of the delegates wanted it, he would seek a fourth term if nominated by the Democratic National Convention.

The day following the dinner Frank Walker came to see me and said that Flynn had repeated his arguments against me, and that my chances for the nomination were not as good as they had been; he said that Douglas and Truman were now strong possibilities. Shortly afterward Leo Crowley, who had been in the President's office, came through the East Wing of the White House to call on me. He said that Mr. Roosevelt had told him of Flynn's opposition to me.

In order to clarify matters, with Crowley present, I called the President on the telephone, and said, "Leo is here is my office and has repeated his conversation with you. I would like to know if you have changed your opinion about my being a candidate."

He replied, "You are the best qualified man in the whole outfit and you must not get out of the race. If you stay in, you are sure to win." He made other statements in a similar vein, which I repeated to Mr. Crowley, who sat nearby.

On the morning of July 13 I went to the President's office on some piece of official business. When this was disposed of, Mr. Roosevelt said that he wanted to talk politics. Wallace, he told me, was to have lunch with him that day, and the Vice Presidency was to be discussed. He was certain that Wallace could not be nominated, but knew he would insist on running unless the President told him to withdraw; Ickes and Rosenman, he added, had "talked to Henry about withdrawing, but he had declined to discuss the matter with them." I said I could understand Wallace's attitude in view of the ill feeling between Ickes and himself growing out of Ickes' desire, and years of strenuous effort, to take the Forestry Service from the Department of Agriculture.

The President replied, "Yes, and Henry possibly knows that Sam Rosenman has been advocating the nomination of Henry Kaiser." Mr. Rosenman seemed to admire Mr. Kaiser, who during the war built the Liberty Ships. The President appeared amused that Wallace had told them he would discuss his affairs with the President but not with them.

I said that while I differed with Mr. Wallace about many things, in view of his personal loyalty to the President I did not see how he could tell Wallace to withdraw. The President agreed and said that if Wallace did not voluntarily withdraw, he (Roosevelt) would give him a letter stating that if he were a delegate to the convention he would vote for Wallace, but that as President he would not urge his nomination. I said that if he did that, of course he could not thereafter express a preference for anyone else. He said he would not do so, and because he had previously talked to me about being a candidate, he wanted me to know what he was going to do. He also said that in reaching my decision, I could rely upon his promise that he would not express a preference for anyone.

I told him that while at first I had not thought well of it, if he intended leaving an open field, I would probably be a candidate. I would resign as Director of War Mobilization, because if I should keep an office in the White House after announcing my candidacy there might be a question of the sincerity of the President's statement about how he would vote were he a delegate to the convention. Mr. Roosevelt objected, saying that it was neither necessary nor desirable for me to resign; he hoped I would consider that point very carefully, because while the convention was on he was going to Pearl Harbor to discuss Pacific strategy and would be out of the country for several weeks. He wanted me to be in charge in his absence.

As I left the President's office to return to my own in the East Wing, I encountered Sidney Hillman and a man who was a stranger to me going to the President's office by the colonnade used by occupants of the White House residence. That evening Mr. Roosevelt left for Hyde Park, where he was to remain for a few days before going out to San Diego and beyond.

On Friday the fourteenth, Walker and Hannegan asked me to meet them for lunch at Leo Crowley's apartment. They told Crowley and me that, as matters then stood, if any of FDR's friends should question them about the President's position on his running mate, they would have to say he favored Truman or Douglas. I replied that this did not square with the President's statement to me on the previous day, which I repeated to them in detail. Hannegan said, "I don't understand it."

Neither did I, and I decided to clarify my position—and that of the President. I remembered that in 1940, after Mr. Roosevelt had been nominated, he told me that he would decline to run if the convention refused to accept his recommendation of Wallace for Vice President. I knew how effective his threat had been. I knew also that through the big-city bosses he would be in even more complete control in the 1944 convention. I therefore had no intention of running unless I was assured that he would tell them either that he favored me or had no preference and would not interfere with the convention's selection. Though I already had the President's assurance that he would leave the field open, I did not like the way Hannegan was now talking. So after lunch I asked Crowley to accompany me to my office, telling him I was going to telephone Mr. Roosevelt at Hyde Park. In advance I wrote out several questions which needed an answer. I read those questions to the President and took down his answers in shorthand. There follows a transcript of the material portion of our conversation:

Byrnes—I understood from you that you would write a letter to Henry Wallace. It was my understanding from your statement to me yesterday that you would not authorize any person to quote you as saying you preferred any candidate other than Wallace.

The President—I am not favoring anybody. I told them so. No, I am not favoring anyone.

Byrnes—Bob Hannegan and Frank Walker stated today that if at the convention they were asked about your views, they would be obliged to say to their friends that from your statements they concluded you did not prefer Wallace but did prefer Truman first and Douglas second, and that either would be preferable to me because they would cost the ticket fewer votes than I would.

The President—Jimmy, that is all wrong. That is not what I told them. It is what they told me. When we all went over the list I did not say that I preferred anybody or that anybody would cost me votes, but they all agreed that Truman would cost fewer votes than anybody and probably Douglas second. This was the agreement they reached and I had nothing to do with it. I was asking questions. I did not express myself. Objection to you came from labor people, both Federation and C.I.O.

Byrnes—I have a letter from Al Whitney asking permission to take charge of my candidacy in the Ohio delegation. He sent his legal representative and friend, Mr. Miller, to see me this morning. I just wanted to know if Walker and Hannegan would be correct in stating to their friends that you believe I will cost more votes than others.

The President—They can state their own opinion but they cannot state mine. I have not given my opinion to anyone.

Byrnes—If they make the statement, notwithstanding your letter to Wallace, that you have expressed a preference for Truman and Douglas, it would make it very difficult for me.

The President—We have to be damned careful about language. They asked if I would object to Truman and Douglas and I said no. That is different from using the word "prefer." That is not expressing a preference because you know I told you I would have no preference.

Byrnes—I made the statement to you that should I decide to become a candidate, I would resign. I now believe that would be unwise because it would create the impression of a disagreement between us.

The President—I think that is right.

Then we discussed the platform, the President expressing the hope that I would go to Chicago and help Hannegan. He asked, "Will you go on and run?"

I replied, "I am still considering it. Before deciding, I wanted to know your answers to these questions and whether you had authorized Hannegan and Walker to make the statement that you preferred other candidates."

Mr. Roosevelt said, "After all, Jimmy, you are close to me personally, and Henry is close to me. I hardly know Truman. Douglas is a poker partner. He is good in a poker game and tells good stories."

I telephoned Hannegan and read him the transcript of the President's words. He only repeated, "I don't understand it." At the time I did not understand his skepticism. Of course, I did not know what it seems Walker knew—that Hannegan had in his pocket a letter signed by the President which was postdated July 19, the day before the nomination for Vice President was scheduled to take place, but which evidently had been given Hannegan on the thirteenth, the same day the President told me I could rely upon it that he would not express a preference. That letter read:

July 19

DEAR BOB:

You have written me about Harry Truman and Bill Douglas. I should, of course, be very glad to run with either of them and believe that either one of them would bring real strength to the ticket.

Always sincerely,
FRANKLIN ROOSEVELT

Reading this letter one will note that the President did not use the word "prefer." That may explain his emphatic statement to me over the telephone that "We have to be damned careful about language." It is possible that Hannegan may have been impressed by the President's statement which I read to him, in which he emphatically protested he had not expressed a preference for anyone. However, the fact is that if in our conversation he had told me that he had written such a letter to be made public the day before the voting, I certainly would not have become a candidate unless he wrote a similar letter regarding me.

Knowing nothing of the letter, Crowley and I went to Hopkins' office a few doors down the corridor, and there I repeated my conversation with the President, telling Hopkins that, relying upon Mr. Roosevelt's statement that he would express no preference and that there would be an open field, I would become a candidate. Hopkins repeated that the President was satisfied that if I entered the race I would be nominated. I then informed several friends of my decision and telephoned Senator Truman in Independence, Missouri.

Referring to a news story on the ticker that he had that day issued a statement from Kansas City that he would not be a candidate, I asked if this was true. He confirmed the report and added that if I should be a candidate he would support me and would help me as far as he could with the Missouri delegation. I thanked him and asked if he would nominate me. This he promptly agreed to do. I did not tell him that the President would support me. As of that moment it would not have been true. Had it been true, I would have known I was certain to be nominated.

The next morning, Saturday, I received a call from Ed Kelly in Chicago. Hannegan, he said, was in his room and they were expecting the President to arrive in Chicago, en route to the West Coast, about three that afternoon. He and Hannegan proposed to meet the President's special train at the depot, and he would tell the President that Flynn's opinion of the Negro voters' attitude to my candidacy was unsound; that he had talked with some of his Negro leaders and their view was that the colored voters would support Mr. Roosevelt regardless of who was nominated for Vice President.

About an hour later there came another call. Hannegan and Kelly had seen the President on his special train and the matter of the Vice Presidency was "settled." Kelly told me, "The President has given us the green light to support you and he wants you in Chicago." Kelly asked that upon arrival there I come to his apartment. I left Washington for Chicago reasonably sure of my position. Leo Crowley, who had been close to me in all this, was on the train and was delighted at the news.

We arrived in Chicago on Sunday morning. I was met by the Chicago Fire Chief's automobile and taken to Mayor Ed Kelly's apartment. Hannegan was the only other guest. As we ate breakfast, they repeated that when they had discussed with Mr. Roosevelt the attitude of the Negro leaders in Chicago, he had said, "Well, you know Jimmy has been my choice from the very first. Go ahead and name him." Hannegan had been given a copy of the letter which the President had written to Senator H. M. Jackson, the permanent chairman of the convention, about his position on Wallace's candidacy. Plans were discussed for releasing this on Monday night, when they would also announce publicly that they were supporting me. Privately, during the day, they would advise leaders of the President's statement to them at the depot. They got busy immediately.

In the afternoon and early evening of Sunday, news of the President's approval of my nomination began to leak to the radio and to spread among the assembling delegations. Senator Alben Barkley, who was a potential candidate, in his book *That Reminds Me* writes that when he reached Chicago he "had a talk with the late Mayor Edward Kelly, a Roosevelt lieutenant and a friend of mine. He gave me the word that Roosevelt wanted Byrnes and that 'it was in the bag for Jimmy.'"

That night I attended a dinner with Hannegan and other political leaders in an apartment placed at his disposal by one of his friends. Both he and Kelly told the group of their conversation with Mr. Roosevelt at the depot. There was general approval and plans were discussed for Monday's announcement, which would be made at five o'clock, immediately after the release of the Wallace letter. (Hannegan, Kelly and others would announce that the letter did not bind them; that they had the President's permission to support me for Vice President, and would do so.) The general estimate of the group was that we could rely upon about seven hundred votes. Frank Walker told me, "You know my position; I'm for whoever the President wants; now that he has told these fellows to nominate you, I'm for you."

However, at the end of the gathering, while we were standing and just about to leave, Hannegan turned to Kelly and said, "Ed, there is one thing we forgot. The President said, 'Clear it with Sidney.'" Kelly agreed that the President had made that request at the depot meeting. Kelly asked if I felt free to talk to Hillman or to Phil Murray. I told him that Murray was on my War Mobilization Advisory Board, that I knew him pleasantly and would be glad to talk to him; but I declined to approach Hillman. Hannegan then undertook to do this.

The next morning I got a call from him, asking me to use a room next to his suite at the Blackstone as an office. Various matters, he expected, would come up and he would want to consult me. Before I could leave my room Al Whitney, president of the Brotherhood of Railway Trainmen, arrived and told me he had just talked with Sidney Hillman, who had breakfasted with Mr. Truman. I thought it was well to make a note of what Whitney told me. Hillman had said he was for Wallace first and Truman second. Whitney had then said of Truman, "He is out of the race," to which Hillman replied, "Well, he may get back into the race." Whitney argued with Hillman on my behalf and against Truman, but without success. He reported saying, "I think with Byrnes we could get Ohio," and concluded by telling me,

"Hillman seems determined to have the C.I.O. name the Vice President." He also reported that all but one of his delegation would support me. Frank Hague, of New Jersey, telephoned that he had informed the President that he would support me.

After I went to Hannegan's headquarters at the Blackstone, I had a friendly talk with Philip Murray. He said that the C.I.O. membership was overwhelmingly in favor of Wallace, and because of this he too had to be for him. However, if the nomination did not go to Wallace, the C.I.O. would still support the President regardless of whom the convention named as Vice President. When I told Hannegan of this conversation, he was entirely satisfied. And so the situation stood when the National Committee met on Monday afternoon.

Soon after the meeting adjourned, Hannegan returned to his suite at the Blackstone and gave me a detailed report of what occurred. Ed Flynn, as he has written in his book *You're the Boss* (Page 182), arrived just as the proceedings were getting under way. When he learned that there was unanimous agreement for me, he became very angry. He swore that I would cause Roosevelt to lose New York. Perhaps I should quote Mr. Flynn's own description of his part in these deliberations. "As I entered, Hannegan rushed me over to a corner and said, 'It's all over. It's Byrnes.' . . . I browbeat the Committee. I talked, I argued, I swore, and finally they said if the President would tell them again he was for Truman, they would agree."

After Hannegan had told me of Flynn's violent opposition at the meeting, he said that Hillman, Murray, and Flynn were coming to his suite for dinner and that Flynn was insisting that they get in touch with Mr. Roosevelt by telephone. I did not want to be there when they arrived, and immediately left for my suite in the Stevens. After dinner I heard from Crowley, who had been asked by Hannegan to report to me on the lengthy conversation between the President, Hillman and Flynn. Crowley reported that Hillman had repeated his argument that organized labor would oppose me because it felt that as a result of the Hold-the-Line order on wages, it had lost many of its gains under the New Deal. Flynn repeatedly asserted to the President that my nomination would cost the President 200,000 Negro votes in New York and that he would lose the State of New York and probably the election. Finally, Mr. Roosevelt had told the labor leaders and Flynn that in view of their statements he would withdraw his approval of my candidacy and would go along with their desire to nominate Truman.

Notwithstanding his promises, he specifically expressed a preference for Mr. Truman.

About an hour later, Mr. Truman himself came to see me. This was the second time we had met at the convention, though our previous meeting at his apartment late Sunday evening had been at a purely social gathering with a number of my former senatorial colleagues, and no mention had been made of the Vice Presidency. He told me he had learned from Hannegan that the President had telephoned, asking that he (Truman) run for Vice President. Mr. Truman felt he should comply with the President's wishes and therefore must withdraw his promise to support and to nominate me. I told him that Leo Crowley had just relayed to me Hannegan's message about the President's decision; that I fully understood his position and, of course, released him. He asked if I would run anyway. I told him I did not think so, but I wanted to think it over that night.

On Tuesday morning I told the friends who called on me what had occurred, and that I had decided not to allow my name to be presented. That day, the eighteenth, I dictated a letter to Senator Maybank, chairman of the South Carolina delegation, saying that I did not wish my name presented to the convention. The letter was dated the nineteenth and marked for release that day at ten A.M. because, before it was made public, I wished to tell Ed Kelly of my decision, and had learned he would not be available on the afternoon of the eighteenth.

Before leaving Chicago on Thursday afternoon, I told Maybank that if the vice-presidential contest became one between Wallace and Truman, as I anticipated, I hoped my friends would vote for Truman. I am certain that most of them did.

With the advantage of hindsight, I think Hannegan's real desire was to defeat Wallace. From the President's statements to him for several weeks before the convention, he believed the President wanted me named, and he therefore urged my nomination to accomplish his primary purpose. When on Monday night the President switched to Truman, I think Hannegan was pleased because as head of the Democratic machine in St. Louis he was friendly to the Pendergast organization of Kansas City. Hillman and Murray, while pretending to go along with the rank and file of the C.I.O. who favored Wallace, actually favored Truman; and on Monday night, when they got the President to agree to Truman, they decided to let the delegates they controlled vote for Wallace on the first ballot. They knew the several men nominated as "favorite sons" would get enough support to require a second ballot. They did. Then the word was spread that Wallace could not win; that Roosevelt wanted Truman and that they should stand by the President. The contest was over. Truman was nominated.

I freely admit I was disappointed, and felt hurt by President Roosevelt's action. Not having wanted to be involved, I was angry with myself for permitting the President to get me in it. But I cherished no animosity toward him. I realized that he was looking after his own interests; that he desired always to carry his home state; that when Flynn insisted that I would cause him to lose 200,000 Negro votes in New York, it was too much to expect that President Roosevelt should continue to urge my nomination. Nor did I harbor any ill feelings toward Mr. Truman, whose position I fully understood. I had assured him of this on Monday night when he called to tell me that in view of the President's expressing a preference for him, he felt he should be a candidate and asked that I release him.

I have set forth how I came to allow my name to be discussed. Why I caused it to be withdrawn is set forth in a letter to Senator Byrd of Virginia only a few days after the convention, on August 3, 1944:

DEAR HARRY:

Thank you very much for your cordial letter of the 26th. Your statement that had my name been presented to the Convention the Virginia delegation would have voted for me, makes me feel very close to Virginia and very close to you.

The first time I have an opportunity I will tell you of the assurances I received which prompted me to permit my name to be discussed in connection with the Vice Presidency. When on Monday night I was advised that the President had changed his mind and had advised Hannegan and his other political leaders that I should not be nominated and they should go ahead with Truman, I had to decide whether I would permit my name to be presented.

Knowing that the political leaders who had expressed their willingness to support me would follow the President's wishes and support Truman, and knowing also that the C.I.O., having expressed to the President its opposition to me, would continue that opposition to the end, it really meant that I would receive very little support outside the South.

If I went into the race, I would have to make statements as to what had occurred. I could not do this without first resigning. I tried to resign last February and the President would not agree. I announced two months ago that when the Office of Demobilization was established I would not accept the appointment. Therefore, I was not interested in a job. But I was greatly embarrassed. The President was going to be away for weeks and had left believing I would be here to run things. I knew that I would be needed here while he was away. Events prove I was right. I had left the Supreme Court to do a job in time of war and I felt that under these circumstances, I should not resign for the purpose of becoming a candidate for another office.

To one friend I wrote, "I got off the Supreme Court to serve my country—not Mr. Roosevelt. I owed a debt to the more than 15,000,000 men and women in the armed services."

After this political interlude, I returned to the White House, continued to discharge my duties as Director of War Mobilization, and later announced my support of the Roosevelt-Truman ticket. In late September I visited the European front with General Marshall. On my return the President wrote me:

THE WHITE HOUSE
October 18, 1944

DEAR JIMMY:

Now that you are back I do hope that you can act favorably on some of the many demands for you as a speaker. I have known of several places that wanted you and while you were away I told them all they would have to "hold their horses" until you returned. I think you ought to decide on dates fairly soon because, as you know, I want you, of course, in the campaign and you can speak not only well but authoritatively.

As ever yours,
FRANKLIN D. ROOSEVELT

I told the President I would comply with his request, and when the National Committee official in charge of radio time called me the next day, I arranged to speak on the evening of October 30. In some ways I think this was my most effective political speech. I criticized those who talked as if it were more important to put an end to the New Deal than to put an end to the war, and added, "I have never regarded myself as a New Dealer. I am a Democrat." I continued: "The war is not over, either in Europe or Asia. We must continue to maintain national unity and a truly national administration of the war effort. This is no time for anyone to urge on partisan grounds a wholesale housecleaning to purge the administration of either Republicans or New Dealers. This is no time to impugn the good faith or honesty of people we do not like or do not agree with. This is no time to return to politics or business as usual."

All this did not prevent me from expressing the pride I felt as a Southerner in the strong support and active leadership that southern Democrats in the Congress had provided in matters involving international co-operation in the war and in the peace. But the spirit of my address was neither sectional, narrow nor partisan, nor did it show lukewarm support of the Democratic ticket. One man at least was highly pleased with it. Before I left the studio I was called to the telephone. On the other end of the line was Franklin Roosevelt, congratulating me on what he termed a "really good speech." He was good enough to say that "as a master of old English, I think your diction superb."

Having described from my personal knowledge some important features of the process by which two recent Vice Presidents came to hold this place in government, I want to make some general comments about the past and future of the office. Since Thursday, April 30, 1789, when George Washington took the first oath of fealty to the Constitution on the balcony of the Federal Hall in New York City, our country has enjoyed the services of thirty-three presidents—and thirty-six vice-presidents. Of the latter, seven to date have come to hold the position of Chief Executive as a result of the death of a President. The office of Vice President has certainly had a mixed history. Such an authority on the Constitutional Convention as Madison's *Journal* indicates that its establishment was an afterthought; in any event no mention was made of it until thirteen days before the Convention adjourned. Those who drafted the Constitution provided that each member of the Electoral College should cast his vote for two persons, the one receiving the majority to be elected President and the one receiving the second largest vote to be Vice President, regardless of any differences in the political beliefs of the two concerned. This resulted in the Federalist John Adams having as his Vice President Thomas Jefferson, an intense anti-Federalist. After the election of 1800, when Jefferson and Burr received the same number of electoral votes, the contest went to the House of Representatives. When thirty-five ballots were taken before it was decided that Jefferson was to have first place, it was evident that some change in the electoral machinery was necessary. But only from then onward was the Vice President nominated and elected as such.

The Constitution provides that the Vice President shall be president of the Senate, "but shall have no vote, unless they be equally divided." In actual practice, of course, the Vice President presides in the Senate Chamber for only a very limited time each day. That duty is mostly performed by the senator who has been elected president pro tempore of the body or by another member designated by him. However, the Vice President must be available if leaders anticipate a close vote. Research indicates that in our history the Vice President has cast a deciding vote on nearly two hundred occasions. However, I do not think his intervention in this way is necessary or desirable. If a motion does not receive a majority vote, it should be considered lost. It is not wise that the Vice President, a representative of the executive branch of the government, should affect the will of the legislators by casting a decisive vote. In short, participation by the Vice President in Senate voting, either in support of his own views or the President's, constitutes a violation of the spirit of the fundamental provision of the Constitution that the three branches of our government shall forever be separated.

A forward step, in my view, would be to amend the Constitution so that the Vice President is relieved of the duty of presiding over the Senate. After all, this activity offers no training for the position of Chief Executive. Furthermore, a President is limited in the use he can make of the Vice President's abilities by the requirement that the Vice President shall be available to the Senate to vote in case of a tie. In recent years, though the Senate has been almost evenly divided between the major political parties, there have been very few tie votes on any issue.

Because the Vice Presidency has been given few vital functions to perform, the office has often been the subject of jest. The theater public, for example, was never offended by the note of playful ridicule struck by the comedian Victor Moore as Vice President Throttlebottom. Earlier in our history, John C. Calhoun thought it desirable to resign from the Vice Presidency in order to serve in the Senate; and when Benjamin Harrison was offered the nomination on the ticket with Grant, who was reputed to be in bad health, he said, "I am not ambitious to enter the White House following a hearse." Yet the fact remains that under law the only useful function of a Vice President is that he shall be qualified to act as an adequate replacement for the Chief Executive.

It is not reasonable to expect a man to be an adequate replacement for the President if his experience is only that of a "waiter"—waiting around the Senate to see if there is a tie vote and, when the Senate is not in session, waiting around the Capitol to see if the President comes safely through the day. The only place the Vice President can receive adequate training to replace the Chief Executive is in the executive department. Assuming adoption of this constitutional amendment, the next step would be to provide training in the executive branch. It would not be entirely new.

Before the question of President Eisenhower's health arose in 1955, Congress had taken steps—the first I can recall—to supplement the constitutional duties of the Vice President by providing in 1949 that he should be a member of the National Security Council, an organization established to co-ordinate policies relating to defense and national affairs. Five years later President Eisenhower went a step further by announcing that Mr. Nixon would preside over the Council in his absence. But other Presidents before Mr. Eisenhower had sought to give the Vice President duties of some scope and importance. In 1921 Harding encouraged Coolidge to join in Cabinet deliberations; and under Mr. Roosevelt, Garner, Wallace, and Truman also attended. Vice President Garner was also asked to represent the President on a number of visits to foreign countries. Again, President Roosevelt appointed Vice President Wallace to the chairmanship of the Board of Economic Warfare, a post with considerable executive authority. I have related elsewhere how this experiment failed, largely because the powers of that Board and of the Reconstruction Finance Corporation were not clearly defined and because of the clash of personalities. But it was a step in the right direction. It is certainly important that the Congress, or the President by executive order, should authorize the Vice President to attend meetings of all policy-making groups so that if he should be suddenly called to the higher office, he could carry on without impairing the efficiency of government.

There are many important duties that could be delegated to the Vice President. If during the war President Roosevelt could delegate to me wide powers over domestic problems and the settlement of controversies, even between Cabinet members, surely President Eisenhower should be able to install the Vice President in White House offices and delegate to him duties that would relieve the Presidency of a measure of its burdens. I think a Vice President who has been elected by the people would be assured of a degree of co-operation from department officials and members of Congress that would not be accorded any one not so elected. The people and the politicians will realize that he may at any time become President. On the other hand, gratitude and ambition would surely inspire a Vice President to perform duties given him by the Chief Executive to the very best of his ability. After all, every Vice President is aware that he owes his place to the President's victory; and if he has further political aspirations, he knows his election as President will depend upon the record of the administration in which he has served. If under such an arrangement serious personal difficulties should develop between the two men, the President, who under law retains the primary legal responsibility, could promptly rescind the executive orders by which he had delegated special powers to the Vice President.

Men of ability may still hesitate to seek the Vice Presidency if the candidate for President is to continue selecting his running mate the night after his own nomination and after conferring hurriedly with a few political bosses and labor leaders. It might be well to have the nomination for the Vice Presidency precede the nomination of the President. The candidates for President would be so busy with their own contests that they could hardly interfere with another contest. Of course, the surest way to improve the method of selecting a nominee would be to arouse the people to the importance of the office. You cannot get people excited about selecting a Throttlebottom or a Joe Smith, but you might interest them if the Vice President, as a result of the delegation of powers by the President, was made in effect an assistant President.

The solution of these two problems is only incidental to the problem of the incapacity of the President, which at long last is receiving the attention of the Congress as a result of the relatively short illnesses of President Eisenhower in 1955 and 1956.

Many recall the long indisposition of Woodrow Wilson and the arguments over whether he was really capable of performing his duties or whether presidential authority should have been passed on to the Vice President. During that period Vice President Marshall continued to preside over the Senate and refused even to comment on the President's illness. The question then and now remains: Who has the right to determine if an ill President is seriously incapacitated? Admittedly the Constitution is vague. It has been proposed that by congressional enactment there should be formed a committee composed of the Vice President, the Speaker of the House, the majority and minority leaders of the Senate and House, and the Chief Justice of the Supreme Court. This group, in case the President was ill, would select medical specialists to examine him. After receiving the professional medical advice, the committee would pass upon the capacity of the Chief Executive to perform his duties. Under this plan, if it was considered necessary for the Vice President to assume the Presidency and the elected President then recovered, he would not be allowed to resume his former status. There are other somewhat similar proposals.

I can think of several reasons why such a proposal would be unwise and possibly dangerous. It sounds like an ouster of the President, who has the right under the Constitution to hold office for four years.

Suppose, for example, such a statute existed today and President Eisenhower became ill; the committee meets and the Democratic members vote for a medical examination of the President, while the Republican members vote against it; and Chief Justice Warren casts the deciding vote in favor of the examination. However, the President asserts that he is not incapacitated and refuses to submit to examination. Who will enforce it?

Assume he does submit, and that after the examination the Democratic members and Chief Justice Warren vote that the President is incapable of performing his duties, but the President again denies such incapacity and further denies that Congress even had the power to authorize the appointment of the committee. In due course the question would probably go to the Supreme Court. For the sake of argument, assume the Chief Justice and four of the justices should vote that the committee had the power to oust the President. But, assume the President, still asserting his capacity, says that in Article VI the Constitution provides that "This Constitution, and the laws of the United States which shall be made in Pursuance thereof . . . shall be the supreme Law of the Land," and in Article II, Section 2, provides that "The President shall be Commander in Chief of the Army and Navy of the United States." How would the Supreme Court enforce its decision ousting the Commander in Chief of the Army and Navy of the United States?

The mere statement of the possibilities should be sufficient to cause Congress to decide that in a matter of such importance it should not attempt to legislate, but after careful consideration should draft and submit to the states an amendment to the Constitution which would make certain that which is now very uncertain.

Should Congress continue to discuss the problem but fail to act, there would be less demand for drastic action in an emergency if there was already in the White House a Vice President actually vested by the President with some of the presidential powers. Moreover, every President, however blessed with health and strength, needs all the assistance he can be given. Surely we should raise the status of the Vice President and legally amplify the duties and responsibilities of that office in order to insure that the Chief Executive is given all possible help in carrying his crippling load.

# 14   RECONVERSION

Shortly before the Democratic convention, the half-yearly production report compiled at the end of June, 1944, had indicated that the gradual slackening off which I feared would come with news of our successes had indeed occurred. Munitions output for June was generally below that of May and 3 per cent under schedule. Our production figures for ships, guns and ammunition needed to be increased. In the closing days of July, while our troops were making rapid advances on several fronts, critical shortages appeared in the supply of heavy guns and ammunition, bombs, radar equipment, trucks, tanks and tires. Aside from the effects of slowing down and strikes, many of the deficiencies were due to labor shortages in plants producing war matériel, and it was plain that there was a gradual flow into civilian jobs.

For three days we held a series of meetings with representatives of the services and agencies to meet this threat. It was decided that a new and sweeping directive should be issued—"the last legal step short of a national service law." This was announced on August 4 and placed ceilings on nonessential industries in areas where labor shortages had developed. Stating that the move was intended to prevent prolongation of the conflict, the directive continued, "Our war needs will come first and civilian production must not interfere . . . we have the enemy on the ropes; he is dazed and his knees are buckling. This is not the time to take a holiday and give him time to recover"— wording which would indicate that I watch the prize fights. By strengthening the hand of the Manpower Priorities Committee, I hoped to improve manpower distribution in the critical areas; and thereafter some general improvement did take place.

238

On the day the directive was issued, the President wrote me from the Pacific, where he had been since the Chicago convention. He did not know my plans for the future. His "peace feeler" read, in part:

But the more I think of it the more convinced I am that the time has come to press for the Universal Training Bill in one form or another—one year in the service of the government and enough military and educational features can be put into such a program to make it extremely valuable for our defense. The main point is that if we were to take one million and a quarter boys each year, ages from 17 to 23, they will be trained in discipline and physical fitness and they could be paid as were the C.C.C. boys—$30 a month with the bulk of it going back to their families straight.

I am out in the far Aleutians—stormbound at the moment. We have done a grand job out here and have built an excellent base—14,000 Army and 8,000 Navy at the present time. Incidentally, the Seabee battalions of the Navy present a picture of how to use the older men who are too old to be in the regular armed forces.

Just before Mr. Roosevelt reached Washington on August 17, he sent a further message asking that I see him upon his arrival to discuss the George-Kilgore reconversion bill, which made my office permanent. Referring to the many efforts being made to weaken our wage policy, he added, "Tell me about the coming WLB decision in Little Steel."

Two days later he explained his universal training scheme to the press, showing that it was really on his mind. To the newsmen, he emphasized that he did not approve military training programs as such but wanted our young people to learn "how to live in harmony with others."

He had been absent from the country for about a month. Before the convention he had left with me, as he had done on previous occasions, an interesting form of blank check. These were signed sheets on which executive orders might be issued in a grave emergency, after consultation with him by cable. At the time of his journey to Cairo and Teheran, when we were plagued by the coal strike and the President had decided, under certain conditions, to take over the mines, he had left two versions of an order, one directing the Secretary of War to effect the seizure, the other the Secretary of the Interior. In a covering note he wrote, "I am sending both to you to hold in escrow. I hope it will not be necessary to issue either one. Unless new circumstances arise, I prefer draft No. 1. . . . Let us pray that neither one has to be issued."

The early fall months saw us continuing with reconversion plans, though it was difficult always not to impair the current production program in doing so. It now seemed probable that Germany could not last many months and that we would soon be concentrating on the Pacific fronts. In accordance with the direction of Congress I prepared a report on the progress of reconversion which was issued the day after my statement of September 8 that while production of critical war materials had increased in August, output was far behind schedule.

The OWM report was made only after a series of conferences over a period of several months with the procurement agencies. The effort involved in reconversion measures may be judged by the fact that we found 350 people already engaged in contract termination work in the War Department alone, and it was estimated that any effort to end contracts more speedily would require the services of 25,000 trained persons. In the end additional people were trained in special courses provided for certain employees of contractors who might help.

My published report gave details of the cutbacks already made, totaling 18 billion, and stressed that the war against Japan would also require large quantities of war materials. However, there could be, I estimated, a 40 per cent reduction of our total war effort after V-E Day, and the work week might be reduced in most cases to forty hours again. Our military food program would then decline about 50 per cent, and war controls would, of course, be quickly modified to stimulate civilian production.

The report also stated that fear of prolonged unemployment at the war's end was exaggerated, but urged the states to be prepared to liberalize their unemployment insurance legislation; price controls, fairly administered, should be continued, the wartime excess profits tax repealed, and Congress should appropriate at least $2 billion to support farm prices in the transitional period.

During the month of September, Congress passed both a surplus property bill and a bill establishing an office of War Mobilization and Reconversion. This was one "home front" bill I did not urge the Congress to pass. These measures were signed by the President on October 3, but he asked at the same time for further action to improve them. He felt especially that the industrial reconversion measure did not deal adequately "with the human side of reconversion." On the same day by executive order all records, funds and personnel of OWM were transferred to the Office of War Mobilization and Reconversion, which meant in fact that they stayed where they had been since the establishment of the agency. The President also announced that I had agreed to continue as head of the new organization until Congress reconvened, when an appointment could be sent to the Senate.

Meanwhile, I set about selecting the newly created three-man Surplus Property Board. Senator Gillette agreed to serve, as did former Governor Hurley of Connecticut. Fortunately, I usually could induce able men to accept appointments without having the President add his weight to the request. But in the case of the third possible appointee to the Surplus Property Board, David Lilienthal, Director of TVA, I brought Mr. Roosevelt into the picture, since I not only wanted the benefit of Lilienthal's services but thought that a change of post for him would be helpful to the administration. Lilienthal was an idealist, a gifted man and a good administrator. However, he did not get along with Senator Kenneth McKellar and Senator Tom Stewart, who had once been loyal followers of the President. Lilienthal frequently charged the senators with embarrassing him by making requests for political appointments to TVA; they replied in turn that he was domineering, insulting even, and had used the TVA organization in efforts to defeat them. As a result of this controversy the two Democratic senators from Tennessee had changed their attitude toward the President, and when they had doubts about a question in the Senate they resolved those doubts against Mr. Roosevelt.

McKellar told me that if Lilienthal should be reappointed to TVA a few months hence, he would see to it that he was not confirmed by the Senate. That would be embarrassing to the President as well as his appointee. I therefore suggested to the President that he could avoid that trouble by making Lilienthal chairman of the Surplus Property Board, which would not require confirmation. When I mentioned it to Lilienthal, he said that he wanted to think it over but that he did not believe he could accept the post. This I reported to the President, telling him that he would have to "turn on the charm" when Lilienthal came by with me the next morning.

In the President's office I sat quietly by, watching to see the magic work. Mr. Roosevelt said enthusiastically, "Dave, I greatly enjoyed your recent magazine article. It was grand. You ought to tell the people more about the wonderful work you are doing. I would like you to get on the radio some Sunday evening and picture for the people the future of TVA." Lilienthal beamed as he developed the idea of how a similar authority might be introduced to lands like India and Africa, showering blessings upon mankind. Dave soared to heights of eloquence. He said if he had ever done anything of value with TVA, it was entirely due to the inspiration he had received from a speech made by the President on the capitol steps at Montgomery, Alabama, movingly repeating some of the President's words on that occasion and their effect on all who heard them. Then the President took off, as if in a jet, flying equally high. I was left alone, grounded with my sordid appointment to the Surplus Property Board. I tried to get the conversation back to earth, but it was of no avail. Lilienthal told the President that because of his insistence he would consider the appointment further, but, once away from the charm, he declined. Later that day, when I saw Mr. Roosevelt alone, he asked me how he had done. I replied, "Overdone!"

I recall another occasion when the President's charm failed him. Before we left for Yalta, he told me he had arranged to visit Ibn Saud on the way home. The President hoped he might be able to make some progress in bringing about better relations between the Arabs and the Jews on the Palestine question. When I left him at Yalta, in parting I expressed the hope that he would soon be rid of his cold and that he would have good luck when he met Ibn Saud. Some days after the President's return I asked what progress he had made with the Arab leader. He quickly said, "Oh, I want to tell you about that a little later," and began discussing another subject. I was greatly interested and later made another inquiry. When he just as quickly evaded answering, I said, "Mr. President, I fear you were not very successful." He said, "Oh yes, I had an exceedingly pleasant meeting with Ibn Saud and we agreed about everything until I mentioned Palestine. That was the end of the pleasant conversation."

Of course it was expecting too much of the Roosevelt charm to think it might bring together the Jews and Arabs.

For a year there had been no signs of an armistice in the WPB war between Donald Nelson and Charles Wilson. In April, 1944, Wilson had again resigned and once more I had persuaded him to continue for awhile. However, in June he asked that I remind the President of his desire to leave, and FDR finally determined he would have to act.

He proposed to send Nelson to China to investigate and report on economic conditions, and asked me to sell the idea to him. Nelson agreed and made his plans to leave in August. The story of his trip leaked to the press, which quoted Nelson as saying that the assignment was temporary and that he would be out of Washington for only a few weeks. On August 17 the President made the formal announcement of Nelson's mission, saying it might well occupy "several months" and that Charles E. Wilson would act as chairman of War Production Board in his absence.

At this time it was stated by some members of Congress that Nelson's trip would affect his reconversion program, which was one of the causes of disagreement between him and Wilson. A day or so later the President denied that any change in WPB policy was indicated. Wilson was not happy over this development. He was sure that Nelson lieutenants in WPB would be out to discredit him. He reiterated to me his desire to resign and suggested that Lieutenant Commander Krug succeed him. Krug, who had once been with the Tennessee Valley Authority, was a former vice chairman of WPB and a friend of Nelson. Apparently he also enjoyed Wilson's confidence.

Notwithstanding Wilson's recommendation and mine, the President hesitated to appoint Krug, saying that Leland Olds of the Federal Power Commission had told him Krug was no longer friendly to public power. It was surprising that he seemed more interested in Krug's views on this issue—one really not within WPB's jurisdiction—than in the man's qualification as an administrator or in his knowledge of production problems.

Meanwhile, Wilson, accompanied by Sidney Weinberg, his personal assistant and close friend, came to me with another letter of resignation. A few changes were suggested, and while Sidney rewrote it, I busied myself drafting a letter for the President to sign accepting the resignation and expressing appreciation of Wilson's services to his government. Within a few minutes after this had been sent over to the President, together with the resignation, Grace Tully telephoned that it was signed and had gone to the press room for release. The Krug appointment was made and proved to be an excellent one. Krug was a patient man, who never sought headlines and had a capacity for getting along with the people around him. The war crises had brought together in the War Production Board the greatest galaxy of "stars" in our industrial world. When the feuding at the top ended, conditions eased both within WPB and between that agency and the armed services.

Toward the end of September, 1944, I received a request from General Marshall that everything be done to increase the supply of ammunition for General Eisenhower's heavy artillery in France. After his explanation of the situation there, I ordered the War Production Board to give this first priority. Eisenhower had reported that the matter was most urgent because our lines were in advance of his original plans for the period, and soon our troops would be facing fortified positions that could be reduced only by concentrations of heavy artillery fire if we were not to suffer a disproportionate loss of life.

To relieve the shortage immediately it was necessary to tackle the transportation as well as the supply problem, and Franz Schneider of my staff, who devoted his time to shipping problems, told me that the greatest bottleneck was lack of unloading facilities in the port of Cherbourg. Here ships loaded with the ammunition so vitally needed were unable to dock and had come to be regarded more as warehouses than ships. It was hoped that the docks at Antwerp, which had been bombed out, would be repaired and open to us in December, but we could not wait on that development. General Marshall told me he was going to SHAEF to confer with General Eisenhower and hoped I would go with him, spending a day or two at Cherbourg consulting with the Corps of Engineers officers there who were in charge of repairing the berthing facilities, as well as with those directing the transportation of the munitions by truck and rail to our advancing forces.

I was anxious to go with him and on October 5 we boarded the presidential plane, the *Sacred Cow,* piloted by Colonel Henry T. Myers of Georgia, and flew nonstop to Paris. This was said to be the first nonstop flight to Paris since Lindbergh's. We were met by General Eisenhower and Generals Omar Bradley and Bedell Smith. At Cherbourg some of the shipping problems in which I was interested were worked out and plans made to relieve the harbor congestion.

I was able to appreciate by how close a margin we had escaped disaster when we were taken to see one of the launching sites in that area for the Nazi V weapons. It was located in what had been an old rock quarry and was well camouflaged. The Germans had not quite completed the construction of a fully protective concrete roof when they were driven off. Had invasion been delayed many weeks beyond June 6, 1944, it is entirely possible that from such sites flying bombs would have rained on English installations so effectively that we might never have succeeded in gathering and launching our enormous invasion forces.

My companion and military aide was Major Donald Russell, who some months before had been transferred from OWM to SHAEF headquarters in France. Together we flew to visit General Hoyt Vandenberg's air headquarters. It was interesting to see actually in use the end product of so many of our plans and efforts to provide supplies, and inspiring to meet the men, of all ranks, into whose hands the vast military machine created by our domestic efforts had been entrusted.

We then went to the headquarters of General Bradley's 12th Army Group. The next morning General George S. Patton arrived; after he had concluded his business, he told me that he was free that day since his headquarters was being moved. He proposed to drive to the Montfaucon area where he had been severely wounded during World War I, and asked Russell and me to accompany him. With our party was a major, referred to by everyone as "Shorty," who, Patton explained, was a Texas ranger and a former sergeant in his outfit in 1917. Shorty, it appeared, had also been wounded in the same engagement. As our jeep cavalcade neared Montfaucon, Patton ordered his driver to stop, and when Shorty's jeep had caught up, jumped out. "Shorty," he said, "the whole place is changed, but I remember this tree. I'm sure this is where we camped the night prior to the fight." When Shorty expressed his doubts, Patton said: "If we did not camp here, we should have." He offered to wager that when we had driven a half mile farther down the road, we would find a side road, and off that road would be a creek.

To my surprise, after we had gone that distance, we found both road and creek, and within sight a monument erected by the State of Pennsylvania in memory of those in the Pennsylvania National Guard who had fallen there. In a few moments Shorty had found the spot where he had received his wound, but Patton could not locate the place where he had been when wounded. Unfortunately, what had once been a wooded area was now cultivated land, and after some thirty minutes the General gave up in disgust.

After a short visit to Montfaucon, we returned to General Bradley's

H.Q. Noticing the huge wall map of the front, I asked Patton to tell me of his own part in the rapid advance of our armies following the Normandy landings. Dropping on one knee beside the map, he described the movements of his soldiers, with some criticism of Montgomery for not keeping pace. Those delays, he thought, had given the Germans an opportunity to bring up further reinforcements. In the middle of this story he turned and said, "You know this advance was planned by Bradley; but [turning back to the map] I was the only man who could have executed it."

Later at lunch I was able to observe the attitude of some thirty officers who watched him as he talked. Most of them were young men, and every face reflected admiration and confidence in him. It was wonderful to see how he conveyed his own self-confidence to others. He hoped I could help to have his Third Army transferred to the Pacific war as soon as Germany surrendered. He was confident that with the Third he could conclude that war successfully in short order. Of course, he complained repeatedly and bitterly about the lack of gasoline and ammunition supplies which had stopped his drive into Germany. As I left him he asked me to deliver two notes for him when I returned to Washington, one to his wife and another to his daughter, whom he adored and who resembled him in many ways. I am no military expert, but I think that my military friends are right in regarding him as one of the most brilliant field commanders ever to wear our country's uniform.

During the early days of November I held a series of conferences on the manpower shortages with all key officials, and after our talks I gave to the press a letter dated November 16, reading in part: "While a shortage of material and weapons exists in relatively few programs it is sufficient, if not speedily overcome, to prolong the war." I then summarized the deficiencies in our program, dealing with such items as heavy bombers, heavy artillery and ammunition, trucks and radar, and drew attention to the manpower situation in certain key areas, from which there was a drain of skilled personnel who were switching to employment in civilian industries. I continued: "Much of the manpower trouble is due to the mistaken belief of some people that the war is about over. Two hundred thousand able-bodied men, willing to do hard work, could break the bottleneck in the critical programs and shorten the war."

At this time the need to obtain the maximum manpower and to expedite our production to the front lines was so great that for the first time I permitted an increase in my staff. At many of our office conferences involving War Department affairs, Major General Lucius D. Clay had been present as one of the department representatives, and during the discussions would often come up with solutions to our most pressing problems. I came to have the highest regard for his judgment, and drafted him as my deputy director for war programs and general administration, though he remained in the Army and continued to wear his uniform. On his recommendation, we added to our force several additional deputies, including J. B. Hutson, formerly an Assistant Secretary of Agriculture, who came to assist in adjusting our agricultural programs from war to peacetime conditions.

At the same time the President accepted my recommendations for the War Mobilization and Reconversion Advisory Board, provision for which had been included by Congress in the recent legislation. Its members were the Honorable O. Max Gardner, chairman; Mrs. Anna Rosenberg and William H. Davis, representing the public; Eric A. Johnston, George H. Mead, and Nathaniel Dyke, Jr., management; William Green, Phillip Murray, and T. C. Cashen, labor; and Edward O'Neal, A. S. Goss, and J. G. Patten, agriculture.

Toward the close of 1944 a dispute arose at Oak Ridge over the jurisdictional rights of several labor organizations. I had first learned about the nature of the work being done there one day back in 1943 while I was discussing with the President some of the problems of war mobilization, and he then told me the story of the Manhattan Project. I listened, fascinated, as he pictured the race between the German scientists and our own. He said that prior to 1939 it was known that our enemies had made some progress—but we had little information. When he described the possible consequences of an atomic weapon bringing victory to either side, I was frightened as well as awed.

Even before this talk I had had considerable curiosity about the project, for as Mobilizer I was expected to ensure that it had top priority in men and in material. I noted too that some of our most skilled technicians were involved and that it required the services of more than a hundred thousand workers. I had not asked the President about the project and had refrained from mentioning it to Secretary

Stimson, who had it under his personal supervision. Then one day the subject came up in a conversation, and it was easy to see Stimson's surprise when he learned that I had knowledge of what was being done with the important resources involved.

During my work as War Mobilizer I had no further connection with the Manhattan Project, beyond continuing to see that it was accorded top priority in labor and materials, until the Oak Ridge dispute arose. This had been referred to the National Labor Relations Board, which, at the request of the War Department, had several times postponed the public hearing required by law because of the need "to maintain a secrecy beyond that of any other project." In mid-December, Under Secretary Bob Patterson and Major General Leslie R. Groves, in charge of "Special Weapons," came to the office to enlist my aid in inducing the labor representatives to accept further delays. Groves pointed out that at such hearings damaging revelations about the number of workers involved and indications of the relation of a particular unit to the project as a whole would surely be made.

Both my visitors agreed that it would be April of next year before they would be in a position to know whether the atomic weapon could actually be developed. With this in mind I arranged a conference with Joseph P. Clark of the International Brotherhood of Firemen and Oilers and Al Wegener of the International Brotherhood of Electrical Workers. These two labor leaders had authority to represent the other organizations. I told them I knew that we could not expect them to co-operate unless they were given very substantial reasons, and that we would take them into our confidence. Binding them to secrecy, I told them that the work involved a new weapon which we hoped would shorten the war, and that it justified the waiving of their rights under the Wagner Act and their continued co-operation with General Groves. As a result we obtained their full co-operation and the promise was kept for the duration of the war. Their attitude was encouraging, as was that of the few congressional leaders who, knowing the nature of the work, resisted the temptation to tell their colleagues and thus divide the responsibility for the vast appropriation that was being spent on what was still an uncertainty.

It was just at this time that the mid-December Nazi counteroffensive struck our advanced troops in Belgium and Luxembourg. When the surprise attack began, the President was absent at Warm Springs, where he had been since early in the month. It threw a scare into all of us. I sent him an appraisal of our domestic situation which perhaps is worth quoting at length only because it shows the wide range of the problems of my office:

December 20, 1944

1. The continued shortage of manpower in war industries indicated a need for more drastic action. Therefore, I authorized the Director of Selective Service to amend his regulations to increase the induction of men between the ages of 26 and 37 not employed in essential war industry. I am advised that this action has already shown excellent results in bringing about the transfer of men eligible for the draft from less essential industries to war industries. . . .

2. The tire production program continues to lag and the provision of sufficient tires for military purposes will be most difficult during the early part of 1945. All possible steps have been taken to augment our own production and in addition, the Army has been asked to place experienced production experts at work in bringing French and Belgian tire industries into production at the earliest possible date. These factories will be utilized first to retread and repair worn tires.

3. I have also asked the Army to survey the French munitions and explosives industries to ascertain the possibility of utilizing their industry to reduce the demands on our own country. The Army ammunition program involves a considerable expansion and manifestly we should utilize any available facilities in France to reduce its extent.

I have also asked the Joint Chiefs of Staff to review the Navy munitions program to determine if some of the Navy's capacity can be diverted to Army use during the next few months.

4. I have asked the Joint Chiefs of Staff to review the shipping requirements for 1945 at the earliest possible date to permit intelligent consideration to be given to our shipbuilding program for the last half of 1945.

5. I have been disturbed to find that the requirements for high octane gasoline are already in excess of the established production. Since the construction of new facilities for this purpose will require a minimum of fifteen to sixteen months, it is apparent that our air effort during this period must be governed by the available supply of gasoline.

A letter which I have written to the Joint Chiefs of Staff on this subject is also attached.

6. I have authorized the Army, Navy and Foreign Economic Administration each to proceed with the disposal of their surpluses abroad under policies to be established by the Surplus War Property Board. This problem is particularly acute with the Army, which is abandoning installations in

North Africa and the Middle East which are no longer required for the war effort. . . .

7. I have authorized the Dutch Purchasing Commission to acquire certain power equipment belonging to a magnesium plant at Lake Charles, Louisiana, which is not now in operation. The Dutch are in desperate need of this equipment to provide the power for pumping operations which must be undertaken in that part of their country inundated by enemy action. We not only have secured an advantageous price but also have enabled one of our Allies to obtain desperately needed material promptly for its rehabilitation, thus increasing its capacity to contribute to our common war effort. . . .

My letter reflected a certain urgency which grew in the following days as news of the Nazi successes continued to pour in. Just at this time it was proposed that the Los Angeles race track be reopened. The local California office of the Manpower Commission had decided favorably on the application, but I announced that I had asked the War Production Board and the Office of Defense Transportation to prevent the use of critical materials, services and transportation in the operation of all race tracks. This "request" became effective January 3, 1945, and I made it clear I would find the means to enforce it, if need be. The racing fraternity soon indicated that it would comply. It is difficult to estimate exactly how much was saved in manpower, railroad transportation, tires, and that particularly scarce item, gasoline, used by thousands following the races. Paul Porter, chairman of the Federal Communications Commission, informed me later that 19,000 miles of leased wire circuits with more than 700 extensions, previously used for dissemination of racing information, were being made available for more essential purposes; in addition, large numbers of telephone instruments, which were in short supply, were reclaimed for more essential uses.

Early in the New Year I asked General Hershey of Selective Service to investigate the large number of young men, between the ages of eighteen to twenty-six, allegedly unfit for military service, who were featured in professional athletics. He set the local draft boards to work. Although some ardent sportsmen were incensed at the curtailment of their pleasures, the fact that the American troops in combat were without any diversions was sufficient reason for our course.

There was another brief flurry of this sort in late February, when we decided to issue an appeal for places of entertainment throughout the nation to close at midnight, reserving the right to exercise the powers of

WPA, OPA, the Manpower Commission and the like to ensure co-operation should it be necessary. Our aim, of course, was to save any further drain on coal, electricity and particularly manpower. I soon received a call from Mayor La Guardia of New York. Fiorello talked as if New York City would secede from the Union if its night clubs were forced to shut down so early; he expressed doubt that I had any power to "invite" the closing and told me that such activities would continue in New York City until one o'clock in the morning.

I did not argue with him but got in touch with General Marshall, who was glad to issue an order to military personnel in the New York area that any club failing to comply would be placed off limits. The Navy, through Admiral King, issued similar orders. The main reason for these drastic measures, which the country as a whole was prepared to accept patriotically, was contained in the first sentence of the press release on the curfew: "We must convince our fighting forces that the home front is prepared to sacrifice for their support."

# 15  WITH FDR AT YALTA

In late December, 1944, I had occasion to go to the President's study for a discussion of some shipping questions. When we had concluded our talk, he said, "Jimmy, I want you to go with me on this trip to the Crimea." I knew, of course, of the arrangements for a conference between Stalin, Churchill and Roosevelt which was to be held at Yalta within a few weeks; but in view of my heavy responsibilities on the home front, I had no idea of being asked to go. I therefore expressed genuine surprise at the President's statement and told him I felt I should not be away from the country at the same time that he was. He said that the shipping problems we had just been considering illustrated the reason for his request; that at Yalta major issues would be discussed which would affect our programs for reparations, Lend Lease, and other matters on which I could be of great help to him. But I was not convinced. Among other things the "work or fight" bill was pending in Congress; because it affected so many individuals and families directly, people felt strongly about it, and their differing views were reflected in the positions taken by their representatives. If I should leave, I knew that my deputy director, General Lucius D. Clay, would be confronted with this very serious problem. I told the President that I would have to think about his request and give him an answer later.

Upon returning to my office I found my staff unanimously of the opinion that I should go, and so, despite misgivings, on the following day I agreed. But the misgivings persisted and on the day we were to leave Washington, January 22, 1945, I went to the President's offices to tell him again I should not go. While I was waiting, Pa Watson and

Steve Early told me that Ed Flynn was to be a member of the party. They were curious why he was to be included. Oddly enough, when I asked the President who was going, he mentioned everyone but Flynn. He explained that although regulations prohibited a woman from traveling on a naval vessel, he had obtained permission for his daughter Anna Boettiger to accompany him.

Now I asked once more to be excused from the trip, but he continued to insist, adding jocularly, "We are the only two well men in the crowd." Later I recalled that comment, for the President suffered from a stubborn cold and sinus infection throughout his absence from the United States; Harry Hopkins was quite ill most of the time at Yalta, and delayed his return home to rest in Africa's sun; and Pa Watson died on the return journey. I thought it possible that perhaps there was only one truly physically fit person on that trip—myself.

Why the President insisted on my going I still do not know. Perhaps it was because I had a reputation with the Congress and the public for being more conservative than other members of our delegation, such as Stettinius and Hopkins. Or perhaps it was because he knew better than those close to him the state of his health.

I boarded the train for Norfolk at the underground track used at times by the President during the war. This is a secret subway that leads from the place where one boards the train, under one of the government buildings, to the main line of the railroad. The President invited me to join him in his car, and said he was very uncomfortable from a cold he had caught at the inaugural ceremonies two days earlier; he was drinking orange juice as a remedy.

The next morning, boarding the U.S.S. *Quincy*, he said his cold had grown worse but he hoped it might be improved by sunshine on the voyage. Unfortunately, we had bad weather most of the trip and, except for lunch and dinner in the dining room, the President stayed in his cabin. His general appearance concerned me, but both Dr. McIntire and Mrs. Boettiger assured me that he was not really ill. She thought my impression came from observing him during the showing of films in the evening when she usually sat on one side of him and I on the other. She explained that his sinus trouble, now aggravated by his cold, caused him to hold his mouth open and that this naturally made him look bad.

Only a few days after we left Washington, my opinion that it was not wise for me to leave was confirmed by messages I received about developments on the home front. On January 16 we had had a meeting in the President's office with a congressional group and General Marshall and Admiral King to discuss the need for the national service legislation mentioned by the President in his recent State of the Union Message. In it he had asked that all possible use be made of the more than one million men exempted from military service as 4F's and suggested other measures to help production. At our meeting Congressman May, chairman of the House Military Affairs Committee, told us that there was serious opposition to the legislation and he needed assistance to get it passed. It was decided that support must be mobilized, and I prepared a letter addressed to May for the President to sign, writing others for my own signature to May, Speaker Rayburn and Senator Thomas, chairman of the Senate committee. In the letter I tried to express the long view:

If we are to have the most effective use of our manpower in this period, to insure that essential production for the Pacific is not disrupted by the drift of workers into civilian industry, the government must be endowed with sufficient authority to see not only that men work or fight, but that they work where they are most needed.

However, we must be prepared, when Germany is defeated, to replace promptly those young men who are deferred because of their present need in war production so that they will then have the opportunity to serve their country in combat. To the fullest extent possible, these young men should be replaced by soldiers of comparable skills who have had many months of battle service.

After my departure for Yalta the agencies and military services, whose representatives had agreed to support this "work or fight" measure, began suggesting various amendments and in a few days were again at war with each other about the bill. From General Clay I received a letter setting forth their differences, which he felt might be fatal to the legislation. He also enclosed an editorial on the subject from the Washington *Post*. I read it carefully because the writer took the occasion to criticize strongly my absence from Washington:

. . . the differences between the contending groups are not broad. We think they can be bridged by a clear understanding of objectives and functions, such an understanding as Mr. Byrnes might have been able to impart to legislators on both sides if his time and energy had not been diverted to international affairs that lie outside of his official assignment.

We cannot imagine that the man who is the administrator of the entire home front can have any mission on the foreign front which can justify his absence at this critical moment, legislatively as well as actually, in home-front affairs. The pilot clearly should be with his ship. . . .

. . . as the president of the home front, he is at the very spearhead of the struggle to get Congress to authorize more manpower controls. . . . He, too, has slipped out of town for an overseas jaunt, doubtless in response to superior orders.

That hurt! I agreed with most of the views expressed, but unfortunately could make no reply. In fact, I found it necessary to wire Walter Brown not to make any statement correcting the newspaper story. He wanted to tell the press that I had not gone on a "jaunt" but had gone reluctantly, complying with an urgent presidential request. However, I took some comfort from the editorial writer's inference that I had responded to "superior orders." As to the "work or fight" bill, Clay worked hard, but its passage was delayed until after my return.

On the *Quincy* one of the topics of small importance but of interest wherever two or three were gathered was the presence of Flynn on board. On the train to Norfolk, Steve Early, Pa Watson, and Ross McIntire had all questioned Admiral Leahy and me about why Flynn was going. Neither of us had an answer to give to them or to the military personnel traveling with us who made similar inquiries. When we stopped at Malta, I think the first question asked me by Harry Hopkins, who joined us there, was "What about Flynn?" Averell Harriman was equally curious. On the first Saturday we spent aboard ship the President facetiously announced, "Father Flynn will say Mass tomorow morning." This caused someone to suggest that perhaps the President had asked Flynn to go to the U.S.S.R. to inquire about the treatment the Catholic Church was receiving there. It is a fact that before the Yalta Conference adjourned, Mr. Roosevelt asked Stalin to have arrangements made for Flynn to make certain trips through Russia, and later the press recorded that he visited the Vatican before returning home.

There were, of course, more urgent matters to occupy our attention. The first day out from Norfolk the President received a cablegram from Mrs. Roosevelt and Sam Rosenman urging that he take some action in support of Henry Wallace, whose nomination for Secretary of Commerce was being bitterly opposed. They suggested that he sign an executive order transferring the loan agencies from the Department of Commerce, as this move would disarm some of the opposition to Wallace. The President said he was opposed to this plan and did nothing. Two days later they sent a second appeal. In this they asked whether, should Senator George's bill proposing to transfer the lending powers be passed, he would sign it. Handing me the message, with little indication of personal interest, he asked what I thought. I told him I would approve it, and he said that was his view, too. I could easily picture the situation on the floor of the Senate and, grasping the urgency of the request, promptly drafted an affirmative reply for his signature, addressing it to Senator Barkley. By acting quickly we were able to dispatch this message on the special plane flown from the Azores, and fortunately it was received by Barkley fifteen minutes before the vote on the bill. With the even division in the Senate, it was probably this favorable statement from the President that saved the passage of the George bill by a few votes, which in turn made possible the confirmation of Wallace's nomination for Secretary.

At meals on board ship I was seated next to the President, and on many occasions we talked about the subjects that would probably come up at the conference. However, because of his indisposition, he was to all appearances doing little paper work on the voyage, and I did not know until the day before we reached Malta that the State Department had prepared a great deal of briefing material for his consideration en route. I spent some hours going through it, and later, as I heard him at the conference table, I marveled that he made such a good presentation apparently with little preparation.

One evening at dinner on board ship I told him that Ben Cohen, who had worked with the Dumbarton Oaks committee in drafting the proposal for the United Nations Organization, had convinced me that in view of the rule of unanimity required for action by the Security Council, there should be some provision for collective action by the member states if the Security Council were prevented by a veto from taking action. After we had talked of it, the President professed to agree with this view. At the conference table I was disappointed to note that he had not changed the draft treaty in this respect before presenting it. Later I learned that the Secretary of State, Stettinius, and other representatives of the State Department who were at the Conference, persuaded the President to stand by the draft that the Department had prepared. This omission was remedied in some degree at the San Francisco organization meeting, when Article 51, which allows member states to take all effective measures in their own self-defense, was included in the charter.

The U.S.S. *Quincy* moored in Grand Harbor, Valetta, Malta, at one minute after ten on February 2. The weather was sunny and all Malta seemed to be lining the quays to greet the President. As soon as the vessel was secure a traffic of important visitors started from and to the shore. Within a few minutes of our arrival Stettinius, together with our Ambassador to Russia, Averell Harriman, and Harry Hopkins, fresh from preliminary talks with the British in London, came aboard. About a quarter to eleven, Winston Churchill in naval uniform, accompanied by his daughter, Section Officer Sarah Oliver of the British Women's Auxiliary Air Force, came to pay a short courtesy call on Mr. Roosevelt. Churchill had been in Malta for three days while the Combined Chiefs of Staff had been in session there. Earlier, while plans were being made for the rendezvous, he had cabled the President in characteristic vein:

We shall be delighted if you will come to Malta. I shall be waiting on the quay. You will also see the inscription of your noble message to Malta of a year ago. Everything can be arranged to your convenience. No more let us falter! From Malta to Yalta! Let nobody alter!

At one o'clock precisely, the Prime Minister and his daughter returned for lunch in the President's cabin. The other guests on this occasion included Stettinius and his British counterpart Anthony Eden, Admiral Leahy, and me. There was some general discussion, particularly between Mr. Churchill and Mr. Roosevelt, about the physical arrangements at Yalta. The Prime Minister had previously expressed himself firmly on the difficulties of getting there and on the insalubrious nature of the place—in fact, he had told Hopkins that if ten years had been spent in research, no worse location in the world for a meeting could have been found! However, the President was able to report that a medical team from our floating communications center, the U.S. auxiliary vessel *Catoctin*, anchored at Sevastopol, had done an effective debugging operation at the conference site.

After the British guests had left, the President went ashore for a two-hour drive. There was a discussion with the U.S. Chiefs of Staff after his return and before the arrival in the evening of Churchill and a British party. There followed another small dinner party in the

President's quarters. Shortly after ten, Churchill and Eden left and by eleven our party went ashore to Luqa airfield, where planes were waiting to take us the rest of the way—fourteen hundred miles—to the Crimea.

The Air Transport Command had the formidable job of conveying conference-bound personnel totaling at least five hundred to Saki airfield over an unknown route in blacked-out night flights. But the entire operation went off with precision, the fourteen C-54's, escorted by fighters, arriving safely at exactly ten-minute intervals. The President traveled in the *Sacred Cow*, a plane especially equipped for him with an elevator. Just as the door of the ordinary plane opens to allow passengers to alight by a flight of stairs, a door opened in the bottom of the *Sacred Cow* through which a small elevator was let down. With equal ease it could be drawn up. This was one of the few times President Roosevelt used the plane, for he disliked airplanes as much as he liked sailboats. However, the next day he said he had been resting when the plane left the runway at Malta.

When our delegation reached Saki on February 3, Foreign Minister Molotov and other high officials were there to meet us and explain that Marshal Stalin had not yet arrived in the Crimea. The President remained in his plane until Mr. Churchill's plane touched down. He was quickly out and came over to greet the President. The two leaders, Mr. Roosevelt riding in a jeep, Mr. Churchill walking by its side, then approached the guard of honor. Arms were presented and a band played the three national anthems. After this ceremony our convoy proceeded to the Livadia Palace, near Yalta, eighty miles distant. The first part of the early morning drive was through a snow-covered countryside on roads that were very poor in comparison with our well-paved highways, and past many reminders of the war, such as burned buildings and German rolling stock abandoned in the enemy's hurried flight. The troops guarding the route included many girl soldiers—girls with guns. As its headquarters the British party was given Vorontzov Villa, the former residence of a Russian prince, twelve miles or more from Livadia.

Formal conference sessions were to be held at Livadia Palace, which was also headquarters for the U.S. delegation. This was the former summer palace of the Czars, built in 1911 of white granite in Italian Renaissance style. It had fifty rooms and commanded a splendid view of the mountains and the sea. After the revolution the Soviets turned it into a rest home for tuberculosis patients. During the German occupation it had been used by the High Command and left in very bad condition, but it was soon evident that our Russian hosts had accomplished wonders with only three weeks' advance notice in repairing and refurnishing it for our use.

The President was quartered on the first floor where the former Czar and his son had lived. Here he had ready access to the large room, once used for balls and banquets, where the plenary gatherings of the conference were held. On the second floor the Czarina and her daughters had had their suites. General Marshall occupied a beautiful room on this floor, which was originally the imperial bedroom, and the boudoir adjoining was assigned to Admiral King. I slept on the ground floor not far from the billiard room, which had been turned into a private dining room for the President.

In passing, I should like to correct a mistaken impression given by John Gunther in his widely read *Roosevelt in Retrospect*. In dealing with the supposed inaccessibility of the President there, he writes: "It was hard enough even for Byrnes or the highest Generals to get to Roosevelt at Yalta." The writer was misinformed. Actually the President and I had both lunch and dinner together throughout the week except on two or three occasions when an official engagement took us elsewhere. Every evening before dinner I was in his apartment and I saw him not only at the conference table every afternoon but at other times. I did not attend any private conference between Roosevelt and Stalin. However, I had ample opportunity to make my views known to him, though the record will show that my advice was not always followed.

As we began the work of the conference I became acquainted with several State Department officials for the first time. Among these was Freeman Matthews, Director of the Office of European Affairs, who is now Ambassador to Austria. It took only a short time for me to become a sincere admirer of "Doc" Matthews, one of the many able men in the career service.

A more controversial figure was also present. The day following our arrival, the President handed me a paper prepared by the State Department containing proposals for a European High Commission to control liberated areas, and requested me to give an opinion on it after talking to the department representative in charge of this question. Alger Hiss was then brought to my room by Hopkins. He was one of Mr. Stettinius' three special aides and had already participated in the departmental discussions at Marrakech in North Africa and at Naples on matters to be considered at the conference. This was my first meeting with him at Yalta. He told me several members of the Department had contributed to the document which the President had given me. Some of its provisions did not accord with my thinking, and when I conveyed my objections to the President there were some revisions made before he presented the proposal at a plenary session.

Mr. Hiss has been frequently pictured as exercising a dominating and detrimental influence upon the President at Yalta. My opinion is that, if he did, it was indirect. For example, the evidence indicates that before our party ever arrived in the Crimea, the State Department group had decided to recommend to the President that he try to bring about agreement on the desirability of securing the maximum degree of unity between the Chinese Communists and the Nationalist government. According to Stettinius, he stressed this point of view in talking to Mr. Eden at Malta, and Eden had agreed and said he hoped that the Soviets could be persuaded to do what they could to further it. Later this was to be described as an instance of Mr. Roosevelt's willingness to "surrender" to the Communists, but it was a British-American policy agreed upon by Eden and Stettinius before reaching Yalta.

It is plain that Hiss had easy access, for good or evil, to Stettinius and Hopkins, who were, of course, trusted advisers of the President. Hiss did not sit at the conference table, as has often been stated. He attended the third plenary meeting, at which the Dumbarton Oaks proposals for a world security organization were under discussion; then I believed him to be present because of his employment in the relevant division of the State Department. He sat in the rear of the room and was frequently consulted by Mr. Hopkins and Mr. Stettinius. The record shows that while he did not sit at the conference table, he did subsequently attend all other sessions, as well as the meetings held by the Foreign Ministers throughout the conference.

One question which interested me before we even left the U.S. was the desire expressed by the Soviets, through diplomatic channels, that areas of the U.S.S.R., such as Byelorussia and the Ukraine, neither an independent state, should be granted membership and votes in the

United Nations. At a Cabinet meeting shortly before the Yalta Conference the President referred to this request, terming it ridiculous and saying he had told some members of the Senate Foreign Relations Committee that if such a proposal should be offered he would ask that at least two of our states be granted votes. Both the senators and the Cabinet members had agreed with the President's position.

In the course of the fourth plenary session, February 7, after the Soviets had agreed to accept the United States proposals for voting procedures in what would be the Security Council of the world organization, Stalin presented his request for membership for Byelorussia and the Ukraine. In so doing, he emphasized that their inhabitants had endured great suffering at the hands of the Germans. Mr. Churchill expressed warm sympathy for this request, but the President was more guarded, saying that he was reluctant to depart from the principle of each state's having one vote only, and that the question should be referred to the Foreign Ministers for consideration. This was done, and at the next full session Eden reported, on behalf of the Foreign Ministers, a recommendation that the U.S. and U.K. should both support the application of these Russian states for United Nations membership at the forthcoming organizational conference. No mention was made of any additional votes for the U.S. as a compensation, and the President accepted the recommendation.

That evening the leading delegates were entertained at dinner by Marshal Stalin. Before the dinner I expressed to the President my strong conviction that a serious mistake had been made, but he told me he had raised no objection because he did not want to endanger the entire proposal for a world security organization. He said that the next day he was having Churchill for lunch and I could talk with him about it then, though he feared it was too late to make a change.

The next day, while Mr. Churchill and I were awaiting the President's arrival in the dining room, I explained to him the predicament we would be in upon returning home if there should be an agreement to give the Russians three votes to our one. Mr. Churchill recognized at once how embarrassing this would be politically and said he would be glad to vote for allotting three votes to the United States.

A little later he repeated our conversation to the President and I contributed a story to illustrate the point. In 1920, I said, when I was campaigning for the Democratic party, I had a joint debate with a Republican orator at Camden, New Jersey. After I had made what

I thought was a convincing speech, a man rose in the audience whose face and voice indicated his origin. In a good Irish brogue he asked, "Is it true that in the League of Nations the United States would have one vote and Great Britain six?" "Yes," I replied, "but—" I never had a chance to finish the sentence, for the Irishman exclaimed, "That's enough for me," and walked out amid audience applause and my embarrassment. Churchill promptly agreed to support a proposal that we have as many votes as the Soviets.

Knowing the influence Harry Hopkins had with the President, I also talked to him about my proposal, and he joined me in urging him to approach Stalin about it. Mr. Roosevelt said he would take it up with him, and on the day I left Yalta he wrote a personal letter to the Marshal expressing concern lest he encounter political difficulties in the U.S. over the number of votes allotted to the big powers in the Assembly. He stated that in order to get the Congress and the American people to accept a world organization, it might be necessary to give parity in votes to the United States; he asked if Stalin would support him in this. He received promptly the following cordial reply:

Koreis, February 11, 1945

Dear Mr. Roosevelt: I have received your letter of February 10. I entirely agree with you that, since the number of votes for the Soviet Union is increased to three in connection with the inclusion of the Soviet Ukraine and Soviet White Russia among the members of the Assembly, the number of votes for the U. S. A. should be also increased.

I think that the number of votes for the U. S. A. might be increased to three as in the case of the Soviet Union and its two basic Republics. If it is necessary I am prepared officially to support this proposal.

With sincere respects,

I. Stalin

One should note that Stalin said that "the number of votes for the *Soviet Union*" is increased to three.

As I have said, I was not at the Conference the last day when those letters were exchanged, but on my arrival in Washington I received a message from Harry Hopkins:

FOR JUSTICE BYRNES FROM MR. HOPKINS:

The President has received completely satisfactory replies from the Prime Minister and Marshal Stalin on additional votes to achieve parity for the United States, if necessary. In view of the fact that nothing on this whole subject appears in the communique, the President is extremely anxious no aspect of this question be discussed even privately.

At first I did not understand the need for secrecy on this point, but later was told it was in order that France and China might be informed of the agreement before it became general knowledge. Thinking the matter settled, I concentrated on the problems that had accumulated in my office during my absence, and did not follow developments in the State Department. A few months later I learned that at San Francisco Secretary Stettinius, chairman of our delegation, had agreed to the membership of Byelorussia and the Ukraine with no mention made of the agreement giving the United States three votes.

The only explanation for this that I have seen since was a report of a press conference the President had at Warm Springs on April 5, just seven days before he died. Then when a reporter referred to a "leak" of a secret agreement that we should have three votes, the President was quoted as saying: "This plea for votes was done in a very quiet way," and that if he were a member of the delegation he would probably vote yes. The newspaper story further quotes the President:

Then I said, "By the way, if the Conference in San Francisco should give you three votes in the Assembly—if you get three votes—I do not know what would happen if I don't put in a plea for three votes in the States." And I said, "I would make the plea for three votes and insist on it."

It is not really of any great importance. It is an investigatory body only. I told Stettinius to forget it. I am not awfully keen for three votes in the Assembly. It is the little fellow who needs the vote in the Assembly.

Question: They don't decide anything, do they?

The President: No.

This explanation is inconsistent with the written agreement of Stalin quoted above, but I assume the condition of the President's health was such that he did not recall what had taken place.

Later, while serving in the General Assembly of the United Nations, I had to listen to three speeches from the Soviet government on every controversial issue and hear three votes cast for every Soviet proposal. I frequently regretted that the United States had not demanded at San Francisco the three votes that had been agreed to by Churchill and Stalin at Yalta. In the deliberations of the U.N. when a two-thirds' vote is required, there are times when Russia's three votes may provide her with the strength necessary for hampering action.

One of the vivid recollections I have of the Conference was the flurry over trusteeships which occurred when Mr. Stettinius had begun to read the section of the Dumbarton Oaks proposals dealing with this question. He began, "I have a brief statement as to Dumbarton Oaks. It is agreed that five governments which have permanent seats on the council should consult each other prior to the United Nations Conference as to the establishment of trusteeships."

He was interrupted by Churchill, who said vigorously:

I absolutely disagree. I will not have one scrap of British territory flung into that "area." After we have done our best to fight in this war and have done no crime to anyone I will have no suggestion that the British Empire is to be put into the dock and examined by everybody to see whether it is up to their standard. No one will induce me as long as I am Prime Minister to let any representative of Great Britain go to a conference where we will be placed in the dock and asked to justify our right to live in a world we have tried to save.

At this point the President asked that Stettinius be allowed to finish what he had started to read, as it had no reference to what Mr. Churchill had in mind. Stettinius started off again, explaining that the policy makers were not considering the British Empire. But Churchill had previously read the proposal and, as he understood it, wanted no part of it. He grudgingly admitted that some form of trusteeship might be created for some of the former enemy territories, but he again proclaimed the general integrity of the British Empire.

At the end of these rather heated statements I suggested to the President that he declare a fifteen-minute recess for the usual afternoon tea. During that interim, after talking to Doc Matthews, I took occasion to assure Mr. Churchill that the drafters had no idea that their language would be given the interpretation he had put on it. When I told him what the Secretary had meant to say, he interrupted to inquire, "Well, why doesn't he say what he means?"

When the session was resumed, Stettinius presented a statement that entirely satisfied the Prime Minister. As I again took shorthand notes of his colorful comments, I noted that Marshal Stalin was considerably amused by the incident. In conversation later I referred to it, and he indicated, with a grin, that it was always a delight for him to listen to Churchill.

It was always a delight to me, too. In his personal contact Winston Churchill had all the charm that made him so popular in the United States. Of course he was unorthodox. He did the unusual and unexpected without an effort. At the conference table he could be expected to be forceful, logical and even dogmatic. He spoke frequently and usually at some length, but no one could say he was ever boring.

Stalin himself was different from all other men I have known. He was direct in his conversation and his sentences were short and emphatic. Unlike his countrymen whom I met, he had a sense of humor. At times he indulged in "needling" Churchill, whom he seemed to admire although it was apparent he had a deeper affection for Roosevelt. He dominated those around him. This was made evident the first time I met him when I saw him turn to a general and order him to bring him a cup of tea. That was not the last evidence, however, of his domination over those who served with him.

His government worked under the rule of unanimity but I was satisfied when Stalin made a demand there was unanimity at the Politburo—or else.

Molotov had little resemblance to Stalin. There was nothing direct about him. His ways were devious; his thinking was devious. He was, however, able and a tireless worker. When the average American negotiates on any subject his action usually is based upon his experiences but no American has had any experience to qualify him for negotiating with Molotov. He is not cool—he is cold. He is a chain cigarette smoker. As he smokes and smiles he makes charges calculated to offend you and I have sometimes felt that his greatest pleasure was in seeing his opponent lose his temper.

The Conference finally agreed to hold the organizational meeting for the establishment of a United Nations organization in San Francisco, and the President talked with me about the choice of our delegates. I thought first of Senators Connally and Vandenberg of the Senate Foreign Relations Committee and Congressmen Bloom and Eaton from the Foreign Affairs Committee of the House. The President added that he had in mind as representative at large, Harold Stassen, who was then in the Navy. I knew he would also want an alternate Democrat for Cordell Hull, who was to be named senior adviser, so I suggested Governor Lausche of Ohio. The President approved and the day after I left Yalta a telegram was sent to the White House authorizing the release of the list of U.S. delegates, but Governor Lausche had been eliminated and in his place was Dean Virginia Gildersleeve of Barnard College. However, that the President had passed on my recommendation of Lausche to Stettinius is evident from a memorandum in the Secretary's handwriting, which came to my attention in 1954. On his memorandum pad, Secretary Stettinius had written simply, "Lash of Ohio, Alternate for Hull," which later puzzled the historians of the State Department, who asked me to identify the unknown.

While we were occupied at the conference, I was disturbed over various unfavorable developments at home. A strike was threatened on the Bingham & Garfield Railroad, a short line essential for the transportation of copper, and General Clay forwarded an order for the President's signature to have the government take over the railway. Manpower difficulties prompted Secretary Forrestal to write urging me to return by plane rather than ship "because of several urgent problems I believe you can solve." I needed no persuasion to travel by air: time was always of such importance to me that only once in my extensive travels during and after the war did I go by ship, except to Yalta with Roosevelt and to Potsdam with Truman.

When on February 10 the conferees agreed to end their deliberations on the following day, I told the President at lunch that I would like to leave with Admiral King that afternoon; that it would not be necessary for me to attend the last day's session. As we had discussed the urgency of matters in Washington, he agreed to this plan. Steve Early was present and said that the communiqué reporting the work of the conference had been prepared, and Mr. Roosevelt suggested that I hold a press conference on it upon my arrival in Washington, as he was going to Saudi Arabia before returning by ship.

Later I was to learn that shortly after my departure Stalin requested the President to stay on for another day because he wished to discuss a very important matter with him. There is no doubt about the importance of the subject discussed, for it concerned Soviet requests for a warm-water outlet on the China coast. Admiral King and I were crossing the Atlantic when this last meeting took place, and it was many months later before I heard that an agreement had been reached on several subjects in the Far East, and kept secret.

Admiral King and I had a significant interlude with our Russian hosts at the beginning of our long journey back home. Leaving the Crimea, we had an uneventful trip until we reached Simferopol, where the Russians had provided a special train with a vice admiral and a junior aide assigned to welcome us and escort us to our plane at Saki. We were shown our compartments, and shortly afterward I walked out into the section used as a dining room. Here was a table laden with bottles of vodka and wine. Going back to Admiral King's compartment, I warned him that our hosts were anticipating a big night. He said that during the war he had been very temperate and thought he should become a teetotaler right away. Our hosts were most insistent upon our joining them in drinks; as I recall it, the Admiral took one glass of sherry and I confined myself to a glass of some other wine which the Russian admiral particularly urged upon me when I declined vodka. The dinner was not a gala affair, to say the least, with our hosts as insistent that we drink as we were firm in our determination to abstain.

At its conclusion Admiral King was presented with a paper detailing the Soviet government's pressing need for ships, matériel and supplies, together with a list for his approval. He had a hard time explaining that he had no authority to allot ships and supplies to an ally, though he promised to present the request to the Secretary of the Navy when he reached Washington. The Soviet admiral stubbornly persisted in trying to change King's attitude; I never thought failure could make a man look quite so disgusted.

About five o'clock in the morning following this dinner, we reached our destination and got into the automobile that had been sent to take us on to Saki airfield. Our car was driven by a Russian army officer accompanied by a woman in army uniform—a Russian officer seemed invariably to be accompanied by at least one other person. This "Wac" spoke good English and was a graduate of Moscow University, where she had specialized in languages. I enjoyed talking to her while we waited two hours for mechanics to clean the ice from the wings of our plane.

I was back in Washington by February 13 and, following the President's suggestion, I held a press conference. The first question asked me was in what capacity I had attended the conference. This gave me the opportunity to say that I had not wanted to leave the country and had so told the President up until the very day of our departure, but that he had insisted that I could be of service, particularly during the discussions on various questions concerning reparations and domestic affairs with which he was not overfamiliar. Asked about the voting formula agreed upon for the world organization, I stated that the conference had adopted "the proposal of the President" but that I could not make known the details. Of course, I relied on the cabled information from Hopkins that my proposal to give the U.S. additional votes had gone through, and I promised that the President would make a statement on the formula on his return.

An embarrassing question concerned Mr. Flynn's trip to Moscow. I could not answer that one. Referring to our demand for free elections in the Balkans, a reporter asked, "He isn't going to supervise the elections, is he?" I replied that I knew nothing of the purpose of Mr. Flynn's mission, not having discussed it with him or with the President. I was then questioned about the reason for my "very precipitous return." I said that as soon as the communiqué on the proceedings had been brought to the President and he expressed the opinion that they would adjourn the following day, I made plans to come home with Admiral King. "I returned because my job was finished," I told the reporter. "I thought you had some job to do here in a hurry," he said. I told him I had had one before I left.

In this story of Yalta I have endeavored to refer only to events of which I have personal knowledge. From this policy I must divert in order to bring into the story the much-discussed agreements about China. Those agreements were not signed, or discussed at the conference table, while I was at Yalta. At Potsdam I heard some State Department official—I have now forgotten who—refer to a private agreement, and President Truman in a conference with Stalin referred to an understanding reached by President Roosevelt at Yalta.

Soon after the Japanese surrender I again heard that there was an understanding; this story was supposed to be based upon data in the Map Room in the White House. I should have inquired about it then, but I did not, and it was not until February 10, 1946, when I was Secretary of State, that I knew there was a formal agreement signed by the Big Three at the conference table at Yalta the day after Admiral King and I had left. As a result of an inquiry by a reporter at my press conference, I asked Charles Bohlen, who had been at Yalta throughout the meeting, whether there had been a formal agreement about China affairs, and he told me there was a written agreement in Admiral Leahy's office in the White House. I telephoned President Truman about it, and within a few hours he had it sent to the State Department to be filed. The following day I released the exact language to the press.

From my inquiries I learned that late in the afternoon Admiral King and I left Yalta, Stalin and President Roosevelt had met privately and tentatively reached the so-called secret agreement. In addition to Bohlen, Ambassador Harriman was present, and it was said Hopkins was also there. The next day the agreement was prepared, and after some changes were made it was formally signed. The record of that meeting shows that with the President were Stettinius, Leahy, Harriman and Hopkins. Prime Minister Churchill also had some members of his staff there. Admiral Leahy writes in his book that the Big Three decided the agreement should be kept secret because it was feared that if it should be made public the Japanese would anticipate Russia's entering the war and invade Russian territory before the Soviets could transfer troops from the German front.

It is understandable that I was not later informed of the agreement, because I was not then an official of the State Department. As a matter of fact, I resigned as Director of War Mobilization a few weeks later, April 2, and in those weeks was kept busy in my own office.

When I read the signed agreement, I was troubled by the specific pledge given by the United States and the United Kingdom that "these claims of the Soviet Union shall be unquestionably fulfilled after Japan has been defeated." The record shows that Roosevelt and Churchill acted because their military advisers told them the invasion of Japan planned for the following fall would result in a million casualties. Their decision was made early in February when the German army was still fighting, but in the six months that followed our enemies surrendered in Europe and in the Pacific. Today many will say that Churchill and Roosevelt should have had the foresight to anticipate these events and should have refused to woo the Soviets. This is not written in their defense, but we must remember that hindsight has some advantage over foresight.

# 16  TYING UP THE LOOSE ENDS

When I returned from Yalta I was confronted with the problem of the National Service Act, generally known as the "work or fight" bill. Because of changes made by the Conference Committee the report was adopted by the House but in the Senate it was defeated. Some members who had voted for the original bill changed their position because they believed the war was about to end and the legislation would not be necessary.

Now much of the work of the office was centered around plans for the period after V-E Day, when new arrangements for the disposal of surplus property for emergency relief in Europe as well as industrial reconversion would be necessary. Also, as the law establishing the office of War Mobilization and Reconversion required the Director to file a report every quarter, my second report would be due on April 1. I had already decided that when this report was submitted to the President and the Congress, I should resign from government service. I was convinced that whoever was to assume responsibility for the major reconversion moves after V-E Day should take over as soon as possible, and I had long made it plain that this task would not be mine.

By mid-March, messages from Europe indicated that the German collapse was imminent; there was news of a German surrender in Italy, and by March 24 Montgomery's army had crossed the Rhine in force. We hoped that V-E Day was at hand, and in fact my office began to co-ordinate the elaborate plans for the various ceremonies which had been made by representatives of the Army and Navy, together with Elmer Davis of the Office of War Information, and my deputy, General Lucius Clay. The object of this program was not

270

only to celebrate fittingly Hitler's overthrow but to remind our citizens that the struggle against Japan had still to be won. I had long feared that total war might be followed by moves toward total relaxation. A memorandum covering the program was sent to the President on March 27. His comments showed his close interest and that he was thoroughly in accord with the "work and worship" theme of the arrangements. I am glad that President Roosevelt had the opportunity to approve the announcement of the great victory, though death prevented him from issuing it as he had expected to do.

On the day of the Rhine crossing, because I knew Mr. Roosevelt was leaving for Hyde Park that evening, I prepared a letter of resignation and took it over to him. It set forth my position in these terms:

Last June when the Congress was considering the Bill to expand the Office of War Mobilization into the Office of War Mobilization and Reconversion, I advised the Committees of both Houses that I would not remain to administer the reconversion program.

In November when I again advised you of my reason for not wishing to remain, we agreed that I should accept the appointment as Director of the newly created office with the understanding that I would continue only until V-E Day. This announcement was made by you. I remind you of this only because I hope that having remained for nine months after expressing my desire to leave, you will view with sympathy what I now feel obliged to write.

I think V-E Day is not far distant. My knowledge of the nature of the work now confronting the office causes me to conclude I should not remain longer. The office has already embarked upon the development of a program of reconversion. I have organized committees composed of representatives of the various agencies which have been at work for some time developing the program. In the report I shall submit to you next week that program will be outlined.

I am convinced that the person who is to direct the reconversion program should take charge of this office now. He would then have an opportunity to familiarize himself with the plans we have made and can modify in such manner as he deems wise the plans he will be called upon to administer.

Therefore, I tender my resignation to become effective April 2. I fix that date because the law requires a report to be filed with you and with the Congress on April 1 and I think it my duty to file that report.

After he had read it, we began to talk. He said my reasoning was sound if I was going to insist on leaving by V-E Day, but he had hoped that I would stay to assist with the important tasks which would then present themselves.

I told him I had willingly resigned from the Supreme Court to help during the war, but after my years in public service I did not want to wind up in peacetime as a bureaucrat in a rapidly shrinking reconversion bureau. When I insisted, he asked me whom he could appoint in my place. I suggested Fred Vinson, but the President said that he disliked to move him since he had only recently been put in charge of the Reconstruction Finance Corporation. As an alternative, I told him the most competent man I had found in the executive departments was General Lucius Clay, whom I had made my deputy because of his rare ability and his understanding of government and people. When I had finished outlining Clay's qualities, the President said, "I have never known you to be so enthusiastic about anyone in government." I replied, "I do not know another Clay. Give him six months and he could run General Motors or U.S. Steel."

The President asked that I bring the General over to talk to him. I then added that Secretary Stimson and I had already discussed Clay's going to Germany temporarily as assistant to General Eisenhower, with a view to his later becoming our High Commissioner there. I emphasized that this would certainly be a good selection for a most difficult task, where a man in uniform was needed, and the conversation came back to Vinson. I again stressed that he would be my first choice, for I did not believe the Congress would like the idea of having a man in uniform in the White House as "Assistant President." Some years later, when General Eisenhower was elected President, I realized that times had changed, or that I was a poor judge of public sentiment.

Before I left, the President told me that he had always thought he had asked too much of me when he got me to leave the Court; that he believed there would be a vacancy in the near future and would reappoint me when it took place. I reminded him that he had asked me to get a leave of absence, not to resign, and that the resignation had been my decision. I have no idea which justice he thought would retire or resign, but I believe he was quite sincere. However, I told him, he could not reappoint me because, no matter how untrue it was, it would be stated in unfriendly quarters that we had had a secret understanding that this would be done.

The next morning the President telephoned from Hyde Park. He told me he wished to withdraw the agreement he had made the previous afternoon on my leaving. My answer was emphatic that it was time for me to go. Had I known at the time how ill he was, my decision would have been different; but as so often happens, those who are frequently with sick persons fail to detect their gradual physical deterioration. Mr. Roosevelt wrote me the same day:

I was, of course, knocked off my feet yesterday when you told me you felt you ought to resign this Spring instead of on V-E Day. I am distressed but I, in part, appreciate your reasons. It will be, of course, next to impossible to find anyone to substitute for you.

Give me a few days more to decide between Fred and the General— and I will try to see the General, if you could bring him in, next Thursday morning. My inclinations are toward Fred, as he is such an old friend, but if we shifted Fred at the present time, we would have to find somebody else to handle the loans.

You have certainly done a grand job under very great difficulties—pulling your weight in the boat to the satisfaction of everybody. I just hate to have you go. I shall miss you and Maude more than I can tell you, but be sure before you take up anything else to get a real bit of rest.

I told General Clay of the possibility of his being asked to succeed me. He was opposed to this, giving many reasons why he should not. I soon received a wire from the President, asking me to bring Clay to his office when he returned from Hyde Park, as he would stay a day in Washington before proceeding to Warm Springs. When we went into the President's office on Thursday, we found Mr. Roosevelt extremely nervous. Instead of letting Clay speak, he began to talk rapidly and without rest, saying he had learned about Clay's experience as an Army engineer building a large dam in Texas, and suggesting that he consider the possibility of building a great power development in central Europe, but never giving Clay an opportunity to reply or to make an observation. At the end of ten minutes or so, Steve Early came into the room and mentioned that he had others waiting outside. Clay left us and I remained a moment or two with Mr. Roosevelt. He asked me to inform Vinson that he would be appointed, saying that he would telephone Fred before he left for Warm Springs. He also authorized a release stating that Clay would go to Germany. After this, with a word of good wishes for his vacation, I withdrew. It was my last meeting with FDR.

As I rejoined Clay on the way back to my office, I said jokingly, "General, you talked too much." He replied, "Mr. Justice, even if the President had given me a chance, I doubt that I could have talked to him because I was shocked at his appearance. He is not going to live."

That was the first time I fully appreciated the seriousness of the President's condition. From my office I called Vinson to tell him I was resigning and that the President had authorized me to ask if he would accept the appointment. When he agreed, I telephoned Grace Tully, requesting her to have the President call Vinson before leaving the city. But Mr. Roosevelt left his office earlier than expected without telephoning. I called him the next afternoon at Warm Springs and he told me that in the rush of leaving he had overlooked the Vinson matter, but that we could go ahead, using one of the signed nomination blanks which were kept in the office.

On March 31 I held a press conference to discuss my second quarterly report. In this report I put more emphasis than I had in the earlier one on the problems of reconversion, adding many reminders that the war against the Japanese homeland had still to be fought. It was possible, I said, to look forward after V-E Day to the end of the midnight curfew, the ban on horse racing and to more liberal travel restrictions. I also told the press that the various military cutbacks would reduce the "hard goods" going into weapons production, freeing considerable amounts of raw materials for the manufacture of items for civilian consumption. I estimated that, while this would actually amount to a cut of about $18 billion in our total procurement program of about $60 billion a year, because of the nonconvertibility of some items the actual gain for the civilian economy would be only $13 billion. At this a correspondent with an inquiring mind asked what would happen to the $5 billion worth of hard goods not converted. I remarked, "I guess I got off the sled at that point," but added that it would be "disposed of as surplus property."

In an endeavor to set the right atmosphere for V-E Day I said, "I hope the American people will make the day one of work and worship. I recommend that all government agencies observe the spirit of this request." I also urged that Congress pass the manpower bill which was then before the Senate, since I was sure that manpower legislation would be needed not only in the post-V-E Day period but also to help facilitate reconversion and the production of essential civilian goods. I called for a continuation after V-E Day of price controls and rationing and also of private savings, warning that the pent-up demand represented by the $140 billion our citizens had set aside during the war was an inflationary hazard if released too quickly into the economy.

Of the postwar period itself, I said that free enterprise would then be given an opportunity to prove that it could provide full employment and urged that "we should not be stampeded into large public works programs." I also recommended that the War and Navy Departments be consolidated into a "fully unified" department of national defense; because despite their splendid co-operation in the war, there had been, and remained, many duplications of effort which had resulted in substantial expenditures that might have been avoided.

Congress, I told the press, should authorize the President to consolidate and curtail agencies; and in view of the fact that our public debt totaled $233 billion, representing a per capita obligation on each of our citizens of $1,680, I thought it well to add a solemn warning on the state of our national finances: "No nation that has lost a war hitherto has had saddled upon it a public debt as large as the debt we as victors must pay." As for postwar rehabilitation projects, I added that while we would do our part as a Christian, humane people to relieve suffering and distress, the government should give consideration to the people of this country who would be called upon to pay the bills.

After the press conference I remained in Washington for a week waiting for Vinson's confirmation by the Senate and for him to wind up his affairs at the Reconstruction Finance Corporation. During this time I received several memoranda from the President, indicating that he was attending to business, and on several occasions I talked with him by telephone. His voice, I noted, was stronger; though Clay's comment on his appearance had made a deep impression on me, I felt his vacation was doing him good and the familiar process of "bouncing back" was under way. On April 7 I left for my home in Spartanburg, where I expected to remain as a private citizen. Circumstances, however, were to decree otherwise.

# Part V

---

# SECRETARY OF STATE

# 17  THE A-BOMB

I arrived in Spartanburg on April 8 to receive a heartwarming welcome from my neighbors there. It was nice to feel that although I had been living in Washington for the greater part of the past fifteen years, they regarded my return as "coming home." My first task was to address myself to the mail which the postmaster, Mrs. Helen DuPre Moseley, an old friend, had been accumulating since my departure from Washington had been announced. Letters had come in from many parts of the country and from persons both in private and official life. One, dated April 7, I will always remember with much interest, for it was the last message I received from Mr. Roosevelt. In it he asked me about a citizen of South Carolina who had been jailed for embezzlement and was applying for a pardon. Before I had a chance to investigate, the President died.

Some of the communications were from members of the Supreme Court with whom I had served and one was from Chief Justice Hughes. There was one I might mention from Justice Wiley Rutledge, my successor on the Court. Rutledge was generous in his reference to my past public service and most unselfish with regard to my future, for he said in part, "When I first learned of your retirement, I considered, frankly, whether I should not come to you and ask your permission to discuss with the President my own possible resignation and your reappointment here. . . . If it is your desire to return to the court at a future time, I for one, would be delighted if it should work out that way." Such unselfishness is rare in political life, and I quickly wrote him that I, along with all his other friends, would certainly object to his leaving the Court.

Some days later I was shocked to learn through one of the staff of a local radio station of the President's sudden death. In a few minutes Secretary Forrestal telephoned, urging that I come to Washington and offering to send his personal plane for me. I readily agreed, and flew from Spartanburg airport that night at ten, accompanied by Walter Brown.

Early next morning I called on President Truman. Understandably, he was overwhelmed by the task that had devolved so suddenly on him and was trying to familiarize himself with the more urgent problems confronting him. Some of them I was able to discuss with him, for I had not been absent long from my White House office. He asked that I accompany him the following morning when he went to meet the funeral train on which Mr. Roosevelt's body would arrive, and then ride with him on the journey to Hyde Park. After the funeral, on the train returning to Washington, he invited me to be his representative at the forthcoming United Nations Conference in San Francisco. I expressed my appreciation, but said that I believed it unwise because the delegates had already been approved, and I knew from President Roosevelt's experience in sending Ray Moley to the London Conference that the presence of a personal representative is apt to cause dissension. President Truman accepted this view.

The next day I was again summoned to the White House. The President told me that he wished to appoint me Secretary of State; though in order not to lessen the prestige of Secretary Stettinius, who was going to San Francisco as chairman of the United States delegation, he would make no public announcement of the move until the United Nations Conference ended. I said I had left Washington because I did not wish to serve as a peacetime bureaucrat, but that the same reasons which prompted my resignation from the Court in wartime made me wish to assist, in any way I could, with the making of the peace, and I would gladly accept.

The task of the President at that time was unusually heavy. President Roosevelt had found it unbearably hard to conduct our foreign affairs in time of war and at the same time keep pace with events on the domestic front. He had had years of experience in the office and had learned to live with his problems as they accumulated; in contrast, President Truman was facing without warning unfamiliar hazards both at home and abroad, with his Secretary of State necessarily absent from the capital. While I remained in Washington I saw him daily, giving him what help I could.

At a dinner given by Lord Halifax at the British Embassy, I met Sir Anthony Eden and his principal associates, who were en route to San Francisco. During a pleasant evening we discussed several of the issues that were expected to arouse differences at the Conference. Lord Halifax told me he was worried because he had heard from several persons who had been at Yalta that Prime Minister Churchill did not look well. I replied that Mr. Churchill had looked fit to me, but was himself concerned about Mr. Roosevelt's state of health. As President Roosevelt had commented that he believed his friend Churchill was not entirely fit at the Conference, I thought it ironic that these two old comrades in arms should leave the Crimea, each believing the other to be in ill health.

On the day I left Washington to go gack to Spartanburg, I called on President Truman to assure him that I would be free to return whenever he wished. At this time I handed him a letter given to me by Justice Felix Frankfurter in which he said that in a talk with President Roosevelt some months previously, the President had mentioned that when he died he hoped there would be no talk of erecting a monument to him in Washington. He hoped the Justice would see to it that if any memorial were to be erected, it would take the form of a simple slab, inscribed, "In Memory of Franklin D. Roosevelt, Thirty-first President of the United States," which might be placed at the Apex, east of the Archives Building. Whether any consideration was given to this, I do not know. But more important than a marble slab is the memorial at Warm Springs, Georgia, which was always dear to the President's heart.

Before leaving the White House I went over to the residence to say good-by to Mrs. Roosevelt. She was in the President's bedroom, packing his books and personal belongings. As I looked around, my mind was flooded with memories of the many personal conferences I had had with him in that room over the twelve years of our close association. As I talked to her, I felt I was not talking to Mrs. Roosevelt, the writer and lecturer, but to Eleanor Roosevelt, the widow of Franklin Roosevelt. My admiration for her courage was mingled with sorrow.

As I went down the steps of the White House my mind was filled with thoughts of the man whose room I had just left. I knew that many writers would try to picture this remarkable personality but that no two would paint the same portrait, because Franklin Roosevelt was not the same to any two men.

I was sure that the President who received suggestions on government problems from Hopkins and Hillman was different from the President who discussed those proposals with Garner, Hull and me. We were bound to see in him different qualities. I always felt that within him there must have been continuous conflict, with his vivid imagination and unbounded curiosity prompting him to embrace new ideas, and a conservative streak restraining him all the while. His stamp collection was often referred to as his hobby, but politics was really his hobby. He loved people and he knew how to play upon their weaknesses, vanities and prejudices. To him men were so many tools to be used for the accomplishment of what he believed to be a good purpose. The plaudits of people stimulated and inspired his imagination and energies. I forgot his weaknesses and thought only of the remarkable qualities that had enabled him to inspire the free peoples of the world to unite in defense of freedom, and to mold the energies of America so that its might brought victory to the allied cause.

At home I resumed the task of putting my own affairs in order, but my mind was concerned with the new President's efforts to familiarize himself with the course of foreign as well as domestic affairs. I therefore took from my files my private shorthand notes of the Yalta Conference. At those meetings I had not participated directly in any of the discussions at the conference table, but rather than "doodle," as did one of our party, I made shorthand notes of much of what was said in crucial sessions. Details of these debates were now to assume a marked importance, and I was able to dictate for President Truman a good verbatim text on many of the key exchanges.

While in peaceful Spartanburg I was also in touch with developments in Washington and elsewhere on the atomic bomb. My connection with this project came about during one of my early talks with President Truman. I had told him what I have written earlier about the Manhattan Project and the conference I had held with the labor leaders over the threatened work stoppage at Oak Ridge. While he knew of the project generally through his Senate committee work, he had not as yet been fully briefed on its details and was interested in all I told him. Then, on April 25, Secretary Stimson gave him a memorandum, the opening paragraphs of which contained the fateful prophecy, "Within four months we shall in all probability have completed the most terrible weapon ever known in human history, one bomb of which could destroy a whole city."

After further elaboration, the Secretary cited a recommendation of General Groves of the Manhattan Project that there be appointed an Interim Committee to make recommendations "to the executive and legislative branches of our government when secrecy was no longer in full effect." During our second talk the President requested me to represent him on this body. Other appointees were Ralph A. Bard, Under Secretary of the Navy; William L. Clayton, Assistant Secretary of State; Dr. Vannevar Bush, Director of the Office of Scientific Research and Development and president of the Carnegie Institution of Washington; Dr. Karl T. Compton, chief of the Office of Field Service in the Office of Scientific Research and Development; and Dr. James P. Conant, chairman of the National Defense Research Committee and president of Harvard. In the absence of Secretary Stimson, George L. Harrison was to act as chairman. Harrison had been president of the Federal Reserve Bank of New York. He had rendered outstanding service through the Red Cross overseas in World War I, and Stimson had called him to the War Department to help him in World War II.

While the discussions of the committee would eventually cover the whole field of atomic energy, its primary and immediate function was to make recommendations on the preparation of a test explosion in New Mexico and, if this proved successful, on the use of the bomb against Japan. We were also to consider the drafting of statements to be published immediately after the bomb's offensive use, and then to consider the prospects for domestic and international control of atomic energy. A scientific panel, including Doctors A. H. Compton, Enrico Fermi, E. O. Lawrence and J. R. Oppenheimer, would assist us, and in addition to these nuclear physicists, whose calculations and experiments had made the project possible, the committee would have the benefit of the views of the industrialists who had actually supervised its large-scale development.

As I heard these scientists and industrialists predict the destructive power of the weapon, I was thoroughly frightened. I had sufficient imagination to visualize the danger to our country when some other country possessed such a weapon. Thinking of the country most likely to become unfriendly to us, I asked General Marshall and some of the others at the meeting how long it would take the Soviets to develop such a bomb. The consensus was that they would have the secret in two or three years, but could not actually produce a bomb in less than six or seven years. One or two expressed the opinion that Soviet progress would depend upon whether or not they had taken German scientists and production experts as prisoners of war for the purpose of having them work on such weapons. No one seemed too alarmed at the prospect because it appeared that in seven years we should be far ahead of the Soviets in this field; and, of course, in 1945 we could not believe that after their terrible sacrifices, the Russians would think of making war for many years to come.

A few days after the committee was appointed, President Truman referred to me a letter addressed to President Roosevelt by Dr. Albert Einstein, dated March 25, which was in President Roosevelt's office at the time of his death at Warm Springs. In it Dr. Einstein requested the President to receive Dr. L. Szilard, "who proposes to submit to you certain considerations and recommendations." After citing Dr. Szilard's reputation in the scientific field, Dr. Einstein went on to say that Dr. Szilard was concerned about the lack of adequate contact between the atomic scientists and the Cabinet members who were responsible for determining policy. Dr. Einstein concluded with the hope that the President would give his personal attention to what Dr. Szilard had to say.

President Truman asked me to see Szilard, who came down to Spartanburg, bringing with him Dr. H. C. Urey and another scientist. As the Einstein letter had indicated he would, Szilard complained that he and some of his associates did not know enough about the policy of the government with regard to the use of the bomb. He felt that scientists, including himself, should discuss the matter with the Cabinet, which I did not feel desirable. His general demeanor and his desire to participate in policy making made an unfavorable impression on me, but his associates were neither as aggressive nor apparently as dissatisfied.

In response to his statement that the younger scientists were very critical of Doctors Bush, Compton and Conant, I asked him his opinion of Oppenheimer. He quickly expressed enthusiastic admiration. I told him then that he should feel better because the following week, upon the suggestion of the three scientists about whom he complained, Dr. Oppenheimer would meet with the Interim Committee. This pleased Szilard and his companions, and the conversation passed to a more general discussion of atomic matters. What they told me did not decrease my fears of the terrible weapon they had assisted in creating.

These oppressive thoughts, and the burden of security, made themselves felt in meetings of the Interim Committee. A few days later, when I mentioned to General Groves the scientists' visit to Spartanburg, he told me that he already knew of it; that one of his intelligence agents had been following the three gentlemen, as they followed others connected with the project. The diligence of Groves impressed me then as it had done before.

I carefully refrained from mentioning to anyone the President's plan to appoint me Secretary of State, though in one special case I was forced to bend if not break a confidence. This was in May, when Will H. Hays, popularly known as the czar of the motion picture industry, came to see me. He was to retire, he said, and was authorized to offer me the appointment to succeed him. The salary would be $100,000 a year, which seemed to me somewhat exorbitant when I recalled that it almost equaled the total compensation for my more than ten years' service in the United States Senate. When I declined with appreciation, he concluded that the figure was insufficient and hastened to say he felt it could be increased. In the face of this good will I did not wish to appear ungrateful, so, binding him to the strictest secrecy, I told him I expected soon to return to public service—and he probably guessed in what capacity.

On June 1, 1945, our Interim Committee unanimously recommended to President Truman that the bomb should be used without specific warning and as soon as practicable against a military installation or a war plant in the Japanese islands. It had been suggested that it first be used against an isolated island with representatives of Japan and other nations invited to observe the test. This alternative was rejected. There was also the question of giving the Japanese fair warning about the time and place of the explosion; but because we felt that American prisoners of war would be brought into the designated area, this idea was not adopted. We were also told by the experts that whatever the success of the test bomb, they would not guarantee that another would explode when dropped. Further, if we gave the Japanese advance notice and then the bomb failed to explode, our optimism would have only played into the hands of the Japanese militarists.

Meanwhile, arrangements for the test firing at Alamogordo went on. People who lived in the area had to be moved away. The task of writing news releases that would tend to allay public fears after the explosion and at the same time guard the secret from the enemy was placed in the skilled hands of William H. Laurence of *The New York Times*. The degree of uncertainty about what power the bomb would actually develop is evidenced by a story he wrote for the *Times* on June 29, 1951. He related that on the day preceding the test, a hundred scientists were invited to participate in a pool, each guessing at the bomb's power in terms of TNT. It had been designed to produce an explosive force equal to 20,000 tons. Dr. Oppenheimer, the director of the Los Alamos laboratory where it had been constructed, guessed 300 tons and most of the others less than 500. Of the participants in the pool at a dollar a chance, Professor I. I. Rabi of Columbia University, who arrived late and found the low numbers taken, won with his estimate of 18,000 tons.

Though it is sometimes said that for many months the success of the bomb was assured, another indication to the contrary is the fact that though we had but three bombs, and could not hope to possess another for many months, our scientific advisers felt it essential to devote one to a test firing.

The awesome responsibility for accepting the committee's recommendations rested, of course, with President Truman. Inasmuch as I represented him, I felt a measure of this responsibility. However, I knew that the Joint Chiefs planned to invade Japan about November first. In our successful efforts to penetrate the perimeter of Japanese defenses in the Pacific, we had suffered approximately 300,000 casualties. Though the Japanese Navy was nearly destroyed, the imperial armies remained intact, and were estimated by our General Staff to number over five million effective troops. At least that number of United States soldiers, sailors and airmen would be involved in the attack on the Japanese homeland, and a fifth of these, it was thought, would be casualties. Under these circumstances, it was certainly essential to end the war as soon as possible and avoid the invasion. The day the committee reached agreement, I communicated its decision to President Truman. He said he had been giving thought to the problem and, while reluctant to use this weapon, saw no way of avoiding it. Thereafter, Secretary Stimson formally presented him a written statement, setting forth our recommendations in his lucid and convincing style.

# 18 POTSDAM

By the time the A-bomb was successfully tested the war in Europe had ended triumphantly, but the diplomatic struggle with the Soviet Union had just begun. Prior to his death, President Roosevelt had been told by Stalin that it would be impossible for Molotov to attend the San Francisco Conference. However, after Mr. Roosevelt's sudden death Stalin informed President Truman that "President Roosevelt has died but his cause must live on." In order to let the world appreciate his attitude, he thereupon announced that the Foreign Minister of the U.S.S.R. would attend the San Francisco meeting.

Before Molotov reached Washington, President Truman had had an opportunity to read the various exchanges between Stalin and the western leaders on the Polish question and other issues, all of which revealed a surprising and dangerous deterioration in our relations. As a result he conferred with Stettinius, Stimson and Forrestal; and Molotov, upon his arrival, found the President very critical of the Russian attitude. From Chip Bohlen, who was present as interpreter, and from Mr. Truman himself, I learned that this meeting had been anything but harmonious, and that Molotov had appeared to be offended. In any event, on reaching San Francisco, he did everything he could to promote disunity. Stettinius had solicited the support of some of the Latin American republics on admitting the Ukraine and Byelorussia to the U.N., and they in return urged that the United States favor the admission of Argentina, a development that Molotov opposed bitterly. Even more damaging to hopes of future harmony in the United Nations was Molotov's insistence that the right of veto should extend to procedural questions.

During the month of May, while the conference continued, Harry Hopkins, at President Truman's request, visited Stalin in Moscow to see if co-operation with the Soviets could be restored. Chip Bohlen accompanied him, as did our Ambassador to Moscow, Averell Harriman. These gentlemen heard Stalin voice a number of complaints, not only concerning Poland and Argentina, but on the swift discontinuance of Lend-Lease shipments to Russia after V-E Day. They explained to him that under our law such supplies could leave the United States only for the purpose of prosecuting the war, and since the Soviet Union was not at war with Japan it was no longer eligible to receive them. When they reminded the Russian leader of the United States' liberal attitude during the war, Stalin admitted that this was so. Further, though Molotov had taken the position at San Francisco that a dispute could not even be discussed in the Security Council without the unanimous vote of the five permanent members, Stalin overruled him. Hopkins also secured from Stalin an agreement that he would meet with Truman and Churchill in the Berlin suburbs in mid-July, when it was hoped that such difficulties as had arisen over Poland, reparations, and other matters might be eased.

At the same time the President had sent to London the Honorable Joseph E. Davies, a former Ambassador to Russia, who found Prime Minister Churchill most anxious for an early meeting of the new leadership. Eventually July 15 was decided upon. I had been kept generally informed of these developments, and was present when Ambassador Davies reported in person to Mr. Truman. It was now apparent that the first international conference I would attend as Secretary of State would be a most crucial one.

On July 3, 1945, I took the oath in the White House rose garden.

Because we were to leave for Potsdam on the sixth, I did not attempt to make any changes in departmental personnel prior to my departure. I did, however, tell Donald Russell and Walter Brown that I wanted their assistance, and I immediately appointed Ben Cohen as Counselor of the Department of State. He had long been a student of foreign affairs, was familiar in some degree with the department's work, and by appointment of Secretary Hull had worked on the committee that had produced the first draft of a United Nations Charter. He was able, loyal and modest.

Cohen had recently helped me draft a proposal to create a Council of Foreign Ministers. In presenting this proposal to the President, I expressed the hope that we might avoid some of the pitfalls of the

Versailles settlement after World War I if such a Council should start promptly preparing treaties with the enemy nations of lesser military importance, while at the same time the principals sought to agree on how Germany should be governed. This plan met with President Truman's approval. Ben Cohen; Freeman Matthews, chief of the European Division (now Ambassador to Austria); and Charles E. Bohlen, until recently Ambassador to Russia, traveled with us on the cruiser *Augusta*. The four of us spent hours each day reviewing departmental memoranda and recommendations and preparing proposals for the President to consider for discussion at the conference. I had gone to Yalta only in the capacity of economic adviser and there I had felt that our lack of preparation was too conspicuous for comfort, especially when compared with the Soviets' clean-cut written proposals. About once a day President Truman sat in on our discussions, and on the last day aboard ship he spent some hours with us studying the various papers.

When our ship docked at Antwerp we were greeted by the Ambassador to Belgium, Charles Sawyer of Ohio, who was later to become Secretary of Commerce, and whom I knew well. He had organized a drive through the streets of Brussels, where the entire population, it seemed, had turned out to greet the President of the United States. We then boarded planes for Potsdam. President Truman and I could not travel together, for under the law at that time, in the event of the President's death, there being no Vice President, he would be succeeded by his Secretary of State. The precaution was a sound one, though it was a depressing reminder of life's uncertainties.

On landing at Gatow airport, the presidential party was greeted by a large delegation, including Secretary Stimson and other officials of the State, War, and Navy Departments, who had preceded us, as well as Lieutenant General Clay and other military officers from headquarters, Berlin District.

Babelsberg, where we lived, was a fashionable suburb of Berlin. The house assigned to the President, soon known as the "Little White House," had been the residence of the head of the German movie colony. Though a civilian, he had been arrested and sent by the Soviet forces to serve in a labor battalion in Russia, and his wife was now a charwoman in one of the nearby houses assigned to the State Department staff. This large stucco house, located in a beautiful garden which sloped down to a lake, had been stripped of its original furnishings and was rather oddly equipped with furnishings brought in from other dwellings.

On our arrival we were informed that Stalin, who traveled by train for health reasons, would be delayed for a day. However, the Prime Minister was already in residence; his quarters, about a mile away, he had designated as "10 Downing Street, Potsdam," this address appearing on the dinner menus when he entertained. Stalin's quarters were more remote, located in the vast wooded park surrounding Cecilienhof Palace, where the meetings were to be held. Though we received official invitations to visit his quarters on several occasions, it was obvious that their location was a well-guarded secret to the Conference personnel generally.

We spent a morning with our military advisers, and in the afternoon the President, Admiral Leahy, and I drove into Berlin. Here we saw what remained of the German Chancellery and other relics of the broken regime. But our small party had no monopoly on sightseeing. On our return I heard from Will Clayton and Ed Pauley (our representative on the Reparations Committee) that they had seen machinery from a manufacturing plant which had been moved from the U.S. zone of Germany into the Soviets' shortly before our arrival. It was now standing in an open field. They also had heard stories of all kinds of materials and even herds of cattle being taken to Russia. We knew that in our quarters the original bath fixtures had vanished, others having been hurriedly substituted for our use, and there was plain evidence that the Soviets were unilaterally awarding themselves reparations, both in large and small quantities.

About noon the next day, July 17, Stalin called on the President. It was, of course, their first meeting. Molotov accompanied him and from that moment things began to happen. For more than an hour the four of us remained in conference, Chip Bohlen and Pavlov doing the interpreting. After an exchange of greetings, and some remarks on his long and tiresome train journey, Stalin launched into a discussion of Russia's entry into the Japanese war. He reported that the Japanese had already made overtures to him to act as mediator, to which he had given no definite reply since they did not provide for an unconditional surrender. But he left me with the distinct impression that he was not anxious to see an end to the fighting until Soviet entry into the war could help secure the concessions he expected of China. He said he had not yet reached an agreement with the Chinese Premier, T. V. Soong, on certain matters, and that this was necessary before he could declare war. Negotiations had been halted until after the Potsdam meeting, he said, and mentioned, among other unsettled questions, arrangements for the

Port of Dairen. The President commented that the United States wanted to be certain that Dairen was maintained as an open port, and Stalin said that would be its status, should the Soviets obtain control of it.

Not having been at Yalta on the day the so-called secret agreement was arrived at, and having been out of government service for three months, I could make no statement of my own knowledge, but having heard a few days before that there had been an understanding between President Roosevelt and Stalin that Dairen should be an open port, I supported the President's statement in a general way, saying that our people understood that at Yalta President Roosevelt had taken the same position. Stalin merely repeated that that would be its status under Soviet control. Nevertheless, I was disturbed about what kind of bargain he might coerce China into making, for the very fact that they had not reached agreement made me suspect that Stalin was increasing his demands. The President told Stimson that night that "he had clinched the Open Door in Manchuria."[1] I was encouraged but not quite that confident. However, the President and I felt that, without appearing to encourage Chiang to disregard any pledges made by Roosevelt at Yalta, we should let him know that the United States did not want him to make additional concessions to the Soviets. Then the President received from Chiang a cable stating that China had gone the limit to fulfill the Yalta agreement. I prepared a message which the President approved and on the 23rd sent to Chiang Kai-shek: "I asked that you carry out the Yalta agreements, but I have not asked that you make any concessions in excess of that agreement. If you and Generalissimo Stalin differ as to the correct interpretation of the Yalta agreement, I hope you will arrange for Soong to return to Moscow and continue your efforts to reach complete understanding."

Our purpose was stated in the first sentence. The second sentence was to encourage the Chinese to continue negotiations after the adjournment of the Potsdam Conference. I had some fear that if they did not, Stalin might immediately enter the war, knowing full well that he could take not only what Roosevelt and Churchill, and subsequently Chiang, had agreed to at Yalta, but—with China divided and Chiang seeking Soviet support against Chinese Communists—whatever else he wanted. On the other hand, if Stalin and Chiang were still negotiating, it might delay Soviet entrance and the Japanese might surrender. The President was in accord with that view.

[1] Herbert Feis, *China Tangle*, p. 329.

The President had learned of the Japanese "peace feeler" a day or two before our conference with Stalin, for we had broken the Japanese code early in the war. But with Russia not yet in the Pacific war, we could not tell Stalin this and that we had intercepted some of the Japanese messages.

As a result of this interception, in 1943 we had been able to shoot down a plane carrying Admiral Isoroku Yamamato, the Commander in Chief of the Japanese Navy. After the surrender, one of our naval officers in Tokyo could not resist the temptation to tell the story of the interception and it was published in a Japanese newspaper. Its publication caused the Japanese officer in charge of communications to threaten to commit suicide. However, he was finally convinced that our achievement had not so sullied his honor as to require his death.

I have been diverted from an orderly account of our proceedings at Potsdam by these events which looked to the ending of the Pacific war. The two were so intertwined in the making they cannot easily be separated in the telling.

In what I shall have to say of this and other international conferences, it must be understood that I am not writing a history of those conferences. That has been done, or will be done, by the Department of State. I am recording only some of the highlights and my sketchy stories do not purport to be a complete account of the events or of the debates. Inevitably, however, I must touch on some matters that I have already covered more fully in an earlier book.[2]

The first plenary session began the afternoon of July 17. Representing the United States, in addition to the President and me, were Admiral Leahy and former Ambassador Joseph E. Davies. As different subjects were considered, we were joined by various specialists from the State Department, though throughout the conference there was a general understanding that no country would have more than ten persons in the room at a session. The Soviets, I may say, took this very seriously, and acted as if suffering from an acute inferiority complex. For example, once my staff inadvertently numbered twelve, and almost immediately the Soviets rushed in two additions to their own. On another occasion Miss Connor brought me some papers and had to wait a few minutes. She had scarcely seated herself when two women from the Russian staff promptly came in and took chairs by the side of their male associates.

At the first session President Truman presented some of the papers

[2] *Speaking Frankly*, New York, Harper & Brothers, 1947.

we had prepared on the *Augusta*, asking that they be included on the conference agenda. Among these were the proposal to create a Council of Foreign Ministers to take charge of drafting plans for the peace conference, the political and economic principles that would govern the occupation of Germany, the enforcement of the Yalta declaration on liberated Europe, and a new policy toward Italy. He made it clear that others would be forthcoming. Stalin, as I had anticipated, produced quite a list of his own, which appeared to have been carefully prepared, while Churchill limited himself to some trenchant comments, declaring that the British proposals would be submitted in writing. There was an agreement that the Foreign Ministers should fix a formal agenda before the next session, but Stalin and Churchill both questioned the advisability of including China in the proposed Council of Foreign Ministers.

The following morning I met with Molotov and Eden and we reached a general agreement on the extent of China's participation in the proposed Council, and the part France would play as signatory to the various treaties. When our recommendations were submitted to the plenary conference that afternoon, they were accepted without much discussion.

Churchill mentioned the question of submitting the treaties to the United Nations, and I explained that the Charter provided for this; whereupon Stalin commented that this was superfluous, as the powers present would represent the interests of all. This confirmed an impression I had gained at Yalta that the Russian leader had little faith or interest in the world organization, and that it was only because he believed President Roosevelt to be enthusiastic for it that he had paid it lip service. I also feared that his ready acceptance of the idea of a Council of Foreign Ministers meant that he expected it to be of little importance. However, the Russians often seemed to blow first cold and then hot, and I was heartened again a few days later when Molotov, in discussing plans for our September meeting in London, gave the impression that we might reach prompt agreement on the treaties with Italy and the Balkan states.

On a related subject—the implementation of the Yalta declaration on liberated Europe—there was little evidence of harmony from the outset. In our prepared paper we proposed joint action to reorganize the Bulgarian and Rumanian governments so that all democratic groups in those countries might participate. Free elections, to which all three states would send observers, would also be a prerequisite to diplomatic recognition of these new regimes. Churchill was particularly critical of conditions there, declaring that "an iron fence has come down around our representatives in the Balkans." Stalin dismissed these allegations as "fairy tales."

The following day at the Foreign Ministers' meeting Molotov presented a paper attacking conditions in Greece, which brought angry denials from Eden. It was Soviet tactics to counterattack in a different quarter whenever they were hard pressed. I said that while the United States disliked any involvement in foreign elections, we were willing to join with others in supervising elections in Italy and Greece, as well as in the Balkan states, because only if our people were convinced that the governments of those countries were the result of free and unfettered elections would we recognize them.

Many hours were to be spent by us and by the chiefs of state in discussing this subject. Molotov once indicated that if we would first recognize Bulgaria and Rumania, the election proposal would go through. He would put the cart before the horse! I told him our recognition of a country must be based upon our opinion of its regime and was not a subject of bargaining.

It was only at the end of the conference that we made some headway on an Italian peace treaty. Included in the protocol was a statement that the three powers would take up the preparation of a peace treaty with Italy as the first among the tasks of the new Council of Foreign Ministers, with concurrent preparation of treaties with the other countries, if this were found to be feasible. We would not give way on the question of diplomatic recognition, merely agreeing to examine it separately "in the near future in the light of conditions then prevailing."

Another issue soon presented itself—that of trusteeships. At the outset Stalin had declared that the Soviet Union wished to discuss trusteeships, as his country "would like to have some territory of the defeated states." President Truman made clear our belief that such matters should be determined at the peace conference and in the United Nations. Without delay Churchill voiced strong opposition, picturing Britain's losses in lives and property, her recognition that these could not possibly be recouped, and her determination to make no territorial claims. Stalin simply remarked that he wanted to learn if Italy would lose her colonies; if so, "we can decide to which states they should be transferred for trusteeship." This, of course, looked toward the establishment of Soviet positions of strength in the Mediterranean, and to postpone the controversy the President suggested it be considered by the Foreign Ministers. When Molotov brought the matter up again in our meeting, I reminded him that such a decision was linked to the peace treaties and that work on these would begin within a month. With this he was content—for the moment.

At Yalta the Soviets had said that they did not seek territory save for security reasons, stressing the two invasions of Russia through the Polish Corridor. Their effort to secure possession of Italian colonies in the Mediterranean convinced me their talk of security was pure hypocrisy.

Additional evidence of their expansionist policies appeared when the chiefs of state discussed the control of the Dardanelles. Churchill had expressed his willingness to join in a revision of the Montreux Convention which would ensure free passage through the straits for both naval and merchant ships of the Soviets in peace or war. He emphasized, however, that Turkey would be justifiably alarmed by Russia's request for the provinces of Kars and Ardahan, and for a naval base in the Straits.

Stalin declared that Turkey was too weak to give guarantee of free passage effectively, and therefore it was right that the Soviet Union should be able to defend the free use of the Straits by force. The President pointed out that we believed the Straits should be a free waterway, open to all and guaranteed by all. By stating this he clarified the issue: Russia wanted the passage to be essentially under her own secure control; we wanted free navigation guaranteed by the United Nations.

In this connection President Truman brought up for discussion a paper that proposed free and unrestricted navigation of various inland waterways in Europe. But Stalin stuck to his point about the Dardanelles and Molotov brought in the present arrangements with regard to the control of Suez, to which Churchill replied that these had operated for seventy years without complaint.

As usual when an impasse was reached, the United States' proposal was referred to the Foreign Ministers. But on the several occasions when I endeavored to get Molotov to consider it, the only progress I made was to secure the appointment of a subcommittee, with a Soviet representative—who never attended a meeting! The deadlock continued until the closing hours of the Conference, when efforts were being made to agree upon a protocol. The President and I then insisted that the record must show, and it does, that this proposal had been discussed and had been referred to the Foreign Ministers' Council.

On July 25 the Conference temporarily recessed to allow Churchill and Attlee to return to London, there to learn the British national election results. At dinner the night before they left I talked to each sepa·

rately about the outcome. To my surprise both professed to have no intelligent guess how the voting had gone. Since it had been several weeks since election day, I felt that in our country, under similar circumstances, political experts would have had a very good idea of what had happened. I asked Mr. Churchill what the opinion of the gamblers was. He said they seemed confident that the Conservatives were in by a substantial margin. The modest Attlee agreed with this prediction, though he felt sure his own Labour party had made a good showing. Bearing these statements in mind, I was amazed to learn twenty-four hours later that the Labour party had been overwhelmingly elected. I now had a new colleague, Ernest Bevin, who returned with Attlee as Foreign Secretary in the latter's government.

About the same hour we heard of Churchill's stunning defeat, the President received a message of approval from Chiang Kai-shek, endorsing what was to be known as the Potsdam Declaration. The history of this declaration is that before we left Washington, on July 2, Secretary Stimson, as chairman of the Interim Committee, had submitted to the President a draft of a final warning to the Japanese, which Mr. Truman turned over to me. Then, in Potsdam, when we learned of the success of the bomb test, and before Churchill left, I finished drafting the warning. The copy in my files indicates that several suggestions made by Churchill were incorporated, and the President inserted one or two with his pen. The final version was sent off to Chiang Kai-shek for his concurrence, and on July 26 the Declaration was made public. It contained no advance warning about the bomb, nor did it refer specifically to the status of the Emperor. It did, however, declare that the ultimate form of their government should be left to the Japanese people.

The Declaration solemnly warned of the inevitable destruction of the Japanese armed forces and of their homeland as well, and urged immediate and unconditional surrender. This warning to Japan went out immediately through diplomatic channels and was simultaneously released to the press. Out of courtesy, I sent a copy to Mr. Molotov's residence.

His interpreter telephoned a request that the Declaration be held up for several days. When told it had already been released, it was apparent that Molotov was going to protest, but I hurriedly explained that I deemed it inappropriate to consult the Soviet Union about the document when his government was not at war with Japan. He had no answer to this but said that, while he desired to make no change, he felt he might have been consulted.

Two days later Secretary Forrestal arrived and told me in detail of the intercepted messages from the Japanese government to Ambassador Sato in Moscow, indicating Japan's willingness to surrender. He also quoted General Eisenhower as saying that President Truman had told him his principal objective at Potsdam would be to get Russia in the war. I told him it was most probable that the President's views had changed; certainly that was not now my view. Forrestal replied that he thought it would take an army to keep Stalin out, with which I agreed.[3] In fact, I would not have been surprised if the Soviets, sure that they could obtain what they wanted from a divided China, had declared war without waiting to complete their negotiations with Soong.

My days at Potsdam were exacting and exhausting. Each morning, after seeing the three or four members of my staff to make decisions on important matters submitted to me by the Under Secretary, I had to attend the meeting of the Council of Foreign Ministers. At the conclusion of our meeting a report had to be prepared for the plenary session in the afternoon.

At luncheon the President usually had guests from among the many top officials and military representatives then in Potsdam. After lunch I would brief the President on matters that the Council had considered during the morning meeting. After the plenary session, which usually lasted from 3 to 5:30 or 6, we would return to the "Little White House" for dinner. The President always had guests unless we were to be the guests of either Mr. Churchill or Stalin. Always after dinner I spent time on matters brought to me by Dunn and Matthews, as well as the problems that during the afternoon session had been referred to the Council of Foreign Ministers for consideration the next day.

Molotov called one day to inform us that the Generalissimo was temporarily indisposed but had instructed him to discuss the early entry of the Soviet Union into the war with Japan. In his opinion the best course would be for the United States, Great Britain and the other Allies to address a formal request to the Soviet government to declare war. He added that he assumed agreement between the Chinese gov-

[3] *The Forrestal Diaries* state at page 78: "Talked with Byrnes, now at Potsdam . . . Byrnes said he was most anxious to get the Japanese affair over with before the Russians got in, with particular reference to Dairen and Port Arthur. Once in there, he felt it would not be easy to get them out."

ernment and the Soviet Union would be reached in advance. The President said he would consider the suggestion. But we both were disturbed.

The Russians had a nonaggression pact with Japan, such as the one they had had with Nazi Germany. In the latter case the pact had been broken by the Nazis. In this case it was certainly preferable for the Soviet government to be solely responsible if it decided to end its agreement with Japan, which was not due to expire for nearly a year. We had, of course, begun to hope that a Japanese surrender might be imminent and we did not want to urge the Russians to enter the war.

As there were no meetings that day, Ben Cohen and I spent the better part of the afternoon thinking of some way to avoid a positive refusal without committing ourselves. Finally Ben suggested that we draft a letter for the President, drawing the attention of the Soviet government to the Moscow Declaration of October 3, 1943, in which the Soviets and the Allies had undertaken "to consult with each other ... with a view to joint action on behalf of the community of nations," pending the establishment of law and order and a system of security in the world; also to Article 103 of the U.N. Charter, which provided that in the event of conflict between the obligations of member states of the United Nations under the Charter and previous international under-takings, the Charter should prevail. The draft we submitted to the President concluded: "It seems to me under the terms of the Moscow Declaration and the Provisions of the Charter, above referred to, it would be proper for the Soviet Union to indicate its willingness to con-sult and cooperate with other great powers now at war with Japan with a view to joint action on behalf of the community of nations to maintain peace and security."

The President approved the letter and sent it to Stalin with a covering note in which he said that if, after negotiations with China, he wished to make the letter public, it would be in order to do so. The British agreed with this course. Stalin expressed his appreciation, though when the Soviet statement of reasons for attacking Japan finally came out, it contained no reference to Article 103.

When Prime Minister Attlee and his Foreign Secretary Ernest Bevin reached Potsdam, I learned with interest that the differences in British political thinking which had caused them to replace Churchill and Eden were not evident in their foreign policies. With a similar change in United States leadership I am afraid there would not have been a like continuation in policy. I believed the lesson to be one worth learning and I determined to do all possible to bring about a truly bipartisan spirit in our peacemaking.

I have not yet mentioned the Polish question, which in a sense dominated the Potsdam Conference. The fundamental difficulty was the determination of the Soviets to maintain in power the Lublin government which they had sponsored. Under pressure they agreed that some representation should be given to the political parties that had fought in the war against Germany and later maintained a Polish National government in London, but they strongly contended that any such representation would be a mere addition to the Lublin government and in effect superfluous. They also alleged that any representation which differed from the Lublin group would be hostile to the Soviet people and that, while occupying Germany, they could not afford to have an enemy across their lines of communication.

Another difficult factor was the Polish boundaries. At Yalta, Churchill and Roosevelt had agreed that at the peace conference they would support the Soviet claim for recovery of Polish territory that had formerly been Russian, and that the eastern border of the new Poland would follow the so-called Curzon Line. At the same time Roosevelt had forcefully argued that the Soviets should make some concessions to their Polish neighbors, especiaaly around the city of Lvov.

To this Stalin replied that he, a Russian, could not be expected to take a less favorable view of his country's rights than had Curzon, who was English. Churchill admitted that when the Poles lost this territory, they should be compensated by German territory in the west, the Oder River becoming the eastern frontier of Germany. However, neither the President nor the Prime Minister had favored any transfer of territory prior to a peace conference, and Mr. Roosevelt had emphasized that it could only be accomplished by a treaty, which he expected to place before the United States Senate.

Just before Potsdam it had been reported that the Soviets, by unilateral action, had transferred to Polish administration territory, both east and west of the Oder, which was part of the Soviet occupation zone. In the early days of the conference we asked the Soviet representatives about this and found it to be correct. Both President Truman and Prime Minister Churchill protested vigorously, but Stalin said that part of the Russian zone had to be administered by someone and the Poles were best qualified. He also declared that the western frontier question was still open and that the Soviet Union was not bound to cede anything to the Poles.

Later Attlee echoed Churchill's protests, but neither he nor Mr. Truman knew of any way to force the Soviets to oust the Poles and take back the administration of the territory concerned, short of resorting to force. It was unwise to start something we were not prepared to finish. With the yearning for peace in a tired and war-sick world, I do not believe that either the people of Britain or the United States would have been willing again to resort to arms to force the Soviets, instead of the Poles, to administer that part of the Soviet zone. We had to be content with a positive statement in the final communiqué that the permanent disposition of the territory concerned would eventually be decided by peace treaty.

The President and I discussed whether or not we were obligated to inform Stalin that we had succeeded in developing a powerful weapon and shortly would drop a bomb in Japan. Though there was an understanding that the Soviets would enter the war with Japan three months after Germany surrendered, which would make their entrance about the middle of August, with knowledge of the Japanese peace feeler and the successful bomb test in New Mexico, the President and I hoped that Japan would surrender before then. However, at luncheon we agreed that because it was uncertain, and because the Soviets might soon be our allies in that war, the President should inform Stalin of our intention, but do so in a casual way.

He then informed the British of our plan, in which they concurred. Upon the adjournment of the afternoon session, when we arose from the table, the President, accompanied by our interpreter, Bohlen, walked around to Stalin's chair and said, substantially, "You may be interested to know that we have developed a new and powerful weapon and within a few days intend to use it against Japan." I watched Stalin's expression as this was being interpreted, and was surprised that he smiled blandly and said only a few words. When the President and I reached our car, he said that the Generalissimo had replied only, "That's fine. I hope you make good use of it against the Japanese."

I did not believe Stalin grasped the full import of the President's statement, and thought that on the next day there would be some inquiry about this "new and powerful weapon," but I was mistaken.

I thought then and even now believe that Stalin did not appreciate the importance of the information that had been given him; but there are others who believe that in the light of later information about the Soviets' intelligence service in this country, he was already aware of the New Mexico test, and that this accounted for his apparent indifference.

One of the most difficult issues was that of reparations. Our representative on the Reparations Commission, Ed Pauley, had been unable to reach any agreement during more than a month of negotiation in Moscow. The Soviets contended that at Yalta President Roosevelt had agreed to exact reparations from Germany to the extent of $20 billion, one half of which was to be awarded the U.S.S.R. In the meeting of Foreign Ministers at Potsdam, when the point was first discussed, I quoted President Roosevelt as having said at Yalta that he agreed to the sum named only as a "basis for discussion." Molotov and Stalin were not impressed.

All the evidence which we continued to amass at Potsdam—apart from our personal observations—supported our belief that large quantities of equipment and materials which could not possibly be classified as "war booty" had been moved to Russia. Finally I raised the issue firmly with Molotov, asking that he give us a statement of the value of these removals. He offered to reduce the $10 billion by $300 million to account for them, and when I pressed him further for an accounting he said he would reduce his demands to $9 billion if I would stop talking about it.

I also raised the question of the removal of coal by the Poles from the Silesian mines in the Russian zone and asked for an accounting. This was one of the few occasions in the year and a half during which I dealt with Molotov that he lost his temper. I felt I was making progress.

All this took place with a background of reports from General Clay, who was daily experiencing difficulties in the Allied Control Council in Berlin. I realized then that there was no possibility of the three powers ever agreeing on which plants were to be regarded as war plants and therefore subject to removal. Reluctantly I concluded that we must abandon our hope of treating the German reparations question as a whole, and now conceived the idea that each of the three powers should look to their respective zones for reparations, with certain adjustments to be made to balance the preponderance of industry in western Germany against the rich food- and coal-producing areas of the east.

I arranged for a private interview with Molotov, who I was convinced would try to wear us out with his endless discussions, and told him that for days we had made no progress; that we had three issues outstanding and must reach agreement on all three that afternoon because the President and I intended to return to the United States the next day. I outlined the compromises we had proposed during the previous three days and asked him to inform Stalin so that he could come to the Conference that afternoon prepared to accept or reject them.

Our first proposal embraced two objectives: demilitarization and reparations. It would reduce Germany's war potential while satisfying the reparation demands of her neighbors who had suffered at the hands of Hitler's armies. Germany was to be left with only enough industry to maintain average European living standards without asssistance from other countries.

In discussing our reparations proposal Molotov told me that Mr. Maisky, their representative on the economic commission, had "not done so well." At the time I did not appreciate the significance of that statement, but never again during my service did Maisky appear at a conference, nor have any of our representatives in Moscow to whom I have talked seen anything of Mr. Maisky. He was talented and had previously served for ten years as Ambassador to Britain. I fear he continued to do "not so well."

The other outstanding issues were our proposals dealing with Italy and the Balkan states, and with the Polish border and the Polish administration of the territory turned over to her by the Soviets. At the afternoon session Stalin expressed disapproval of "the tactics of Mr. Byrnes" in insisting upon the consideration of three problems in one package, but he proceeded to discuss the package proposal. He demanded a fantastic increase in reparations. When we held firmly to a 10 per cent figure to go to Russia from the western zones without exchange, and 15 per cent from our zones in exchange for food, coal, timber and the like from the Soviet zone, he finally agreed to the "package." Molotov abandoned his proposal for a joint administration of the Ruhr. The Polish occupation was declared to be an interim one and there was agreement to fix the final borders of Germany at a peace conference. Stalin also agreed to reverse some control pro-

cedures in Rumania, Bulgaria and Hungary to meet our objections—
but did not live up to his agreement.

At the next meeting the communiqué committee presented a report
of the work of the conference which was most comprehensive. There
was one statement in the communiqué agreed to by the three governments worthy of note then as it is now: "The three Governments have
no doubt that in view of the changed conditions resulting from the
termination of the war in Europe, representatives of the Allied press
will enjoy full freedom to report to the world upon developments in
Rumania, Bulgaria, Hungary and Finland."

There has not been a time since 1945 that the Allied press has enjoyed freedom to report in Soviet Russia or her satellites.

With the adoption of the communiqué the conference adjourned. We
were not satisfied, particularly with regard to the arrangements for
eastern Europe, but we had forced some concessions by Stalin. Everything depended upon whether the Soviets carried out their agreements,
and by this time I had little confidence in their pledges. Nor did I
believe their attitude toward Germany gave much hope for the Council
of Foreign Ministers to make headway on a German peace treaty. As I
wrote later, the Potsdam Conference was a success that failed. It did
provide a basis for the early restoration of stability in Europe, but
the failure of the Soviets to live up to their agreements robbed our
efforts of any real value.

After the adjournment the President and I flew in separate planes
to a point near Plymouth, where the *Augusta* awaited us. King George
VI had come from London to greet the President and he entertained a
small party at lunch on the battle cruiser *Renown*. At the luncheon
table I sat next to the King. I observed him closely, for it was the
first time we had met, though as it happened I was pleasantly acquainted with his elder brother, the Duke of Windsor. I recalled that
newspaper stories at the time of King George's accession indicated that
he had little interest in affairs of state. On the contrary, he showed the
keenest interest in everything that had taken place at Potsdam, reviewing with me some of the problems encountered and showing some
familiarity with details. He evinced particular interest in the atomic
bomb test, about which he said Prime Minister Churchill had kept
him fully informed. After a brief inspection of the British ship we
returned to the *Augusta*, where the King paid a brief return call on
the President. Within a few minutes of his departure, we were under
way.

## 19 THE JAPANESE SURRENDER

When we boarded the *Augusta* for the return trip, we had an accumulation of letters and memoranda from various people at the conference on many subjects that for lack of time had not been considered. Among these papers was a memorandum from Harriman at Moscow about the Sino-Soviet negotiations.

Though, as I have related, we had sent a message to Soong shortly after reaching Potsdam for the very purpose of assuring him that we did not want him to make further concessions, the President and I concluded to comply with Harriman's request for instructions along the line he suggested, which he could use with the Soviets; and I sent him a message stating that while we had no intention of withdrawing our support of any Yalta understanding, we believed that Soong had already met the Yalta requirements and we hoped very much that Generalissimo Stalin would not press for further concessions. The message stressed that no agreement should be made involving further concessions by China that might adversely affect our interests, without consultation with us.

The message impressed upon Harriman that "our public opinion is much opposed to an arrangement which might be construed to prejudice our historical open-door policy."

On August 6 the President and I were lunching with the crew when Captain Frank Graham of the President's staff brought in a message telling of the first successful atomic attack against Hiroshima. Before leaving the messroom, Mr. Truman told the sailors of the message, and turning to me said, "It's time for us to get home." Two days later, when we were back in Washington, the second bomb was dropped on Nagasaki. This was August 8, and on the following day the U.S.S.R. entered the war against Japan. Early on the morning of the 10th we received through the Swiss government a message from the Japanese that they were ready to accept the terms of the Potsdam Declaration "with the understanding that the said declaration does not comprise any demand that prejudices the prerogatives of His Majesty as Sovereign Ruler." This qualifying statement disappointed me, for the Potsdam declaration had specifically stated that the ultimate form of government in Japan should be established by the freely expressed will of the Japanese people. It appeared to me that they were now attempting to add a condition to their acceptance.

That morning, at a conference in the President's office attended by Stimson, Forrestal and Leahy, Stimson urged that we agree to their proposal. While equally anxious to bring the war to an end, I had to disagree, pointing out that we had to get the assent of the British and Soviets; that we had their concurrence to the Potsdam Declaration with the words "unconditional surrender," and any retreat from those words now would cause much delay in securing their acquiescence. Since the Japanese were patently anxious to surrender, it was not the time for them to present conditions. The President requested me to draft a reply. I went to my office and wrote a message which met with his approval.

It said that the Japanese Emperor's authority and that of his government to rule the state would be subject to the authority of a Supreme Commander of the Allied Powers and that the Emperor personally should sign the terms of surrender; that it would be left to the freely expressed will of the people of Japan to determine their own form of government. It was sent immediately for approval by the governments of Great Britain, the U.S.S.R. and National China. Stimson telephoned me his hearty approval of the message.

We heard from the British government in record time, certainly within six hours. The only modification suggested from London was that the Emperor, rather than signing himself, should require his agents to sign on his behalf. President Chiang replied the next day that he was in full accord with the original draft. However, in Moscow, Ambassador Harriman was dealing with a government that was plainly anxious to maintain its forward drive in Manchuria and, as I had anticipated, contended that the Japanese had not accepted unconditional surrender.

Molotov's first response to Harriman was that he doubted Japanese intentions, but that a formal reply from his government would be forthcoming next day. He was then asked firmly to present the matter without delay, that night. This produced a reply—and a further condition to which Harriman objected strenuously: that if the Japanese accepted our draft, the allied powers should "agree on the candidacies" for representation on the High Command to which the Emperor and his government would be subordinated. This, of course, would have involved long negotiations, with every prospect of a Soviet veto on anything short of key positions for them in administering occupied Japan.

Harriman told Molotov that the condition was unacceptable; before he had transmitted the Soviet reply to Washington, Molotov informed him that Stalin had been consulted and that there had been a misunderstanding: the U.S.S.R. only wanted "consultation" and not "agreement" on this point. Stalin then also agreed to delete any reference to "candidacies." In this, as in some other incidents, I wondered whether Molotov had deliberately given the impression that he was responsible for their first unreasonable position, so that if it had to be modified it would appear to be the concession of the generous Stalin.

Our message, now approved by the principal Allies, went to the chargé d'affaires of the Swiss legation, Max Grassli, for transmission to Tokyo via Berne on the morning of August 11. There was little doubt that the Japanese government would respond favorably, but meanwhile the war went on and every hour meant a tragic waste of life. Never have I known time to pass so slowly! I telephoned our Minister to Switzerland, Leland Harrison, that when he received a reply he was to telephone me at once without waiting for coding.

Meanwhile important steps were taken to prepare for the surrender, and General Douglas MacArthur was designated and approved as Supreme Commander on behalf of the Allied Powers.

On August 14 at about four o'clock I was in my office talking to the Duke of Windsor when a telephone message came through from Berne and Harrison read me the message from the Japanese government. It was a complete acceptance of our terms, and I asked that it be put on the wire as rapidly as possible. It was only a few steps across West Executive Avenue to President Truman's office, and I hurried over to give him the momentous news. In the Pentagon the War Department had set up a teletype exchange with London, Moscow and Chungking. By this method I informed the Foreign Ministers in the three capitals that we now had complete acceptance of the Potsdam Declaration and suggested that the news be simultaneously released at 7 P.M. that evening. As usual there were differing views on the time set and, knowing from experience the difficulty of getting Molotov to agree to anything, I concluded that we should not permit disagreement on this unessential point to delay giving the wonderful news to the world. Therefore I told the Foreign Ministers that President Truman would make his announcement at that time and hoped the other governments would accommodate themselves to that hour.

By six o'clock the cable from Switzerland transmitting the Japanese message in full was in my hands and I took it to the White House so that the President might have it before him when he made the official announcement of the ending of the world's most terrible war—to date.

Even before receiving the message from Japan, the Great Powers had agreed that General MacArthur would represent all powers in accepting the surrender. Then another war started. The Secretary of the Navy began an offensive to have Admiral Nimitz join General MacArthur in the surrender ceremonies, arguing that in the Pacific the war was a naval War and a naval victory. At first I urged that it was not important, but made no headway. He was attacking from land and air as well as sea. Late that night Forrestal telephoned to say he had an idea—the surrender should take place on the battleship *Missouri*. It was an "idea" the Army man would describe as a "Navy trick." I joined him in recommending it to the President because I feared if I did not, Forrestal would next suggest that while the surrender was taking place on the *Missouri*, a Navy band should play "The Missouri Waltz"!

Much has already been written in explanation of the Japanese delay in surrendering after having indicated to the Soviets their willingness to do so a month earlier. From documents that came into possession of the United States (after the war was over), it appears that five weeks before the surrender the Japanese did not know definitely that Russia intended to enter the war against them. In view of the fairly wide knowledge of this fact—certainly as early as Yalta in February—this is surely a reflection on the effectiveness of the Japanese inteligence service.

On July 6, when the Foreign Minister of China, T. V. Soong, was in Moscow negotiating with the Soviets, Admiral Togo apparently had some suspicions about what might occur, because in referring to these talks he said, "It is *even* reported in some quarters that the

Soviet Union may soon enter the war against Japan." But his use of the word "even" indicates surprise and disbelief.

Nor does Japanese Ambassador Sato in Moscow seem to have been successful in securing any definite information. Judging by the messages we intercepted before the war ended and the documents we acquired later, he certainly displayed courage in the messages he sent to his homeland. When he was told to ask the Soviets to act as mediators, he informed his government that its message was so general in character that the Soviets would not consider it, and that unless Japan was ready to surrender, any diplomatic approach by him would be a waste of time. He added that he knew his views were not in accord with the Emperor's communication, but "even though my offense is great I want to preserve the lives of hundreds of thousands of people who are about to go to their deaths needlessly." He emphasized that Japan had no choice but to accept unconditional surrender.

But as late as July 21 the Japanese militarists caused their government to wire the Ambassador, "We cannot consent to unconditional surrender under any circumstances. Even if the war drags on, so long as the enemy demands unconditional surrender we will fight as one man against the enemy in accordance with the Emperor's command." That cable, which we intercepted, depressed me terribly. It meant using the atomic bomb; it probably meant Russia's entry into the war. There is no question in my mind that only the havoc wrought by our new weapon, which was used only twice, caused the war lords of Japan to surrender when they did.

In view of developments since, it is well to call attention to the records of the Japanese Foreign Office, which show that on August 10 the Soviet Ambassador in Tokyo delivered a note to Foreign Minister Togo stating that the Soviets endorsed the Potsdam Declaration and announcing the existence of a state of war with Japan. Simultaneously, Foreign Minister Togo handed the Soviet Ambassador for transmission to his government a copy of the message sent to the United States that morning, through Switzerland, stating Japan's willingness to surrender, upon condition we made no demand "prejudicing the prerogatives" of His Majesty as a sovereign ruler. This message from Japan is the one I answered on the 11th which resulted in the surrender just four days after the Soviets announced their entry into the war. Certainly their entry with full knowledge of Japan's willingness to surrender indicates that the Soviets were determined to get into the war!

It is doubtful whether ever before in history a government delivered a message indicating willingness to surrender and simultaneously was handed a declaration of war.

A few days after the Japanese surrender I attended a meeting with the President, Secretary of the Treasury Vinson, and Leo Crowley, who administered Lend-Lease. Crowley reminded us that immediately upon the surrender of Germany he had stopped shipment of supplies to Russia, since it was the clear intent of the law that any such aid should cease with the ending of hostilities; the Soviets were not then at war with Japan and therefore there was no justification for continuing to send them Lend Lease. His action had brought bitter complaint from Stalin. He now proposed that in order to comply with the law he inform all Allies that this type of aid was at an end and further assistance could be secured only as a result of legislation by the Congress.

We all agreed with Crowley's view and the President authorized him to act promptly. Later, in conversation, Crowley told me he had estimated that the Soviets were indebted to us for Lend Lease deliveries amounting to approximately $11 billion. He said that after V-E Day, when he informed the Soviet representative that if they wanted any of the supplies which were "on order," but which had not been shipped, they would have to arrange payment for them, he was told the items would be carefully screened, because it was doubtful if any of them would be needed.

From this I judged that if the supplies were shipped under Lend Lease, they wanted them; but that if they had to arrange to pay for them, they did not want them. To me that meant the U.S.S.R. never intended to meet its obligations under Lend Lease. During my service as Secretary I called upon them for payment of their debt of $11 billion, but met with no success. I doubt whether to this day one dollar has been paid, but I would continue to ask for payment in the hope that the bills would worry them as my bills worry me.

Crowley told me that in his last conversation with President Roosevelt about April 1 he told the President about a rumor that our government was considering a loan to the Soviets of $10 billion, and that he thought it wise to refrain from making any loan until more was known of their postwar attitude. He said the President agreed. Later, after I became Secretary, an official of the State Department showed me a proposal by Morgenthau urging a loan to the Soviets. Dated January 10, 1945, it was in the form of a memorandum addressed to President Roosevelt and referred by him to the State Department. It suggested giving the U.S.S.R. a credit of $10 billion at an interest rate of 2 per cent, amortized over a period of twenty-five years, for the purchase of "reconstruction" goods in the United States, the amount to be repaid chiefly in strategic raw materials in short supply in the United States. The memorandum stated that Russia could develop substantial dollar assets from her tourist trade and exports to the United States of nonstrategic materials, and could also make payment from her stock of gold. Among other supporting arguments, it held that the credit "would be a major step in your program to provide 60 million jobs in the post war world."

It was interesting that the Treasury proposal was submitted shortly after the Russians had requested that we extend them a credit of the smaller sum of $6 billion at the slightly higher interest rate of 2⅜ per cent. This would indicate that our Treasury officials were not always the coldhearted, glassy-eyed individuals all bankers are supposed to be. When the memorandum was brought to my attention, I had it placed in the "Forgotten File," as I felt sure that Fred Vinson, the new Secretary of the Treasury, would not press it.

During my absence at Potsdam, Joseph C. Grew was Under Secretary of State. Upon my return he wished me to accept his resignation, and I did so with regret. Mr. Grew was an experienced diplomat and had rendered splendid service to his country. I then asked Dean Acheson, who had been Assistant Secretary, to accept the appointment of Under Secretary and he remained throughout my term. He was able, well informed and loyal. William L. Clayton continued to function as Assistant Secretary in charge of economic affairs. There were several new appointments in the first weeks of my secretaryship. In August, William Benton took over our information program, and Donald Russell became Assistant Secretary responsible for administration. Spruille Braden, who had been our Ambassador in Argentina since April, returned to Washington to succeed Assistant Secretary Nelson A. Rockefeller, who resigned in August in order to look after his private business. Braden's sphere of interest was the Latin American republics.

For a period the Department also had the services of Walter J. Brown as special assistant in the public relations and press field.

While I am dealing with these questions of "housekeeping," I should add a general word on protocol. The day after I assumed office the chiefs of diplomatic missions in Washington, which included Ambassadors and Ministers, called. After greeting my visitors I told them that I must ask their indulgence in social affairs; that I could not entertain and be entertained and at the same time meet the demands of that office. It was understandable that my position would not be appreciated by all, but from this policy I never varied, except when an official visitor arrived who customarily would be entertained by the Secretary of State.

I therefore went to few formal dinners during my service as Secretary; but when I did attend one, I noted a change in our position on the protocol ladder. In the office of congressman, and later senator, our places were fixed. But when I went to the Supreme Court I found we had moved up next to the President. Since all offices created by statute outrank those created under executive order, my resignation from the Court and appointment by executive order as Economic Stabilizer sent us to the foot of the table. Now, as Secretary of State, I was back near the top rung, but it did not affect our pride or our appetites.

President Roosevelt always surprised me by his interest in such social problems. When I moved into the White House offices as Economic Stabilizer, I told him that I truly disliked formal dinners and only attended because I considered a presidential invitation a command. He replied that I was at liberty to decline at any time, and thereafter Mrs. Byrnes and I attended only dinners and luncheons of an intimate character.

I recall another conversation with Mr. Roosevelt about protocol. When I was in the Senate he told me he had decided that the Chief of Protocol, who was an official in the State Department, was wrong in seating members of the Senate ahead of governors of states; he believed that a Governor, having power to appoint a senator to fill a vacancy, should outrank the senator, saying the creature should not outrank the creator. Accordingly, he had instructed the protocol officer to advance the governors, and was telling me about it so that if I heard any complaints from my senatorial colleagues, I could explain his position. At the next formal dinner I attended he had seated at his right Mrs. Gifford Pinchot, wife of the Governor of Pennsylvania. No senator complained to me, but Mrs. Byrnes reported a vigorous objection from the wife of a western senator. Frequently I had tried to explain the President's political decisions to senators—often without success—but when it came to explaining his social decisions to the wives of senators, I told him he would have to explain it to the Married Women's Union.

## 20  WHEN FOREIGN MINISTERS MEET: LONDON

On September 5, I left for the first meeting of the Council of Foreign Ministers at London. In spite of the signs of Soviet expansion in the Far East, in eastern Europe and in the Mediterranean area, and the disappointments of Potsdam, I was optimistically determined to make the machinery of the Council work if possible—especially as it had been established as a result of my initiative. With us at the planning sessions on the *Queen Elizabeth* was John Foster Dulles, who had been foreign affairs adviser to Governor Dewey, the Republican candidate for President, in the last presidential campaign. I had invited him to accompany us because he was unusually well informed in foreign affairs and deeply interested in establishing a bipartisan policy.

After the conference had opened on the 11th at Lancaster House, my optimism began to wane. In the discussion over arrangements and agenda, the Soviets made clear their desire to deny any real participation to the smaller states and to confine the task of peacemaking to themselves, the United States and Great Britain, which would have made the idea of the Council itself superfluous. And though experience with the Soviets had indicated that on occasion we might make more progress in private conversation than in the public sessions, at London both types of negotiations were generally acrimonious and unprofitable.

Heated debates took place almost daily. At one point we circulated a memorandum on the proposed drafting of a Rumanian peace treaty, the opening paragraph reading: "This suggested directive is submitted by the United States delegation with the understanding that the United States will not negotiate a treaty of peace with Rumania until there has been established a government broadly representa-

313

tive of all democratic elements in the population and pledged to the earliest possible establishment through free elections, of a government responsive to the will of the people."

This preamble seriously offended Molotov, who urged repeatedly that it be withdrawn. If not, he would have to make a reply. I told him that was a matter for his decision. He began an impassioned argument, comparing the Italian and the Rumanian governments to the former's disadvantage, and alleging that the United States maintained relations with fascist governments in Spain and in Argentina. In short, our objections to the Groza regime in Rumania resulted in an attack against the United States. In reply, I argued that we had recognized the government of Poland, though subsequent events in that country had disturbed us; we had recognized Finland; and we were making no reservations with regard to Hungary because we expected free elections to be held there as had been agreed at Yalta. In Rumania the Russian representative, Vishinsky, had given the King two and a half hours to install a government suggested by him which we did not consider a representative one.

I also complained of the delays experienced by the United States officials in entering Rumania and of the censorship of press reports from there. Molotov retorted, "As long as the Rumanian people are satisfied, American correspondents will have to realize that changes will not be made to suit them." Ernest Bevin proposed that a commission of investigation be sent in, to which Molotov replied, "We have too many commissions in Rumania already." He made it clear that he sought action on recognition of the Balkan states before turning to the Italian treaty, and to this I would not agree.

London was my second meeting with the Soviets as Secretary, but I felt I had learned little about them. Bohlen told me that I was not alone in this—that he had been talking with a member of the Soviet staff, and the Russian said, "I do not understand your Secretary of State. We have been told that he is a practical man, but he acts like a professor. When is he going to start trading?" Bohlen explained to him that in matters involving what we believed to be a principle we did not trade, but doubted he had been convincing enough.

When the subject of an Italian peace treaty was finally reached, we found that the Soviets were demanding $6 billion in reparations from that country. This we opposed as utterly impractical, especially as we were already granting financial relief to the new Italy, and did not want to subsidize the Soviets indirectly by these payments. Molotov then switched to his government's demands for a trusteeship of one of the Italian colonies. He quoted a letter from Stettinius, which he construed as a promise to support Soviet claims, and also referred to a similar undertaking by an American "high official," who, it developed, was Harold E. Stassen, a delegate to the United Nations San Francisco Conference.

Before this, in one of my private talks with Molotov, I had learned that the Soviet preference was for holding Tripolitania. When the question came up publicly, I told him I could not support or even discuss such a claim, and pointed out that the Stettinius letter had merely stated that the U.S.S.R. would be "eligible" for a trusteeship. This was one of the occasions when the language barrier made itself felt, and, to illustrate, I said that while every male citizen born in the United States is eligible to become President, this does not mean he is going to be. He professed to be unable to understand our arguments and claimed a breach of faith.

We had hoped that after two weeks work we would have reached an accord on the broad principles to be followed in writing the various European peace treaties, but within a few days it was apparent that this was going to be impossible. Aside from bickering over the agenda and procedures, we fell afoul of new and unexpected complications. France wanted to discuss the control of Germany, and the Soviets brought up the question of Japan. Molotov argued that there should be a control council there and that General MacArthur's regime should end, since the problem was now political and economic, not military. He also stated that the Soviet representative in Tokyo had been ignored by the Supreme Commander.

I refused to discuss the Japanese situation on the ground that the subject had not been proposed by him in the communications we had exchanged prior to the meeting, and was not on the agenda. Molotov, however, raised the question on several occasions, as he also continually pressed for our recognition of Rumania and Bulgaria. It was on September 22, after a private meeting with him in the morning during which we again discussed the occupation of Japan, that the Russian Foreign Minister virtually broke up the conference. That afternoon he stated that we should reorganize; that an initial mistake had been made on September 11 when it was decided that France and China might take part in the discussions of peace treaties for Finland,

Rumania, Bulgaria and Hungary. The two powers, he continued, should not be present except at discussions when the fate of countries with whom they had signed armistice agreements was being considered.

This, in effect, would have excluded China from European treaties, and limited France to the German and Italian treaties. After several sessions of harsh debate I saw we were deadlocked and drafted a message which I asked President Truman to send to Stalin, requesting him to instruct Molotov to stand by his agreement of September 11. But Stalin's message in reply showed him to be in full support of Molotov, who maintained his position. It would have been most useful in a matter of this importance if the President could have called up Stalin personally, but while this would be possible technically, it would be difficult linguistically. Direct telephone communication is feasible, of course, in dealing with the English-speaking nations of the Commonwealth since, whatever the differences of opinion and aim, exchanges of views are easy to effect.

The Soviet attitude in effect killed any hope of real progress at London. During this debate I was impressed by the patient dignity of France's Foreign Minister Georges Bidault and his associates in these difficult and humiliating circumstances. I was glad to plead their cause, and that of the Nationalist Chinese, because I believed in it.

Before adjournment we tried to agree upon the customary communiqué enumerating the subjects on which there had been agreement. Molotov refused to sign anything that referred to the original agreement including participation by France and China. He wanted it stricken from the record, even though it had already been made public. Bevin commented that this "was the nearest thing to the Hitler theory" he had ever heard. This insulted Molotov, who started angrily toward the door; but as he neared the exit, he appeared to slow down so that the blunt but good-natured Bevin could withdraw his statement. Bevin retracted it, as Molotov had expected, and the conference continued for several more sessions.

In private conversation, when I urged Molotov to consider our proposal to internationalize the Danube, he said that I was personally unfriendly to the U.S.S.R. and that the United States policy had changed since President Roosevelt's death. On the contrary, I had tried every honorable way to reach agreements with Molotov, and in a private conversation had suggested a twenty-five-year treaty on the demilitarization of Germany under four-power supervision.

When it became apparent that further meetings would do more harm than good, at my suggestion Dr. Wong, the able Chinese representative, who was presiding that day, formally adjourned the conference on October 2. I returned home exhausted in patience and depressed in spirit. Walter Brown, the United States representative on the communiqué committee at Potsdam as well as London, contended that if Job had been forced to reach an agreement with Molotov and his deputies, he would not today have his reputation for patience.

A few days later I made a radio speech explaining what had happened—not what had been accomplished—at London. I said that while agreements in international affairs, as in domestic matters, depended upon intelligent compromise, "compromise does not mean surrender and, unlike surrender, requires the assent of more than one party." Attempting to explain the various difficulties, I reminded my listeners that the Foreign Ministers Council, like the Security Council of the United Nations, acted under the rule of unanimity, thus giving each one a "veto power." The veto power, I concluded, "is a great power and should not be used lightly. We are willing to make concessions but the United States does not believe in agreement at any price." I reiterated my view that all the states both large and small that had fought and suffered in the war should help make the peace.

The reaction to my statement was better than I had anticipated. Well aware of my own disappointment, I had expected that others would feel the same way. But I was heartened by expressions of confidence from legislators, editors and columnists. Writing later about what had occurred, Mr. Dulles said in his book *War or Peace:* "He [Byrnes] would not, for the sake of agreement . . . make a compromise that would sacrifice our country's historic friendship with China and France. At that moment, our post-war policy of 'no appeasement' was born, and, on the whole, it has been adhered to ever since. We refused to pay international blackmail." I like to believe this is a true appraisal of the London Conference.

I have mentioned that on several occasions Molotov claimed that the attitude of the United States had changed, as if he expected Uncle Sam always to play the part of Santa Claus. But President Roosevelt also had his share of troubles with the Soviets. A short time before his death he told me that Stalin would write him an offensive message, which he frequently laid aside in order that he might cool off before answering;

then another would come, this time couched in such friendly terms that he found himself ignoring the first message.

There was also the incident concerning General Kesselring and several senior German staff officers who had indicated through our OSS office in Berne their willingness to discuss a surrender in Italy. The Combined Chiefs of Staff approved General Alexander's plan to send a representative to Switzerland to make contact, and we told the Soviets what was afoot, making it clear that this envoy would do nothing but make arrangements for a meeting at Kesselring's Caserta headquarters, at which a Soviet general could be present. Molotov's response was that unless the U.S.S.R. took part in negotiations from the beginning, it would not take part at all.

Within a day or so Stalin sent an insulting message to President Roosevelt, charging that in return for the surrender of the German Army in Italy the United States and Britain had promised to secure easier over-all peace terms for the Germans, and that as a result three German divisions had been moved to the Russian front. The President denied the charge, saying there had been no agreements and no negotiations, and that the divisions had been moved several weeks prior to Kesselring's peace overtures. He said he resented the "vile misrepresentations," which reflected a desire of some of Stalin's informants to destroy the friendly relations existing between the United States and the U.S.S.R.

Stalin's reply was conciliatory and on April 11—on the eve of his death—President Roosevelt sent a message saying he was glad the incident was over. It is noteworthy too that on the day following, at Warm Springs just an hour before he died, he replied as follows to an inquiry from Churchill about how he ought to handle the question of joint relations with the Soviets in a speech he was about to make in the Commons: "I would minimize the general Soviet problem as much as possible because these problems in one form or another seem to arise every day and most of them straighten out as in the case of the Berne meeting. We must be firm, however, and our course thus far is correct."

At the time of the London meeting I had not yet heard of this exchange, but it was my considered view that we had emphasized patience enough and that henceforth we should stress firmness as well as patience in our relations with the Russians.

It was quite clear to me, nevertheless, that we must find a way to resume negotiations so that peace treaties could be prepared—and signed. Until they were signed the Soviets would have an excuse to keep large military forces in the Balkans and in Austria. Protected by a massive occupation army, their agents could work to take control of, or strengthen the Russian hold on, occupied countries. At London, Molotov had frequently delayed our talks with the plea that he must consult his government. Since we could make no progress by the usual diplomatic correspondence, I thought we had better resume negotiations in Moscow, where Molotov would have less excuse for delay.

Before suggesting that talks be resumed, I thought it well to review our position, particularly on the thorny question of "diplomatic recognition." We considered everything we might do to demonstrate to the Soviets that we would not depart from the spirit of the Yalta and Potsdam undertakings on this question, which was that each case would be investigated separately and decided on its own merits. Acting thus, we found it possible to recognize the provisional government of Austria on October 20, 1945.

Within two weeks we had done the same in the case of Hungary. Meanwhile, Ambassador Harriman was asked to visit Stalin, who was in the Crimea, to point out to him that we had shown our good faith in these cases and to present the reasons we had not acted on Rumania and Bulgaria.

When Harriman reported back to Washington, his reply was surprising. Stalin apparently was not particularly interested in our recognizing these two Balkan states and turned the conversation away from Europe to the control of Japan. Harriman was not prepared to discuss this, but his information about Stalin's attitude was interesting because only a few days previously we had learned that the Soviet military representative in Tokyo, General Kuzma N. Derevyenko, had been called from Japan.

## 21  THE PROBLEM OF SECURITY

In the interval between the London and Moscow meetings, I turned my attention to the organization of the Department. While I was at the London Conference Leslie Biffle, then Secretary of the Senate, who was on his way to France, had called to see me. He said that the President had announced the signing of an executive order transferring to the State Department the employees of the Office of War Information, the Office of Strategic Services and the Office of Inter-American Affairs. This information came as something of a shock to me, since it meant that the State Department now had four thousand more employees than when I had left Washington two weeks before. I had had only two days in the Department before beginning my travels, so I was not familiar with the personnel, but I was certain the Department could not absorb so many employees without becoming an administrative agency rather than a policy-making body. I felt strongly that its functions should be limited to policy making.

Furthermore, I knew that the majority of the four thousand new employees had been recruited when manpower was at a premium. Many of the people in OWI, admittedly a propaganda agency, had been employed when the U.S.S.R. was our wartime ally, and they were sympathetic with Soviet ideology. In view of recent Soviet attitudes I did not like the idea of their being transferred in a block into the Department which controls our foreign relations. Experience had demonstrated the difficulty of firing unsuitable governmental employees because, under the rules of the Civil Service Commission, an employee who was dismissed could demand a written statement of the charges and a hearing before the Commission. This provision had been useful in peacetime to

prevent unfair treatment resulting from petty political prejudices; it
was not foreseen, however, that it might operate to prevent dismissal of
an employee whose loyalty was doubtful but against whom there was
no positive evidence.

When I returned to Washington I expressed to the President my
regret that the transfer had been made. He explained that it had been
decided that these employees should be retained in order not to add to
the anticipated unemployment resulting from discharge of men in the
armed services, and that as they were experienced they would be of
greater service than new employees. He also mentioned that the Budget
Bureau was recommending the establishment of a Central Intelligence
Agency and he thought the employees transferred from the Office of
Strategic Services could be utilized there, and that the Voice of America
might use some of those transferred from the Office of War Information.
Though he paid me the compliment of saying he thought I could handle
the situation better than any other Department chief, this did not provide the aspirin necessary to relieve the headache.

Following my adoption of a policy of firmness at London, I began to
hear of some employees whose statements indicated sympathy with
the Soviet attitudes; they were critical of what they chose to call a
"get tough" policy on my part. This problem was referred to Assistant
Secretary of State Donald Russell, who had been placed in charge of
administration. In order to ferret out some of the difficult cases, he
brought in from outside the department several outstanding citizens,
including Joe Panuch and Carter Burgess. Legal restrictions notwithstanding, he and his staff made some progress, and without fanfare.
When he learned of an employee whose loyalty to our policies was in
doubt, but against whom a case might not stand up in a formal hearing
by the Civil Service Commission, he would have him transferred to a
routine or even disagreeable task which might encourage a resignation.
I recall an instance of one such employee who was sent to work in the
basement of the old German Embassy sorting documents. Shortly afterward he resigned. Without any publicity there were a number of resignations under similar circumstances.

But this, of course, was only a stopgap policy. At an executive session of the Senate subcommittee in charge of appropriations for the
State Department, headed by Senator McCarran of Nevada, Russell and
I reported on our difficulties in securing testimony against suspected
employees, and our inability to take action in view of the right of em-

ployees to demand a hearing before the Civil Service Commission. We suggested that the State Department be given authority to dismiss an employee "for the good of the Service," notwithstanding the provisions of the civil service law. When the appropriations bill was reported to the Senate, the "McCarran Amendment" was added conferring this right on the Department; this made possible the dismissal of certain employees who had previously been troublesome and embarrassing.

For instance, among the employees transferred to us from the Office of Statregic Services was one Carl Marzani. His record came to the attention of our security officials in April, 1946, and a prompt investigation revealed that he was a member of the Communist party. By the time I returned from Paris in July, the McCarran Amendment had come into effect and we could proceed with his dismissal. When he learned of the action about to be taken he attempted to resign, but was forestalled by the order of dismissal.

The most harmful publicity the State Department received in the field of security problems came from the charges against Alger Hiss, a former official of the department. He had been first employed in 1936 while Cordell Hull was Secretary, and during the Stettinius administration was promoted to chief of the Special Political Affairs Division. As I have previously mentioned, I noted at the Yalta Conference that Hiss had Mr. Stettinius' ear, and he was one of his chief advisers at the United Nations Conference at San Francisco. He became Secretary General of the Conference, and afterward I heard favorable comments on his work there from Senator Vandenberg and Mr. Dulles.

I have previously expressed my doubt that at Yalta Hiss exercised any influence directly upon President Roosevelt in the decisions he and Churchill made on the Far East. Rather, it was my impression from what President Roosevelt told me that these decisions were made upon the advice of the Joint Chiefs of Staff that the planned invasion of Japan would result in a million casualties. Whether Hiss, through Hopkins and Stettinius, influenced the President on any matters other than the United Nations proposals is pure speculation and a point upon which partisan opinion will never agree.

After I became Secretary of State I saw Mr. Hiss only once except on the relatively few occasions when I was able to attend a staff meeting. Some years after I had left government service I was told that as early as December, 1945, just a few days before I left for

Moscow, the FBI had sent the State Department a general report in which Hiss was mentioned. This report did not, however, come to my personal attention. This is understandable. I was fully occupied at the time in essential preparations for the Moscow Conference as well as by many other urgent tasks.

It was not until February, 1946, that I learned from Senator Eastland that Hiss was being investigated by the FBI. I telephoned Mr. J. Edgar Hoover at once and he sent me a copy of the report filed by one of his agents. Though it did not contain charges of specific subversive acts by Hiss, it stated that an admitted Communist, Whittaker Chambers, had accused Hiss of being a party member and had said that without success he had urged Hiss to sever all connections with the party.

Sending for Hiss, I personally questioned him, for I was vain enough to think that as a former trial lawyer I was a fair cross-examiner. He denied positively any connection with the Communist party or any affiliated organization, and also any acquaintance with Chambers. I watched him closely for any trace of fear when I suddenly inquired if he would willingly submit to cross-examination by J. Edgar Hoover. He did not flinch and said he would do so at any time. After he left my office I telephoned Hoover to inform him of what had occurred. He expressed regret that I had talked to Hiss because he felt that it might be more difficult in the future to get information from the person he referred to as "the source"; however, he recognized my position when I said that if he could give me any evidence that Hiss was a Communist I would not keep him in the Department overnight, and he told me to send him over.

Hiss was told to make an appointment with Mr. Hoover's office and not to attend, as scheduled, the meeting of the Security Council of the United Nations in New York the following week. When I returned from the Council I learned that Hoover's office in interrogating Hiss had been no more successful than I in securing from him any incriminating admission. I was reluctant, without positive evidence, and with Hiss' positive denial of even knowing Chambers, to ask for a resignation that would ruin a man's life.

Nevertheless, Chambers' statement lurked in my mind and I questioned two career-service men who had worked with Hiss and of whose loyalty I had no doubts. They both seemed surprised; they had not suspected Alger Hiss of Communist affiliations, and both expressed confidence in him. In spite of all this, I took steps to see that certain matters of importance in our foreign relations were not sent to Hiss' office, and some months later welcomed the news that he had been offered a position elsewhere and wished to accept it. The rest of the story is too well known for it to require discussion here. To my mind, a real, but less often remarked, element of the tragedy is that suspicion was thrown upon the entire State Department because Hiss had occupied a position of responsibility.

Assistant Secretary Russell had not been concerned only with security matters. We had decided that urgent steps should be taken to improve conditions in the career foreign service so that we could encourage recruits of quality as well as support loyal and tried employees. After all, the men and women of the service are the eyes and ears of our policy makers. In times of peace they constitute our first line of defense, and as a result of our new position in world affairs their effectiveness is more essential than ever before. The first basic legislation to govern the foreign service was enacted when I was a member of the House of Representatives in 1924. Congressman Rogers of Massachusetts, speaking in support of it, called this unit of the State Department the "stepchild of the government." In the twenty-two years since his day there had been no supplemental legislation to help the service keep pace with the growing power of the United States in world affairs, and for lack of encouragement ambitious young men had almost ceased entering this important arm of our government.

The general indifference of congressmen was understandable. Their influence is of no value to applicants for the foreign service, and few had firsthand contacts with career officers, only occasionally noticing a news picture of some ceremony abroad with those present wearing formal attire. So it was that some legislators often called members of the foreign service "cookie pushers in striped pants."

When Russell began his study of the career service, he encountered conflicting views within the Department as well as opposition from other departments that had representatives abroad. In the State Department considerable thought had been given to the subject, and in the late spring of 1946 Russell had ready a proposed bill which, though it would not give us all we wanted, was all we could hope to secure at that time. The two chairmen of congressional foreign affairs com-

mittees agreed on its merits, but an unusually crowded calendar
made it highly improbable that it could be considered before adjournment. From April to July I had to spend most of the time at the peace
conference in Paris, and when there was a ten-day recess in July
I was so exhausted that I planned to rest in Europe rather than fly
back to Washington for so short a period. However, Russell notified
me of the precarious situation of the foreign service bill and asked
me to return. The two of us then spent most of the week talking with
congressional leaders, and in the closing days of the session both Houses
passed the bill by a unanimous vote. I returned to Paris feeling well
repaid for the effort, but in a day or two Russell telephoned me that
the Bureau of the Budget was urging the President to veto the bill.
Over the telephone I urged the importance of the bill on the President, and after considering the problem he did not use his veto.

After I left the State Department I kept my interest in the welfare
of the career service, and in the hope of arousing support for its
loyal and hard-working members I contributed an article to *Collier's*
magazine in 1955 entitled "Stop Shooting Our Sentries." I pointed
out that the method of recruiting career service people made it certain that they would have no political sponsors, and since we properly
demanded that they should not interfere in domestic politics, it was
our responsibility to protect them against unfair political attacks. If
they are to give us the nonpartisan service we demand, our career
men should not be forced to seek political influence at home and they
must be free to report conditions as they find them—not as some
political official at home may wish them reported. And they should
not have to worry about how a report may be interpreted several
years later by some senator or congressman with all the benefits of
hindsight.

Early in November we were temporarily diverted from the peace conference issue by the question of international control of the atom and of its use in future warfare. Molotov had made a fiery speech marking the anniversary of the Russian Revolution, warning the western powers that they could not long expect to be the sole possessors of the bomb and promising the Soviet people various technological advances. Three days later the Prime Ministers of Great Britain and Canada, Attlee and Mackenzie King, arrived in Washington to discuss with the President a whole range of problems, and Bob Patterson, then Secretary of War, Dr. Vannevar Bush and I sat in on the conferences.

On November 15 a decision was announced to share the atomic bomb secret with other members of the United Nations "just as soon as enforceable safeguards against its use for destructive purposes can be devised." I do not believe in all history there is a record of a more unselfish offer than this willingness to surrender our monopoly of the terrible weapon, nor stronger evidence of our desire for peace.

This was the week before Thanksgiving, a day which I spent quietly, clearing my desk of accumulated papers. While working alone, with only the ticking of an old grandfather clock for company, I had an idea of how we could resume negotiations. After talking with President Truman I sent a cablegram to Molotov, reminding him that at Yalta it had been agreed the Foreign Ministers would meet at least every three months; that they had met informally at San Francisco, Potsdam and London but had not met in Moscow, and I thought it appropriate that the next meeting should be held there. I was confident the Soviets would not refuse to extend the invitation, and

326

I hoped that some understanding on atomic matters could be reached before the United Nations General Assembly convened in London in January. The Soviets fell in with our suggestion and the date for the Moscow meeting was set for December 15.

To mar this encouraging development came serious news from Iran, which had on her soil at this time troops of the three major powers. It had been agreed that all would leave by March 2 of the following year, 1946. Meanwhile, when antigovernment rioting broke out in the province of Azerbaijan, the Soviet occupation forces prevented Iranian forces from entering the area to quell the disturbances. It was a fair assumption that they were actually encouraging a separation movement in the area, which adjoined their own territory. The Iranian government asked for all foreign troops to withdraw. We had the War Department pull out our troops at once, and proposed January 1 as the date for both the British and the Russians to withdraw. By December 3 the Russians had refused, and the British felt they should also remain for a while.

I was due to leave for Moscow on December 12. During the weeks preceding this date, the President and I met often, not only at our standing engagements for 12:30 each Monday and Thursday, but at numerous other times because of the need to discuss the subjects to be taken up at Moscow. We conferred frequently on the developing situation in Iran and the increasing problems of China. The situation in the Far East continued to worsen, and our rapid demobilization was not helping matters. We had materially aided the Chinese Nationalist forces with Lend Lease during the war, but they were now proving unequal to the task of disarming the Japanese in north China and Manchuria, where they were vigorously opposed by the Chinese Communist armies.

Our Marines, under Lieutenant General Albert C. Wedemeyer, were disarming the Japanese forces in areas where we had assumed that obligation, and were to withdraw from China by mid-November. Later, at the request of the Chinese Nationalists the time limit was extended to December 15. It was rapidly becoming evident that if this withdrawal took place, it would be left to the Chinese Communists to disarm the Japanese in North China, thus increasing both their prestige and their weapon strength. Our reports indicated that the Communist forces were being well received by the civilian population in some sections and were picking up many deserters from the Nationalist armies.

Further, and more disturbing, it was reported that notwithstanding Soviet professions of aid to the Nationalist government, in the areas in Manchuria where the Soviet troops dominated, the Chinese Communist forces were rapidly gaining in men and matériel.

At President Chiang's request we agreed that our troops should remain for even a longer period to give the Nationalist government more time to move troops to Manchuria and north China; the Soviets were also asked by Chiang to lengthen the stay of their forces. We undertook to transport some Chinese forces to the north for the purpose of disarming the Japanese, but we avoided doing anything to justify the charge that we were deliberately interfering in a civil war between Chinese forces. On October 11 both sides had issued a joint statement declaring that they still wanted a peaceful solution. Churchill had advocated a unification policy, and Stalin professed to favor it. At Potsdam I had heard him describe the elements opposing the Nationalist government as "revolutionists"—not Communists. And he further said the Nationalists offered the only hope for a stable government.

Before our policy could really adapt itself to the changing circumstances, we were confronted by the resignation of Major General Patrick J. Hurley, who had been in the United States since the end of September. When he came to see me, I showed him our reports, urging him to return to his post because of the urgency of the situation. Finally he agreed to return within a few days. I immediately informed President Truman, but within a few hours I was told that the news ticker was busily bringing word that Ambassador Hurley had released a copy of a speech, to be delivered at noon, announcing that he had resigned.

That day members of the Cabinet were luncheon guests of the President. Before luncheon he and I were discussing the Hurley resignation when we were joined by Clinton P. Anderson, then Secretary of Agriculture, now senator from New Mexico. He suggested to President Truman that General George C. Marshall be appointed Ambassador to succeed Hurley. I immediately agreed it would be an excellent appointment, believing that no one could be more successful in solving the military and diplomatic problems we had there. The President thought well of it. But since Hurley had made the positive statement to me that morning that he would return to his post, after luncheon I telephoned him to inquire whether the report we had heard was true. He said it was, adding that he was sick and at that time could not discuss why he changed his mind. When I informed the President, he telephoned General Marshall and secured his acceptance.

Later it occurred to me that there might be a touch of political strategy in Anderson's suggestion of Marshall. Hurley had been in New Mexico for some time since his return from China, and the press had reported that he was considering becoming a Republican candidate for the United States Senate. It was possible that Anderson, a New Mexico Democrat, had in mind that the news of Marshall's appointment would blanket the report of Hurley's resignation. It did. Later, Clinton Anderson and Hurley became candidates for a senatorial seat. Mr. Anderson was elected and has served with distinction.

During my absence in London, and thereafter, the Under Secretary, Dean Acheson, gave much consideration to the Far East and had called for a new evaluation from John Carter Vincent, chief of the Far Eastern Division. Later I learned that Vincent submitted to Acheson four alternate lines of policy in the light of changing conditions in China. After conferring with War Department officials, Acheson recommended one of the proposals and, after making various revisions, we incorporated it in a memorandum which was forwarded to General Marshall for his consideration. On Sunday morning the ninth he came to my office accompanied by his deputy chief of staff, General Thomas T. Handy, and another officer. We were joined by Acheson and Vincent. Marshall made several suggestions, to which I readily agreed, and I emphasized that, since he was no ordinary ambassador but a "special representative" of the President, he was expected to report directly to Mr. Truman. Knowing that Mr. Truman would not expect him to carry out a policy with which he was not in full accord, I suggested that he and his advisers withdraw to the room across the hall set aside for the use of ambassadors to consider the memorandum in the light of our conversation.

After deliberating for about an hour, Marshall agreed that on the day following I should present the revised memorandum to the President for his approval. On Monday afternoon General Marshall and I discussed the mission with the President and he approved the policy memorandum in its final form. Plans had been made for me to start for Moscow at 9 A.M. Wednesday, so it was Acheson who accompanied General Marshall when he went to the White House on the eve of leaving Washington. He was handed a letter signed by the President and several documents, one of which the President referred to in his letter as "a statement of United States policy toward China which I understand was prepared after consultation with you and with officials of the War Department."

The main objects of the program were to develop a united and democratic China, and to assure that the Chinese government would be able to extend its sovereignty over Manchuria. It was suggested that General Marshall should effect a truce, particularly in the north China area, and induce the Nationalist government to call a conference of representatives of the major political elements in order to bring about a united China.

Our Marines would be kept in north China to complete the disarmament and evacuation of the Japanese, and we would assist the Chinese government to transport essential armed forces and supplies to Manchurian ports. General Marshall was also to complete arrangements for transporting other Chinese troops into North China when he considered this step consistent with the progress of negotiations, or when it was plain that the negotiations had either failed or had no prospect of success and that the movement was necessary to carry out the terms of surrender and promote the interests of the United States in maintaining international peace.

Marshall could also use his discretionary power to induce or compel concessions by the Nationalist government, or by the Communists or other factions. Not in writing, but verbally, he was told by the President that the Chinese Nationalists were not to be left entirely without help, regardless of the success or failure of his efforts to promote a peaceful settlement. Though he was authorized to promise loans, economic assistance, and the aid of military adviser groups, all factions were to be impressed with the fact that if China was ravaged by civil war, the United States would not intervene.

The policy statement added that when conditions in China improved, the United States would consider aid for long-term projects "unrelated to civil strife which would encourage economic reconstruction and reform in China." By these means we hoped to encourage the Nationalists, Communists and others to settle their political differences peacefully and establish a constitutional government similar in some respects to our own, supported by the people themselves.

General Marshall enjoyed great prestige in China, but in September, 1946, after nearly nine months, he reported to the President that it seemed useless to remain there much longer. He was instructed to return whenever he concluded further effort would be of no avail. I was in Paris at the time and I notified the Chinese Foreign Minister of President Truman's position.

Dr. Shih-chieh Wang feared that Marshall's departure would indicate that the United States had lost interest in China's affairs. I assured him that this was not true, but pointed out that it was useless for our special Ambassador to stay when neither faction would accept his advice. Marshall remained in China until January, 1947, when he returned to Washington and to an appointment as Secretary of State.

On Wednesday, December 12, I started on a long and, as it proved, strenuous journey to Moscow. Because of the importance that I attached to the negotiations on atomic energy, I asked Dr. James H. Conant to accompany me. On the way I remembered that it was the custom of participants in conferences to exchange small gifts and, willing to try anything once, I cabled Miss Connor to send me a framed photograph which I could present to Mr. Molotov. This eventually resulted in my receiving in return autographed photographs from both Mr. Stalin and Mr. Molotov, which was at least progress in the social amenities.

Somewhere near Moscow our plane was lost for awhile in a heavy snowstorm and it was with relief that our party landed, even though it was at the wrong airport! The conditions under which we were to labor were far from ideal. In the first place we had to accommodate ourselves to new hours that were particularly trying to me since I have always been of the "early to bed, early to rise" school. In Moscow it is customary for senior government officials to begin work at about two in the afternoon and continue until two in the morning. Again, our Moscow Embassy did not compare with those we have in some other world capitals, either in living accommodations or in communications facilities. But Ambassador Harriman provided us with the best that was possible under the circumstances. He assigned us living quarters in Spasso House (our Embassy) and it was from here that we commuted to the conferences at Spiridonovka House.

We had come with certain aims. We wanted to resume the negotiations on the peace treaties; induce the Soviets to co-operate in creating a commission of the United Nations for the international control of atomic energy; promote the establishment of democratic governments in the Balkans, as had been agreed at Yalta; secure agreement on a

Far Eastern Advisory Commission; and finally, attempt to get the Soviet troops out of Iran.

Our proposal was that the Council of Foreign Ministers should first draft proper treaties for submission to the peace conference. To that conference we wanted to invite all members of the United Nations that had actually waged war with substantial forces against the Axis—a total of twenty-one states. As a reluctant concession to the Russians we were prepared to agree that after a peace conference of those powers had arrived at its recommendations, the final drafts would be prepared by the countries that had actually signed armistice terms with the enemy country. Molotov maintained the position he had taken in London.

While objecting to the participation of India because it was not an independent state, he wished to invite the Soviet Baltic republics of Latvia, Lithuania and Estonia. His intransigence blocked any progress on this particular question for three days, and though we shifted at times to consideration of the Iranian problem, we made little headway on that either.

Finally I learned on December 19 that Stalin had returned from his Crimean vacation, and asked to see him. We met that same night in his Kremlin office at ten o'clock—Stalin, Molotov, Harriman, Chip Bohlen and I. Stalin's interpreter was Pavlov, whom I had come to think of as an old friend. He said that he had been in the Crimea with the Generalissimo, and when for conversation I asked what he had been doing there, he answered, "Reading your speeches." When I congratulated him upon his good taste in reading, he said "That was *must* reading for me."

As soon as the six of us were seated, I handed Stalin the letter I had brought with me from President Truman, the principal paragraphs of which read:

Secretary Byrnes and I have sought to go as far as we have felt able to meet your view with reference to the Allied council for Japan and to the Far East Commission, and I sincerely hope that your government will accept the proposals which we have made. . . .

Secretary Byrnes and I have also gone far in an effort to meet your views on the future procedure for handling the peace treaties, and the difference between us now on this matter is not great.

The letter expressed the hope that the Soviet government "will join in the proposals to have a commission created under the United Nations

Organization to inquire into and make recommendations for the control of atomic energy in the interest of world peace," and concluded: "I hope very much you will see and talk frankly with Secretary Byrnes. He is thoroughly familiar with my purposes and I feel certain that if you had a full and frank talk with him it would be most helpful."

We then began to discuss our difficulties over the peace conference. I pointed out to him that the British had to insist on the presence of India, which had contributed its armed forces to the fighting. If he insisted on including the three Baltic republics, the Soviet Union with five republics would have six votes, and the British Commonwealth six also. Under these circumstances I would demand six votes for the United States, five of them for states of the Union. Stalin replied that he was willing for the United States to have equal votes with the United Kingdom and the U.S.S.R., and reminded me that at Yalta he had agreed to our having three votes in the United Nations General Assembly. Stalin's remark indicated that he shared my amazement at our failure to claim equality at the San Francisco Conference.

My impression that night was that he would agree to our proposal but did not wish to reverse Molotov so quickly and in his presence, so, asking that he give further consideration to our list of states, I went on to discuss Iran. A proposal by Bevin to send an investigating commission into that country had caused an acrimonious debate with Molotov. I reminded Stalin of the pledge given by the three powers at Teheran to preserve the territorial independence of the country, and of the action of the Russian Army in denying Iranian troops the right to travel on an Iranian highway toward Azerbaijan. Stalin gave the weakest excuse I ever heard him make. He said the Baku oil fields in southern Russia lay close to the border, and that he had no confidence in the Iranian government; that it might send saboteurs to set fire to them. The Soviet Union, he said, under its treaty with Iran could maintain troops there until March 15 and "at that time the situation would be examined again."

This meant that in March he might or might not comply with his written pledge. I argued that the right to remain until March could be claimed, but it was not mandatory to exercise it; that there was no right to interfere with Iranian troops. It was important, I said, to avoid even the appearance of violating a pledge given by the three great powers. I also said I had been advised that in January Iran would present her case to the United Nations Assembly, and we would have to support her appeal. "It would surely be unfortunate," I said, "if we should be opposed on such a vital question at the very first meeting," but unless he would agree to withdraw all troops "we would have to support Iran vigorously." To this Stalin replied, "We will do nothing to make you blush," which did not prove to be the case.

At the conclusion of our talk I wired the State Department the substance of Stalin's remarks on this point, as follows:

1. Iranian government is hostile to Soviet Union and there is danger that this hostility will manifest itself in sabotage of Baku oil fields. It is for this reason that Russia continues to maintain troops in Iran.

2. Treaty of 1921 gives Russia right to send troops into Iran if conditions become disturbed in that country. In light of Iranian hostility which creates danger to Russia it will be necessary for Soviet Union to consider later whether Soviet troops can be withdrawn in accordance Tripartite Treaty of 1942 or must be retained under terms of 1921 treaty.

3. Soviet forces are not interfering in Iranian internal disturbances. Reason they are refusing permit additional Iranian forces into Azerbaijan is that they fear clashes between local population and Iranian troops and incidents involving Soviet troops as well. Even now, his troops are suffering and several Russian soldiers have been killed by Iranian detachments.

4. Iranian government is trying to stir up trouble between Russia and Anglo-Saxon powers. We must be skeptical of Iranian complaints.

5. We may rest assured Soviet Union has no territorial or other designs against Iran. Once it feels secure about Baku oil fields USSR will withdraw forces and take no interest whatever in internal affairs of Iran.

I expressed surprise that Stalin considered Iranian government hostile to Russia and reiterated my belief it was important that great powers should always be able to show they were living up to agreements and behaving correctly toward small nations.

At the next afternoon's session Molotov said that they would accept our peace conference proposal. I suspected that after our meeting of the previous night, Stalin had told him to agree. We now sought the concurrence of China and France, and asked France if she would invite the conference to meet at Paris.

As to the Far Eastern Advisory Commission, I found that Ambassador Harriman's report about the Soviets' intense interest in this question was not exaggerated. Molotov reiterated the complaint that their representatives were ignored by General MacArthur. When I reminded him of the agreement that MacArthur was to be Supreme Commander, he said they wished to see a Japanese Control Commission established like the one in Berlin. We had had sad experiences in Berlin and wanted to make certain we did not have the same trouble in Japan. I pointed out that immediately after the Japanese surrender the Soviets had agreed to the establishment of a mere advisory committee, the operation of which had been delayed only because of the attitude of Britain, Australia and New Zealand.

But we made no progress. Each time the subject was discussed Molotov wanted to know when we would withdraw our troops from China. Accordingly, when I again visited the Kremlin I complained to Stalin. In three different sessions, I said, I had repeated to Mr. Molotov that our Marines were in China first because the Chinese government requested it, and further because it was our duty to disarm Japanese troops—that we would withdraw them just as soon as our obligations under the surrender terms were discharged. With a smile I told him that his Foreign Minister evidently could not understand me, or liked the sound of my voice, because he made the same inquiry day after day, and each day I gave him the same information. Stalin laughed, but Molotov kept his dead-pan expression.

Then, putting some matches on the table, I indicated the location of the Japanese armies in China and of our Marines, who numbered less than fifty thousand. Stalin leaned across the table to see the positions indicated; suddenly he looked up and said, "Now where is that Chinese army of a million men with reference to your troops?" When I told him, "I know nothing of such a force and am satisfied there are no Chinese troops in that particular area," he replied, "Well, the Chinese were always terrible liars." I told him of Marshall's mission and the President's statement of our China policy, a copy of which I had given to Molotov.

In our conversation Stalin agreed it was essential that we should rehabilitate China and promised to declare publicly his support of the Nationalist government. He also agreed to reaffirm "adherence to the policy of non-interference in the internal affairs of China." When I asked when the Soviets would withdraw their troops from Manchuria, Stalin said their withdrawal had been delayed at the request of the Chinese, but would take place by February 1.

My conversation with Stalin helped secure an agreement on an Advisory Council for Japan with such limited powers that the Soviets did not seriously interfere with the plans of General MacArthur, who proved he was a statesman as well as a soldier. He did such a good job that he won the respect of the Japanese and the gratitude of all patriotic Americans.

At Moscow we also decided to create a commission, with representatives of the United Kingdom, China, the U.S.S.R. and the United States, to work out an agreement for a four-power trusteeship for Korea, for a period up to five years, the aim being the "establishment of the national independence of Korea." The agreement was sound, but as usual the Soviets, with their armed forces in northern Korea, intended neither to withdraw them nor to allow the commission to operate.

By December 24, after much negotiation in which personal conversations with Stalin were an important feature, I discerned our first real progress and was able to wire the President as follows:

We have reached complete agreement as to the peace conference and resumption of the work on peace treaties with Italy and enemy Balkan states. China has concurred. We have not definitely heard attitude of France but I hope to talk with Bidault this afternoon and secure the agreement of France.

In my first conversation with Stalin on the peace conference he supported Molotov's position but later Stalin telephoned making concessions which made possible our agreement. As a result of a long conference with Stalin yesterday afternoon, I now hope that we can make forward steps toward settling the Rumanian-Bulgarian problems. We also discussed the Chinese situation, Iran and atomic energy. As a result of our conversation, I hope that this afternoon we will be able to reach some agreement on these issues. Yesterday Molotov held out for complete subordination of the Atomic Energy Commission to the Security Council, making it a subordinate agency of the Council, and objected to any reference to a plan being developed by stages. We are in general accord as to Far Eastern issues. The situation is encouraging and I hope that today we can reach final agreement on the questions outstanding and wind up our work tomorrow.

It being Christmas Eve, Stalin entertained at a dinner for Mr. Bevin and me. There were about thirty guests, including members of the Politburo. Molotov acted as toastmaster, and when he proposed a toast to Conant he said he had the assurance of the Secretary of State that Conant did not have an atomic bomb in his pocket. Stalin, at whose right I was seated, asked about Conant; when I told of his contribution to the development of the atomic weapon, he was deeply interested. He had said nothing before, but now rose and said he thought Mr. Molotov was wrong in speaking so lightly about the American scientist; Stalin said that he himself was no scientist and had no knowledge of physics, but he thought Conant and his associates deserved the plaudits of all peoples. Dr. Conant, disregarding the rebuke to Molotov, appropriately expressed his appreciation. Within the past year I have thought Stalin's attitude toward scientists may account in some measure for the encouragement given by the Soviet government to scientific developments.

Later, while coffee was being served, I mentioned to Stalin my proposal for a twenty-year treaty among the four powers to keep Germany demilitarized. Recalling his statement both at Yalta and Potsdam that the Soviet attitude toward neighboring countries was due to their determination to ensure Russian security, I suggested that such a plan should remove all fears and that I had been somewhat surprised, when I mentioned it to Molotov in London, that he did not respond favorably. Stalin said Molotov had mentioned it, but he gave the impression the discussion had only been a casual one. After listening to my explanation, he said it seemed by far the best proposal he had heard on the question, and I told him we would prepare a draft which could be circulated for suggestions.

Upon my return I told President Truman of Stalin's reception of the idea; he was delighted, and agreed that I should submit a draft to the Chief of Staff for consideration from the military viewpoint. Enthusiastically the President said this would be known as "the James F. Byrnes Treaty." Vandenberg also heartily approved the proposal. About a month later the draft, which had been approved by our military authorities, was submitted to the three Foreign Ministers. From Britain and France came prompt approval in principle; Molotov said he would want to discuss certain amendments. This was to be expected, but later at Paris he flatly rejected the whole idea.

To return to the Moscow Conference: I had been over-optimistic in expressing to the President any hope that we could conclude our work on Christmas Day, though there was less trouble than I had anticipated over the proposal that the United Nations establish an Atomic Energy Commission. Molotov was told that there could be no question of our eliminating any of the language as to safeguards and finally abandoned his opposition to the provision that the plan be developed only "by stages."

As to Iran, on Christmas afternoon in a private conversation, Molotov told me that he thought the British plan to send an investigating commission there was acceptable. However that evening he suggested one particular amendment which left in doubt the date when the Soviets would withdraw their troops. Both Bevin and I rejected this, and when the subject was again discussed next day Molotov took the position that since Iran was not on the conference agenda, an exchange of views was all that was necessary. We had reached a complete impasse and in this matter Stalin proved to be just as intractable as his Foreign Minister. Again I decided that no agreement was better than a bad one, and that if necessary we would fight it out in the Security Council.

We also continued to have trouble over the recognition of Rumania and Bulgaria, as we again attempted to hold the Soviets to the Yalta declaration on the liberated areas. This stated specifically that each controlling power agreed "to form internal governmental authorities promptly, representative of all the democratic elements in the population pledged to the earliest possible establishment through free elections, of governments responsive to the will of the people." In view of the gross violation of this pledge by the Russians, we had agreed at Potsdam only to "examine" the situation in Finland, Hungary, Rumania and Bulgaria and act favorably on recognition before the peace conference—if we felt the actual conditions warranted it. After the election in Hungary, a free election in which the Communist party was not victorious, the United States had recognized the new government.

Stalin now argued that our recognition had been granted only because of the Communist defeat, and that we could show our sincerity by accepting the regimes in Bulgaria and Rumania. He denied any pressure by the Red Army in Bulgaria and said he could not force reorganization on the Bulgarian government. I told him I was confident that if he would advise the Bulgarian government to include in its ranks truly representative members of two important political parties not then represented, his advice would be taken; then we would again consider the question of recognition. As to Rumania, I insisted that Clark Kerr, the British Ambassador in Moscow, and Ambassador Harriman should accompany Mr. Vishinsky to Rumania to arrange for a reorganization of the government with adequate guarantees of civil rights.

This did not modify either of the Yalta or Potsdam agreements; on the contrary the purpose was to enforce them. Stalin's attitude on this was hopeful, but again the next day Molotov and Vishinsky refused absolutely to agree to the language we proposed. I concluded it would be useless to spend additional time in going over the same ground, and proposed that the conference adjourn. The questions outstanding, I suggested, could be considered when we attended the coming January meeting of the United Nations in London. Bevin concurred and Molotov was forced to agree.

The staffs were instructed to prepare the communiqué in Russian and English. This took surprisingly long and during the waiting period Molotov again approached me privately about recognizing Bulgaria and Rumania. On this occasion I purposely used the word "*nyet*," since he did not seem to understand "no."

It was not until two o'clock on the following morning that we met again at the conference table to sign the documents. I had signed the several copies and had left my chair to say good-by to members of the British delegation when the Russian interpreter came to say that Mr. Molotov would like me to return to the table. Once more he attempted to bargain on the Rumanian and Bulgarian question, and when he saw we would not yield he announced that the Soviet Union would agree to the British and United States proposal that ambassadors of all three powers should be sent to Rumania! It was a complete reversal, and Bevin asked him facetiously if he would look in his pocket to see if he could find another agreement there on our Iranian proposal. Molotov good-humoredly said he could not. The protocol was then amended and at 3:30 A.M., some four hours before our plane was scheduled to leave, it was signed, and the conference ended.

We were all extremely tired. I packed, took a short nap, spoke briefly to the American newspaper and radio correspondents, and then left for the airport. Colonel Hugh A. Kelly of Jersey City, our military aide, who had had some time to move about Moscow, had met Father Braun, a Catholic priest who had been in Moscow for twelve years and was now vainly trying to leave for London. There were no transportation facilities and so he had asked Kelly if we would let him travel as far as Berlin in our plane. When in the early morning we decided upon adjournment and fixed the time of our departure, I told Kelly that if he could get Father Braun out to the airport in time he could go with us. Despite the short notice, Father Braun was waiting for us at the plane when we arrived. (The Berlin airport was closed and we had to fly to Naples.) He stayed with us all the way to the States and was able to visit his mother in New England before returning to Europe.

When we were in the air I found I could not sleep and I began to reflect upon the activities of the past two weeks, which had probably been the most strenuous of my life. I knew then what other Americans have since come to know—that negotiating with the Soviets is likely to inflict enormous nervous strain. I remembered too the remark of Dr. Conant on the previous evening, that he thought the president of every American university should have the opportunity of attending such a conference in order to see the difficulties inherent in negotiating with the Soviets.

I knew also that my staff had had a most difficult time. Bohlen and Matthews, for example, had done much more than assist in planning the agenda and attending the sessions. During the morning hours they had presented to me any messages from the Department requiring personal attention, and in turn they prepared messages to the Acting Secretary of State on Conference developments, this being the regular procedure at international conferences. When of sufficient importance, reports thus sent are communicated by the Acting Secretary to the President. This type of communication was, of course, transmitted in code through the Embassy.

In some capitals our Embassy could also get in touch easily with the Department by telephone, but the Moscow service was awful. This was impressed upon us on Christmas Eve, when a member of my staff spent six hours trying to get a satisfactory connection through to Foreign Minister Bidault in Paris. The message was not one requiring the strictest secrecy and we felt we could risk a telephone call, even though Harriman had warned us that our telephone line might well be tapped. He also told us that the room in Spiridonovka House in which we held our private conferences might have devices to record our conversations, and I can picture now the half-comic scene of a number of men in a huddle in the center of the room well away from the walls.

I may add that during the first few days so much of our time had been consumed in discussing agenda and procedure that the telegrams sent were few, and that those which were sent on the 17th and the 18th of December were of little interest. It was not until after Stalin's return from the Crimea on the 19th that I could send a cable of significance.

This conference had provided some examples of the class distinctions in Soviet society. There had been little time for recreation, but Bevin and I had attended two or three functions planned for our entertainment. One evening we were officially invited to see the ballet *Raymonda* at the Bolshoi Theater. We were both surprised to find this supposedly "most democratic" country so much more class-conscious than either the United Kingdom or the United States. Between the acts we were invited to a room where the refreshments included tempting and even rare delicacies. But only our party was given this pleasure, and as we left to return to our box I noticed members of the diplomatic corps emerging from a different room and the press and staff members from yet another.

On another occasion Molotov invited the Ministers and their staffs to take refreshments in the attractive quarters used at Spiridonovka for social affairs. Both Ambassador Harriman and Bohlen, who had spent years in Moscow, told me that so far as they knew no Ambassador of the United States had ever been invited to the home of a Soviet official in Moscow, though he might be frequently feted in this official setting. On this afternoon Mme. Molotov was present, and while talking with her I noticed across the room M. Litvinov, the former Russian Ambassador to the United States. Had I followed my inclination I would have gone over to speak to him and his attractive wife, who was a native of England, for during their service in Washington I had had the pleasure of knowing them. But I had to check this impulse because there was considerable doubt about how well he stood with the "powers" in Moscow. I was told he was thought to be overfriendly to the British and ourselves, so I thought it wiser when we met to content myself with a handshake, offered without any show of enthusiasm. It was returned in about the same manner. Thus protocol and politics have to be reckoned with even at official Russian social events.

The following summer, when we were in Paris at the home of the Russian Ambassador, I again noted even more pronounced class distinction. On that occasion, Senator Connally and Senator Vandenberg with their wives accompanied Mrs. Byrnes and me, but found themselves escorted into a large room with many guests while we were taken to a small one with a most exclusive group, including Molotov and the leader of the French Communist party! As soon as I could with reasonable grace, I asked the privilege of joining my Senate associates.

Not only did Moscow educate us in Russian protocol but we suffered from much argument over details of procedure. At all international conferences it is essential that there be agreement on simultaneous release of a communiqué. At this meeting I finally succeeded in fixing a release hour acceptable to our own wire and radio services, which had often complained in the past that the British public got the news from international conferences before it reached the public in the United States. The first paragraph of the cable containing the communiqué read that it was "for release at ten P.M. Washington time on December 27th and simultaneously in the other two capitals, London 3 A.M. December 28th and 6 A.M. Moscow December 28th." I had informed the American correspondents who were waiting for us at our Embassy of this agreement on the release time, and while getting a hurried breakfast we gave them some general information about the subjects agreed upon, without, of course, going into any details.

Before I left Moscow at seven that morning I was assured by Ambassador Harriman that as soon as he could get his staff to the Embassy, he would have the communiqué coded and sent by the usual method to the State Department. He obviously made a very special effort to do this because the record shows that his long message in twenty-six sections began to come over the Department wires in Washington at 6:30 on the morning of December 27, fifteen hours before the release time. As it was Christmas week, many officials were away from Washington when the communiqué started coming through. The President had gone to Independence, Missouri, for the holidays, but I was told that Mr. Acheson made special arrangements to transmit the communiqué to him there.

On Saturday morning we landed at Stephenville, Newfoundland, where our plane was checked and refueled. While we were waiting I asked the commanding officer at Harmon Field to send the War Department this message: "December 29th 1945. Relay to State Department for Acheson from the Secretary. Please ask Assistant Secretary William Benton to try to arrange for broadcast Sunday night preferably ten o'clock. If necessary ask White House help."

As it turned out, this was a wasted telegram. With a skeleton force on duty in the Department, the watch officer (the official who is on duty in the Secretary's office at night and on holidays) took the message and telephoned it to Mr. Acheson at his home about 12:35 P.M. By then I had already reached Washington airport, our plane coming down at two minutes past noon. Acheson was among those who met me.

Mrs. Byrnes, Donald Russell and Miss Connor were at the airport and went with me to my hotel. Before we had lunch I asked Miss Connor to place a call to the White House to ask for an appointment with President Truman, for I wished to report to him and to discuss making the broadcast. Informed that he was on the *Williamsburg* with a party of friends, she then asked that my request be relayed to him. About an hour later I received this message through the White House Secret Service officer on duty there: "Happy to hear of your safe arrival. Suggest you come down today or tomorrow to report on your mission. Arrangements can be made for you through the Secret Service. We can then discuss, among other things, advisability of broadcast by you. Please advise time of arrival."

By four o'clock that afternoon I was on a plane headed for Quantico, where I boarded the *Williamsburg* and had a cordial meeting with the President. We talked for more than an hour in his cabin. When I told him of the last hectic night in Moscow and of the surprise agreement by Molotov at 2:30 in the morning to send our ambassadors to Rumania and Bulgaria, he said he then understood why he had not heard of the adjournment until after the news was on the radio. I pointed out that the hour of the formal adjournment was 3:30 A.M., and that radio information came instantly whereas telegrams sent through the Embassy, with all the delays of coding and decoding, took many hours. I told him of my reaching Washington as early as a telegram I had filed at Newfoundland.

He said he understood and expressed pleasure at the progress we had made; he particularly approved of my warning to Stalin that we would support Iran. Of Stalin's promise, "we will do nothing to make you blush," he was as skeptical as I. He urged me to make the radio report, and insisted that I stay for dinner. During the meal, at his request, I told his guests of the more important things we had already discussed. At the conclusion, when the table was cleared for poker, I asked to be excused, saying it was necessary for me to leave in order to get my statement prepared for the next evening. The President said he would be listening and urged that I return to the *Williamsburg* for dinner on New Year's Eve. I must confess that I felt the need of rest more than a party, but because of his cordiality I accepted the invitation to join him in ushering out the old year.

The next morning I was up early to begin work on my radio report, which had to be prepared in advance of broadcast time in order to be available for the press. In it I stated that the agreement reached at Moscow on the peace machinery "meets our insistence that all states which took an active part in the war should participate in the peace," and described in detail the procedure to be followed at the conference to be called not later than May 1.

Referring to the fact that since the London Conference we had found it possible to recognize the governments of Austria and Hungary, I emphasized that there was still a wide divergence between our viewpoint and Russia's over Rumania and Bulgaria. "Our objections . . . have been not only to the exclusion of important democratic groups from these governments, but to the oppressive way in which they exercise their powers. Until now our objections have been little heeded by those governments or by the Soviet government." I then spoke of the tripartite commission of ambassadors which would proceed immediately to advise the King on broadening the basis of representation in the Rumanian government. I stressed that we would recognize the Rumanian government only when our government decided that adequate safeguards had been taken for free elections and for freedom of speech, of the press, religion and of association. Attention was also called to the pledge of the Soviet government to advise the new Bulgarian government to take similar action. These agreements, I said, did not go as far as I should have liked, but were a great improvement over the generalities of Yalta and Potsdam. As time soon proved, they were so good from our point of view that the Soviets proceeded to ignore or to violate them.

I next reported on the agreement on the Far Eastern Commission, which could now function: no basic allied policy could be adopted without the concurrence of our government. Further, the Council in Tokyo, composed of representatives of the Soviet Union, the British Commonwealth, China and the United States, would be under the chairmanship of General Douglas MacArthur, whose decision "will be controlling on all but three reserved questions." Nor could the Council take action on these three questions without our agreement. I emphasized that I was "determined to assure that the outstanding and efficient administration set up and exercised by General MacArthur should not be obstructed."

I was also glad to report that the Soviet government had pledged to remove its forces from Manchuria on February 1 and had affirmed its adherence to the policy of noninterference in the internal affairs of China. I wish I could say now that the Soviets had carried out this last pledge, but obviously I cannot.

Finally, I explained the agreement on the establishment of a U.N. Commission on Atomic Energy, which was based essentially on the accord reached in November by President Truman and the British and Canadian Prime Ministers. I made it clear that I had told Molotov that the root of the matter lay in the problem of providing safeguards in relation to every phase of the subject and at every stage, and that we could not "be expected to share our armament secrets until it was certain that effective safeguards had been developed to insure our mutual protection."

The next day I held a press conference. The Associated Press commented, "In high good humor at his first news conference since his return from Moscow, Byrnes reported that 'President Truman and Cordell Hull are pleased with the results of the meeting. Hull sent heartiest congratulations on the progress made.'" Walter Lippmann was generous in writing, "The verdict of our people is bound to be that the Secretary of State has earned our confidence and support as a practical negotiator." Many similar comments of approval doubtless contributed to my good humor; a congratulatory message from Secretary Stimson certainly did.

With long experience in politics, I knew the normal disposition of senators and congressmen to criticize the achievements of public officials of opposing political parties, and I was agreeably surprised that so few expressed any serious objections to what had been done. Late in the afternoon I went back to the *Williamsburg* to have New Year's Eve dinner with the President and his party. In greeting me, President Truman said that he and those with him at the time of my radio broadcast the previous evening commended it unanimously. We spent a pleasant evening, all the group joining in singing the old year out.

After the President returned from the short holiday on his yacht, I talked to him about the United Nations meeting in London, suggesting that, since Molotov would not be present, I remain there only until the resolution creating the U.N. Atomic Commission was adopted. With his approval I appointed a committee to draft plans which our government could present to the U.N. Commission when it began to function. It was composed of Under Secretary of State Acheson, former Assistant Secretary of War John J. McCloy, Dr. Vannevar Bush, Dr. James B. Conant and General Groves. Because some of the anti-administration press continued to criticize the language of the resolution, I issued a statement just before I was to leave for London in which I said:

The language of the resolution [to establish the atomic commission] makes clear that even as to the exchange of basic scientific information for peaceful purposes, the commission has authority only to make recommendations. Therefore unless the United States concurs in the recommendation, it could not be adopted. If the United States concurred and the Security Council adopted the recommendation, it would still be for the government of the United States by treaty or by Congressional action to determine to what extent the recommendation should be acted upon. If action is required by treaty it would take a two-thirds vote of the Senate to ratify the treaty.

Some years later a statement was published that at this time, the first week in January, there was a serious difference between the President and me over the decisions at the Moscow Conference. That there was no basis for the statement is evident from what the Presi-

dent said at his press conference on January 8, when he repeated the
commendation of my course at Moscow which he had wholeheartedly
given me on the *Williamsburg* upon my return. This was gratifying
because I have always held that inasmuch as the President is primarily
responsible for foreign policy, there should be complete accord between
him and his Secretary of State. When such accord does not exist, the
Secretary should resign. The newspaper reports of the President's
press conference were similar to the one that appeared on page 1
of *The New York Times*: "President Truman unqualifiedly endorsed the
Moscow decisions and Mr. Byrnes' actions, including atomic control
and supervision of Japan in his approval. He reserved the right to
withdraw recognition from Rumania, Bulgaria and Yugoslavia if they
fell short of the Yalta provisions for freedom."[1]

I left Washington on January 7. Senator Connally and Senator
Vandenberg, members of the United States delegation, had preceded
me, and when I reached London I invited them to dinner, after which
we discussed plans for the meeting. Vandenberg had some doubts about
the adequacy of the safeguards provided for in the Atomic resolution,
but I pointed out that the language of the draft was precisely that
agreed upon the previous November by Attlee, Mackenzie King and
President Truman, and I reminded him that he, Connally and I had
been present when the statement was made public and that we had
approved it. Vandenberg then said he had been misled by a newspaper
story emanating from Moscow. He seemed entirely satisfied when I
explained that the wording to which he had objected was the only

[1] Felix Belair, Jr., in *The New York Times,* January 9, 1946.

"WASHINGTON, January 8—President Truman today gave his personal imprimatur
to the recent Moscow agreements of the Big Three, including the proposed United
Nations Atomic Energy Control Commission, but reserved the right to withhold
even conditional recognition of the Rumanian, Bulgarian and Yugoslav Governments if they fell short of the democratic processes agreed to at Yalta.

"Insisting on his position as sole arbiter, so far as the United States is concerned, of whether Yalta agreements were complied with, the President repudiated
any suggestion that they had been modified at Moscow and said he would continue to insist on free and untrammeled elections and the other freedoms agreed
to by President Roosevelt, Prime Minister Churchill and Generalissimo Stalin.

"President Truman's replies to all questions in the foreign affairs field constituted
a blanket endorsement of all that Secretary Byrnes had undertaken during and
since the Moscow meetings. These included the proposed United Nations Atomic
Energy Commission, the appointment by Byrnes of a special committee to study
controls and safeguards of United States atomic secrets during United Nations
consideration of the subject, and arrangements for Allied participation in policy
decisions governing Japan's occupation."

part of the resolution to which Molotov objected, and that I had told Molotov it was the heart of the resolution and we must insist on it if we were to have any resolution at all.

Senator Connally, serving on the steering committee which first considered the resolution at the conference, ably supported it. When it came to the floor I opened the debate, urging acceptance, and it was unanimously adopted.

There was no further criticism of the atomic energy agreement at Moscow, either by Republicans in Congress or in the press. I am confident that if Vandenberg had been with us at Moscow there would not have been any misunderstanding on the subject, and from that day to the end of my service as Secretary I insisted upon his accompanying us to every international conference. Senator Connally and I had no serious differences with him.

On January 19, the Iranian representative filed his country's protest with the Security Council against Russian interference in Iran. The Soviets, in the belief that Great Britain had encouraged the move, promptly appealed to the Security Council to order the British out of Greece. The Ukraine, with Russian concurrence, called for British forces to leave the Netherlands Indies. At the same time the Arab countries of Syria and Lebanon threw into the Council's lap a complaint about the occupation of their territory by the British and French.

The Council found itself deadlocked because the permanent members were unable to agree on any solution. Since none of the powers would openly question the proposition that no state had a right to keep troops on the soil of another independent state without its consent, the United States representative on the Security Council, Edward Stettinius, was instructed to present to the Security Council a general resolution to this effect. After many days of debate a majority accepted it, and on February 15 the Security Council agreed without a dissenting vote that British and French troops should leave Syria and Lebanon. The Soviets abstained from voting because the language was not sufficiently strong.

A Soviet representative said that Soviet troops would leave Iran on March 2, and the Security Council voted to turn the Soviet-Iranian dispute back to the two countries for settlement by direct negotiation, retaining the right to request information on its progress.

I was not in London for these disputes because I left for Washington after the atomic energy resolution was agreed to on January 24. But as

I learned of these developments they convinced me that the Soviet attitude was hardening and that my own pessimism was generally justified.

In February, Mr. Churchill was in Miami and I flew down to visit him, taking Mr. Baruch with me. Unfortunately, Mr. Churchill had contracted a heavy cold. Lying in bed, he talked about public affairs and then told me of his engagement to speak at Fulton, Missouri, outlining the speech he proposed to deliver. When I commented upon a phrase he had used, he said a man should not be "a slave to phrases but should make phrases his slaves." This reminded me of an evening at the British Embassy when, surrounded by a group of friends, he had seemed to me to be trying out some phrases and new ideas. I commented on this to one of his party who sat near me. He told me that on occasions of this kind Churchill was likely to do exactly that; and if the ideas and phrases went over well, one could expect to hear them in future speeches.

I was given a rehearsal of the famous Iron Curtain speech in its final form when Mr. Churchill passed through Washington on his way to Fulton. The British Ambassador, Lord Halifax, invited me to dinner, after which Mr. Churchill and I went to his suite and I read the address in full.

The next morning, when I gave President Truman a résumé of the contents of the speech, he decided not to read the advance copy that was to be sent to him. Anticipating that the Soviets would charge the British and Americans with "ganging up" on them, he could truthfully say he had not read the speech prior to its delivery.

About this time General Eisenhower told me that Army reorganization was progressing more rapidly than anticipated. This was more comforting than his statement the previous October. At that time, recalling Theodore Roosevelt's advice about speaking softly and carrying a big stick, I had thought it wise not to voice publicly my concern when we had only a twig with which to defend ourselves. But in the light of General Eisenhower's comments I accepted an invitation to address the Overseas Correspondents Club in New York, thinking it a good audience for the speech I had in mind. I sent an advance copy of my proposed speech to the President, as was customary in the circumstances, and received it back with the notation, "Jim, I've read it and like it—A good speech! I've marked some phrases I particularly like. H. S. T." Accordingly, on February 28 I addressed the club, among whose membership I could claim a number of old friends. I knew they realized that, though speaking to them, my words were intended for the Kremlin when I said:

> All around us there is suspicion and distrust, which in turn breeds suspicion and distrust. Some suspicions are unfounded and unreasonable. Of some others that cannot be said. We have covenanted not to use force except in defense of law as embodied in the policies and principles of the Charter. We intend to live up to that covenant. . . . We have a responsibility to use our influence to see that other powers live up to *their* covenants. And that responsibility we intend to meet. . . .
>
> Much as we desire disarmament and much as we are prepared to participate in a general reduction of armaments, we cannot be faithful to our obligations to ourselves and to the world if we alone disarm. . . .

I then went on to declare that in order to banish war, nations must refrain from doing the things that lead to war, expressing the conviction that despite the gathering tensions "satisfactory solutions can be found if there is a stop to this maneuvering for strategic advantage all over the world." Speaking for the benefit of the Russian leadership, and as a reminder to Stalin of our talk in Moscow, I repeated: "We have no right to hold our troops in the territory of other sovereign states without their consent and approval freely given. . . . We must not conduct a war of nerves to achieve strategic ends. We do not want to stumble and stagger into situations where no power intends war but no power will be able to avert war. . . . If we fail to work together there can be no peace, no comfort and little hope for any of us." In my opinion that statement is just as applicable to our relations with the Soviets today as it was in 1946.

While European affairs, and particularly relations with Russia, dominated our thoughts, developments in other areas of the world also caused concern. In Argentina Colonel Juan D. Perón was in the ascendancy and found it popular to make false charges against the United States. Spruille Braden was our Ambassador to Argentina at the time. He had spent many years in South America, where he first went as a representative of Westinghouse Electric Corporation; prior to his service in Argentina, he had lived in the neighboring state of Chile. He accurately appraised Perón as a dangerous dictator and, because in answering Perón's charges he expressed himself freely, Perón attacked him as well as the government he represented.

Some time after Braden came home to replace Nelson Rockefeller, who had resigned, the State Department issued a blue book tracing the connections between the Argentine militarists and the German Nazis. Perón denied everything and blamed the publication of the book on the presence of Braden in the State Department. This I promptly denied, and President Truman stated at a press conference on January 31 that he had read the documents that Perón complained of before their publication and had authorized their use.

He also said that the Chief Executive and not the Department of State was responsible for our foreign policy. This prompted a reporter at my press conference the following day to ask if Mr. Truman's remark indicated a rift between the White House and the State Department. I replied that I would regret it if the President's comment was so interpreted, because there was certainly no rift; the President had merely stated a fact. I added, "No man as Secretary of State could ever have had more complete support than I have had from the President."

Another newsman said he had interpreted Mr. Truman's words as evidence that the President approved my record as Secretary. I replied, "I have never had any evidence to the contrary at any time."

On February 28, Secretary Forrestal asked if it would be agreeable to me if the Navy sent a task force to the Mediterranean. I promptly told him that I hoped it would, and suggested that the force accompany the battleship *Missouri*, which we planned to have take to Turkey the body of the Turkish Ambassador, who had just died in Washington. Forrestal's proposal was timely. He and I thought it would give encouragement to Turkey and Greece. When I told the President of the plan, he approved it and Jim Forrestal was delighted.

A few days after this the Iranian Ambassador told me his government had instructed him to file a protest with the Security Council against the refusal of the Soviets to withdraw their troops from Iran. As the period fixed in the treaties for the withdrawal of troops expired March 2, I assured him his protest would receive our support. The Soviets, however, took the position that Iran did not have the right to present its case to the Security Council. I thought that if such a precedent were established, denying any country, large or small, the right of appeal to the Council, the United Nations would not and should not live. Consequently, I went to New York to present our views personally.

In opening the debate at the meeting of the Security Council I said,

"If the United Nations is to endure there must be no excuse or need for any nation to take the law into its own hands. . . . Questions affecting world peace must not be treated as questions of honor which cannot be discussed. Questions of honor between individuals are no longer left to the ordeal of the duel. Questions of honor between nations cannot be left to the ordeal of battle."

As representatives of other governments stated their views, there was a tense situation in the chamber when I moved that the Security Council recommend "that the Soviet government, in accordance with its obligations under the Charter of the United Nations and its treaty obligations, withdraw its armed forces immediately from the territory of Iran."

I further moved that upon the withdrawal of Soviet troops from Iran, the Council immediately proceed to consider any unsettled grievances between the two countries and use every effort to effect a fair and just solution. I argued that peaceful and honest negotiations could not be carried out under the shadow of marching armies.

When the Iranian Ambassador, a man of small stature physically but of great courage, arose to present the cause of his country, the Russian Ambassador, Andrei Gromyko, dramatically walked out of the chamber. It was the first time a member of the Security Council had indulged in that exercise, but it was not to be the last. That meeting of the Council was a splendid demonstration of the power of the United Nations to focus the world's attention upon a government's violation of its treaty pledges and the principles of the Charter. The Soviets could not stand the spotlight, and the Security Council did not have to act formally upon the grievances between the two countries. Stalin shortly announced, not to the Security Council but to a representative of a news agency, that his government was withdrawing its troops. The announcement demonstrated to my satisfaction the wisdom of our position at London and at Moscow that firmness as well as patience must be our policy in dealing with the Soviet government. Now that we were militarily stronger, we could emphasize firmness.

During March the deputies of the Foreign Ministers continued to work in Paris on the drafts of the peace treaties and made some progress. But it was quite clear that unless some extraordinary effort was made the peace conference itself would not be held, as agreed at Moscow, "after completion of the drafts" and "before May 1st." In

view of this I asked the three Foreign Ministers if they would meet in Paris to help facilitate the deputies' labors. I suggested Paris because the peace conference itself was to be held there. Furthermore, since the Soviets were at the time courting the French Communist party, I felt they would find it difficult in that setting to deny France the right to participate fully in our discussions.

In anticipation of another extended plane trip and many weeks of intensive activity away from home, upon the urging of Mrs. Byrnes I went to the Naval Hospital at Bethesda for a checkup on April 12. What I had expected to be a routine physical examination actually resulted in bringing to an end my long service in the United States government.

---

**U. S. NAVAL HOSPITAL**
NATIONAL NAVAL MEDICAL CENTER
BETHESDA 14, MARYLAND

12 April 1946

SECRETARY OF STATE JAMES BYRNES

    The Secretary came to the hospital this date apparently on his own volition for a recheck of his cardiac status and for a blood sugar determination. He states that he has been feeling about as usual and that there have been no essential changes insofar as he knows since his

---

4-12-46, Electrocardiograph: Rhythm-sinus; Rate-64 per minute; P-R Interval-0.19 seconds; QRS Occupies-0.09 seconds; T Waves-Upright in leads 2 and 3; inverted in leads 1 and 4; Conclusion-Since tracing of 1/13/45 $T_1$ and $T_4$ have become inverted.

    In view of the evidence of added myocardial damage which is interpreted as indicating chronic coronary sclerosis, the patient was advised to refrain from excesses of physical exertion and mental strain and to avoid

---

After an electrocardiograph had been taken, the technician and the physician in charge showed me a tracing made in January, 1945, and said that comparison with the one just made showed there had been "additional myocardial damage." I was frightened when the doctor said, regretfully, that I would have to avoid excessive mental and physical strain and slow down my activities. I had had no pain, nor any previous indication of cardiac damage, but two days later I was even more concerned when I received the written report confirming the verbal warning.

Having experienced the physical strain of flying from one continent to another about once a month, as well as the mental strain of long conferences with the inflexible Molotov, I knew what was ahead of me at the Paris meetings, so after several days consideration I decided I should offer the President my resignation. In my letter I said:

Last week I had a medical examination. I was advised that I must "slow down." I know myself. I cannot slow down as long as I hold public office, particularly the office of Secretary of State.

The only way I can comply with the advice of the Doctors is to resign. Therefore, I am tendering my resignation to take effect July first.

I select that date because there is a meeting of the Council of Foreign Ministers in Paris next week to be followed by a Peace Conference and it is impossible to tell how long those Conferences will continue. I think it my duty to attend those meetings. Again, by fixing July first, you will have time in which to select my successor.

Some weeks ago several newspapers published a story that I had resigned and you had selected my successor. You stated it was untrue. It certainly was untrue because we had never discussed the subject. I presume these newspapers now will state that their story was true, but I cannot be deterred from doing what I believe to be right simply because it may give the appearance of truth to that which is false.

In resigning, I wish to say that since I became Secretary of State you have given me your wholehearted support. When I think of the controversial character of the problems that have confronted us, it is rather remarkable that we have never failed to agree as to foreign policies.

Recently I have been made happy by the increasing evidence that the people recognize and appreciate the skill and courage with which you are performing your duties. I know what a terrible task it is and I know too how much you deserve that appreciation.

I want to assure you that as a private citizen I shall give to you my hearty support—not only because of my sincere affection for you personally, but because of my honest belief that your splendid administration of the office of President deserves that support.

I made the effective date July 1 because, in mistaken optimism, I felt that by that time we would have the treaties signed. I had done so much work on those treaties that it seemed to be my duty to finish the job, regardless of the health risk; on the other hand I felt it equally my duty not to start work on the crucial German treaty when informed that my physical condition was such that I might not be able to finish work on it.

On the morning of April 16 I gave Mr. Truman this letter of resignation and read to him the part of the medical report that dealt with the condition of my heart. He was very sympathetic and seemed better informed about heart ailments than I. He comforted me somewhat by telling me of a friend who had been warned of heart damage but had thereafter experienced no serious trouble.

The President expressed appreciation of my reference to his record as President and to the harmonious relations that had existed between us. At his suggestion I agreed that regardless of the July 1 date I had set, I would remain until whatever date the treaties were completed.

Because I was worried about my heart condition and hoped for a more encouraging medical opinion from another doctor, the day before leaving for Paris I went to Dr. Walter A. Bloedorn for a second check. After a stethoscopic examination he encouraged me by saying that he did not detect anything wrong with my heart and that, while he did not have the equipment of the Naval Hospital, he would make an electrocardiograph on his smaller instrument. In a few minutes he told me that his machine did not show the tracing that had caused the Bethesda diagnosis, which I had shown him. This examination improved my spirits considerably. I felt as a prisoner must feel when paroled during good behavior, but I had some doubts about which machine was right.

I decided to keep to myself the results of the physical examination and my resignation, not telling even members of my family. But we usually make some exceptions in a matter of this kind, and mine in this case was to tell Senator Vandenberg, who, as Republican adviser and an old friend, I felt should be informed in confidence. Van kept my secret. He surprised me when he took from his pocket a small bottle of tablets which he carried, he said, because of his own heart condition. He had had it for several years, and while it required him to report to his physician once a month it had not slackened his pace. In the days that followed I too forgot the "slow down" injunction.

In January, 1947, when my resignation had finally been accepted and while I was awaiting the arrival of my successor, General Marshall, curiosity prompted me to return to the Naval Hospital for examination by the same physician, same technician and same machine. I was then told that the tracings on which they based their opinion the previous April were no longer the same and that there was no indication of the additional myocardial damage about which they had warned me. They assumed that at the time of the previous examination I had been under some heavy strain. Of course that was a normal condition for me. I decided that if in the future I received an alarming report based on an electrocardiograph tracing, I would certainly appeal from the decision of the machine.

## 24 THE PARIS MEETING

I traveled then to Paris to the Foreign Ministers' meeting with Connally, Vandenberg and the usual State Department staff. Our delegation was quartered in the Hotel Meurice, where I was assigned the suite previously used by the commander of the German occupation forces. Meetings were held in the centuries-old Luxembourg Palace in the heart of the city.

The first meeting brought a surprise concession from Mr. Molotov. Georges Bidault, as Foreign Minister of the host country, proposed rules of procedure which provided for all four delegations to participate in discussions on all five treaties. No one demurred, though in London Molotov's refusal to allow France to participate had been made into a "vital principle" and the main reason for stalemate. Now all was changed. But after this promising beginning we might as well have been back at Lancaster House in London. There was immediate disagreement on the agenda, including a complete refusal to consider Austrian affairs, and a negative response to a draft treaty for the disarmament and demilitarization of Germany for twenty-five years, which I now formally proposed.

I resorted again to the device of a private talk with Molotov and Vishinsky, inviting them and their interpreter Pavlov to dinner. Ben Cohen and Chip Bohlen were with me. A few minutes after our guests arrived in my suite the fireworks began, Molotov complaining bitterly of my attitude in the Iranian case when it had come before the Security Council in New York. I told him that in his conversation with me and in the Soviets' communications to Iran, they did not definitely state that they would withdraw their troops in accordance with their

357

pledge; they had said only that they would do so unless "unforeseen circumstances prevent." Molotov said this phrase was to safeguard against the establishment of a new Iranian government hostile to the Soviet government; that when this was no longer regarded as a danger, the Soviet government had withdrawn the qualifying clause. This was an admission that Russia had kept its troops in Iran in order to influence the political developments in that country.

That evening he convinced me we had no hope of helping Austria get rid of Soviet troops. First Molotov said five treaties were more than enough for that session. Then Vishinsky said that the process of denazification in Austria had not proceeded far enough to consider final settlement. Molotov further charged that in the Iranian dispute I was conducting a propaganda war against the U.S.S.R. I replied that at the Moscow Conference I had told him at least half a dozen times, and Stalin too at meetings with him, that if Soviet troops did not leave Iran according to treaty obligations and written pledges, and the case came before the Security Council, we would support Iran. The fact that our action seemed to surprise him convinced me that our solemn warnings had not been taken seriously, nor had those of the British, and that whenever in the future we made such statements we should have to make our intentions unmistakably clear and definite.

With this sort of argument as an hors d'oeuvre, it was plain that the rest of our dinner would not be enjoyable or helpful, and it was not. When next morning I told my senatorial advisers what had occurred, they agreed that the outlook was dim. However, even they were not so pessimistic as to believe that we would spend the remainder of the year in angry debate with Molotov and Vishinsky, though this turned out to be the case.

It is useless to record in detail all the arguments in which we became involved. Our most difficult hours were spent on Italian matters. Here we found the Soviets demanding that Italy cede to Tito's Yugoslavia all of the Venezia Giulia area, including the city and port of Trieste, join with the U.S.S.R. in a trusteeship for Tripolitania, and in addition pay $100 million to the Soviet government for reparations. Whatever the arguments on the other questions, the last point irritated me. The United States was already advancing considerable money to prevent starvation in Italy, and I did not intend to see Italy turn this money over to Moscow as reparations. With no progress in this and other matters, I finally suggested that since we could not agree on all

questions, we mark the first anniversary of V-E Day, May 8, by calling
the peace conference for mid-June. By then, at least, the deputies could
record and circulate the agreed clauses, and the four delegations could
set forth their views on the disputed ones.

My French and British colleagues agreed, but Molotov replied that
under the Moscow agreement no peace conference could be held until
agreement had been reached on the "basic" issues. Here again it was
evident that the Soviet definition of what was "basic" would provide
opportunities for indefinite delay. A week later, on May 16, we resorted to adjournment for a month, which would bring us back to
Paris on June 15. Back home, in accordance with custom, I made a
frank radio report. I tried not to be overpessimistic, saying that
"building a people's peace in the world at this time is a long hard
process, requiring patience and firmness." But, I added, if the conference was not called to meet that summer, we would seek action in
the United Nations General Assembly, since we were bound "to take
the offensive for peace just as we took the offensive for war. There
is no iron curtain that the aggregate sentiments of mankind cannot
penetrate." This offended Molotov, who attacked me in Moscow with
the statement that America was aiming at world domination and in-
stigating aggressive warfare against the U.S.S.R. It was at least interesting to know that he was following my statements so closely.

Back in Paris on June 15 we resumed our disputes. After two weeks
we agreed to postpone formal action on the Italian colonies for a year
and, if in the meantime no agreement had been reached, to leave
the decision to the United Nations General Assembly.

On the same day the Soviets made a truly surprising concession. I
was presiding and stated, "Now we come to the subject we have discussed many times—'The Dodecanese Islands.'" Molotov quickly said,
"The Soviet Union agrees to the transfer to Greece of the Dodecanese
Islands." I said, "Do I hear you agree?" Slowly puffing his cigarette and
smiling, Molotov said, "The Soviet Union is always willing to make
concessions."

I had known all the time that they had no real objections to the
transfer. The justice of Greece's claim was so apparent that they knew
we, and the British, would favor it; therefore they opposed it, so that
when they finally agreed it would appear to be a generous concession.
If it had not weighed so heavily on the peoples affected, it would have

been interesting to watch this strategy at work.

There was now further discussion of reparation claims against Italy. As part of reparations, I suggested to Molotov that Russia accept four naval vessels. He countered that these constituted war booty—traditionally not a source of reparations. In reply, I said this was true—and as war booty, strictly speaking, they should remain the property of Great Britain and the United States, whose forces had captured them. But, said Molotov, at Potsdam President Truman and Mr. Churchill had given the U.S.S.R. some of the captured German naval vessels. I explained that a gift on that occasion was no guarantee of another gift every time we met; that the war was over and they should not expect us to act like Santa Claus at every conference.

Finally we reached a working agreement on how the Italians should pay: reparations would come from wartime industrial equipment, from Italy's assets in the Balkan states, and the balance from current production, providing the Soviets would furnish raw materials essential to such production. After this, I really thought we might begin to issue invitations to the peace conference, but again Molotov thought otherwise.

The next day he proposed that the four powers draft the rules to govern the peace conference. Bevin, Bidault and I firmly rejected the proposal. I declared repeatedly that the United States would feel free in the peace conference to accept or reject any amendment or any new proposals on their own merits. After four days of debate it was finally agreed that the rules of procedure accompanying the invitations should be regarded only as "suggestions." We adjourned, with many issues unsettled, to meet again in Paris on July 29 for the peace conference.

It was good to be home for a few days, relieved of the strains of negotiation. Dean Acheson could usually be counted on to help furnish some of that relief. I remember that one morning we both arrived at the "official" elevator at the same time. He had been in the Department for some years and through those years had traveled miles up and down on that elevator, with the same operator, going to the same floor. This day he stepped in, as usual, and the operator, as usual, looked up at this well-over-six-feet-tall man and said, "Floor, please?" Dean turned to me and said, "That is God's way of keeping me humble."

Though more than a year had passed since the war's end, and there was some disillusionment, the majority of our citizens were still hopeful that Russia would abandon its obstructionist tactics and join the other allied nations in making possible troop withdrawals from Europe. There was evidence of this yearning for peace when the *Washington Post* suggested editorially, a few days before our delegation again left for Paris, that we should be given a rousing send-off by the people of the District of Columbia.

At short notice and with little preparation, the streets of the city in the area of the White House and the old State Department building were lined with well-wishers and there were an estimated five thousand gathered at the airport. Also present were the President, members of the Cabinet, Chief Justice Vinson, Speaker Rayburn and a host of senators and congressmen. Expressing what I feel was a general sentiment, President Truman said of this demonstration, "If this is not a wholehearted send-off I have never seen one; the country is behind Mr. Byrnes and his efforts to get a just peace for the world, a peace founded on the Atlantic Charter and on the Charter of the United Nations, on which this country stands now and from this time forward. Good luck, Mr. Byrnes!"

Back in Paris the conference opened in the lofty Senate Chamber of the Luxembourg Palace. As usual the French sense of occasion did not fail and there was a spectacular showing of guardsmen, motionless as statues in their brilliant uniforms of red and white, heavily trimmed with braid, who lined the approaches and the long stairway leading to our meeting place. Some 1,500 delegates representing fifteen countries crowded in beneath the statues of French statesmen of the past, who from their niches in the chamber walls appeared to supervise the proceedings. Among the delegates themselves there was a general absence of the spats and striped trousers so much in evidence at Versailles a quarter of a century before. Indeed, the most spectacularly dressed was Sir Khizar Hayat, Minister of State for Punjab, India, who wore a billowy white turban and a striped coat which reached to his knees.

For all of its opening formalities, the conference proved to be just another round of the same fight. I am sure that many representatives of the smaller states had believed, before reaching Paris, that the press had exaggerated the Soviet delaying tactics in the meetings of Foreign Ministers. Now they saw those tactics in use and many came to offer me their sympathy.

In my opening speech to the conference I stated that I had reserved the right to vote on every procedural proposal on its merits, and the British representative, Ernest Bevin, followed with a similar statement. Molotov immediately charged in harsh words that we were violating an agreement. I read from the record six different statements I had previously made of my intention and said that, in the light of that record, he was the only representative of any government who would make such a charge. I thought this strong language to use against the representative of a great country, but it made little impression upon Molotov.

After procedural matters were finally settled, I asked Senator Connally and Senator Vandenberg, who were still in Washington, to return to Paris to help with the committee work. At the same time our Ambassadors to Great Britain, France and Russia, Averell Harriman, Jefferson Caffrey and Bedell Smith, joined us and also served on committees.

The conference dragged on for weeks, with the Soviets demanding a roll call on every question in every committee, as well as on every question in plenary sessions. Molotov or Vishinsky spoke almost daily, aiming their tirades at the United States and Great Britain and frequently at Italy and Greece. Representatives of the satellite states were coached to join in the vituperative chorus.

I shall not forget the day when Prime Minister De Gasperi of Italy appeared to plead his country's cause. He had had no part in establishing fascism in Italy, and when he had come before the Foreign Ministers' Council in London had impressed me most favorably. Now at Paris he and his delegation were seated in the last row, looking for all the world like prisoners in the dock. When called on to speak, De Gasperi walked down the center aisle of the long chamber to the speaker's stand where Bidault presided. There was no outward evidence of sympathy from any delegate as he made a courageous and appealing statement. His words apparently fell on deaf ears. Some ten years later, one of his compatriots, Signor Guerriero, in describing the event, wrote: "When he had finished speaking, there followed a cold and hostile silence. At that moment only one of the delegates of the many countries there represented stood up to shake his hand: the American Secretary of State, Mr. Byrnes. There was in that a symbolic gesture; only one hand was extended to Italy in a friendly spirit and it was the hand of the United States."

I thought De Gasperi had suffered enough at the hands of Mussolini and the Nazis without the Allies' inflicting further suffering on him. But aside from humanitarian considerations, there was every reason for peace-loving people to win the confidence and friendship of the new Italy. From the time of the London meeting of the Foreign Ministers' Council in September—in fact, as early as at the U.N. Conference in San Francisco—the Soviet ambition and effort to obtain direct control of one of Italy's Mediterranean colonies, or indirect control through a trusteeship, had been apparent. Now the U.S.S.R. was determined to use the Italian treaty to further its goal of a base in the Mediterranean. By holding firm, Britain, France and the United States prevented this.

Yet I was not naïve enough to think that the Soviets had permanently abandoned their ambition solely because of persuasive talks around the conference table. I had agreed with Forrestal that we should add to our Mediterranean fleet—he had needed no urging. And I agreed with Walter Lippmann when he wrote for the North American Newspaper Alliance: "Mr. Byrnes' success is due in the last analysis to the decision to reinforce the United States Mediterranean fleet. That decision made plain in language that the Kremlin fully understands that the United States has a vital interest of her own in the Mediterranean. This American act spoke louder than all the long speeches."

Over two years before, in December, 1943, President Roosevelt had told us in a Cabinet meeeting after his return from Teheran that during an argument, when Churchill quoted an opinion of Pope Pius, Stalin had asked, "How many divisions has he got?" Either the President or some Cabinet member repeated the story elsewhere, for in a few days it appeared in the press. Since then, the statement has been attributed to Stalin at Yalta as well as at Potsdam. I was at those conferences and did not hear it, and the record does not show it. But from many things I did hear Stalin say, I am satisfied that the remark correctly expressed his view of the persuasiveness of military might.

The Soviets were in no hurry to complete the conference's work. They made speeches on every majority and minority report. While I ignored most of their attacks on the United States, there were one or two occasions when I could not resist the temptation to reply. When Molotov declared that "certain large powers had enriched themselves during the war," I said that "if he could possibly mean the United States, we have spent over $400 billion fighting the war; we have sent to the Soviet Union more than eleven billion dollars in Lend Lease, and we now seek neither territory nor reparations." It had no effect on him, but it helped me feel better to keep the record straight.

The long negotiations at Paris were not entirely useless, for we learned much about some of the countries represented. For instance, one day when Vishinsky was criticizing the United States, declaring that we were trying to achieve world domination by "handouts," I saw two of the Czechoslovak delegates, who were seated just in front of us, enthusiastically applauding his attack. It happened that I had just learned from Under Secretary Acheson that Czechoslovakia had applied for a credit of $50 million for the purchase of surplus property to meet emergency needs. Simultaneously we learned that this needy applicant intended to transfer $10 million of this credit to Rumania at 6 per cent interest plus an administrative fee of 7 per cent. Since they would be obligated to pay us only 2⅜ per cent interest, our response to their "emergency needs" would net them a nice profit.

The attitude of the Czechoslovakian delegates influenced me to send instructions to the Department of State to refuse the credit. Some days later, Jan Masaryk, Foreign Minister of Czechoslovakia, accompanied by Vladimir Clementis, a Communist in their delegation, came to ascertain our reasons for refusal. I mentioned the details of the bargain with Rumania, and said that they could not act as a broker in dispensing funds appropriated by us for relief; also that we did not wish to offend people who regarded our generosity as a "handout" made for the purpose of controlling their government. Masaryk was obviously embarrassed, and later that day he told me privately that he had not heard of the plan to transfer funds to Rumania and sympathized with my position. Masaryk was a patriot, and it was with regret that I learned about a year later that his body had been found below his window. Whether he had killed himself or had been murdered, there is no doubt that he was a victim of the Communist seizure of his country.

During the peace conference Tito also revealed something about his attitude toward the United States. Our supply planes traveling between Austria and Udine in northern Italy could not fly a direct course without passing over the tip of the Yugoslav peninsula. To avoid doing so, pilots had to fly over rugged mountain peaks sometimes 18,000 feet high, and frequently they lost their way. When two of our transports were shot down by Yugoslav fighter planes, Tito claimed that his country had been invaded by more than one hundred United States planes within a month. The attack cost the lives of five of our Air Force and an officer of the Turkish Army who was a passenger. A few passengers and crewmen were arrested and confined to a Belgrade hotel.

On hearing the details, I invited Eduard Kardelj, the Vice Premier of Yugoslavia, who headed that delegation, to come to my office. When he said he had no information about the outrage, I demanded that he obtain an explanation. I also sent a cable to Acheson, instructing him to demand formally through our Ambassador that the hostages be released within forty-eight hours, or we would bring the matter before the Security Council for appropriate action. Our note called the act an offense against the laws of nations and the principles of humanity as well as a violation of the Charter. In addition to a satisfactory explanation and the release of those held as hostages, we demanded indemnity for the families of the deceased flyers and compensation for loss of the planes.

Soon after these demands were made known in Paris, I saw Molotov and Kardelj in a huddle and suspected what they were discussing. Within the time limit our men were released and the Yugoslav government announced that military honors would be paid to those who had lost their lives. They also agreed to pay the various indemnities. After much consideration, Washington decided, with my approval, not to ask for action by the Security Council. But I told Kardelj that the American people would not soon forget this grossly unfriendly act by his government.

During the long summer we received information of a change in the Soviets' attitude toward Germany. At Potsdam, a year before, certain general principles for the control of Germany had been agreed upon, and I made every effort while in Paris to induce the Soviets to get their Deputy Foreign Minister to work on a German treaty. I was unsuccessful. At a private dinner in April, I had asked Molotov to tell me his objections to the draft of the twenty-five-year demilitarization treaty I had forwarded him. At first he said that it might delay German disarmament and that it had been agreed at Potsdam to effect that at once. I assured him that the treaty would mean not only immediate disarmament but continued disarmament. Further, it would make certain that the United States bore its full share of the burden of keeping the peace. He seemed to agree to the importance of such a treaty not only for Germany but for Japan, but continued to repeat that he wanted immediate disarmament.

Next day at the open Council meeting, I insisted upon discussing the matter. Molotov now made half a dozen excuses: the period was too short; it should be forty instead of twenty-five years. I agreed. He said the language on disarmament was not sufficiently comprehensive. I told him it was the language previously agreed upon by his representative, Zhukov, as well as Eisenhower. It was soon apparent that under no circumstances would he consider our treaty proposal.

About this time Molotov made a short trip to Moscow, and when he returned he brought with him a new policy toward Germany, which he announced on July 10. Though he had never before released a speech to the press prior to its delivery, on this occasion he freely distributed advance copies. It was the first offensive in what I later called "a battle for the minds of the German people."

Molotov's performance was a clever one. Knowing that the people of Germany had reacted violently to the so-called Morgenthau Plan published in our press in the fall of 1944, he now emphasized that "it would be incorrect to adopt a course of Germany's annihilation as a state or that of its agrarianization, including the annihilation of its main industrial centers." Time and again he emphasized the point: "Our purpose is not to destroy Germany but to transform her into a democratic and peace-loving state which, besides its agriculture, will have its own industry and foreign trade."

Nothwithstanding the fact that the Soviets had already turned over to Poland a part of their zone and were promoting Polish claims to Silesia and all the territory east of the Oder and Neisse rivers, Molotov brazenly stated, "No territory should be separated from Germany except as the result of a plebiscite." He also made plain Soviet intentions regarding a peace treaty with Germany when he said, "It is first necessary to solve the question of setting up an all-German government . . . but even when a German government has been set up *it will take a number of years to determine what this new German government represents and whether it is trustworthy.*" (Italics added.)

This statement of policy was carefully worded and quite plausible. It was also well timed. The war had been over for a year, and the German people wanted a definite statement of what their fate was to be at the hands of the conquering Allies. As was to be expected, they welcomed the news that the Soviets were opposed to destroying their industries and turning Germany into a pastoral country. The fact was, our policy toward Germany had not been satisfactorily clarified. I had hoped we could first agree upon the five treaties. Now I felt our policy should be announced promptly and in such a manner as to impress the people of Germany and of Europe.

I sent for General Clay and General Mark W. Clark to get their views about the effect the new Soviet tactics were having in Germany and Austria. Both told me that they thought Soviet propaganda was making headway and that further clarification of our own aims would be helpful. I decided to make a major policy speech and asked Clay's opinion as to the advisability of making it in Germany. He was enthusiastic about the idea and from that moment took charge of all the arrangements. When my statement was ready it was sent to the President and he approved it.

On September 5 we arrived at Berlin's Tempelhof air base. General Clay had arranged for us to be met by a guard of honor and an excellent Army band began to play "The Star-Spangled Banner" just as we landed. With the General were many high-ranking Army officers. As we were driven from the airport to the residence of General and Mrs. Clay, some of our party saw for the first time the devastation that had so greatly depressed me when I went to Potsdam. Ambassador Robert Murphy and his family joined the Clays in making our short stay in Berlin pleasant, and late that afternoon we left for Stuttgart, in the train that had been luxuriously equipped for Hitler's private use. It was better than our President's private car. By some miracle it had escaped destruction, and the roadbed had been restored by our Army. Mrs. Byrnes and I were assigned the suite formerly used by Hitler and Eva Braun.

After daylight the train attracted considerable attention as it passed through the countryside, news that it was making a special run evidently having got around. Whenever we stopped, crowds came to the car window to ask for autographs and to pass in bits of paper and newspapers. I quite willingly gave autographs, but later learned that General Clay had become seriously concerned when he heard what was happening, fearing that some irresponsible person might take the opportunity to do me some harm. This had not occurred to me.

Upon arrival at Stuttgart we were honored with another official welcome from a military contingent, and the German Minister Presidents of the three districts of the United States zone, Bavaria, Greater Hesse and Württemberg, called on us. After talking with them about some of their problems for half an hour, we went on to the old State Opera House where the meeting was to be held, it being the only building of any size in the city which had not been badly damaged. General McNarney and Ambassador Robert Murphy accompanied Senator Connally, Senator Vandenberg and me to the stage. Clay, avoiding the spotlight as usual, took a seat on the front row among some German officials and representatives. I noticed that along with his other thoughtful arrangements he had had my speech translated, and mimeographed copies were being distributed to the Germans in the audience.

As we entered the hall the band played "Stormy Weather," and I thought of asking Clay if an order for symbolic music was part of his planning, but the tune quickly changed to "Dixie," which seldom fails to stir an audience and which certainly made me feel at home. The Opera House accommodated only about 2,000 and it was filled to capacity, many of our military personnel being present as well as German citizens.

General McNarney made the introduction, and I launched upon what I believe was my most effective speech.

At the outset I said, "I hope the German people will never again make the mistake of believing that because the American people are peace-loving they will sit back hoping for peace if any nation uses force or the threat of force to acquire dominion over other people and other governments. We intend to continue our interest in the affairs of Europe and of the world." Because we believed the United Nations would stop aggressor nations from starting a war, we would support that organization "with all the power and resources we possess." Offering hope to the German people, I said that freedom from militarism would give them the opportunity, if they would but seize it, "to apply their great energies and abilities to the works of peace—and in time to take an honorable place among the members of the United Nations."

I explained that the levels to which the principal German industries would be reduced were set on the assumption that the resources of the country would be available for all, and that products not necessary for use in Germany would be available for export, to pay for necessary imports. The levels of industry that had been fixed were only sufficient to enable the German people to maintain living standards comparable to that in other European states. I stated that as of that date the Allied Control Council was not governing Germany, nor permitting the people of Germany to govern themselves, essential control administrative departments not having been established.

I urged that to secure the greatest possible production and the most effective distribution of food, a central department for agriculture be set up without delay. "Germany," I said, "is a part of Europe and recovery in Europe and particularly in the adjoining states will be slow if Germany with her great resources of iron and coal is turned into a poorhouse."

Calling attention to the fact that at the time of the surrender there had been no German government with which the Allies could deal and that we therefore had had to take over temporarily the responsibilities of the state, I then said, "It is the view of the American government that the German people throughout Germany, under proper safeguards, should now be given the primary responsibility for running their own affairs."

For the benefit of these people and for the leaders of the Soviet Union as well, I said, "I want no misunderstanding. We will not shirk our duty. We are not withdrawing. As long as an occupation force is required in Germany the army of the United States will be a part of that occupation force." I gave all possible emphasis to this statement, and the editor of the *Stars and Stripes*, the G.I. newspaper, wrote, "That was the medicine the patient needed."

On the subject of boundaries, I said that we had agreed to support in a peace conference the ultimate transfer to the Soviet Union of the city of Königsberg, and also that, pending final decision on Poland's western frontier, Silesia and other eastern German areas should be under the administration of the Polish state; however, "as the protocol of the Potsdam Conference makes clear, the heads of government would not agree to support at the peace settlement the cession of that particular area." If the Ruhr and the Rhineland desired to remain united with Germany, the United States would not oppose this. I concluded the address by saying again that America wanted to return the government of Germany to its people and to "help them win their way back to an honorable place among the free and peace-loving nations of the world."

As I finished, the Army band played "The Star-Spangled Banner," and Vandenberg expressed my view when he said, "It was never played like that at home."

Upon leaving the Opera House our party was taken to the Villa Reitzenstein, built shortly after World War I by a German princess, where we were served luncheon while an orchestra played Viennese waltzes. From Stuttgart we went by train to Murnau in Bavaria, where we stayed at the Hochheim estate, owned by Jacob Loeb and leased by our government, which, fortunately for its owner, preserved it. We were made welcome here by our military governor for Bavaria, General Walter J. Muller, and Mrs. Muller.

The next day was fully occupied with sightseeing—that week end, incidentally, was my only holiday during my service in the State Department. We were shown the Ettal Monastery and told that here had been located the largest Messerschmidt factory in Germany, with the entire works underground. Seven thousand workers had made airplane parts under a one-hundred-foot ceiling. We stopped at the famed summer colony of Berchtesgaden and made the spectacular climb from there to Hitler's "Eagle's Nest" in jeeps. Little was left of the recently flourishing colony, and Hitler's house had been largely destroyed by Storm Troopers before they left. From Murnau we went to Hochheim, arriving late in the evening on Saturday, September 8. A young officer, Captain Asselin, sang grand opera arias to us during and after dinner, and General Clay exclaimed, "A man who can sing like that can't shoot a gun!" General Muller explained that the captain was his top military counterintelligence man and came to him after being demobilized. I often wonder if Asselin, who had been trained for opera, returned to make a career in it.

We returned to Paris Sunday afternoon, and seemed to make some progress. The British, hoping to influence the Soviets, announced they would not press their claim against Italy for $11 billion in reparations. The Commonwealth nations joined us in urging that reparations demands on Italy be limited. The Secretariat notified the eight committees that their work must be finished by October 5 and that the conference must adjourn by October 15 because of the United Nations General Assembly meeting on October 23. We agreed to shorten the time that delegates could speak upon any question and now looked forward to bringing the conference to a close.

Heartened by the bipartisan support evidenced by the splendid co-operation of Senators Vandenberg and Connally and by the press reactions to the policy we had been following with the approval of the President, I was shocked to learn of the speech made on September 12 by Secretary of Commerce Henry A. Wallace, denouncing what he termed my "Get Tough with Russia Policy." This was at a Madison Square Garden meeting, of which one of the sponsors was the Political Action Committee of the C.I.O.

The *Herald Tribune* described Wallace's speech as proposing "a delimitation of Russian and American spheres of influence, although he was very hazy about the limits. Russia was to be given a free hand to 'socialize' eastern Europe; the United States was not to be interfered with in democratizing western Europe, the western hemisphere and Japan: China was to work out her own destiny on the basis of a hands-off policy by outside powers. Within the Russian sphere the United States would merely insist upon freedom to trade —a freedom which Russia thus far has shown a lively interest in blocking."

A teletype message from the State Department reported a storm of criticism of the address at home as well as abroad. In reporting the President's press conference the day following, the Associated Press said that "Mr. Mylander, correspondent of the Minneapolis *Star-Journal and Tribune,* called the President's attention to this statement in Wallace's speech: 'Just two days ago when President Truman read these words he said they represented the policy of his administration.' Mr. Truman replied that was correct. Mylander, pursuing the point, asked, 'does it apply just to that paragraph or to the whole speech?' Mr. Truman said he had approved the whole speech. At that point Raymond Brandt of the St. Louis *Post Dispatch* came in with this question: 'Mr. President, do you regard the Wallace speech as a departure from the Byrnes policy?' Mr. Truman said that he did not."

I noted, however, that the editorial writers agreed overwhelmingly that Wallace's speech was in definite conflict with the policy that the President had approved and that we had been following.

Next day the President evidently felt he should clarify his position and he issued a short statement to this effect:

There has been a natural misunderstanding regarding the answer I made to a question asked at the press conference on Thursday, September 12 with reference to the speech of the Secretary of Commerce delivered in New York that day. The question was answered extemporaneously and my answer did not convey the thought I intended it to convey. It was my intention to express the thought that I approved the right of the Secretary of Commerce to deliver the speech. I did not intend to indicate that I approved the speech as constituting a statement of the foreign policy of this country. . . . There has been no change in the established foreign policy of our government.

The day after this the press reported that at the end of a two-hour conference with the President, Secretary Wallace read to the White House correspondents a penciled memorandum stating that he and the President had reached an agreement. The Associated Press reported that Wallace read, "with a grin," this statement: "The President and the Secretary of Commerce had a most detailed and friendly discussion after which the Secretary reached the conclusion he would make no public statements or speeches until the Foreign Ministers' conference in Paris is concluded." He then added that he was remaining in the Cabinet.

Of course, this statement, issued with the implied approval of the President, indicated only that Wallace's attack on our foreign policy would be suspended for a few weeks. As the Paris conference was scheduled to adjourn by the middle of October, he would have time to speak during the political campaign preceding the November elections. He frankly announced that he stood by his New York speech and intended within the near future to speak on the same subject again.

Meanwhile the incident was particularly embarrassing to us because President Truman was quoted in the Paris edition of the New York *Herald Tribune* as saying that he had approved Wallace's speech. I decided not to attend the meetings of the conference until the issue was settled. Although the State Department reported that our representatives in various world capitals were being asked whether or not, in my several public statements, I had correctly presented American policy, I decided that it would be inappropriate for me to reply —that answer must come from the President.

Senator Connally issued a statement that he supported the foreign policy we had announced and had been following. Senator Vandenberg, in a statement characteristic of him, said he wanted to co-operate with the administration but that he could co-operate with only one Secretary of State at a time.

I was kept posted on developments not only by the press but by messages from Assistant Secretary of State Donald Russell quoting various newspapers. Columnists pointed out the contradictions in the policy announced by Wallace and that previously approved by the President. Arthur Krock in *The New York Times* described Wallace's statement that we had no business interfering in the politics of eastern Europe as being in conflict with the compact entered into by Britain, the Soviet Union and ourselves at Yalta and again at Potsdam—that before we recognized Rumania, Bulgaria or Hungary they would have to establish democratic governments by free elections and ensure certain freedoms to the people.

I could not understand the President's sudden change of views, and concluded that either he did not have strong convictions about them or that he hoped Wallace's speech would attract little attention and did not wish to antagonize him just a few weeks before the election. I recalled that in the fall of 1945 President Truman had told me there were two persons he had to have on his political team, Secretary Wallace and Mrs. Eleanor Roosevelt—Mr. Wallace because of his influence with labor and Mrs. Roosevelt because of her influence with the Negro voters. He said he could "take care of Henry," but he wanted me to find an appointment for Mrs. Roosevelt in the field of foreign affairs. The following week, in recommending a list of delegates to the first meeting of the United Nations Assembly in London, I placed Mrs. Roosevelt's name at the top of the list, expressing the belief that because of her husband's deep interest in the success of the United Nations she might accept. Truman telephoned to her immediately, while I was still in his office, and she did agree to serve. To the surprise of some of the other members, she proved to be a good team worker, rendering outstanding service, and was warmly congratulated by other delegates.

Knowing Mr. Truman's concern about the political influence of Henry Wallace at that time, I could appreciate his dilemma when asked to endorse Wallace's speech. As for myself, I would soon be out of office in any case; for, as I have explained, my resignation was to take effect upon the signing of the treaties, and it now seemed probable that would be within a month or two. I reminded the President of that resignation in a message I addressed to the Department for Will Clayton or Russell to present to him. I said among other things: "If it is not completely clear in your own mind that Mr. Wallace should be asked to refrain from criticizing the foreign policy of the United States while he is a member of your cabinet I must ask you to accept my resignation immediately."

This message was not made public, but I discussed it "off the record" with one or two newspaper friends who respected my confidence. And this seems a good place to pay a deserved tribute to the press. In my long years of public service, I often discussed my problems off the record with them, and never once did one of them violate my confidence.

My next information from Acting Secretary Clayton was that he had been in conference with the President, who would see Wallace the next day and call me after their meeting. When he tried to get me, however, after some delay, the Paris operator impatiently reported that there was a third person on the channel and the line could not be cleared. We were frequently warned that our telephones might be tapped, and I thought it best to ask if a teletype conversation could be arranged, knowing there was equipment for it both in the White House and in our Paris Embassy. The President agreed. This method of conferring was not as satisfactory as a telephone conversation, but was considered more secure. Before going to the Embassy I hurriedly prepared a brief memorandum, and as soon as we got the "go ahead" the operators began sending my statement over the wires. The President's "talk" to me was recorded on an incoming machine at the same time that my message to him was being recorded on the White House machine. After our two prepared statements had been sent, we "talked" informally. This is the teletype record:

*The Secretary:* I realize that in reaching the agreement announced by Mr. Wallace you were trying to reconcile the difference in views held by us on the one hand, and by Mr. Wallace on the other.

But Mr. Wallace's last statement leaves the representatives of our government abroad, as well as other governments, in more doubt than ever as to just what American foreign policy will be. Mr. Wallace has reiterated that he stands by his New York speech which he does not deny was intended to be critical of our foreign policy. There is little difference in a member of the Cabinet issuing to the press statements that he stands by his criticism of your foreign policy and making such criticisms from a platform.

Mr. Wallace has promised to refrain from speaking until the present Paris Peace Conference concludes, but the form of his statement indicates that he will continue to press publicly his own ideas on foreign policy which differ from your ideas and that you recognize his right as a member of your Cabinet to do so. When the administration itself is divided on its own foreign policy, it cannot hope to convince the world that the American people have a foreign policy.

. . . When this conference ends and the Council of Foreign Ministers meets to make the final decision, each day I would be confronted with statements of Mr. Wallace in conflict with views expressed by me. I would then have to insist upon being relieved. It is far better for the administration to let us come home now, rather than for us to return October 23, by which date we hope the conference will adjourn.

If Wallace is influenced by any ill feeling toward me it is possible that if you accept my resignation he might be willing to support your foreign policies or at least refrain from attacking such policies.

To me the important thing is to try and restore confidence in our policies.

I sincerely hope that when you appoint someone you can announce that you are wholeheartedly and undividedly behind the foreign policy of the United States as it has been heretofore determined by you and as it is being carried out; that our foreign policy is an American foreign policy and not the policy of any party or faction; that no change in American foreign policy is desired or contemplated by you. If for any reason you wish to modify your policy in any way, I hope that whatever policy you determine upon you will announce it as the American policy to which we are going to adhere, and that while a private citizen can express his views in opposition, that no member of your Cabinet can express views in conflict with your policies.

. . . I do not want to ask you to do anything that would force Mr. Wallace out of the Cabinet. However, I do not think that any man who professes any loyalty to you would so seriously impair your prestige and the prestige of the government with the nations of the world. . . . You and I spent 15 months building a bipartisan policy. We did a fine job convincing the world that it was a permanent policy upon which the world could rely. Wallace destroyed it in a day.

*The President:* I had a lengthy conference with Henry Wallace yesterday and informed him that I stood firmly behind our established foreign policy which you are carrying out in Paris at this time and further advised him that his speech had caused great concern throughout the world and I showed him a number of cables received from our representatives in various countries. A thorough discussion was had and an agreement was reached that Wallace would make no public statements or speeches until the Peace Conference in Paris ended. At the conclusion of the Peace Conference the situation will be re-examined and Wallace will then be informed as to whether he may make, as a Cabinet member, any speeches or statements affecting our foreign policy. There is no agreement or commitment that Wallace is to be permitted to speak on this subject as soon as the present conference ends. I am in wholehearted support of your stand and your actions in carrying out our established foreign policy. For your information, I am having a press conference tomorrow (Friday) morning and I shall read a statement to those present. Such statement will be a full reaffirmation of my support of your efforts and will express complete confidence in you and the delegation. The wording of the statement will be worked out today with Mr. Clayton. You and the delegation must stay on the job and finish it.

*The Secretary:* No one will quarrel with Mr. Wallace making his speech on foreign policy if it is in support of the policy determined by you, but every man knows he cannot help you by attacking your policy.

*The President:* That is correct.

*Secretary:* I agree heartily that Wallace should speak on other questions. I agree that he can speak on foreign policy if he is going to support your policy, but I do not think you can leave any doubt about your re-examining the question in the last week of October as to whether he can make a speech criticizing the policy fixed by you.

*President:* You misunderstood me. It is a re-examination whether we will let Wallace speak or not. The foreign policy will stand as it is.

*Secretary:* I am sorry I misunderstood you. I hope that it will be cleared up tomorrow and the delegation here can go back to work. I regret greatly that you have had trouble in the field of foreign affairs but my conscience is clear and I have done my best to minimize your difficulties.

*President:* No speeches by anyone will be approved unless they are in accord with the foreign policy as it now stands. Mr. Wallace may want to make speeches on other subjects and I do not want to feel that I will have to muzzle him completely. The situation will be made perfectly clear tomorrow. There will be no misunderstanding; the statement to you was on Wallace's right to speak and had nothing to do with the foreign policy. You have done an excellent job. Nobody appreciates it more than I do and I shall continue to support you with everything I have.

*Secretary:* You certainly have done it up to this time and your statement makes me feel good.

We heard nothing more until the next day, when to our surprise we learned that the President had not only made it clear that he did not approve a change in our foreign policy, but had asked for and received Mr. Wallace's resignation as Secretary of Commerce. Our delegation went back to work.

It is generally believed that in recent years the attitude of the French people toward their German neighbors has begun to change, but in 1946 there was overwhelming evidence that France found it hard to forget the repeated invasions of her soil by Germany in 1870, in 1914 and again 1940. After World War II, as the French leaders grew aware each day of the imperialistic ambitions of the Soviet Union, they began to fear that another peril had replaced the German one. Yet they doubted if the new menace was generally recognized by the people at large. Probably it was because of this that an official of the French government said that he wished I would find occasion to speak to his countrymen on the aims of our foreign policy. His interest, and my desire to emphasize that the President was firmly behind the policies I had been advocating, prompted me to accept an invitation to address the American Club of Paris on October 3.

On this occasion I referred to the United States' failure to follow Woodrow Wilson and to join the League, stating, "America is determined this time not to retreat to a policy of isolation." Pointing out that President Truman had recently made plain to the world that the foreign policy begun by President Roosevelt would be continued, I said, "This can be relied on, because it is supported by Republicans as well as Democrats and will be adhered to regardless of which political party is in power." I also made a direct reference to my speech in Germany, saying that I was happy to repeat in France that as long as there was an occupation army in Germany the armed forces of the United States would be included in it. I emphasized that we had actually offered to enter into a treaty for twenty-five or even forty years to keep Germany demilitarized. Our only ambition, I said, was "to see Germany disarmed and democratic, ready to respect the fundamental freedoms of her citizens and the security of her neighbors."

*Pravda* called me "the protector of Germans" and scoffed at my address as an attempt to allay French alarm over the Stuttgart speech. I believe, however, that it helped allay French fears that we might return to the isolationist policies of the early twenties.

Before ending my brief description of the peace conference, I should add that Senator Vandenberg and Willard Thorp, representing the United States, together with Ernest Bevin, were successful in getting adopted a joint resolution affirming the principle of free commerce and navigation on the Danube.

Vandenberg and Connally were excellent committeemen, patient when necessary but always ready to take up the challenge when they were subjected to the disagreeable tactics of the Russians. They took a skillful and lively part in the debate in committees, but by custom only the Secretary of State and the other Foreign Ministers conducted the debate in the Council of Foreign Ministers itself. This was trying for the senators because everything I said had to be translated into both Russian and French, and even if it was a good statement to begin with, it became boring to listen to three recitals of it, two of them in a foreign tongue.

Before our adjournment I was invited to dine privately with Molotov. That afternoon he and I became involved in a very harsh debate about displaced persons, during which he severely criticized the United States. At eight o'clock, the hour of the dinner, there was still no prospect of adjournment, and when we finally finished more than an hour later, Molotov was the last person I wanted to sit down with at dinner. I asked Bohlen to tell him that since it was then so late I assumed he would not expect us. When Bohlen returned, he said that Molotov was greatly disturbed and had said he would be terribly disappointed. We knew he felt he owed us this courtesy in return for our hospitality six weeks earlier, so we went. At quite a late hour we arrived at the Soviet Embassy to find a most gracious host. I took advantage of his affability to tell him that I had found it possible in my career—whether on the Court or in the Congress— to differ sharply with men without using intemperate language; that I did not understand why, when he had positive instructions from his government on an issue, he did not tell me privately so that we could for the time being postpone further discussion rather than enter into long and intemperate arguments such as we had engaged in earlier that day without any hope of agreement. At the end of my conciliatory remarks, he said with a smile, *"ya-soglasyen"* (I agree). I suspected he really did not agree, but I asked, "Why, then, don't you tell me what you really want on the subject of Germany?" "The Soviet Union," Molotov replied, "wants what it asked for at Yalta—ten billion dollars in reparations—and it also wants to participate with the United States, the United Kingdom and France in a four-power control of the industries of the Ruhr."

From his expression and his manner, I firmly believed he was telling the truth in stating their desires. At that time, of course, they wanted the Ruhr industries more than anything else. But our inability since that time to get them to agree to anything reasonable on any subject proves how impractical it would have been, and how wise we were in opposing it.

There was further discussion of the problem of displaced persons during the dinner, and I told Molotov we took the position that we must give asylum to these political refugees because that was historically our attitude, not because we bore ill will toward the Soviets. I said it was a serious problem and we were frequently perplexed about what to do with the displaced persons in our zone in Germany. At this Vishinsky, who had been listening, said something and laughed heartily. I inquired about the cause of his amusement and Bohlen replied, "Mr. Vishinsky says if you don't know what to do with the displaced persons, he does," and, with his thumb extended, pointed to the floor. Because of Vishinsky's laughter I thought it possible that I did not appreciate the Russian brand of humor, and I was in some doubt about his meaning. On our way home Bohlen said he was in no doubt whatever—Vishinsky meant that he would put the displaced persons underground. Vishinsky was one of the ablest advocates of the Russian delegation, but after this, whenever listening to him, I recalled his heartless remark and was disposed to believe the published reports of the cruelty with which he had conducted the purge of many Russian citizens in 1936.

Upon my return to Washington I promptly reported to the President. He received me cordially, but did not mention the Wallace affair. In the election the next week, the Republicans carried the Senate and House. At least one news commentator thought that many admirers of Wallace who ordinarily voted the Democratic ticket did not vote. However, Mr. Wallace did make a public statement urging the election of Democratic candidates, and if Mr. Truman felt that his attitude contributed to the election results he did not indicate it to me.

In my radio report to the nation on the Paris meeting, I explained that though the treaties were not written as we would write them if we had a free hand, nor as other governments would if they had a free hand, they were as good as we could hope to get by negotiation and agreement with other nations. Admitting that tensions between the Soviets and ourselves had increased, I said:

Back of the debates and divisions were real and deep differences in interest, in ideas, in experience, and even in prejudices. It is better that the world should witness and learn to appraise clashes of ideas rather than clashes of arms. If this peace is to be lasting, it must be a people's peace.

In our efforts at Paris we have been criticized by some for being too "soft" and at times for being too "tough." I dislike both words. Neither accurately describes our earnest efforts to be firm but patient. It is possible that the failure or inability of the Soviet leaders to rid themselves of the idea that war is inevitable lies at the root of our difficulties. We will not be able to rid the world of that belief if we ourselves become victims of it. War is inevitable only if states fail to respect the rights of other states to ways of life they cannot and do not share.

After this broadcast Stalin, in answer to inquiries made by Hugh Baillie, president of United Press, said he disagreed with my statement that tension had increased between the United States and the Soviet Union. He said that the most serious threat to peace was Mr. Churchill and "those like him in Great Britain and the United States." I admit I shared Mr. Churchill's views and now feel I was in good company.

# 25 MY LAST CONFERENCE

On November 4, the Council of Foreign Ministers convened at the Waldorf Astoria in New York to consider the recommendations of the Paris Peace Conference. As host, I had quite a problem in finding accommodations because the General Assembly of the United Nations was also in session at that time. The Waldorf generously put at our disposal the very large suite of the president of the company for use as a conference room, and in addition provided seventy-three rooms for offices. To insure security for the leading delegates and their official papers, we had 150 military police and a large number of FBI agents on hand as well as New York City police. Notwithstanding these precautions, we had one unfortunate incident during the conference.

The Ukraine delegation to the United Nations General Assembly had their offices at the Plaza Hotel. One night after midnight, two members of their staff went to a delicatessen to buy food, and while they were being served by the woman proprietor a gunman walked in with a pistol in hand. He took $65 from the cash register, and because one of the Ukranians did not immediately comprehend the order to raise his hands, the gunman fired, striking the man in the thigh. The bandit then fled and the wounded man was taken to a hospital. I at once expressed my regret to the Ukranian Foreign Minister and assured him that every effort was being made to arrest the gunman.

However, the Minister gave the newspapers a statement charging "political banditry" and demanding that I do something about it. The Commissioner of Police admitted to me that he would probably not succeed in catching the gunman because the description as given by the delicatessen proprietor indicated that he was a Puerto Rican and it was exceedingly difficult to get assistance in the neighborhood where most of them lived. Because the Ukrainian Minister continued to assert that it had been a political shooting, I called on Molotov, gave him the report of the Police Commissioner, and told him that we could not possibly provide Secret Service men or military police escorts for every clerk of visiting delegations, nor could we anticipate that a clerk would be visiting a delicatessen after midnight. Molotov seemed reasonable and gave me a smile when I said that if I inspired political shootings, an unknown clerk would be in no danger; but the chief delegate of the Soviet Union might be, if he continued his practice of making long speeches.

At the outset of the Foreign Ministers' meeting we were pleasantly surprised by the very cordial and co-operative attitude of Molotov. Recalling the hours spent in discussing procedure at previous meetings, we were astonished by his prompt agreement on this occasion. But after the preliminaries were over, he became normal, disregarding the recommendations of the Paris conference and repeating the proposals he had offered at the spring meeting and again at the peace conference. In the discussion of the first question on the agenda, Bevin, hoping to help the situation, said that notwithstanding the position he had taken in Paris, he would now support any proposals that had received a two-thirds' vote at that conference. But this had no influence on Molotov; he demanded a vote on each of the recommendations. He did, however, refrain from making the disagreeable attacks upon the United States that he had made in Paris.

The Yugoslav delegation repeated their demands for the city of Trieste and said again that if the Trieste proposal was not changed they would refuse to sign the treaties. Thereupon the British and French delegations supported my motion that any nation not signing the treaties could not benefit by their provisions. Even Molotov supported that motion. About the fourth week of the meeting, Molotov called at my apartment and asked what suggestions I could make to facilitate our deliberations.

I told him that since he felt it his duty to reject nearly every recommendation that had been adopted at the peace conference by a two-thirds' vote or a simple majority, I had reluctantly reached the conclusion that there was no chance for us to agree upon the treaties. I said that I was not complaining about his attitude but simply answering his question. I then expressed the hope that since the General Assembly of the United Nations was in session, we could agree to disagree without attacking each other and hurting the cause of peace. I realized, I told him, that he had to follow instructions from his government and that it was not his fault, nor mine, that we could not agree; that in a year or so our successors could undertake the negotiations and, because we had narrowed the issues, they might eventually come to an agreement. Molotov said I was unduly pessimistic and he believed we could reach agreement now.

The next day Mr. Simic, then Yugoslav Ambassador to the United States, came to see me and said that if we would agree to a modification of the boundary between Yugoslavia and the free territory of Trieste, they would make concessions about the reparations to be paid them by Italy. I suspected this was Molotov's approach to test the sincerity of my statements to him, and told Mr. Simic it was useless to talk about changing the recommendation of the peace conference; that I had already told Molotov we should wind up our work; that Italy would be satisfied if we announced disagreement and Yugoslavia would not be hurt.

The next day Molotov asked me, "Are you still pessimistic?" "Certainly there has been no reason for me to change my mind," I replied. When the Council convened a few minutes later, Molotov announced a willingness to agree to some of the Paris recommendations "with slight modifications." That was to save face. The modifications were slight changes in language, not substance. This again demonstrated that whenever he concluded that nothing more could be gained by delaying tactics, he would do an about-face turn without the slightest embarrassment, smilingly agreeing where he had stubbornly opposed. Churchill, in describing Soviet methods, once told Jim Forrestal: "They will try every door in the house, enter all the rooms which are not locked and when they come to one that is barred, if they are unsuccessful in breaking through, they will withdraw and then invite you to dine that evening."

We decided to hold a meeting of the Council of Foreign Ministers in Moscow on March 10, 1947, to begin work on the German and Austrian treaties. Before agreeing on Moscow I insisted upon a commitment from Molotov, which he announced, that newspaper correspondents would be given the same privileges there as they were granted in New York. However, he refused my request that the

Moscow agenda should include a proposal to withdraw all occupation troops, though he promised to discuss the question at that meeting.

For some time I had been seriously concerned about the Soviet attitude toward Turkey. It will be recalled that at Potsdam Stalin had pressed for a naval base in the Straits, only to be rebuffed by the British and ourselves. But the Russians never give up! After Potsdam they called on Turkey to grant them naval base rights and to cede them the provinces of Kars and Ardahan. Turkey refused, but the continuing war of nerves forced her to maintain an army of approximately 800,000 men, which prevented the rehabilitation of her economy. In September, 1946, the Soviets advised Turkey that the "establishment of a regime of the Straits should come under the competence of Turkey and other Black Sea Powers."

We then notified the Soviets that our government considered that the Potsdam agreement contemplated only an exchange of views between the three powers and Turkey as a preliminary to a conference of all interested powers, including the United States, concerning a change in the Montreaux convention. I pointed out that in our opinion Turkey should continue to be primarily responsible for the defense of the Straits; and that should they become the object of an attack by an agressor, it would be a matter for action by the Security Council.

I had been informed by officials of Turkey that they needed both military and financial assistance. We had pending in Congress a bill for relief funds out of which Turkey would receive a generous allotment, but we had no authority in the absence of legislation to extend military assistance.

We had a similar situation with regard to Greece, which was also a prime target for Soviet abuse. In Paris the Greek Prime Minister, Tsaldaris, told me that their borders were constantly invaded by Communist guerillas trained in Yugoslavia, Albania and Bulgaria, and that Greek soldiers and civilians were being killed. A few weeks later in New York he told me that conditions had worsened, and just before the adjournment of the United Nations meeting I had a long talk with Molotov about the Greek situation. He insisted that Tsaldaris' statements were unfounded.

Because the information he had from sources upon which he relied, or pretended to rely, was so different from that given me by the

Prime Minister, I persuaded Molotov to agree to the appointment by the Security Council of a commission to investigate the border strife. I appointed Mark Ethridge of Louisville, Kentucky, our representative on this committee, which was directed to report not later than January 15. The statements of Tsaldaris were completely confirmed by the investigation.

When Tsaldaris, during our New York conferences, described to me the desperate plight of his people, he shed tears. I invited him to come on to Washington for further consultation, and, after talking to President Truman about the situation, Will Clayton and I explored the possibilities of getting aid from the Export-Import Bank, or any other source, but without success. As in the case of Turkey, we needed legislative authority to furnish any military assistance.

Tsaldaris told me that the British had warned his government that because of financial difficulties they would soon be forced to withdraw their troops, which had been a stabilizing force in Greece. No date had been fixed for the withdrawal when I left the Department in January, but it was thought to be imminent; Under Secretary Acheson believed the Congress, without delay, should be asked for the authority to grant the necessary aid. When the British finally announced their intention to withdraw on March 31, President Truman consulted congressional leaders, who reportedly advised him that authority for military aid would not be granted unless he personally appeared before Congress. He did appear, vigorously presenting the case for military and economic assistance to Greece and Turkey and asking an appropriation of $400 million, which was granted.

When the Foreign Ministers' Council adjourned on December 12, I prepared a speech on disarmament for the General Assembly, setting forth the United States position on the pending resolution. I stressed that "it is not the desire of the United States to be a leader in an armament race. We prefer to prevent, rather than to win the next war," and cited our efforts to establish effective international controls for the use of atomic power which would outlaw atomic weapons and promote the development of atomic energy for human welfare.

The day following this address I met with Mr. Baruch, our representative on the Atomic Energy Commission, and we agreed that he would press for a vote on the adoption of the United States plan, which had been under consideration for months. We knew there would be changes in the representatives of governments on the Commission on December 31 and that this would be used as an excuse for further delay. After six months of negotiations with the Soviets, Mr. Baruch forced the resolution to a vote, which was carried 10 to 0, the Soviet Union and its satellites abstaining. It was a great victory for Baruch and his associates, Herbert Swope, Ferdinand Eberstadt and Fred Searls.

On December 30 the Commission submitted its report to the Security Council, recommending that a comprehensive international system of control and inspection be defined by a treaty in which all the United Nations would be entitled to participate. It spelled out what would constitute a violation and the penalties for such violation; it recommended that the treaty embrace the entire program for putting the system into effect, the Commission to determine when any particular stage had been completed and subsequent ones were to begin.

In the years since this treaty was proposed the Security Council has made no progress toward putting the program into effect. The Soviets have insisted that the plan shall be considered only as part of an agreement controlling all armaments.

One reason for their insistence on merging the two proposals is to get away from the agreement Molotov reached with me at Moscow. If they lived up to that agreement, representatives of the international organization who were nationals of another government could inspect Soviet plants. That would be in conflict with their whole scheme of government, which is based on secrecy. Since then the Soviets have been making many different disarmament proposals solely for propaganda. In dodging an agreement for international inspection, they follow the usual Soviet policy, which I am sure is based on the advice given by the lawyer to Chichikov in Gogol's *Dead Souls:*

Remain calm, let nothing embarrass you, however bad things may get. Never despair of anything; there is no case that can't be saved. . . . If you see that the matter is approaching decision, don't try to justify and defend yourself: no, just mix things up by bringing in new elements. Mix things up, and mix them up again, that's all. Introduce extraneous factors, so that the first thing to do is to complicate them. Why, you can complicate things, if you want to, so that no one will ever be able to make head or tail out of them . . . after all, you can only catch crayfish in muddy waters.

## 26 LEAVING THE DEPARTMENT OF STATE

A few days after my return to Washington I called on President Truman to remind him that my letter of resignation, given him in April, was to take effect upon the completion of the treaties. As this was now accomplished, I hoped that he could release me. He said he hoped I had forgotten it. In a very friendly talk he gave several reasons why he felt I should remain. I told him that during the war Mr. Roosevelt had often called me his "secretary of resignations" because most of the "czars" of that period were constantly bringing me their resignations, but that in many cases, I found, they hoped to be persuaded to stay at their posts. But I was sincere in wishing to leave. As Mr. Truman and I had been friends since he first came to the Senate, we talked long and freely. He asked what I thought of General Marshall as a successor, and my answer was that it would be a splendid appointment and would be well received.

Some days later the President told me he was going to appoint General Marshall, but that the General wished to take a short rest and could not take office until about the middle of January. He said he hoped I could remain until then, and of course I readily agreed. He assumed that the treaties would be ready for signature by then and he wanted me to sign as Secretary of State since I had conducted the negotiations.

That I had resigned in April had been a well-kept secret and so was the fact of its acceptance in December, but in the afternoon of January 7 my friend Arthur Krock, for many years chief of the Washington Bureau of *The New York Times,* telephoned me. Had I been smart I would have been "in conference," but I was not. Among

387

his many talents, he is an expert cross-examiner. This time he asked
me directly whether I had resigned. In reply I asked where he got
that idea and made several evasive answers which were no more
convincing to me than to him. After he hung up I went to see the
President and told him of the conversation and my belief that the
*Times* next day would carry a story speculating on my resignation;
under the circumstances I thought he might as well announce it, and
also Marshall's appointment. He thought this wise and within an
hour or so he released the announcement of my resignation. In his
published letter to me he was good enough to say:

I realize full well how arduous and complex have been the problems
which have fallen to you since you took office in July 1945. Big events were
then impending and the months that have ensued have presented problems
of the utmost moment, with all of which you have dealt with rare tact and
judgment and—when necessary—firmness and tenacity of purpose.

Yours has been a steadying hand as you have met the difficult problems
which have arisen with such unvarying succession.

For all that you did during the war, and in the making of the peace, you
have earned the thanks of the Nation. So I say: Well done, in the hope that
we can continue to call upon you for the counsel which you can give out of
so rich and varied an experience.

It so happened that on the same evening the President was holding
the annual reception for the diplomatic corps, and Mrs. Byrnes and
I attended. Unexpectedly the occasion proved to be a delightful
"farewell party" for us.

On January 20 at 9:30, in the ornate high-ceilinged Room 474 of
the old State Department Building, I formally completed the task
upon which we had been working for more than a year. Senators
Connally and Vandenberg were with me when I signed the treaties
of peace with five nations, performing my last official duty of any
importance.

The next morning I went to the President's office when General
Marshall was sworn in. He and I went to lunch at Blair House and
I took the opportunity to tell him about some of the problems waiting
for him, assuring him of my willingness to assist him in any way possible.

As I write these words (March, 1958) there is much discussion about a summit meeting proposed by the Soviets to relieve tensions and much doubt about the wisdom of a meeting of the heads of state without prior agreement at a lower level on the scope of the discussions. I think President Eisenhower is right in insisting that there be adequate preparation if the purpose is accomplishment and not propaganda.

What I have written about the difficulty of reaching an agreement with the Soviets, even on agenda and procedure, should leave no doubt on that point. My experience, and the Soviet record for violating agreements, might even cause some persons to doubt the wisdom of any negotiation with the Soviets. However, I do not think we can refuse to discuss the problems of peace with them. Even a battle with words is better than a battle with bombs.

At the close of the war, we tried to work out the problems of the peace in close co-operation with the Russians. Having been allies in the war against Hitler, in good faith we made an effort to be partners in making the peace and in establishing the United Nations as an effective instrument for the maintenance of peace. At that time the hopes of our people were high and there would have been great disappointment, if not resentment, had we not tried to work with the Russians.

It soon became apparent, however, that it was not going to be easy to work with them. They knew what they wanted—they wanted to expand their territory and their control over peoples. They took extreme positions and rigidly maintained them. Moreover, they soon made it clear that they considered themselves the sole arbiters of the meaning of any agreements affecting their action in areas under their control, and, in effect, rendered such agreements meaningless.

In the light of the high hopes of the American people and of world opinion, it became necessary to give increased publicity to the course and content of our negotiations, so that public opinion would be better informed about the difficulties. My prayer was for a people's peace, and I said at the time, "statesmen must share their trials as well as their triumphs with the people." Although increased publicity helped to inform and alert public opinion, it also unfortunately helped to convert the conference table from a forum of negotiation into a forum of propaganda.

As the hard realities became better and more widely known, American as well as allied public opinion was sorely troubled and divided.

At one and the same time I was attacked (by Wallace and others) for being the leader of the "get tough with Russia" crowd and (by Admiral Leahy and others) for continuing to negotiate and talk with the Russians at all. It was and remains my view that, without raising false hopes or expectations, it is better to keep talking in an effort to make step by step progress toward peace than it is to cut all contacts and increase the risks of total war.

I would not say that conferring at all times and on all occasions is wise. Obviously, with the seizure of power by the Communists in Czechoslovakia, the Berlin blockade and the Korean war, it became increasingly difficult to hope for results from the conference table; yet even during this tense period the limited contacts maintained with the Russians in and through the United Nations had important and constructive consequences in the ultimate lifting of the Berlin blockade and in the ending of the Korean war. Moreover, it is highly doubtful whether the Austrian treaty could have been concluded when it was if at London, Moscow and Paris we had not insisted on negotiating, even though the chances of final and definite agreement seemed extremely remote.

The angry reaction of Molotov to the manner in which I espoused the cause of Iran in the Security Council in 1946 convinced me that the Soviets still had fear of, if not respect for, world opinion. My regret is that in one or two other instances we have not more effectively championed the cause of the smaller state against aggression.

It is frequently said that we should negotiate only from positions of strength. I would rather say that we must maintain sufficient military strength to hold our own at the conference table. We cannot protect the interests of ourselves and of the free world at the conference table if our power is not equal to Soviet power. But we should not allow ourselves to believe that strength or power is a satisfactory substitute for peaceful negotiation.

For some years, perhaps decades, we must live in a divided world. In this nuclear age, neither we nor the Soviet Union can hope to attain such strength or power that we can count upon surviving total war. Both we and the Soviet Union, however great and irreconcilable many of our interests may be, have an overwhelming common interest in guarding against a war—whether it comes by design or by accident—which would totally destroy both of us.

It is, therefore, very much in the interest of the United States and the Soviet Union to maintain continuing contacts at all levels, official and nonofficial, to avoid in time misunderstandings that might lead to war. And we should at all times take the greatest pains to show to the world that we are not trying to find excuses to avoid them.

Of course, public opinion must be informed regarding what may and may not be expected to come from peaceful discussion and negotiation at various levels. Certainly in the short run, no great victories for one way of life over the other may be expected. Agreements, within the realm of achievement, must be based on common interest, which rules out any spectacular diplomatic victory for one side or the other. Since there are differences even in parts of the non-Soviet world as to the binding character of treaties and agreements, unless they provide their own means of enforcement, we must expect them to be adhered to only so long as they serve the common interests of all parties.

The intensity of the cold war, aggravated by Korea and other incidents, has long dampened serious discussions between us and the Soviet Union at all levels. Too frequently contacts have been renewed only to gain opportunity for the resumption of a war of words and propaganda. If serious discussion and negotiations are now to be resumed, we must first explore, through diplomatic channels, the possibilities of agreement. Of all contacts, summit conferences are the least likely to result in the solid settlement of disputes, particularly if the groundwork has not been done. A summit conference may break the ice which has frozen the pattern of negotiation at lower levels, or it may remove major obstacles in the way of the final conclusion of prepared agreements which diplomats at lower levels have not the authority to tackle. But a summit conference like Geneva will not accomplish much of lasting value, even if it appears at the time to be successful, if it does not serve to vitalize contacts at other levels.

In conferring and negotiating with the Soviets we must remember, first, that the Soviets will keep an agreement only so long as it is to their interest to keep it; and second, they will believe it to their interest only so long as the western powers maintain equality in military strength.

# Part VI

## AND BACK TO SOUTH CAROLINA

# 27 PRIVATE CITIZEN

The President, in accepting my resignation, said he would call on me, and did in fact call upon me for advice several times. The first instance was two weeks later in connection with the conference to be held in Moscow in March. I also went to see him on several occasions. In February, on one such visit, he told me that he was going to Texas to receive a degree from Baylor University and asked if I would request our friend Jack Garner, the former Vice President, to be present. Characteristically Jack sent me back a reply written in pencil, saying he wished he could attend the ceremony but that his wife Ettie was not well. After a brief description of his daily routine, he closed with the words, "My health is good, my disposition worse. Give Maude Ettie's love and my love and take a big part for yourself." It was a typical Jack Garner note, which I forwarded to President Truman.

I also saw the President again in March to tell him of my plans to write the account of our peacemaking efforts which later became *Speaking Frankly*. He volunteered that he would direct that any records I needed should be made available to me, and I certainly had no difficulties in this respect.

In writing to me about the forthcoming Moscow Conference, the President had concluded by saying:

Another thing in which I am very much interested—the little school at Fulton, which conferred the honorary degree on Winston Churchill, is very anxious to perform the same ceremony for you. It would be an excellent chance for you to make a good hard-boiled Foreign Relations speech and I am rather of the opinion that General Marshall would not disagree, al-

395

though I have not discussed it with him. If you are going to be up here any time during the month of February I'd like to talk with you further about it, as well as about the . . . matter.[1]

I appreciated the honor, but, having retired, I preferred not to make the speech, as I told the President when I saw him in Washington, unless he was really interested in having me do it. When he said he would regard it as a personal favor, I laid aside my objections. However, when April came, Secretary Marshall was still in Moscow and, it appeared, would be there for several weeks longer. I decided it would be inappropriate for one so recently Secretary of State to speak criticizing Soviet conduct while his successor was in daily conference with the Soviet Foreign Minister. Consequently, in order not to add to General Marshall's difficulties, and with the President's concurrence, I canceled the engagement.

After retiring from the State Department I did, however, receive honorary degrees from several universities. Not having attended college in my youth, I concluded that late in life I was being educated by degrees. Of course all the citations were flattering, but I hoped there was some truth in one sentence of the Yale citation: "He has shattered the tradition that energy ends at the Mason Dixon Line."

While establishing residence at Spartanburg, I also opened a law office in Washington in partnership with Donald Russell. We took offices with the law firm of Hogan and Hartson, with the designation "of counsel." Because many of the officials of various government departments had been appointed upon my recommendation during the war, we declined to accept any employment that would require us to transact business with these departments. The one exception was the Interstate Commerce Commission, a quasi-judicial body. We accepted employment in an advisory capacity, and appeared only in the United States Appellate Courts.

In March, 1948, while I was still commuting between South Carolina and Washington, I dined one evening at the home of Jim Forrestal, who was then Secretary of Defense. Another guest was Kenneth Royall, then Secretary of the Army. Both these gentlemen were much interested in the re-enactment of the Selective Service Act, which they felt was necessary to bring the Army to its authorized strength. Congress was hesitating to re-enact what its members regarded as war-

[1] This reference concerned the work of the Department of State.

time legislation. Forrestal and Royall believed that it would be helpful if I made a speech urging the legislation.

I recalled that I had received an invitation to deliver an address ten days later at the 105th anniversary of the opening of South Carolina Military College—The Citadel. This seemed a good opportunity for a speech of the character Forrestal wanted me to make, and the next morning I sent a telegram to General C. P. Summerall accepting his invitation.

Forrestal and Royall furnished me information on the status of our armed forces, and I am sure Forrestal inspired the extensive publicity in newspapers and newsreels. Referring to the Soviet threat to Turkey, Greece, Italy and France, I said:

The Soviet government seems to have ignored the policy of the United States, as recently declared by the President, that the United States will support free peoples who resist attempted subjugation by armed minorities or by outside pressure. They have evidently concluded we will do no more than protest as we did in the case of Hungary and Czechoslovakia. It is our duty to let the Soviet government know that they must not be misled by our forebearance in those two instances; that if the independence of these four countries, or any one of them, is threatened by the coercive methods the Soviets have followed in other countries, we will not write a letter of protest—we will act.

Arguing that we needed an Army in uniform and not on paper, I urged Congress to re-enact the Selective Service Law in order to secure the authorized strength, saying that "Mr. Molotov does not understand English but to him, action speaks louder than words of any language." My speech concluded with a statement that is just as true now as then: "If we are going to talk strong, we must be strong. America must be strong if Americans are to be free!"

Some weeks later I sent a copy of this speech to Winston Churchill. It was forwarded to him in France, from where he wrote me: "We are now confronted with the designs and ambitions of despots as wicked as Hitler and even more absolute. How right you were to stand up firmly to them about Persia in 1946!"

Until the spring of 1949 I continued to spend four days a week in Washington, returning home each week end. At that time I decided that the weekly journey was too strenuous and that I wanted to spend more time in my state.

Upon reaching home after a long automobile trip, our colored chauffeur, Willie Byrd, who is an important member of our household and a very religious man, invariably exclaims, "Thank you, Jesus, for a safe trip!" He says this reverently in full realization of the perils of the highways. After any long trip I find myself exclaiming, "Home again!" Much of the joy in such an exclamation is the hope of a greeting from a friend or neighbor that he is glad to see us back, and I confess I was delighted when, shortly after my return from Washington, John Temple Graves, the brilliant newspaper columnist and lecturer of Birmingham, Alabama, wrote an article about my return, under the title "He Can Go Home Again."

Though his headquarters are in Birmingham, the South is his home, and I was flattered by his welcome. Other writers in my state were generous, and, possibly because of this, many invitations came to me to speak at various educational institutions.

In the spring of 1949, Frank Gaines, president of Washington and Lee University, told me that President Truman, who had been invited to deliver an address on June 18 at the celebration of the university's bicentennial, could not accept, and urged me to make the speech. I have always found it difficult to refuse a request of Frank Gaines, so I accepted.

During the years 1947 and 1948 I had found myself differing with President Truman about many domestic policies he was then advocating, but I had not publicly expressed my views. In 1948, sincerely wishing to stay out of politics, I had taken no part in the political campaign, refusing to be considered as a delegate to the Democratic State or National Convention, or even to attend political meetings.

Two thirds of the Washington and Lee speech was devoted to a discussion of foreign affairs, with which I am sure the administration was in entire accord. One third—or less—was devoted to domestic affairs, in which I expressed my oft-spoken criticism of the concentration of power in the federal government. I pleaded that "the states be given a chance"; that "Congress repeal some of the excise taxes, so the states can levy additional taxes in that field and provide for many worthy causes and still leave the people with more money and more liberty."

A few days before this speech a columnist had published the story that while I was in New York at the meeting of Foreign Ministers in December, 1946, I had heard that the President intended to appoint General Marshall to succeed me and that I had wired a protest, insisting that my resignation as Secretary of State be accepted promptly.

For years it had been my policy not to correct untrue statements about me that appeared in the press. As a rule, the friends whose good opinion you value will not believe ill of you. Your enemies will believe, or profess to believe, evil of you regardless of your denial. But at times it is hard to remain silent, and I now varied from my usual policy and wrote the columnist that I knew the accuracy of his statements depended upon the reliability of the source of his information and that in this instance he had been misinformed; that I had never telephoned or wired the President about my resignation; that on the two occasions I had spoken to him about it, our conversations were most cordial, and the fact was that I had recommended Marshall's appointment.

At the same time I wrote to the President, sending him a copy of my letter to the columnist. The President replied, thanking me and saying, among other things, that since he never read that particular columnist or listened to him, he had not known his statement had appeared. In typical Truman style he expressed his opinion of the columnist. He went on to say that he never read or listened to four other columnists, whom he named and about whose veracity he commented.

After signing this letter, the President added a postscript in pen. I was surprised by the postscript and wrote him a letter in longhand saying:

DEAR MR. PRESIDENT:

I am sorry you added to your personal note the postscript "Since your Washington and Lee speech I know how Caesar felt when he said 'Et tu Brute.'"

The implication is not pleasant and not justified. In that speech I spoke approvingly of the foreign policies of your administration. In discussing domestic policies I spoke very critically of new programs seriously proposed and of the danger of giving too much power to the state. I did not mention you.

I did not mention any one political party. On the contrary, my warning was followed by the statement that "each political party tries to outpromise the other." You may have regarded it as a criticism of you because you have approved certain proposals pending in the Congress. But surely if a personal friend expresses criticism of a proposal pending in the Congress which you approve, or criticizes a proposal submitted by you, you are not going to consider it a betrayal by your friend.

I hope you are not going to think of me as a Brutus, because I am no Brutus.

I hope you are not going to think of yourself as a Caesar, because you are no Caesar.

With best wishes for your health and happiness, I am

Sincerely yours<br>JAMES F. BYRNES

The cordial tone of the typed portion of his letter as compared with the unfriendly postscript caused me to believe the President had probably dictated the letter Friday afternoon with other mail, but before it was presented to him for signature on Monday had read my speech in the Sunday newspapers, and then added the postscript. The words "*since* your Washington and Lee speech" indicate that before reading the speech he was not unfriendly.

I received no further communication directly from the President. Thereafter, on one or two occasions, I learned indirectly of some unkind remarks that he had made about me, which convinced me that my reference to Caesar had gone deeper than intended. They hurt because, as I have surely made clear in the course of this book, we had had a close and continuing friendship from our Senate years right up to the date of my Washington and Lee speech. After I left Washington we naturally saw each other less frequently, but we had kept in touch through cordial notes, some of which I have already had occasion to quote from. Another, which was typical, thanking me warmly for a birthday telegram I had sent him, closed with the informal postscript: "P.S. My best to Mrs. Byrnes. The front door over here isn't locked!"

In spite of the abrupt break in our relations following the Washington and Lee speech, I was considerably startled when in March, 1952, there appeared in *Mr. President,* a biography of President Truman written by William Hillman, what was described as a "memorandum-letter"[2] dated January 5, 1946, in which Mr. Truman took me severely to task for alleged derelictions in the performance of my duties as Secretary of State. This letter, Mr. Truman claimed, was not sent, but was read to me.

January 5, 1946

HON. JAS. F. BYRNES, SECRETARY OF STATE

My Dear Jim: I have been considering some of our difficulties. As you know I would like to pursue a policy of delegating authority to the members of the Cabinet in their various fields and then back them up in the results.

---

[2] From *Mr. President* by William Hillman, Copyright 1952 by William Hillman and Alfred Wagg. Used by permission of the publishers, Farrar, Straus and Cudahy Inc.

But in doing that and in carrying out that policy I do not intend to turn over the complete authority of the President nor to forego the President's prerogative to make the final decision.

Therefore it is absolutely necessary that the President should be kept fully informed on what is taking place. This is vitally necessary when negotiations are taking place in a foreign capital, or even in another city than Washington. This procedure is necessary in domestic affairs and it is vital in foreign affairs. At San Francisco no agreements or compromises were ever agreed to without my approval. At London you were in constant touch with me and communication was established daily if necessary. That procedure did not take place at this last conference. I only saw you for a possible thirty minutes the night before you left after your interview with the Senate Committee.

I received no communication from you directly while you were in Moscow. The only message I had from you came as a reply to one which I had Under Secretary Acheson send to you about my interview with the Senate Committee on Atomic Energy.

The protocol was not submitted to me, nor was the communiqué. I was completely in the dark on the whole conference until I requested you to come to the *Williambsurg* and inform me. The communiqué was released before I ever saw it.

Now I have infinite confidence in you and in your ability but there should be a complete understanding between us on procedure. Hence this memorandum.

For the first time I read the Ethridge letter this morning. It is full of information on Rumania and Bulgaria and confirms our previous information on those two police states. I am not going to agree to the recognition of those governments unless they are radically changed.

I think we ought to protest with all the vigor of which we are capable against the Russian program in Iran. There is no justification for it. It is a parallel to the program of Russia in Latvia, Estonia and Lithuania. It is also in line with the high-handed and arbitrary manner in which Russia acted in Poland.

At Potsdam we were faced with an accomplished fact and were by circumstances almost forced to agree to Russian occupation of Eastern Poland and the occupation of that part of Germany east of the Oder River by Poland. It was a high-handed outrage.

At the time we were anxious for Russian entry into the Japanese War. Of course we found later that we didn't need Russia there and that the Russians have been a headache to us ever since.

When you went to Moscow you were faced with another accomplished fact in Iran. Another outrage if ever I saw one.

Iran was our ally in the war. Iran was Russia's ally in the war. Iran agreed to the free passage of arms, ammunition and other supplies running into millions of tons across her territory from the Persian Gulf to the Caspian Sea. Without these supplies furnished by the United States, Russia would have been ignominiously defeated. Yet now Russia stirs up rebellion and keeps troops on the soil of her friend and ally—Iran.

There isn't a doubt in my mind that Russia intends an invasion of Turkey and the seizure of the Black Sea Straits to the Mediterranean. Unless Russia is faced with an iron fist and strong language another war is in the making. Only one language do they understand—"How many divisions have you?"

I do not think we should play compromise any longer. We should refuse to recognize Rumania and Bulgaria until they comply with our requirements; we should let our position on Iran be known in no uncertain terms and we should continue to insist on the internationalism of the Kiel Canal, the Rhine-Danube waterway and the Black Sea Straits and we should maintain complete control of Japan and the Pacific. We should rehabilitate China and create a strong central government there. We should do the same for Korea.

Then we should insist on the return of our ships from Russia and force a settlement of the Lend Lease debt of Russia.

I'm tired babying the Soviets.

Sincerely,<br>HARRY S. TRUMAN

Of course, such a letter was never sent to me, nor read to me. Had this occurred, with my deep conviction that there must be complete accord between the President and his Secretary of State, I would have resigned immediately. My first knowledge of the "memorandum-letter" came with its appearance in the Hillman book. The only explanation Mr. Hillman gives of this unusual action is that "One day the President said that sometimes he wrote letters which he never sent but wished he had sent."[3] As an example, he quotes another letter to an unnamed journalist, which the President told him he wrote but did not send.

I sympathize with this journalist who may some day read the critical letter the President wrote but failed to send, and may suffer the shock I experienced.

The entire letter flabbergasted me, and particularly its implication that I had "babied the Soviets." That was the last charge I ever expected to have leveled at me; I had too often been accused of just the reverse! It would be tiresome and fruitless to review here all the pieces of evidence that reveal the complete inconsistency of the "memoran-

---

[3] *Mr. President*, p. 46 (followed by text of letter).

dum-letter" with the facts; they are scattered throughout the preceding sections of this narrative and, I hope, speak plainly for themselves.[4] However, I might point out that its inaccuracy is conclusively proved by the President's own statement made on January 7, 1946, just two days *after* the date of the disingenuous letter, when at his press conference he publicly endorsed all of my actions at Moscow.

I might also mention that in my letter of resignation, which I handed him in April, 1946, three months after the date of his alleged "memorandum-letter," I said, "When I think of the controversial character of the problems that have confronted us, it is rather remarkable that we have never failed to agree as to foreign policies."

He did not then question the accuracy of that statement—and it is hardly the wording I would have used had he ever expressed to me the sentiments contained in his memorandum.

May I add, too, that it seems strange to me, if he felt as he now says he did, that he should thereafter have urged me to remain on as Secretary of State until the five peace treaties were settled; and that during the Wallace episode he should have refused to accept my resignation when I urged it.

In August, 1952, during the presidential campaign, the President sent me a copy of the book in which he had traduced me. It was a beautiful de luxe copy of a limited edition, twice autographed. One autograph reads:

*To my former good friend, with kindest regards, whose friendship I would still value most highly.*

*Harry Truman*

---

[4] See, for example, p. 347 (Press Conference, Jan. 8, 1946); p. 317-318 (beginning of policy of firmness in London); p. 332-333 (letter to Stalin, December 19, 1945); p. 333-334 (talk with Stalin about Iran); p. 327 (failure to consult with President); p. 336-337, 340 (failure to keep him advised); p. 343 (visit to yacht *Williamsburg*); p. 334 (radio broadcast, December 29, 1945); p. 345 (New Year's Eve on yacht).

To this I could not respond.

It was puzzling that he should seek my friendship if he had ever felt about me as his memorandum made it appear. As he had publicly misrepresented me I thought he should correct his misrepresentations publicly, instead of courting my friendship privately.

## 28 THE GOVERNORSHIP

During the years following my retirement, while engaging in research for speech material, I became deeply interested in the problems of public education in South Carolina. Studies made by competent people confirmed my fears that our facilities were inadequate. This was understandable.

Following the War Between the States, with the privation of the Reconstruction period, the state had little revenue. The public schools of 1,200 school districts were supported by taxing local real estate. In counties where there was a large city, the revenue from real estate was sufficient to provide good schools for both races. But school districts in rural areas could not provide adequate schools for white or colored children. Too often when local revenues were reduced, the Negro schools were the first to suffer. After some years state aid was provided, but not sufficient to remedy the condition. A new source of revenue was necessary. The more I thought of it, the more I realized that the federal government had pre-empted nearly all available sources of revenue.

One important factor contributing to this problem was the increasing number of federal aid programs for activities that many of the states never would have inaugurated but that well-meaning people in Washington had induced Congress to adopt. The states were being impoverished trying to match federal funds. Some people regard federal aid as "government money," never realizing it comes from their own pockets. Others feel they must match federal funds, even when they do not believe the expenditure essential, because otherwise they will lose their share.

Early in 1949, I accepted an invitation to address the Southern

405

Governors' Conference at Biloxi, Mississippi. I told that group that if we wished to prevent the further concentration of power in the federal government, we should call a halt to the establishment of additional federal aid projects. I recalled voting for the emergency measures adopted during the depression, which were supported by Republicans as well as Democrats; but said that when the emergency was over, my efforts had been just as energetically devoted to repealing those emergency measures. We should not have a continued crisis.

I knew I would be charged with inconsistency, but conditions had entirely changed. Again it was unimportant whether what I thought twenty-five years ago was right or wrong; it was important to be right *now*. I recalled also that on one occasion when Senator Ashurst of Arizona was criticized, he answered: "It is useless to attempt to tell the country that I am not inconsistent; but let me say that whoever in his public service is handcuffed and shackled by the voice of consistency will be a man not free to act as various questions come before him from time to time; he will be a statesman locked in a prison house the keys to which are in the keeping of days and events that are dead."

In support of his position, Senator Ashurst quoted Emerson's statement, "A foolish consistency is the hobgoblin of little minds, adored by little statesmen and philosophers and divines."

It may have been because of my discussion of the problems of state governments that letters came to me from people in all walks of life throughout the state, urging me to become a candidate for Governor. Some pointed out that while I had spent many years in the service of the federal government, I had served my state only for two years as prosecuting attorney in my early life.

Whether it was the old horse in the Fire Department responding from habit to a fire alarm or just susceptibility to flattery, I announced my candidacy. As I had been away from the state so much during the war years, it was surprising that, with three opponents, I received nearly 80 per cent of the votes in the Democratic primary. This was equivalent to election, since I had no opponent in the general election.

When a man has been honored as I have been by the people of my state, every problem that confronts them is of concern. However, this is not a history of the state or its people, and I shall comment on only a few of the many problems that occupied my attention while Governor.

In my inaugural address in January, 1951, I referred, among other things, to the Ku Klux Klan, which had been active in an area near the North Carolina border, and in some instances had arrogated to itself the authority to punish several persons thought by the Klan to be violating the law. I urged the enactment of a law making it a criminal offense for persons over sixteen years of age to "parade on the streets or highways while masked," and also prohibiting such persons from "entering upon the premises of a citizen to threaten or intimidate him." Declaring that we must have a government of the people under law, I said that I did not need the assistance of the Ku Klux Klan, nor did I want interference by the National Association for the Advancement of Colored People.

The General Assembly took but a short time to enact the legislation requested. The Klan resorted to leasing private property for meetings, but our state law enforcement officers were so active in policing the meetings that Klansmen in a border county took a man across the state line into North Carolina to administer punishment in the mistaken belief that officers of that state might not be so diligent as those at home. They were arrested and convicted in North Carolina. The leader, who really possessed some qualities of leadership, announced from jail that he would quit the Klan, and when he was released he lived up to his promise. Since then there have been attempts to revive it, but today there is no effective Klan organization in South Carolina.

Between the time of my nomination in June and inauguration the following January, my study of the revenue problem had convinced me that the only source from which we could raise the money necessary to improve our educational facilities was a sales tax, which had previously been urged and rejected. It is a burdensome tax, but one of the few sources of revenue left to the states.

Therefore, in my inaugural address, I urged that adequate school facilities must be provided through a state-wide program which would require the issuance, over a period of twenty years, of $75 million worth of bonds.

Outlining the necessity for levying a sales tax of 3 per cent, to be used only for public school purposes, I stated, "It is our duty to provide for the races substantial equality in school facilities. We should do it because it is right. For me, that is sufficient reason. If any person wants an additional reason, I say it is wise."

I called attention to the fact that laws on segregation similar to our laws existed in seventeen states of the Union and said, "except for the professional agitators, what the colored people want, and what they are entitled to, is equal facilities in their schools. We must see that they get them."

Fortunately, at the time I submitted the school building program, there was a legislative committee which had been appointed at the previous session and had given study to the school problem. The committee agreed to the necessity for the sales tax; the legislature adopted it. It provided for improved bus transportation and authorized the consolidation of school districts. To carry out the educational program we established the State Educational Finance Commission, of which the Governor was chairman. Later, the limit of the bond issue was increased.

Our program was rightly called an "Educational Revolution." In our little state we had more than 1,200 school districts, which we reduced to 102. That required the consolidation of many districts and the abandonment of many inadequate schools. At the end of four years we had eliminated 824 totally inadequate schools in rural areas.

Whenever a district was abolished, the pride of the trustees was hurt because for them it meant a loss of prestige. It meant, too, that the schoolhouse, which in many cases was the social and civic center of the community, was to be abandoned. Most of these 824 inadequate schools had only one or two teachers. A teacher had to teach pupils from six to sixteen years of age. Competent teachers could not be secured for such a task in any community and certainly not in an isolated section. This situation affected the economy because ambitious mothers insisted that their families leave the farm for towns or cities to seek better educational opportunities.

One of the chief complaints about consolidating schools was that children would have to travel a great distance. How this was answered is disclosed by the figures: in 1951, only 142,000 pupils were transported to school. Four years later, 241,000 rode to school daily.

Because the greatest improvement was in the consolidation of Negro schools, this resulted in increasing by 50,000 the number of Negro pupils daily transported to school by bus.

At the end of four years, our Commission reported that $124,329,394 had been allotted from the proceeds of bonds sold and the sales tax— Negro schools receiving two thirds of the amount, even though Negro pupils comprised only 40 per cent of the total enrollment. This was over and above funds from local taxation for school purposes, the only previous source of funds.

In collecting the sales tax some unfriendly merchants would ask the customer for "Jimmie's tax." It was not calculated to increase my popularity but I am proud of what the tax accomplished in our educational program.

There was now at least one first-class high school for colored students in every district, and in many instances these schools were better than those provided for white students because they were newer.

There were also adequate elementary schools for both races. Almost immediately it became apparent that the improvement in elementary schools in rural areas would result in students' continuing in school for more years, and certainly we would require additional high schools. It also became apparent that the vastly improved high schools with increased attendance would stimulate a greater demand for college training.

At the 1953 session of the General Assembly it was evident that at the end of the fiscal year the state would have a surplus. I called to the attention of the legislature that if we were to attain a balanced program of public education, the colleges must be properly supported, and urged the allotment of most of the surplus to the colleges. Because legislators, as a rule, are more interested in appropriating funds for schools attended by the masses, rather than for colleges attended by relatively few, it provoked a hard fight, but we won.

At the same session I urged, and the legislature authorized, the issuance of revenue bonds by state educational institutions under certain restrictions. The bonds were payable primarily from funds the colleges derived annually from tuition fees. Later they were authorized to issue revenue bonds payable out of dormitory revenues. The funds from these sources made it possible for the state university and the state colleges so to improve their physical plants that today returning graduates cannot recognize the place of their studies or the scenes of their crimes. But more important than the building program has been the increased funds made available by the General Assembly for faculty salaries. Now I am proud of our educational system and particularly proud of the improvements at the State College for Negroes.

Another program that made my service as Governor seem worth while was the improvement at the state hospital for the mentally sick.

When elected, I was ashamed of our state hospital; now I am proud of it. That institution had no alumni to solicit support from legislators for improvements, but the legislature responded generously to my appeals and we provided not only modern buildings and equipment but highly skilled psychiatrists and staff. It was heartening because at times I fear the mentally sick are the forgotten people—forgotten even by relatives.

To enlist the co-operation of legislators in the building program for the mental hospital, I appeared at a joint session of the two houses and invited all members to join me in visiting the hospital. We first visited an old building occupied by the more violent patients, which I wanted to have replaced. I was gratified that approximately 150 legislators were with me, but I was told by an attendant that my enthusiasm was not shared by a patient on a second-floor balcony who, when he looked over the large group approaching, headed by the resident physician and me, excitedly exclaimed, "Good Lord, we are over-crowded now; we can't take in all those nuts!"

In 1950 we had an excellent training school for mentally defective white children, but mentally defective colored children were sent to the hospital for insane colored persons. There were just as many, or possibly more, mentally defective Negro children, but most of them were in the rural areas and in most cases the parents were not willing to let them leave home.

There was no appeal to me from any organization of colored or white people for a school for mentally defective Negro children, but I made it my pet project. Because of the terrific demands upon the legislators for funds for many deserving purposes in the closing days of the legislature, the conferees on the appropriations bill eliminated the funds to construct this school.

I still smile at what followed. When informed of that action, I met with the conferees. They said that they had eliminated the item in order to maintain a balanced budget and not because of opposition to the school. When I asked whether they would restore the item if I should find the necessary funds, they agreed, the chairman asking in which pocket I had a million. To their surprise I was able to tell them that on the books of the state treasurer there was a special fund of nearly a million dollars that could be used to start the building. That fund had been established in 1943, out of a surplus that year, to invest in revenue bonds of some state colleges issued some years before and then selling at a discount. By wise handling of the fund, a profit had accumulated. Accordingly, language was written in the bill transferring the special fund to the general fund, and the appropriation was restored to the bill to start Pineland School for mentally defective colored children. Later, additional funds were appropriated, and the school has now been operating for several years.

It was surprising that I should be called upon to give so much time to the effort to obtain industries for the state, but it was rewarding. A prudent businessman moving a plant for any reason makes a careful survey before deciding on a new location. I recall working with one prospect for three years before he reached a decision. In fact, he did not actually start construction until my term had expired. This effort to "sell" the state as the best place for the location of an industry provided some interesting experiences.

On one occasion, while urging upon the president of an industrial enterprise who was a guest at luncheon the soundness of our state government, I told him that under the rules of our House of Representatives the bill providing appropriations to operate the state government could not be passed unless the total of appropriations was less than the revenue estimated for the next fiscal year. My visitor immediately asked why, during my long service in House and Senate in Washington, I did not have the federal government adopt that policy. I did not try to answer that one.

Because this guest was a good friend, as we approached the end of our luncheon I told him the state had a balanced budget because it was economical even in little things. To illustrate, I said that the colored maids and butler who were waiting on the table were not paid by the state; that they were prisoners who, as a reward for good behavior, had been trained for housework and then were assigned by the superintendent of the penitentiary to the Governor's House for this much-sought-after service. He asked, "What are they in for?" When I told him, "murder and manslaughter," he expressed surprise—and I thought some fear—so I assured him that the five who were at the Governor's House had only committed crimes of passion, the two men having killed their wives and the three women having killed their husbands. However, when I told him one of the women had poisoned her husband, I wondered thereafter if he was sincere when he said, "I never eat desserts."

At first I did not like the idea of having prisoners at the Governor's House, but later realized it might contribute to their rehabilitation. We came to like them, and they must have liked us because every Christmas morning since we left the Governor's House, by permission of the present Governor, they have come to visit us, and, with my wife playing the piano, we all join in singing Christmas carols and Negro spirituals.

After I had started our educational program, counsel for the N.A.A.C.P. abandoned a suit that had been previously brought in Clarendon County for equal facilities in a school district and brought a new suit asking the court to declare unconstitutional the laws requiring separation of the races in public schools. A three-judge court upheld our segregation laws and this judgment was sustained by the Court of Appeals for the Fourth Circuit.

When the case was appealed to the United States Supreme Court, President Truman directed his Attorney General to intervene in the name of the United States and urge the Court to declare our laws unconstitutional. In the original suit, E. S. Rogers had represented the school district. When the constitutionality of our laws was attacked, Robert McC. Figg, Jr., was employed by me, as Governor. When the case reached the Supreme Court, I requested the Honorable John W. Davis of New York to argue the case for us. Davis was in the U.S. House of Representatives when I was first elected and I regarded him as the ablest constitutional lawyer of his time.

After studying the record, he said he would make the argument because, in the light of previous decisions of the Supreme Court on the subject, he believed the judgment of the lower courts right. After the argument he declined to accept any compensation, and on his next birthday the State of South Carolina presented him with a beautiful silver service.

At the time there were four similar cases pending in the Court. The case for the plaintiffs was argued by Thurgood Marshall, counsel for the N.A.A.C.P., and by an attorney representing the Department of Justice. While only four states and the District of Columbia were directly affected, similar segregation laws existed in seventeen states and would be affected by the decision of the Court. But the Court could not reach a decision and after many months invited counsel to reargue the cases at the next term. This was the status of the litigation when a change in the national administration was effected by the voters in 1952.

The action of the Democratic administration in intervening and attempting to set aside state school laws offended many staunch Democrats and increased the dissatisfaction with party policies that had expressed itself in 1948. Immediately after the adjournment of the 1948 national convention, the Democratic party of South Carolina and one or two other states had nominated presidential electors who were pledged to vote against Mr. Truman and for a States' Rights ticket, composed of Governor J. Strom Thurmond of South Carolina for President and Governor Fielding Wright of Mississippi for Vice President. That ticket carried four states.

At the time of the 1952 convention I was, of course, Governor and thus almost inescapably became involved in it. The Democratic party of South Carolina, in naming delegates to the national convention, adopted a resolution that the South Carolina party would not be committed to support the nominee of the national party until it knew who was the nominee and what was in the platform; that when the delegation reported back, the South Carolina party would decide what course it would follow. A certified copy of this resolution was filed with the Credentials Committee at Chicago.

At the convention, a group headed by Senator Moody and Governor Williams of Michigan, Senator Humphrey of Minnesota and Franklin D. Roosevelt, Jr., of New York secured the adoption of a resolution providing that no delegation should be seated unless its chairman gave assurance to the Credentials Committee that it would exert every honorable means available to provide that the nominees of the convention appear on the election ballot in the delegation's state, under the designation of the Democratic party. It provided that, for that convention only, an exception would be made for individual delegates who were willing to take the pledge to support the nominees of the party. Later it was amended to add: "Provided that such assurance shall not be in contravention of existing law of the state or of instructions of the state's Democratic governing body."

This loyalty pledge was adopted by a voice vote. I issued a statement and filed a copy with the committee, citing our state's election laws and the resolution adopted at our convention, and added: "I will not give on behalf of the delegates and alternates of the South Carolina delegation the pledge required by the Moody resolution, as amended, because such pledge would contravene the instructions contained in the resolution of the South Carolina convention, which is the governing body of the Democratic party of South Carolina."

Virginia and Louisiana filed substantially the same statement. Georgia and Mississippi took almost the same position, but for some reason those two states were placed on the roll of delegates. We were told that Virginia, Louisiana and South Carolina were not included.

I issued a statement to the press that members of our delegation "do not want to be compelled to act merely as agents of the national Democratic party, seeking to force on the Democratic party of South Carolina candidates or a platform which may be unacceptable to the state convention. . . . We are agents of the South Carolina Convention with limited authority. . . ."

The clerk of the Credentials Committee told us that the names of the three states had not been removed from the roll. Then the temporary chairman of the convention appointed a delegate from South Carolina and one from Virginia on a committee to escort the permanent chairman to the platform. This indicated that we were still members of the convention. Governor Battle, Senator Byrd, Governor Kennon and I met and sent a letter to Chairman Rayburn, asking for a ruling on our status, but received no answer. We decided we would not walk out unless there was formal action to exclude us.

When the roll was called for nominating speeches, Louisiana was the first of the contested states to be reached, and Governor Kennon sought recognition. Some delegate made a point of order that Louisiana was not a member of the convention. I sent Alex McCullough, who was my press assistant, to ask Governor Battle to make the parliamentary inquiry we had agreed upon earlier. When Battle propounded his inquiry as to our status, Rawlings of Utah, chairman of the Credentials Committee, reported that the three states did not meet the requirements. We had agreed that Battle should speak for the three states, and he went to the rostrum. At first it looked as though he would not be allowed to speak, but he patiently persisted, and made a splendid statement of our positions. Congressman Lansdale Sasscer, of Maryland, without any prearrangement, moved that Virginia be seated but made no mention of Louisiana or South Carolina. When the roll call was about completed, it was clear that Virginia had been ousted. With the approval of my delegation, I had told Battle and Byrd that if Virginia should be ousted, we would leave with its delegation. I had similar voluntary assurances from the chairmen of three other delegations. The chairman of the convention, Sam Rayburn, delayed announcing the result of the vote, and while he "dragged his feet" the Illinois delegation—evidently feeling confident Stevenson would be nominated, and fearing the ouster would split the party and defeat the candidate—changed its vote to favor seating Virginia. By this time there were huddles all over the hall. Many delegates had a second thought and wished to announce a change in votes. The changes resulted in Virginia's being seated by sixty-four votes.

Battle now moved that Louisiana and South Carolina be seated. A delegate from Ohio demanded the right to ask a question of the chairman of the South Carolina delegation. Though invited to the stand, I remained at my place on the floor, stood on my chair, and, after answering several questions, read the statement I had filed, repeating the position of the Democratic party of South Carolina. Suddenly there was more commotion around me than usual; when I looked around I saw that two rows behind me a fire, which had actually started where the Montana delegates were seated, was now blazing among discarded newspapers on the floor where our delegation was seated. There were many papers scattered about and the fire was spreading rapidly. State Senator Morrison pulled off his coat and attempted to smother the fire, and others came to assist him. Pandemonium broke loose in the aisle, where members of the press and radio had gathered while I was speaking. When the blaze was under control, in the hope of relieving the tension, I said, "Mr. Chairman, I want to announce that I did not set the place on fire." Later I found that my serious statements were completely forgotten; but people still recalled my denial of having started the fire.

When order was restored, Governor Williams of Michigan rushed to the platform to question me. I answered two or three questions; but when he asked how we failed to meet the requirements, I suggested he ask the chairman of the Credentials Committee, not me. When he began another inquiry covering a point I had already answered, I replied with emphasis but in good humor, "I refuse to be subjected to further cross-examination by the delegate from Michigan." Many delegates applauded. As Williams left the stand, John McCormack, who was presiding, was heard to say what sounded over loud-speakers like "You came up here looking for trouble and you found it."

Chairman Rawlings of the Credentials Committee said the statement that I had filed was substantially the same as Virginia's, and moved that South Carolina and Louisiana be seated. They were seated by voice vote.

Although this must have been two o'clock in the morning, from the many people who later talked to me about the fire, I realized that television had brought national politics into the living rooms of America. To me this is encouraging. It will help educate the people politically, increase their interest in government, and improve the conduct of the delegates in the convention hall.

For President, I favored Senator Richard B. Russell of Georgia, chairman of the Senate Armed Services Committee, who was superbly qualified for the Presidency; but, coming from the Deep South, he could not be nominated. He received few votes from states outside of the South. Adlai Stevenson was nominated.

When the South Carolina convention met ten days later, I stated that we had refused to make a pledge of any kind, but that in my opinion the convention should direct that electors pledged to Stevenson and Sparkman should be placed on the ballot in the column provided for the Democratic party of South Carolina. I said also that the Democrats who did not want to vote that ticket should have the opportunity to vote for the candidate they preferred, which could be done under our law by filing a petition signed by 10,000 electors.

Then I added, "I want it understood that I reserve to myself entire freedom, after listening to the candidates, to vote in November for the candidate I conclude is most likely to bring peace to the war-weary world and happiness to the American people."

Little was said about the platform. Nowadays a political platform is adopted for the purpose of winning the votes of particular groups and is important only to the extent that it may influence the presidential candidate. Members of Congress try to keep the pledges they personally make, but feel no obligation to redeem pledges made by delegates to the national convention.

Later I signed a petition to place on the ballot for presidential electors the names of independent Democrats favoring Eisenhower.

It was after my statement that I reserved the right to decide later for whom I would vote that I received from President Truman a copy of William Hillman's book *Mr. President*. However, that did not influence me to support Stevenson and Sparkman.

Having carefully read what the two candidates had said about many issues, I announced I would vote for the independent Democratic electors pledged to Eisenhower. Among my reasons, I cited a number of issues upon which, after the convention, Mr. Stevenson had altered his position. I called particular attention to his statement that he would use all his influence as President to encourage Congress to limit debate in the Senate, stating that, under the fundamental constitutional doctrine of the separation of powers, a President had no right to use the influence of his office to change the rules of either Senate or House. I cited also General Eisenhower's repeated declarations that he favored, generally, the preservation of the rights of the states.

Of course, I expected criticism. Many of my neighbors believe, with Stephen Decatur, "Our country, right or wrong!" but carry it a step farther to "Our party, right or wrong!"

I was not mistaken in my anticipation of criticism, but I have learned that one who wishes to enjoy the satisfaction that comes from following his convictions in either politics or religion must be willing to stand the criticism of the strict conformists who, instead of thinking for themselves, are willing to adopt the thought of others, even those long ago dead.

Prior to the election, I frequently heard it said that if a South Carolina Democrat voted for a Republican candidate for President, his "grandfather would turn over in his grave." The morning after the election a friend who lives near old Trinity Churchyard in Columbia, where lie the remains of many distinguished South Carolinians, told me that, in spite of election returns which gave Stevenson 173,000 votes and Eisenhower 158,000 votes from independent Democrats and 9,800 from Republicans, neither during the day nor the night of the election had he heard any unusual sounds in the cemetery.

In public life I have seldom deviated from the rule of not offering unsolicited advice to Presidents or others in positions of responsibility. I made no personal requests of President Eisenhower to appoint friends to office, and the only occasion I recall violating, with him, my rule about unsolicited advice was when the Supreme Court ordered a rehearing in the school segregation case, inviting the United States Attorney General to participate.

On a trip to Washington I expressed to the President the hope that he would not feel bound by the position previously taken by the Democratic administration. I said I hoped the Attorney General would follow the decisions of the Supreme Court for over a half century which declared that state segregation laws providing for separate but equal facilities were not unconstitutional. If he did not, I said, I hoped that consideration might be given by the President to the position that the laws of the states should be upheld as being within the authority of a state in the exercise of its police powers to promote education and to prevent disorders.

I called to his attention that under Court decisions the police power of a state is subject to judicial review when in a particular case it is thought arbitrary and unreasonable; and that the Court has held that, even though a law was justified under the police powers of a state at the time of its enactment, if subsequently conditions should change, enforcement might be arbitrary and unreasonable.

Illustrating, I referred to one of the pending cases from Kansas, saying the Court might hold that enforcement of segregated schools in that state, with relatively few Negroes, was not a reasonable exercise of the police power. On the other hand, in the school district in South Carolina which was the subject of litigation, where there were approximately 2,900 Negro students and 290 white students, the Court might hold that it was debatable whether integration there would cause racial conflicts and disorders; and where that question was debatable, it was for the legislature of the state and not the United States Supreme Court to say what should be done in the proper exercise of the state's police power. I thought wonderful progress was being made by the Negro race educationally, and that time would continue to be a great healer.

The President seemed impressed by the suggestion, but said that where a legal question was involved he had to rely upon the opinion of his Attorney General, and requested that I present the thought to Mr. Brownell. The Attorney General expressed interest in the suggestion, saying that it sounded reasonable and he would be glad to consider it.

I made one other request of him. Recognizing that, since the lawyers in the Justice Department during the Democratic administration had prepared a brief urging the Court to declare school segregation laws unconstitutional, they could not well change their views, I said that I hoped he would assign some lawyers to the case who had not previously participated in the argument and could, therefore, study the question with open minds. He said that, too, was a reasonable request.

However, when the brief was filed, a published list of the lawyers who prepared it included the names of at least two who had worked on the brief filed by the Democratic administration, and the argument did not differ substantially from that made by the preceding administration. The Supreme Court took the case under consideration.

It was not until May 17, 1954, that the Supreme Court filed a decision setting aside the provisions of the constitutions of seventeen states requiring segregated schools. Two years before we had established a committee to recommend a revision of our school laws. Under the intelligent leadership of Senator Marion Gressette, the committee recommended many changes, including procedure in assignment of students, which were adopted by the legislature.

After I left the office of Governor in January, 1955, the legislature enacted a law providing that if, by, or in consequence of an order of a court, state or federal, a student was transferred from a school to which he had been assigned by education officials to some other school designated by a court, all appropriations for both such schools should immediately cease. There are similar laws in other states. No such court orders transferring students have been sought by colored students in South Carolina, and thus far we have escaped the serious race riots and disorders that have occurred elsewhere.

I am confident that our foresight in 1951 in adopting a program providing modern and splendidly equipped schools and improved transportation for colored students has contributed to their satisfied attitude. But most credit for our peaceful conditions must be given to the conservative Negro citizens who, expecting to continue to live by the side of their white neighbors, have resisted the efforts of agitators from other states to force prompt integration in the schools. They know it would undo all that has been done during the last fifty years by leaders of both races to bring about improved relations. The educational and economic progress of our colored citizens during that period is something of which I am very proud.

Of course the problem is not solved. It has been suggested that if as a result of a court order a public school is closed in any community, the state should make an allotment to parents to cover tuition fees paid to private schools. Even with aid for both races, it will be difficult for colored citizens to establish and operate private schools, particularly in rural areas. However, thoughtful white Southerners are agreed that the education of the colored children is essential to any wise solution, and they are determined to find a way to ensure that innocent colored children are not denied an education. They believe the school problem is a local problem. They believe that people who advocate immediate integration everywhere are more interested in what they believe to be a desirable social reform than they are in advancing the education of the children of both races.

I fear that in any community in which race tension is such that classrooms have to be equipped with guns and students supervised by the United States Army, as at Little Rock, or by the police, as has been proposed by a grand jury in Brooklyn, there can be no educational progress.

Under the most favorable conditions, it is frequently difficult to get children to study. The presence of soldiers and guns may cause them to study two R's—race relations—but will not encourage them to concentrate on the three R's.

The routine of administering state affairs was broken in 1953, when the President appointed me a representative to the General Assembly of the United Nations. After the first week, it was difficult to believe that it was 1953 and not 1946, when I had spent most of the year negotiating with the Soviets. I commented to Leonard Meeker, a staff member, that we had the same issues, the same actors, and the same frustrating methods employed by the Soviet Union and its satellites. I found myself again making a speech about the outrageous action of the Soviets in refusing to return to Germany and Japan the hundreds of thousands of soldiers held as prisoners of war and the thousands of civilians who had been taken to the work camps of Russia on the pretext of being war criminals. Vishinski was just as vigorous, and vindictive! At the end of the session I had to admit that little real progress had been made toward putting an end to the cold war and to the threat of another world war.

In South Carolina the same spirit of political independence shown in 1952 was displayed in the election of 1956. The names of Stevenson and Kefauver were placed on the ballot as the candidates of the Democratic party of South Carolina. But, by petition, there were also on the ballot electors pledged to Senator Harry Byrd of Virginia and Congressman John Bell Williams of Mississippi.

I cast my vote for the independent electors pledged to Byrd. Givii. many of the same reasons I had advanced in 1952 for not supporting Mr. Stevenson, I said I disagreed, too, with his statement on the unilateral abandonment of nuclear tests and his views about the draft. I said that President Eisenhower had done a fine job in the field of foreign affairs; had brought the Korean war to an end; had preserved peace; and had balanced the budget. However, he had disregarded his pledges to preserve the rights of the states; had advocated federal aid to education; and had made unfortunate appointments to the courts. Consequently, I would vote for the electors pledged to Senator Byrd, who was sound in his views on foreign and domestic affairs and who, I believed, had a more intimate knowledge of the fiscal affairs of government than any other man in public life.

It was said such a vote was only a protest. Concerning this, I stated: "If a man says that a vote for the independent electors is just a protest, I ask what is wrong with a justified protest? Without such a protest in 1776 we might not have won our independence."

Of course a citizen need not vote, but I recalled the words of Abraham Lincoln: "To sin by silence when they should protest makes cowards out of men." I preferred to voice and vote my own views. The independent electors for Byrd and the Republican electors pledged to Eisenhower together received 162,060 votes, as compared to 133,503 given to Stevenson and Kefauver; but the Stevenson ticket receiving a plurality of the votes cast, the electoral vote of the state was cast for him.

On January 18, 1955, I left the Governor's office and public life. Within me was the satisfaction that comes from the consciousness that through the years I had faithfully tried to discharge my duty. I knew I had made mistakes, because I am human. I knew I had made political enemies because I had taken positions on controversial issues and fought to sustain those convictions. But there was compensation in the knowledge that I had made countless friends whose understanding and sympathy had enriched my life.

As I thought of the past, overriding all thoughts of personal relations was my realization that this country is truly the land of opportunity. Now as I think of the future, my hope is that my experiences may encourage others to dedicate their talents and energies to public service, for I believe with Tolstoi that "The sole meaning of life is to serve humanity."

# INDEX

DATE DUE